D0783387

THE SOCIAL BOND

II

THE SOCIAL BOND

An Investigation into the Bases of Law-abidingness

WERNER STARK

Volume II

*Antecedents of the Social Bond
The Ontogeny of Sociality*

New York
FORDHAM UNIVERSITY PRESS
1978

© Copyright 1978 by FORDHAM UNIVERSITY PRESS
LC 76–4712
ISBN 0–8232–1029–4 (*clothbound*)
ISBN 0–8232–1030–8 (*paperback*)

Printed in the United States of America

Contents

Preface

The subject of the present volume is the process known to sociologists as socialization; less technically expressed: the transformation of the newborn baby (who is hardly more than a specimen of an animal species) into a civilized and cultured, and, above all, thoroughly social man. In an introductory chapter I have indicated the starting point and the end point of this great metamorphosis. The starting point is the self-centered and self-preferring organism; the end point, the mentally mature personality, the person in the fullest sense of the word, who is capable of receiving and imparting sympathy, of actively and passively experiencing genuine fellow-feeling. The bulk of the book discusses the stages of this journey and the many problems which it poses for the scholarly observer.

The investigation which I am presenting today constitutes a closed whole and may therefore be read and understood without previous knowledge of the first volume, which appeared in 1976. Yet, on a deeper level, there is, of course, a connection between the two books. This fact is already visible in the subtitles which they respectively carry. The first part is subtitled *The Phylogeny of Sociality*; the present sequel, *The Ontogeny of Sociality*. There I asked whether nature had prefigured and preformed the social bond; in other words: whether the social bond is, in point of fact, based on an assignable organic drive. I found that there is no such natural or organic drive which would constitute the root of sociality. Mammals, including the hominid, congregate merely for selfish reasons—because they, each of them individually, experience fear. But if nature has not made men actually social, she has made them potentially social. She has given them the equipment needed to develop, in freedom and in responsibility, societies and cultures. The latter terms describe, in my opinion, the same reality. In the final analysis, the social bond is a product of culture, just as culture is a product of social coexistence and cooperation.

This insight, this conviction, which dominates the pages of the earlier work, poses the problem with which the present investigation has to grapple. The newborn baby comes to us from the hands of nature; he enters into culture as soon as he leaves the womb. But if he is to be a social being, it is imperative that culture enter into him. My self-imposed task was to show how this happens. What I have to say rests in substance on the teachings of the cultural school of sociology, the school perhaps best represented by the older Durkheim, but also by Cooley, Mead, and even Sumner, and, more recently, by Talcott Parsons. The brief formula which has been handed down within this school—the proposition that human sociality rests on the internalization of norms and values—provides also a terse summary of my own text. But it is not sociological research alone which has provided the bases of my argument; as in the first volume, I have gone out into the neighboring fields and brought home many valuable and, indeed, often invaluable, insights. I have above all striven to see what the recent developments in psychology can contribute to the maturation of sociology; I have found that it is much—very much indeed.

My book is, of course, essentially a scholarly and scientific investigation, but it would be wrong not to draw attention, at least in this preface, to its practical implications. As far as the process of socialization is concerned, there exists a remarkable and regrettable discrepancy between theory and practice. All serious observers agree that the internalization of norms and values is not easy to achieve; the self-regarding body opposes many of its demands. The aims of education must be actively and energetically pursued; the principles of civilized and cultured conduct must be pressed on the developing individual, not merely presented to him. But in the Western countries, at any rate, the widespread opinion prevails that the socialization of the individual is the result of maturation rather than of education or moralization, that it takes place spontaneously, almost of itself, and that it can succeed without social pressures to back it up. Nothing could be more fraught with danger if the level of law-abidingness is not seriously to sag, a possibility which, surely, no sane person can contemplate with equanimity. This is not the place to go more deeply into the matter, but I wanted to emphasize that the ensuing pages contain food for thought for every responsible citizen, and not only for the professional sociologist.

In conclusion, one small detail, to avoid puzzling the reader. I have decided to let the numeration of the sections continue uninterruptedly from the beginning of the first to the end of the last (presumably the sixth) volume. This is why page 1 begins with paragraph 61. But, let me say this once more, that does not mean that this volume is in any sense less than a complete analysis. It covers the socialization—the humanization—of man in all its aspects and presupposes no more on the part of the reader than the perusal of any self-contained book which is generally on the same level of specialization.

W. STARK

Salzburg, June 1978

Self-centeredness and Sympathy

THE CAESURA OF BIRTH

61. There is no man, whatever his age or country or cultural background, who would not prefer a monistic to a dualistic world view; our whole mental constitution induces us to look for unity and simplicity and to shy away from dividedness and complication. Yet the student of man in society has no choice in this matter; the plain facts before his eyes force him to think in dualistic terms. Man undeniably belongs to *two* realms, nature *and* culture, not only to one, and the laws of the latter cannot be shown to be identical with, or even to be in their content dependent on, the laws of the former. We saw how true this is in our first volume where we compared and contrasted animal sociality and human; we shall see the same in this volume where our subject is the socialization of the individual.

That the individual belongs to two separate orders of being becomes obvious as soon as we consider the birth act and its immediate consequences. The expulsion of the fetus from the maternal womb and the severance of the umbilical cord transfer him from an essentially physical to an essentially social environment. True, society had some influence on him even while he was yet inside the parental organism; the nutritive juices which fed him and helped him to develop arrived in a time sequence which was determined by the mother's feeding habits, and these are set by social custom. True, he is destined to remain in the grip of natural necessities even after gaining an independent existence of his own, to be subject to them until he breathes his last. But antenatal life is only remotely controlled by social norms, while postnatal conduct is only relatively loosely connected with physical imperatives. Man must eat, but what he eats, when he eats, and how he eats, indeed, how much he eats, and whether his food intake will be sufficient to sustain him, depend to a greater extent on social than on physical circumstances. Nature is and remains the mistress of every living creature, but to men collectively and to each man individually she has given a generous measure of autonomy, of self-determination.

But we are not laying our finger on the truly decisive fact when we say that the contrast between the prenatal and the postnatal environments consists in this: that the one is physical rather than social, and the other predominantly social and only remotely physical. Far more important—at least in the context of an analysis of the process of humanization and socialization—is another difference. Fetal existence is totally passive; independent life is essentially active. In *Inhibitions, Symptoms, and Anxiety* (trans. James Strachey, Standard Edition of the Complete Psychological Works xx [London, 1959], p. 138)

Freud, while admitting that the "caesura" of birth is very real, argued that the mother's care comes to replace the mother's womb so that there is in fact a good deal of continuity between intrauterine existence and immediate post-natal life. But in the womb the infant has no need to do anything in order to be fed, while at the breast he has to cooperate. We are not unaware of the fact that a certain amount of activity has been observed even on the part of the fetus; thumb-sucking, for instance, is known to go on well before birth. But even if we have here, once again, a contrast which, in principle, is merely one of degree, the degree of difference is so vast that we may, nay must, speak of a difference in essence as well. Prenatal conduct is *in essence* passive; post-natal conduct is *in essence* active. The neonate arrives with an inborn tendency to suck, but how he sucks depends on him, and here lies the first root of his freedom. That freedom is destined to proliferate with every day which comes and goes.

Those who see *Homo sapiens* in zoological rather than in humanistic terms have, not surprisingly, a tendency to de-emphasize the infant's activity. Freud, for instance, insists in practically every one of his writings that the great spring of action is the felt need to remove tensions which have built up within the organism, and he applies this interpretation not only to the acts of the id, i.e., the body, but also to the acts of the ego, i.e., acts which have their origin in the seat of consciousness. Whereas other materialists have considered both pleasure and pain as initiators of behavior, he sees human behavior in terms of a mechanics of pain, with pleasure only a kind of premium which nature at-taches to the resolution of tension, the removal of pain. Such an opinion is far too narrow, indeed, too unrealistic, to command respect. Not only are men activated by the positive aim of securing pleasure as well as by the negative aim of terminating pain, but—and this is decisive—they very often act merely for the sake of acting, without necessary reference to any physical condition. Phil-osophically expressed: activity is a value in itself. Psychologists have proved that this is indeed so. Even "in the earliest stage of development," says Ernest G. Schachtel in his excellent study *Metamorphosis* (New York, 1959; p. 119), "the infant does not only try to avoid stimulation, but also *seeks* it . . . ; pleasure can consist in excitation itself as well as in the decrease of excitation." The nar-rowness of Freudianism (or, rather, of the original and orthodox version of it) lies in its undue fixation on the concrete areas of excitation, the concrete organs in which the pain of tension is located and the pleasure of release is experienced. But, beyond them, there exists such a thing as a general tone of the body, and it should not be forgotten, especially where the ego as well as the id are within the purview. The acting infant feels himself alive, his vitality and the conscious-ness of it are enhanced; he grasps and comes to know that it is *good* to *be*, and this, surely, is a sufficient spur to action, above and beyond mere physically grounded and physically restricted uneasiness. Indeed, with this experience (which should be seen as kindred to, if not indeed as identical with, Henri Bergson's *élan vital*), we stand on the borderline of body and mind and begin to look beyond even Freud's ego, which is seen far too somatically as merely a function of the cortex. Activity which is pleasurable in itself gives us not only, or not merely, pleasure; it gives us joy, and that is something else. One sociologist who knew this very well was Thorstein Veblen whose concept of workmanship is rooted in the correct insight that man is essentially an active creature, deeply desiring, at any time, to be up and doing. This so-called instinct of workmanship (which, as Veblen fully realized, was not a proper inherited instinct, but rather the cultural prolongation and pendant of one—see Josef Dorfman, *Thorstein Veblen and His America* [New York, 1947], p. 324) is the existential basis of the vast development of technology throughout history, but not of technology alone; science, too, the disinterested pursuit of knowledge for knowledge's sake, Veblen's "idle curiosity," has, in the final analysis, flowed from this source. Human activism begins immediately at birth, and therefore prenatal and postnatal existence are contrasts—part and parcel of the great contrast between activity and passiveness.

But even by adding this difference to the difference between a merely physical and a largely social environment, we have not yet completed our description of the gulf which separates fetal and neonatal life. The most painful distinction is still to be considered. Fetal life is largely unproblematical; independence, however, involves us in a profound problematic. Or, to be more precise, any problem experienced by the infant in the womb is an objective difficulty, with no subjective side to it; the problems experienced by that same infant outside the womb are subjective ones, or, rather, intersubjective ones, social ones. The pregnant woman who takes drugs, or merely neglects to get nourishment at regular intervals, will damage her developing child, but since there is to all intents and purposes as yet merely one organism, no problem of relationship can possibly arise. This changes abruptly as soon as there are two bodies, two beings. The whole vast problematic of human relations at once arises, never to be laid to rest until life's whole course is run.

None of us has a conscious recollection of his birth, let alone of the nine months which preceded it. Yet depth psychology has made it clear that there is, in addition to conscious memory, a much wider unconscious memory, indeed, a memory of the body which is different from the memory of the mind. But even if this notion be rejected as too fanciful, it is simply a fact that man has often evinced a yearning for a return to the blissful, problem-free antenatal condition in the womb of his mother, or of his mother's mother, nature, in which there is no anxiety to plague him. A recent expression of this longing is Herbert Read's deeply philosophical novelette *The Green Child*.

The purpose of life, so the hero, Olivero, tells us, is to attain everlasting perfection, but activity cannot lead to it. The conscious self is ever restless and dissatisfied. It must be overcome. Harmony exists in the crystal, and in the material parts of creation of which the crystal is a symbol. It therefore exists before life and after life, but not in life. The body must cast off "the worm" which fills it with itches and desires, and sink back into matter, which alone has stability, proportion, beauty, and perfection (New York, n.d.; pp. 177, 149, 194, 192).

This theme of *The Green Child* can be followed back through the centuries into the realm of saga and legend. The Germanic folk-hero Siegfried and the

Russian folk-heroine Fevronia know the language of the birds; St. Francis of Assisi preaches to them and is understood. Even Rousseau's cry *Retournons à la nature* owes its success, at least in part, to this primal yearning for the warmth of the womb. True, it had a narrower political and psychological background as well: eighteenth-century man had a desire to free himself from the artificialities of the life of the upper classes who oppressed him; and he entertained, as we all do, sentimental regrets for his childhood innocence, which had been lost. But beyond childhood, there is babyhood, and behind babyhood, the womb; behind innocence, total integration, the bliss of unknowing, and it, too, is of real attraction.

Though it is impossible to be dogmatic about the correct interpretation of a primitive rite such as the totemic dance, it is, to say the least, possible that the dance may be explained by the wish to be, be it only for a fleeting moment, back in the womb of nature. The clansman identifies himself with his totemic animal; he mimes its movements; and he dances until he is enveloped in an aura of unreality, until he enters a hypnotic condition in which he is filled with an intense feeling of vitality, but without consciousness of selfhood and separatedness. This experience obviously has a life-enhancing effect, otherwise it would hardly have been developed and periodically repeated. And what can be more life-enhancing than liberation, be it only transient, from the problems of ordinary existence—in other words: return to the problem-free existence which was led in the womb?

But the longing which the clansman acts out, which men like Rousseau and Herbert Read appeal to, is entirely vain. Expulsion from the womb is an expulsion from Eden, and it is final. Man must live his life among thistles and thorns; more soberly expressed: among the manifold difficulties unavoidably inherent in the relationships between the self and others. Even the primal rudimentary interaction between neonate and mother is not without its social problematic. "An element of frustration by the breast is bound to enter into the infant's earliest relation to it," one of our best child psychologists has written (Melanie Klein, *Envy and Gratitude* [London, 1957], p. 4), "because even a happy feeding situation cannot altogether replace the pre-natal unity with the mother." Both individuals concerned may be completely happy and healthy, and yet grievances (Melanie Klein's word, p. 13) will arise. The milk may flow too freely or it may flow too slowly; the time when it is offered may not be exactly the time when it is wanted; and so on. Add to these natural tensions the consequences of human inadequacies—awkwardness in holding the baby, nervousness and distractions on the part of the mother, substitution of the bottle for the breast, and innumerable other interferences—and you have a condition in which all the problematic of human cooperation, all the sorrow of social life, is fully exemplified. The baby who turns from the nipple to suck his own thumb is the archetype of the man who does not get all out of human cooperation that he craves, and retreats from sociality into self-centeredness, to nurse therein his resentments, large and small.

It is necessary to insist on these unfortunate facts because a largely unrealistic view of the roots of sociality is current in the world, and especially in the world of the West. That world has historically emerged from a series of revolutions of which the French upheaval of 1789 was the most archetypal and the most important. Something of the revolutionary ideology still hangs around contemporary thought, even thought which fancies itself entirely scientific. On the eve of the overthrow of a traditional order, there is, at least semi- and subconsciously, a general uneasiness shared by the revolutionary leaders themselves. Will tomorrow really be better than yesterday? Will the new socio-political system be in truth an improvement on the old? Erich Fromm has spoken of a "fear of freedom" and thereby drawn attention to a very important mental mode. To still that fear and to release the forces of aggression, revolutionary movements have to give birth to reassuring ideologies. All these ideologies are of the same pattern: social institutions are bad and spoil man; man himself is basically good. "The fundamental principle of all morality which I have discussed in all my writings," Jean Jacques Rousseau writes in his self-defense before the archbishop of Paris ("Lettre à Christophe de Beaumont," *Oeuvres complètes* [Paris, 1865], III 64), "is that man is a being naturally good and loving justice and order." He is naturally good simply because he is part and parcel of nature, and "the spontaneous tendencies of nature are always right." This conviction has remained; it constitutes an element in the unconscious metaphysics by which modern man lives; it is rarely critically examined, for nobody wants to give up a fond and flattering delusion. But a delusion it is, just as is its opposite, the grim and off-putting doctrine of Joseph de Maistre, according to which man is born with a bent toward evil. In a strictly scientific view, the terms "good" and "bad" cannot be applied to anything which is purely natural; who in his senses would call the laws of gravitation either good or bad? Such terms are therefore meaningless in any discussion of the neonate. But nature has not coordinated human actions (including those of the nursing mother and the nursling child) in such a way that they dovetail into each other as do, for example, the cooperating organs of our bodies. As soon as there are two creatures, mother and child, they are merely referred to each other; they must work out the detail of their relationship, and the process is loaded with a thousand and one difficulties and dangers. Indeed, if a strictly naturalistic view is taken, it appears that conflict rather than harmony is laid on in nature's primary arrangements. The newborn baby is a complete creature endowed by nature with a ruthless desire to survive, to be, and, therefore, to subordinate all others to his own vital interests. Even the mother is, to begin with, no more than a source of food, not to say a milk machine, and for this reason essentially an object of exploitation.

Even the great child psychologist Melanie Klein was, for a while, like most intellectuals, deeply imbued with the Rousseauan spirit. But as time went on, constant observation, coupled with high intellectual honesty, forced her to reconsider and to see the neonate in different colors. In her later writings, such as *Envy and Gratitude* and *Our Adult World* (New York, 1963), she describes *greed* as the most prominent characteristic of the infant; and not just greed pure and simple, but a measureless greed, a greed which is hard to limit. "Greed is an impetuous and insatiable craving, exceeding what the subject needs and what the object is able and willing to give," she writes in *Envy and Gratitude* (p. 7), and in *Our Adult World* she adds:

With greed goes the urge to empty the mother's breast and to exploit all the sources of satisfaction without consideration for anybody. The very greedy infant may enjoy whatever he receives for the time being; but as soon as the gratification has gone, he becomes dissatisfied and is driven to exploit first of all the mother and soon everybody in the family who can give him attention, food, or any other gratification. . . . This situation remains in fundamentals unchanged in the greed of the older child and of the adult" [p. 10].

These words alone (whose realism only an out-and-out utopian could gainsay, as far at least as the "natural" infant, the neonate, is concerned) are sufficient to show how inherently difficult it is to socialize the human animal. Entry into a social situation does not, by itself, change the child. On the contrary. It adds to greed the more social—or, rather, antisocial—trait of *envy*, the great, nay overwhelming, importance of which has recently been demonstrated by Helmut Schoeck (*Envy: A Theory of Social Behaviour*; New York, 1966). Melanie Klein asserts "that envy . . . has a constitutional basis" and that it is an "expression of destructive impulses, operative from the beginning of life" (*Envy and Gratitude*, p. ix; see also p. 81). Like greed, it is, at least in many cases, "insatiable" (p. 8). Klein goes so far as to suggest that envy is a general tendency which "always finds an object to focus on" (ibid.), and that it even focuses on the mother's breast, notwithstanding the fact that this is the source of the life-sustaining, pleasure-giving food, a generous spender (*Our Adult World*, p. 10). Her conception is that the infant considers the breast as not generous enough. Whenever he is hungry or feels otherwise neglected, he imagines that there would be plenty of milk available if only it were given to him, but that it is not given to him because the mother wishes to keep it for her own benefit. We have no need to follow Klein into this extreme speculation; it is doubtful that "there is in the infant's mind a phantasy of an inexhaustible breast . . ." which is hated and envied because it is felt to be a "mean and grudging breast" (*Envy and Gratitude*, p. 11; see also p. 39); we are reluctant to follow her simply because the small child has no definite phantasies at all but merely physical states or conditions which are but meagerly reflected in the mind. But if we reject the notion that the infant is apt to envy his mother, we are all the more inclined to find in the primal feeding situation the roots for the envy of competitors such as siblings, the roots of the enmity between Cain and Abel or Romulus and Remus, and, hence, of all fratricidal tendencies which the socialization process has to overcome. How deep-laid these tendencies are will be understood if one remembers that behind envy there lies the fear of hunger, and behind the fear of hunger, the threat of death.

The hard fact of the matter is that the creature who emerges from the womb is totally self-centered. He is an animalic body containing, it is true, a rudimentary human mind which may come to be filled by a social content, but as yet that mind and that sociality are but preformations, potentialities, and no more. In the beginning there is nothing but the instinct of self-preservation, nothing but an organism of flesh and blood endowed with an elementary drive to exist, and that organism is as yet no different from that of any beast, be it even the most solitary one on earth.

SOMA AND PSYCHE; STRUCTURE AND FUNCTION

62. The infant who is expelled from the womb and propelled into the world reacts to his experience—to the birth trauma, as scientists are wont to call it —by a yell of protest, a yell of pain. He would, if he could, return to the safety of the maternal flesh, but he cannot; that road is blocked. The lure of retrogression may, as we have seen, inspire poetic expressions of deep yearning, but in reality there is only one choice: to go forward, to come to terms with the new environment. But that is not easy to accomplish. Inside the uterus, everything is as it must be, and everything remains as it was before; the setting is simple because it is determined. Outside, however, little is fixed. The fetus leaves a closed world and enters an open one. Openness means riches in the long run; in the short run it hardly means more than uncertainty, difficulty, and problematic.

In his brief, but important, treatise *Biologische Fragmente zu einer Lehre vom Menschen* (Basel, 1951), Adolf Portmann compares the species *Homo sapiens* with other animal species and comes to the conclusion that, even zoologically speaking, there is a tremendous difference between the two: other animal species have a definite, preprogramed habitat, but to *Homo sapiens* belongs *in posse* the whole globe. Portmann contrasts the animal's *Umwelt* with the human *Welt*, a play upon words which is not possible in English, but which is very instructive. The *Umwelt* is a given; the animal is fixed to it. It is either a creature of the steppe or of the forest, of the lake or of the sea. For man, on the other hand, the world is an open field of exploration, and he can settle himself within it, wherever he likes. And not only can he choose his home pitch, he can create a home after his own design within the selected setting. True, animals too build themselves habitations, nests or lairs or burrows, but that hardly diminishes the uniqueness of *Homo sapiens*.

> In contrast with the changes which even the animal may introduce into its environment and which are never more than the transformation of a piece of the fixed *Umwelt* through instinctual activity, human intervention is based on free decision. It can take place anywhere; it can take into account areas which are beyond the purview of our senses; and its background is a knowing relationship to past and future [p. 82].

Portmann here reformulates, from his own bio-zoological point of view, an insight which sociologists, too, have gained through their own efforts: the influence of the deterministic school of geographers, like Pierre Guillaume Frédéric LePlay and his followers, has waned among them, and that of Vidal de la Blache with his "theory of regional possibilities" has grown strong. The animal depends on what its habitat can do for it; man, on the other hand, depends on what he can do with his surroundings. Nature sets an outer perimeter beyond which he cannot go; but within it he is free.

Portmann looks at these important facts from yet another point of view and thereby adds further clarity to what is already clear (p. 84). Even the animal is curious and active and searches all around it, but what is significant for it, what it searches out, is narrowly determined by its physical organization. Man, on the other hand, can interest himself in anything and everything. He decides for himself what is important and what is not. He *bestows* or *attributes* value —sometimes even to things which are hidden from his animal senses. How else could science have developed? To draw a parallel between the chimpanzee who looks for bananas and man who digs into the bowels of the earth to find uranium there because he knows that tremendous energies are hidden in the nucleus of its atoms is to make too much of very little and too little of very much. Science is a search for what *may* have value and probably *will* have value; even the primates restrict their interest to what is *actually* useful to them, and is so *now*.

We are saying all this not in order to exalt the mind of man, not in order to argue for a certain philosophical position, that of idealism, but for a much more sober and scientific reason. Continuing to fix our attention on the neonate, we may assert that to the world of vast potentialities into which he is ushered, there corresponds a vast array of potentialities on his own part; and this, in the final analysis, is the fact which explains why he is able successfully to cope with it. The newborn animal is in almost every detail an exact replica of the grown-up. This becomes sufficiently clear as soon as we set eyes on a newly arrived giraffe or rhinoceros standing next to its dam. The picture of a human mother and her baby is very different: there can be no comparison between her and the bundle she carries in her arms. The bio-zoological explanation of this contrast lies in the fact (to which we shall have to revert) that the period of gestation in *Homo sapiens*—a mere nine months—is too short to produce a virtual adult. Differently expressed: man is born unready, premature, even though "prematurity" is normal for his species. But such a formulation, though correct from the point of view of comparative zoology, is misleading. The term "premature" places the emphasis on the negative aspect, and there is a positive aspect as well. Man is born elastic, so elastic in fact that he can respond to, and adjust to, an elastic environment.

When animal, e.g., primate, potentialities and human potentialities are compared, stress is usually laid on man's larger and heavier brain. That is entirely justified, but by itself it is not enough. Not that man has, to begin with, a more evolved cortex, but that the *functioning* of that cortex can be developed later in a less fixed environment, is the truly decisive circumstance. For about a year or so—the span of time which, biologists and zoologists tell us, measures the comparative prematurity of normal human births—the human fetus or infant (we may use both terms interchangeably because with man we may speak, in a realistic paradox, of an extrauterine fetal period) matures, not under the influence of a uniform environment in the grip of physical laws, but under the impact of a varied environment permeated by freedom. If it be said that in either case—in the womb and out of the womb, in the case of the beast and in the case of man—stimuli impinge on the developing form, then it must be replied that such a formula cannot conjure away what is a very real contrast. Intrauterine and extrauterine, animalic and human, stimuli are so different both in quantity and in quality that only a verbal trick, a verbal fiction, can reduce them to a common denominator. Monism will do as little here as anywhere else.

The awkwardness of traditional dualism has always been to confront body and mind. It is, however, far more fruitful to distinguish behavior (in the sense of Behaviorism), i.e., movements of the body as such, from action (in the sense of Voluntarism), i.e., movements of the body at the command and under the control of the will. When the baby yawns or sneezes, this is something which happens to him, not something which he does; if he feeds, if he actively sucks at the breast, this is something which he does, not only something which happens to him. This distinction is essential and has to be applied on a broad front. Jean Piaget tells us in *The Origins of Intelligence in Children* (trans. Margaret Cook [New York, 1969], p. 89) that the grasping reflex is "not at all comparable to reflexes such as sneezing, yawning etc." and he informs us a little later (p. 90) why. Sneezing and yawning are simply reflexes, but, in grasping, a "functional use" is made of reflexes. To express it in a formulation of our own: sneezing and yawning involve only the mechanisms of the body, whereas grasping (or seeing or hearing or sucking) is triggered by a motion of the will. That will, it is true, is not the conscious and rational will but rather the natural or existential will with which Wilhelm Wundt and Ferdinand Tönnies operate; but it is *will* all the same, and it bears the roots and rudiments of consciousness and rationality within itself.

So important is this difference that even apparently unitary phenomena ought to be conceptually and analytically split up with the help of it. Eating is certainly a unitary phenomenon, but there are two elements in it which are to some extent recognizable as succeeding stages. There is on the one hand stilling one's hunger, and there is on the other enjoying one's food. The former brings peace to our stomachs; it puts them to *rest*. The latter is an *activity* on our part. "The discriminating enjoyment of food is the specifically human quality in eating and drinking," writes Schachtel (*Metamorphosis*, p. 66), "while man has in common with animals the negative pleasure of the relief from hunger." In case even this clear sentence should not yet be fully convincing, let us add, for good measure, a practical and homely illustration. In Italy, it is the custom to eat antipasto (e.g., spaghetti) before the meat. The inherent aim of this habit is to still the hunger, but to preserve the appetite. But hunger is an organic condition, a condition of a specific organ; whereas appetite, though no doubt it is also organic, relates to the whole organism and indeed to the vitality indwelling in that organism and thereby to the person as a whole.

We could also say here that hunger is a condition of the id, whereas appetite relates to the ego; but if we did so, we should use the two terms differently from Sigmund Freud, who has given them so wide a currency within the literature. For Freud, the ego is hardly more than a part of the id, just as thinking is for him "nothing but a substitute for the hallucinatory wish" (*The Interpretation of Dreams*, trans. James Strachey, Standard Edition of the Complete Psychological Works v [London, 1953], p. 567). But, surely, thinking is much more than that; and in the same way the ego is much more than merely a fraction of the id stimulated into awareness by the encounter with reality, with the world. Thought is *pursuit* of reality, not only a *reaction* to it. Granted it is dependent for its functioning on the cortex, i.e., on the body, it is yet the manifestation of a specifically human capacity and therefore depends as much on us as on our physical machine.

The distinction which we have just drawn between "us" and "our physical machine"—that is to say, between *psyche* and *soma*—will of course be impugned by out-and-out materialists and monists, but it is precisely in the context of a study of the infant and his incipient sociality that the reality and justification of it can be most clearly seen. For sociality can only insert itself into the psyche, not into the soma; the body is and remains, and has to remain, within the grip of self-preference. That is how nature has made it. Freud himself has in a manner acknowledged this, for what sociologists usually call the internalized stock of norms and values he describes as the superego, i.e., something grafted onto the ego and not onto the id.

It could not be otherwise. For the internalization of norms and values occurs in and through the ongoing interaction between the as yet non-social infant and the socialized persons around him, and therefore it is part and parcel of an action scheme. It can only be brought about by what in man is prone to action, and the soma is much less so than the psyche. Our bodies react rather than act; it is not in the flesh as such that the energy resides which will build social systems and individual personalities.

To prove this point, let us remind the reader first of all that with the neonate, as also with at least the lower animals, there is little difference between the condition of sleep and the condition of wakefulness. He is, they are, permanently in a state of somnolence. Yet it is not this observation by itself which will support our argument, important though it is; it is rather its analysis which will convince. The neonate and the lower animals are somnolent, passive, undynamical, because they are more body than psyche. Certainly, the body will stir when it is stung by an emotion such as hunger, but as soon as this tension is resolved, it will sink back into inactivity. The body is—to speak with Freud—dominated by the pleasure principle, and "the pleasure principle has as its goal undisturbed quiescence . . ." (Schachtel, *Metamorphosis*, p. 129). Freud was entirely correct when he strongly emphasized this fact. He was wrong only when he went on to assert—setting aside such spontaneous activities, obviously enjoyable in themselves, as play—that the whole man strives at all times for a condition of undisturbed quiescence, with a longing so strong that it can even be described as a "death wish." The quest for knowledge, for instance, is not of this kind. If it is truly awakened in a human being, it will be a permanent spring to action, indeed, a progressive one. Body hunger is sated by feeding, mind hunger is stimulated by it. "The appetite [in this case] grows by eating," as an old proverb has it. And this applies not only to knowledge, usable knowledge which is a means to an end, with the end constituted by the instinct of self-preservation. Man's craving for mental enrichment is not thus restricted (as the scientist, above all other people, should realize); it applies also to the mind's quest for *meaning*, and it applies, above all, to the infant's desire to explore the world of human relationships, to know them, to understand them, to become domiciled within them. To begin with, this desire will also be a desire on the baby's part to manipulate the human relationships in the midst of which he finds himself; to that extent socialization is seriously impeded, and for a long time only a state of semi-sociality is attained. It will take a strong and sustained effort to drive beyond it. But the main point which we have to make here is that the vitality which leads the incipient human being into social interaction and in due time to play his part in it is rooted, not in the fibers of the body, not even in the cortical cells, though they help to implement it on the operational side, but in the capacity, given at birth but as yet not activated, for experience and encounter with a meaningful reality and with other selves.

The connection and the contrast between the cortex on the one hand and mental capacity on the other is a case, an instance, of the connection and contrast between structure and function. Clearly, in practice, the two hang closely together, and yet they must not be considered as identical. A structure is thingly, a set of objects; it belongs to the realm of matter, of physics. A function is processual; it belongs to the realm of life, hence, of biology and physiology. A structure in itself is static; a function is dynamical. A structure is something which exists; a function is something which happens. Perhaps we can clarify the issue with the help of a simple simile. A structure is one of life's tools, like a hammer. But a hammer can be used in many different ways and for many different purposes. It limits the will which wields it, but it does not determine its action. It can be used to drive a nail into the wall; it can also be used to knock a man on the head. Ever the same as a physical thing, it can, in the frame of life, and especially social life, become a servant of many different intentions.

Our sensory organs and our nervous systems are physical structures which admit of multiple human and social uses. In a charming book of recollections, *Das Jahr der schönen Täuschungen* (Wiesbaden, 1952; pp. 209, 210), the novelist Hans Carossa (who was by profession a medical man) recalled his first examination in zoology. He was asked to compare the eye of *Homo sapiens* and of *Sepia* (the cuttlefish), and he launched with gusto into an enumeration of the similarities, which are many. But his examiner, the famous zoologist Richard Hertwig, soon reminded him that near identity in structure may go hand in hand with a great dissimilarity in function. What remained of the sensory tool of the animal in the end, Carossa writes, "was merely the impression of an imitation, of a large, coarse, glass eye, denied every kind of development, while in the optic organ of man the light of the soul and the light of the sun forever strive toward each other." More soberly, but perhaps also more pungently, expressed: the cuttlefish can see only Euclidian space adapted to his (and our) physical inlet; but we can rise to the intuition of Reimannian space and other variants of space as well. As far as the nervous system is concerned, Jean Piaget writes in *The Origins of Intelligence in Children* (p. 8; see also pp. 1, 2): "It is self-evident that if the categories of reason are in a sense preformed in biological functioning, they are not contained in it either in the form of conscious or even unconscious structures." Elsewhere in the book he sheds light on the same subject by explaining the difference between physiology and psychology, or, more precisely, between somatic physiology and psychology in the more-than-somatic sense of the word: physiology describes the inherited mechanisms of man; psychology, the uses to which these mechanisms are put. "This use does not in any way change the mechanism itself . . . . But within the limits of [its] functioning there is room for a historical development which marks precisely the beginning of psychological life" (p. 39). The duality of man's belonging—soma and psyche, nature and culture—could hardly be more convincingly conveyed.

If there should still be anybody who is reluctant to concede what we are asserting here, namely, that the use of the physical equipment which the neonate brings with him from the mother's womb (which is also the womb of nature) enables him to go far beyond the satisfaction of his physical needs—to go so far beyond them that he may add other dimensions, those of culture and sociality, to his being—let us remind him that in the area of life nature is amazingly, overwhelmingly, generous. A small droplet of serum is introduced into our bloodstream: we develop enough antibodies to be safe from smallpox all our days. It is this nature-given excess of organic energy over organic need which has allowed man, both phylogenetically and ontogenetically, to become what he is. Indeed, even more: to turn the tables on nature, to change from her underling into her master. "Although it is man's wants in the earliest stages of his development that give rise to his activities," Alfred Marshall has written in his classic *Principles of Economics* (London, 1938; p. 89), "yet afterwards each new step upwards is to be regarded as the development of new activities giving rise to new wants, rather than of new wants giving rise to new activities." At all events, the problem which occupies us here, the coming of sociality, can only be solved by a reference to that excess energy, for, as we saw in our first volume, the social habit which we all share is not inherited in and with our bodies: on the contrary. What they contain and bring along is merely sociality's chief antagonist—the instinct of self-preservation, which in practice is a comprehensive urge toward self-preference.

HEREDITY AND TRADITION; BRAIN AND MIND

63. The contrast between structure and functioning, between what is antecedently possible and what is actually achieved, between the physical nature of the one and the cultural character of the other, is further thrown into bold relief by the different modes in which they are handed down from one generation to the other. Structures are innate and therefore *inherited*; but the child has to *learn* how to function as a human being.

Luckily, this issue was fought out and finally settled in the nineteenth century. Spencer developed in his *Principles of Biology* the thesis that acquired characteristics are encoded in the body and therefore transmissible just like other somatic traits, blue eyes, perhaps, or blond hair, and he applied this conviction to social life as well, when he came later on to write his *Principles of Sociology*. Activities, he thought, modify the brain, the brain modifies the genes. A warlike society will engender, not only warlike habits, but warlike bodies; these bodies will in turn produce aggressive mentalities and inclusive military cultures. Common observation must surely have suggested from the very beginning that this theory is wrong; children find it no more difficult to acquire a language which their parents have never spoken than a language which they have spoken all their lives. But this matter could be obscured and side-stepped by speaking of predispositions rather than of actual endowments, and predispositions are not easy to prove or to disprove. The Spencerian doctrine of the inheritability of acquired characteristics fell, therefore, only when the heavy guns of scientific biology were trained on it, but then it collapsed for once and for all. Weismannism triumphed. Acquired characteristics are not transmitted by physical heredity. Our parents provide us with a larynx, a tongue, and a brain, but we have to *learn* how to speak. Cooley summed up the common opinion of the biologists around him when he wrote: "The germ plasm . . . bears individuals somewhat as a tree bears fruit, but they do not react upon it; they merely carry it and hand it on, as the apple carries the seed." And he drew the necessary conclusions from this scientific insight. There are *two* modes of transmission between an older generation and a younger: heredity and communication (*Human Nature and the Social Order* [New York, 1946], pp. 9, 48), heredity and tradition (*Social Organization* [New York, 1925], p. 68).

We are by no means denying that the higher animals, too, have tradition as well as physical inheritance, and we would go against the observed facts if we did. Child-care acts are, by and large, inherited among animals, but a monkey mother has difficulties in bringing up her young if she has been isolated in a zoo and thus unable to learn from other monkey mothers. Yet Portmann, in emphasizing this fact (*Fragmente*, pp. 160, 161), shows immediately that tradition here is merely a helpmate to inheritance. Imitation, he says, learning, confirms (*festigt*) innate child-care tendencies or, rather, techniques; it does not create them. But among humans child-care acts are, as L. L. Bernard in particular has circumstantially proved, all learned, all created by culture (*Instinct: A Study in Social Psychology* [New York, 1924], passim).

A minute ago, we mentioned language as one of the specifically social institutions which are acquired by learning, because inheritance supplies only the physical apparatus needed for it and no more, but is language really a social institution? Have animals also not a language of their own, even solitary animals, and is language not therefore a natural, and not merely a human and social, phenomenon? This has been asserted, of course, but, once again, a look at the detail destroys the monistic delusion. Two zoologists, Erich von Holst and Ursula von Saint Paul, write in an article entitled "Electrically Controlled Behavior": "Chickens have a large repertory of gestures and a language consisting of several dozen 'words.' To be sure, their language is not learned, as is the language of man; their sounds and the understanding of these sounds are inborn" (see *Psychobiology: The Biological Bases of Behavior*, edd. James L. McGaugh, Norman M. Weinberger, and Richard E. Whalen [San Francisco & London, 1967], p. 58).

Language remains, therefore, one of the prime distinguishing marks between man and beast, as Portmann asserts (*Fragmente*, p. 161), but the duality of which we are speaking plies not only between beast and man; it is observable even in man himself. We express ourselves partly by words and partly by such means as blushing and paling, or laughing and crying. The difference between the two phenomena consists in this: that we control verbal communication—it is up to us, whether we want to speak or to remain silent—while we do not control our capillary system, which produces blushing and paling, or our facial muscles which are instrumental in laughing and crying. These latter phenomena lie parallel, not to language, but rather to the shout of fear or despair which on occasions "breaks from us" or "escapes us"—which happens to us, we might also say, but which we do not willingly utter, of which we are, indeed, often ashamed. By contemplating this contrast, we can learn a good deal. Blushing and paling, laughing and crying, are physical modes of expression which link us to the animal world, but we are striving to bring them under control. The typical Calvinist did not allow himself to laugh or cry, nor did the classical Confucian; to be self-possessed was not only a cultural and religious ideal, it was to a large extent successfully inculcated in millions by means of education. Of St. Ignatius of Loyola, a man totally in control of himself, it is reported that he would not even blink an eyelid unless his ego gave its consent to it. We see therefore not only that there is a contrast between the unlearned and the learned, the spontaneous and the cultural, structure and function, soma and psyche, but that there is also a conflict between them. The point is more than philosophical. Any education which assumes that man can become a creature of culture without a far-reaching conquest of his native animality, that culture may without break be grafted onto animality (and a good deal of modern educational theory and practice is of this kind), is dismally doomed to failure.

Since we think in words, language in the proper sense of the term—*human language*—is closely connected with thought, and this brings us to the most important instance of the coordination and conflict between an inherited structure and a learned, culturally conditioned, function: the relation of the brain and the mind. However privileged the brain may be among the organs of our body, it shares with all the others the fact that, in the neonate, it is no more than the locus of a capacity. "The brain," writes the neurophysiologist Paul Chauchard (*The Brain* [New York & London, 1962], p. 42), "provides merely the *possibility* of being a man, particularly an aptitude for vocalization. It does not provide a language, the means of thinking; for this it is necessary that man learn socially and culturally how to use his brain, a task that will never be finished." And, in a later context, he emphasizes the importance of learning once again and as strongly as before: "The greatest scientist and the primitive savage have the same brain; they are equally human . . . but what a difference there is in the development of these potentialities thanks to culture and all kinds of educational conditioning!" In other words, to use the language of the medieval philosophers: heredity merely gives us a mind *in posse*; it is cultural tradition, cultural transmission, which gives us our mind *in esse*. We may say quite simply that it gives us our mind.

It is necessary, says Chauchard, that man learn to use his brain. Hence, even the brain is essentially a tool. Yet not only the materialist and the monist but every observer has the tendency to consider the cortex as a commander who issues orders, and not as an underling to whom orders are issued. This is entirely justified, as long as we fix our eyes on part of the picture, on the physical aspect alone. Then the cortex correctly appears as a superordinated instance. But it is not the top of the hierarchy. Above it, there is the will, and that is part and parcel of the whole man; it is the highest concentration of his entire being, and not merely an element of his cerebral apparatus. The brain is the link through which the will operates and ensures that its designs are carried out. Master in relation to the limbs, it is servant in relation to the ego. Of course, the mutual relationship between thought and cortex—an aspect of the interconnection between mind and matter—is an impenetrable mystery and should be left alone in a sociological investigation. But a study of the socialization of the individual would be incomplete without a word on it, especially since this book upholds the thesis that sociality lodges only in the mind and not in the body, and that the body is in fact its permanent antagonist.

Eschewing all metaphysics, and more especially idealistic metaphysics, we can perhaps elucidate the matter to some extent by harkening back to the quotation from Alfred Marshall which we gave in the last section. Marshall sees history as a reversal of powers: at first, wants rule over activities; later on, activities prevail over wants. As we ourselves have the tendency to express it: at first, structure rules over function; later on functioning becomes master of the structure. Something similar has happened in the case of the relationship between brain and will. At first, the brain determines the will, or that capacity to struggle and to strive akin to the will which is characteristic of the animal and the as yet animalic neonate; later on, the will, fully unfolded, manipulates the brain. Not only is this statement in line with commonsensical observation, it is even philosophically entirely unproblematic. The human will and the human mind are the highest achievements of life, and life is greater than matter, greater even than that privileged, because will- and thought-bearing, parcel of matter which we call the cortex or the brain.

This whole discussion has not been only an aside; it has led us to an essential insight basic to any true understanding of the process of socialization. That process, if it is to succeed, must be in the first place a socialization of the human, the individual, *will*.

An issue which invariably arises whenever there is talk of a tension between two elements—here functioning and structure, the self-preferring body and the socialized will—is how strong the influence of the one over the other can become. That the socialized will can come to control the self-preferring body is, surely, obvious, for if it were not so, society would not continue to exist. Parsons distinguishes motivational orientation from value orientation. Motivational orientation determines the what, value orientation the how, of an action. A man has hunger and is driven toward the food (motivational orientation rooted in the body), yet he will normally not pursue the food in any way he fancies, but only in a law-abiding way; he will buy, not steal, it (value orientation learned in the course of social education). Unless value orientation is at least as strong as motivational orientation, the framework of order which we call a society will burst asunder. This is an entirely realistic analysis, but the question arises whether acquired law-abidingness can go as far as to be able to enter into the fibers of the body to transform its organic structures. In Freudian language the question is whether the very id can be changed by learning. Freud denies it, but Parsons asserts it. In his "Social Structure and the Development of Personality," a contribution to the volume entitled *Studying Personality Cross-Culturally* (ed. Bert Kaplan [New York, Evanston, &

London, 1961], pp. 165–99), Parsons points out that the ego and the superego are the products of social life, and nobody will have any quarrel with this assertion. But he goes on to ask "whether even the third of Freud's famous three subsystems of the personality, the id, should be completely exempted from this central interpretation of the importance of object relations [i.e., social relations] and internalization [of social values and social norms]" (p. 167), and he answers with a decided no. "The id, like the other subsystems, is organized about its experience in object relations" (pp. 194–95). "I shall argue," Parsons writes in an anticipated summary of his exposition, "that the interpretation of the id as a manifestation of 'pure instinct' is . . . untenable. Though it is the primary channel of transmission of instinctual energy and more particularized impulses into the personality, it also is structured through internalized object-relations" (p. 167); more simply expressed: through the experience of social life. Who is correct in this case, Parsons or Freud?

We get the answer in a passage from one of psychology's most influential texts. "All impulsive responses are modifiable . . . ," writes Knight Dunlap in *Habits: Their Making and Unmaking* (New York, 1972; p. 29), "and in all cases the modifying processes involve thinking." Read "but" for "and," and you have the solution to the whole problem. If a small paradox is allowed because it will help our exposition, we may translate Dunlap's statement by saying that the id is modifiable to the extent that it is not id, but bears a modicum of the ego within it. This is his decided conviction based on a large amount of experimental work. "Modifications," he says, "occur most conspicuously in those reflexes which are most readily influenced by thought processes directly. . . . From these considerations, we might be led to suspect that the thinking which occurs in connection with the process of modification is the real modifying factor . . ." (p. 27). Later on, Dunlap raises the problem of animal learning. What about the rat who learns to find his way through a maze? Is this not a case where an id is modified through learning? Has a rodent an ego within which modifications can take place? Dunlap expresses himself very carefully, but by no means vaguely. We may be forced to "assume that the rat 'thinks' in learning the maze," he writes in one context (p. 37), and in another (p. 103) he adds: "That thought processes (not necessarily, of course, of the human type) may operate in the lower animal is a live possibility which may prove to be the explanation of the effects of reward on the animal." Another expert in this field, though more of a physiologist than a psychologist—a fact which makes his witness all the more precious—is a good deal more definite than Dunlap. In his book *The Organization of Behavior* (New York & London, 1949; p. xvi), D. O. Hebb writes as follows:

> In mammals even as low as the rat it has turned out to be impossible to describe behavior as an interaction directly between sensory and motor processes. Something like *thinking*, that is, intervenes. "Thought" undoubtedly has the connotation of a human degree of complexity in cerebral function and may mean too much to be applied to lower animals. But even in the rat there is evidence that behavior is not completely controlled by immediate sensory events: there are central processes operating also.

These central processes are processes in a rudimentary vestigial ego, not processes of an id. The id as such simply is not modifiable.

By quoting Hebb's statement with approval, we are by no means retreating from the position, which we have upheld all along, that there is an essential difference between man and animal, for we have always emphasized that the essentiality of that difference may be due to the vastness of a difference in degree. A ray of the sun is, and yet is not, comparable to sunlight as a whole. In any case, there remain other contrasts between human thought and animal "thought" besides the fullness of the one and the near nothingness of the other. Remembering properly so called, for instance, is restricted to human beings. They can recall what is not presented anew to their senses. A rat or a dog can only recognize what enters for a second time into its field of perception (see Dunlap, *Habits*, pp. 147, 148).

The importance of the foregoing discussion concerning the modifiability or non-modifiability of the id for an analysis of the process of socialization will be realized at once if we introduce the simile used by both Freud and Parsons— the simile of the rider and the horse. The ego or psyche is the rider who endeavors to direct the horse (the body or id), and according to Freud he has a hard time of it. Parsons is more optimistic. He assumes that the horse may make the wishes of the rider its own. Real horses no doubt frequently do, but the id is not pliable to the same extent. It had better be compared to the stubborn mule which persists in going where *it* wishes to go and has to be *forced* to accept direction. But in the end the whole comparison breaks down, for even a mule may come to surrender its resistance to an alien will. The human id, as long as it is healthy, and that means healthily animalic, will not do that. Nature has programed it to pursue its own purposes, and these purposes are self-regarding. A man may share his last crust of bread with another, but he will assuredly do so against the protests, and in defiance, of his hungry stomach. A man may also turn the other cheek, but his face will assuredly smart under the blow and wince in anticipation of it. No, the body cannot be socialized, only the personality can; and, in this particular, Freudian soberness, and even Freudian pessimism, are preferable to Parsonian delusion, simply because they are in accord with the facts. To return to the metaphor: the horse, the mule, the id, cannot be broken; but the rider, the ego, the human will, can be strengthened until the sociality which it carries and contains is powerful enough to prevail over the tendency toward self-preference which inheres in the fibers of the body. A realistic theory of society and a realistic practice of education should not forget it.

NATURE AND CULTURE: ANTITHESIS OR SYNTHESIS?

64. In a book which we should not hesitate to call profound, *La Personnalité de base*, the French philosopher Mikel Dufrenne has taken up the same stance as we did in our last section. Nature and culture are opposed to each other like thesis and antithesis; their distinction is clearly visible in the fact that nature appears in the newborn individual, whereas culture lies to start with in the group; in the developing person, nature and culture meet and interfere with each other as long as the process of socialization lasts (Paris, 1966; p. 69). So far, so good. We would only add that the process of socialization lasts all through life. There is nobody whose humanity could not be further improved, and it was precisely the greatest of saints who have most strongly insisted on this fact.

But Dufrenne does not stop there. He asks whether it is legitimate to divide man into two parts, and returns a negative answer to the query. Going very far indeed, he suggests—canceling, we would suggest, his own basic insights— that nature and culture are related to each other as are, in Kant's definitions, matter and form. Now, the distinction between matter and form is a purely mental one; in hard reality form cannot exist without matter and vice versa. A cube must be of ice or of wood or of marble; there is *realiter* no such thing as a cube-in-itself, though, by abstraction, we can develop a "pure" concept of the cube. Is the relation of nature and culture really of this kind? Is nature not resistant to culture and culture not striving to control nature? Can we legitimately proceed from the fact of their antithesis to the assertion that they merge in a synthesis? Dufrenne thinks so and argues along the following lines:

> We must beware of hardening the opposition by reifying nature. She should be conceived as energy [*puissance*] and not as substance. The human nature which we must presuppose is not a ready-made nature which the existence of sociality would modify by exerting on it, from the outside, a causal influence; she is much rather a cluster of possibilities to which only the contact with society can give actual existence and which at the same time bestows on social life a physiognomy of its own. It is not so that there is first nature and then society; rather, there is a nature which realizes itself in society, so that this nature can only be perceived in its social expression, while social expression for its part realizes that nature [pp. 69–70].

This kind of argument is sure to have a very wide appeal. It appears to tally with the facts; more importantly, it falls in with our secret wishes, for who wants to be reminded of the conflict between what, somewhat naïvely, is sometimes called man's higher and man's lower nature; more scientifically expressed: the ego and the id?

Yet, however alluring Dufrenne's argument may appear, it will not stand up to critical examination. For it is obvious that he radically shifts his ground. Where he speaks of nature and culture as an antithesis, he means by nature our physical nature, our body, and that body is surely a substance. It is quite wrong to define it as energy or *puissance*; all that can truly be asserted is that it *carries* or *contains* energy or *puissance*. Where he speaks of nature and culture as forming a synthesis, he means by nature natural capacity and not flesh and blood. That capacity is certainly not a substance and can as certainly be developed in many different directions. So far he is correct. Yet, on the basis of his deductions as a whole, he must be judged wrong. His sentence to the effect that "the human nature which we must presuppose is not a ready-made nature" must, if the truth is to be served, be replaced by two complementary statements. The one would read: "the human nature in the physical sense of the word which we must presuppose *is* a ready-made nature" for, surely, the body is what it is, and though it may further mature after it has left the mother's womb, it cannot be culturally modified. The other statement would run: "human nature in the sense of habitual conduct is not a ready-made nature," but rather the product of habit formation, humanization, and moralization, and as such capable of assuming many shapes and degrees of refinement. Dufrenne, as can be seen, was the victim of ambiguous verbiage, like so many others before him. He who speaks vaguely of "human nature" "in general" is almost bound to slip and fall; only he who knows what nature he means, physical, substantial nature, or habitual conduct (all too often wrongly described as human "nature"—a word which comes close to being a contradiction in terms) will be able to achieve defensible results. There is no antithesis between culture and human nature if by nature is meant a stock of nature-given potentialities; but there is such an antithesis if by nature is meant the parcel of cells imbued with an animal instinct of self-preservation delivered from the mother's womb.

A brief side glance at the history of ideas will show what happens if this all-important problem of definition is not duly attended to. When Cooley speaks of human nature, he means human nature *in posse*—what can be done with the social potentialities which are laid on in man. The body he waves away as if it were no source of trouble. No wonder then that he comes to a picture in which the conjunctive, cultural sentiments, the light hues, so to speak, prevail. When Freud, on the other hand, speaks of human nature, he means human nature *in esse*—the animal *Homo sapiens*, or rather the animal *homo*, a specific kind of primate. The mind is to him only an epiphenomenon, a shining but weak incandescence on the surface of the soma. No wonder that he comes to a picture in which the disjunctive sentiments prevail, egotism, aggressiveness, hate, and so on, a picture of dark and forbidding hues. In either case, the proper balance is lost.

But not only will the proper balance overcome the errors of these two outstanding students of man, it will do away with the whole unfortunate pseudo-problem of nature *versus* nurture over which a whole ocean of ink was spilled in the earlier decades of this century. It is wrong to say that the modalities of human action are owing to nature rather than nurture, for nature provides merely a starting point. But it is as wrong to say that the modalities of human action are owing to nurture rather than nature, for nurture has to have materials to work on: it does not, and it cannot, start from nothing. To think of the body as infinitely plastic because the mind is so, as did Cooley, is profoundly unrealistic. To speak of nurture and nature in terms of an either/or is about as reasonable as to ask whether a child is more the offspring of his father than of his mother or vice versa.

We must be careful, however, not to take our criticism of Mikel Dufrenne too far. There is no synthesis of nature and culture in the Hegelian and Marxist sense of the word, no emergent condition in which the initial antithesis is permanently and totally overcome. But there is an uninterrupted *process* of compromising. Our whole life policy is, and must be, a sustained attempt to satisfy both our native urges and our acquired values, and though some men will yield more to their native urges and others will invest more in their acquired values, all men must to some extent attend to both. Even the Desert Fathers had to have bread and water. Even the most selfish person must set limits to his greed, or he will be destroyed. Our cultural commitments are sometimes described as our "higher" goods, and this creates the impression that our bodily needs are somehow intrinsically "lower." They are so in the context of a moral philosophy because we should in principle prefer the former to the latter. But the most unselfish person has to eat if he wants to remain useful to his fellow-men. Even the moral philosopher is therefore obliged to describe our bodily needs as "more basic" as well as "lower," and our cultural commitments as "more secondary" as well as "higher," if he is to speak in the accents of reason and common sense (see Werner Stark, "Editor's Introduction," to Max Scheler, *The Nature of Sympathy* [London & New Haven, 1954], pp. xv–xvi).

We are emerging then from our bout with Mikel Dufrenne with a reinforced conviction that the socialization and moralization of man can only succeed via man's native potentialities and never via man's native actualities. It has to be brought about by active education; it will not come about spontaneously simply by physical maturation. Not only can the body not be socialized or moralized; it cannot even be absorbed into an abiding synthesis with the cultural norms which we internalize in the course of social life. It has to be continually compelled to abate its demands in an effort which painfully proceeds through piecemeal compromises and stretches all along life's way.

Many fond delusions are current on this head. Melford Spiro, writing in *Studying Personality Cross-Culturally*, has this to say: "By prescribing goals the cultural heritage does not frustrate drives, it merely limits the number of ways in which they may be gratified. . . . A need-satisfaction model is more appropriate than a drive-reduction model as a description of cultural motivation" ("Social Systems, Personality, Functional Analysis," p. 105). But soon this optimism is tempered somewhat. Spiro admits (p. 109) that "the culturally prohibited canalization [of a drive] may continue to persist as a personally preferred canalization, and the culturally prohibited drive may continue to seek expression." Very true; but that is not all. Let us look at Spiro's own illustration. An orthodox Hindu, he writes, is forbidden to eat beef; he normally will not even want to eat it. His nutritional interest or instinct will travel in different directions. But—and this is decisive—in whatever direction or directions it travels, whatever the foods which are permitted and customary in his society, society will have to insist on an all-round mitigation of greed. Are Hindu children allowed to gorge themselves with rice and almonds, even though these sweets are habitual fare? Will they not be urged to be satisfied with a moderate plateful? No, Spiro is wrong. We cannot escape the necessity of working with a drive-reduction model in our social theories. Reality demands it. Who would not prefer a need-satisfaction model? We would not prefer a pleasant to a forbidding hue? But what we cannot have, we cannot have.

THE KNOWLEDGE OF OTHER SELVES

65. We have now seen what the impact of the social forces on the individual cannot do. The time has come to turn to the positive aspect to ask what it can do. The neonate is born with a minimum of sociality. What is the maximum which can be achieved?

The answer is contained in the scriptural injunction: "Love thy neighbor as thyself!" (Lev. 19:18). In principle, we may perhaps imagine an even more highly socialized man, a man who loves his neighbor better than he does himself. But this would be hardly more than a phantasmagoric idea. A society of associates each of whom loves the others as he does himself is for all practical purposes the most ambitious aim human education can set for itself. What it should go for is the development of a sympathetic streak in the personality.

The learning of sympathizing attitudes involves two stages which Cooley has distinguished for us. He speaks of sympathy in two senses: "in the sense of understanding or personal insight," and in the sense of pity or tender emotion (*Human Nature*, pp. 138, 136). The second level obviously presupposes the attainment of the first. Before we can feel sorrow for a fellow-being, we must be able to discern what ails him.

The possibility of understanding others has been presupposed by most sociologists, especially since Max Weber, with his call for an "understanding" analysis, has become a model for many practitioners in the field. But neither Weber nor his admirers have done much to elucidate the modus of mutual understanding. For an effort in this direction we have to go to Max Scheler whose book *The Nature of Sympathy* is a minor, if not a major, classic.

There are, it appears, two traditional theories, one of which may be called the theory of analogical inference. Its basic assumption is that "on perceiving expressive movements similar to those which we experience in ourselves in consequence of our own individual self-activity, we infer a similar self-activity in others" (p. 238). Scheler has two great objections to this doctrine. The first is descriptive; the second, logical. Looking at a baby at the time when it begins to show interest in human faces, and assessing its mental condition at that juncture, can we realistically ascribe to it an ability to draw inferences by analogy? Even if the terms are understood in a much attenuated sense, we cannot. Secondly, "such an argument would be logically correct . . . only if it implied that on the occurrence of expressive movements similar to those I perform myself, it is my own self that is present here as well—and not some other and alien self" (p. 240; emphasis deleted). Differently expressed: if I base my idea of what I see in my neighbor on the traits which I see in myself, I would never come to know him properly. My own self would be a veil which would hide for me forever his true being.

These are powerful, if not decisive, arguments for rejection, but perhaps the weakness of the theory of analogical inference lies even deeper. It is too individualistic a theory. In the final analysis, it sees the self as an enclosed bastion and comes up against the realism of John Donne's dictum that no man is an island. Surely, the fully matured person is capable of understanding others directly, and not only indirectly via the detour of self-knowledge. If it were not so, social intercourse would surely be poorer than it actually is.

The other and competing approach could be called the theory of the *a priori* givenness of a knowledge of other selves. Scheler explains it with the aid of the figure of Robinson Crusoe, "a man, that is, who has never in any way perceived beings of his own kind, or any traces or signs of them, and has no other evidence of the existence of such beings" (p. 234). The question is whether or not such an isolate could know anything of the existence of conscious selves similar to himself and of a community to which he and they belonged. Scheler, showing definite partiality for this doctrine, answers this query in the affirmative. "Crusoe's evidence for the existence of a Thou in general and of his own membership of the community is not merely a contingent, observational, inductive 'experience,' " he writes,

> but is certainly *a priori* in both an objective and a subjective sense and has a definite intuitive basis, namely a specific and well-defined consciousness of emptiness or absence . . . , in respect of emotional acts represented, for instance, by the authentic types of love for other people. In the case of conative acts one might also refer to the consciousness of "something lacking" or of "non-fulfilment" which would invariably and necessarily be felt by our Crusoe when engaged in intellectual or emotional acts which can only constitute an objective unity of meaning in conjunction with the possibility of a social response. From these necessarily specific and unmistakable blanks, as it were, where his intentional actions miss their mark, he would, in our opinion, derive a most positive intuition and idea of something present to him as the sphere of the Thou, of which he is merely unacquainted with any particular instance [p. 235; emphasis deleted].

Scheler, it must be emphasized, does not operate here with the concept of an inborn idea; the knowledge of other selves is based on an experience, but it is the experience of an isolated individual.

Could an isolated individual have such an experience? Surely not. It is difficult to see why Scheler gives preference to this second theory over the first. Daniel Defoe's Robinson Crusoe, or rather that Alexander Selkirk on whose misfortunes Defoe's story is based, was a fully mature man when he lost contact with human society. He knew very well that there are others like him in the world. A true test case would only be an isolate from birth onward, and he would not and could not have that sense of a void, that negative experience, on which, according to the doctrine, the knowledge of an other and others is based. Such a creature would have no mind at all; that inborn capacity would not have become, in his case, an actuality. He would, like an animal, have a somnambulistic awareness of a world of objects, but he would not have a knowledge, let alone an understanding, of other selves and of a social sphere.

It is easy to see, and it is not at all surprising to find, that the aprioristic theory just considered is based on a blunder diametrically opposed to the one which vitiated the theory of analogical inference. It exaggerates the element of sociality, whereas the latter was, as we found, excessively individualistic. True, Scheler was miles away from the assumption of a social instinct, but he assumed, as we have seen, a native givenness of "emotional acts as represented, for instance, by the authentic types of love for other people." Nothing like that is given in the world of hard and merciless facts. Men learn how to love in a circle in which love is offered as well as received. The emotional acts of which Scheler is speaking presuppose the experience, the molding influences, of social life; an isolate would not have this experience and consequently he would not have the outgoing feelings which could give him a longing for other selves and thereby the basis for a knowledge of the existence of a social reality.

As is so often the case in disputes of this kind, neither of the two theories is totally correct or totally false (though the second is correct, up to a point, for a reason different from the one given in Scheler's text). They are, after all, in essence narrower formulations of the wider social philosophies known as atomism and holism, or mechanicism and organicism, or philosophical nominalism and sociological realism. Since society is not only a collection of individuals but something more, and since it is certainly not an integrated body like the body physical but something less, there is the same call here for a third or overarching theory as in sociological thought in general (see Werner Stark, *The Fundamental Forms of Social Thought*; London & New York, 1962/1963). What we must ask, then, is to what extent and in what way the theory of analogical inference tallies with the facts, and to what extent and in what way a truth content can be ascribed to its aprioristic rival.

As soon as we try to answer these questions, we are again confronted with the undeniable fact of duality. The theory of analogical inference makes sense insofar as the life of our bodies is concerned. "The only thing we can never perceive in our observation of others is the experience of their own bodily states, especially their organic sensations, and the sensory feelings attached thereto," Scheler writes (p. 255; emphasis deleted), and it is impossible not to agree with him.

> The pain of another person, or the sensory enjoyment of his food, is something I can never perceive directly. All I can do is to reproduce a similar sensation of my own, and infer that in the presence of comparable stimuli the other person has a similar experience. . . . The various states of the body in sensation and feeling are wholly confined to the body of the individual concerned. Hence an identical sorrow may be keenly felt (though in one's own individual fashion), but never an identical sensation of pain, for here there are always two separate sensations.

Scheler calls grief a "spiritual emotion" (ibid.), and though it might be possible to quarrel over the appropriateness of the term, it is clear that in grief we behold an experience which is different from physical pain. Those who deny the difference (and there have, surprisingly, been some who have) must surely be blind. For the sociologist the salient point is that grief, sorrow, and similar states of mind, are knowable, and that spontaneously and directly.

> Just as we can revive, recall and grieve, more or less, over the same painful experience at different periods in our life, so we can also join with others in grieving at one and the same experience. . . . two people may very well feel the same sorrow. . . . Anyone who holds that mental events are only accessible to one person at a time will never be able to explain the exact meaning of phrases like: "All were fired with the same enthusiasm" . . . [p. 258].
>   The act of internal perception, therefore, is not by nature an act which can only be directed upon the mental life of the percipient himself, as if "internal

perception" and introspection amounted to the same thing. . . . so far as concerns the act and its nature and the range of facts appearing within it, everyone can apprehend the experience of his fellow-men just as directly (or indirectly) as he can his own [p. 256; emphasis deleted].

In and through these quotations, we have reached a truly all-important insight. They show us why it is necessary, especially for the sociologist, to insist on a dualistic philosophy, as we have done from the first sentence of the present book. *Our minds are not as divided as our bodies.* They can be socialized. They are socialized. If Scheler writes that "we actually approach . . . solipsism . . . the more we confine our existence to our own body" (p. 259), then we can add: we come closer and closer to maximum sociality, to the deepest possible knowledge and understanding of our neighbors, the more central our mind becomes to all our being.

It is sometimes said, and not without reason, that a proposition is the more likely to be true the more the history of ideas shows a convergence toward it, and especially if it has been put forward independently in a nearly identical form by several pens. The assertion just made has this support (though it does not seem to us to need it). Cooley and Scheler both present the same theory. "Self and society are twin-born, we know one as immediately as we know the other," Cooley writes in *Social Organization* (New York, 1925), and shortly thereafter he adds: "I am aware of the social groups in which I live as immediately and authentically as I am aware of myself" (pp. 5, 9). This is how Scheler words the identical conviction:

even the essential character of human consciousness is such that the community is in some sense implicit in every individual, and that man is not only part of society, but that society and the social bond are an essential part of himself; that not only is the "I" a member of the "We," but also that the "We" is a necessary member of the "I" [*Nature of Sympathy*, pp. 229–30; emphasis deleted].

This existential connection between the I and the you on which all mutual understanding is based is not difficult to comprehend if we try to see it genetically. At first the infant has a stream of impressions in which nothing is separate, everything is inchoately one. Later on, vortices will form in that stream, nodi as it were, and then the I will divide from the you. But the we is the background of them both (see Cooley, *Social Organization*, p. 8). "Long before the child has ever reached the stage of being capable of a more precise distinction between himself and his mental environment, his consciousness is already filled with ideas and experiences of whose real origin he is completely unaware," Scheler explains (*Nature of Sympathy*, p. 247; emphasis deleted).

We always apprehend our own self against the background of an ever-vaguer all-embracing consciousness in which our own existence and the experiences of everyone else are presented, in principle, as included together [p. 250].

What occurs [in the formative period] is an immediate flow of experiences, undifferentiated as between mine and thine, which actually contains both our own and others' experiences intermingled and without distinction from one another [p. 246; emphasis deleted].

It is possible, therefore, . . . for the same experiences to be given both "as our own" and "as someone else's" . . . [ibid.; emphasis deleted].

Somewhat more precisely Cooley asserts: "I-consciousness does not explicitly appear until the child is, say, two years old, and . . . when it does appear it comes in inseparable conjunction with the consciousness of other persons and of those relations which make up a social group" (*Social Organization*, p. 7).

In the face of these facts, Cooley goes as far as to maintain that "the notion of a separate and independent ego is an illusion" (p. 5). This, however, is not sociology, it is sociologism—i.e., an undue overemphasis on the social element in life. Scheler is a good deal more careful. He writes: "personality is, in effect, a non-spatio-temporal collocation of acts, a concrete whole conditioning each individual act, and a whole whose variations are reflected in those acts" (*Nature of Sympathy*, p. 224). This formulation appears to us acceptable. Personality, we would say, is an action center dwelling in, but not identical with, a bodily organism. Yet, Scheler, too, shows how difficult it is to keep the necessary balance. When he writes (ibid.) that "personality is the substance of which acts are attributes," he comes as dangerously close to excessive individualism as Cooley does to sociologism. The personality is not a substance, in the current meaning of the term. It is a mind and a will carried by a substance, an ego chained to, but master of, an id.

The matter is complicated, but not so complicated that it cannot be understood. When a new human being arrives, he becomes immersed in a stream of life which so far had been flowing along independently of him. That stream will enter his self and leave deposits therein. It will, for instance, anchor words there which will be a possession shared by him and by others, and thereby a common denominator, a basis of mutual understanding. But the linguistic norm will sit lightly on the individual. When the word "dog" is pronounced, one may think of a large animal and one of a small, one of a borzoi and one of a Pekingese. Everybody will entertain a personal variant of the stock of linguistic expressions, but underneath all personal variations there lurks, as a bedrock not to be shaken, so far as mentally normal individuals are concerned, the social theme, the social medium of interpersonal conversation. This social medium is sufficient, and amply so, to ensure mutual understanding.

Needless to say, the disquisition spread out on the immediately preceding pages was something of a work of supererogation, for there is surely nobody who would doubt that human beings come to know and to understand each other. Nevertheless, it was by no means effort wasted, for it is precisely the scholar's office to investigate what everybody else takes for granted, and science is interested not only in the *what*, but also in the *how*. Far more searching is the connected or consequential question concerning the *extent* of our knowledge of other selves, the depth of penetration, as it were, toward the kernel of their personalities. No general statement is possible because no yardstick or tape measure can exist; but a point of principle can and must be made. It is one of the corollaries of the existential difference between body and action center that they cannot be known in the same way. The person is not objectifiable: it is not a thing which can be looked at and taken in by our senses as such. However problematic and partial the apprehension of physical entities may be (a matter which we gladly leave to the epistemologists), the comprehension of a neighbor and his character is likely to be even more partial and problematic. "Personality is that unity . . . ," Scheler writes (ibid., p. 167), "baffling observation and eluding analysis, which the individual experiences as inherent in all the acts he performs," or, as we may add, in all the acts which a neighbor performs. It is at the most a habit system and, as such, though entirely real because it is constantly re-enacted, very difficult to grasp. A strictly scientific knowledge is possible of another man's body, but not of another man's self— which does not mean, however, that our idea of him cannot be deep and true and reliable.

THE COMING OF SYMPATHY: FROM AUTOCENTRICITY TO ALLOCENTRICITY

66. But we must press on. Knowledge of another person is not yet sympathy for him; it is at best the basis and the beginning of that sympathy. We must therefore follow the social forces further in their impact and activity to see how they raise the individual up to the level of true fellow-feeling.

As soon as we enter this new area of investigation, we are once again confronted by the two extreme theories which we encountered before, the one all too individualistic and therefore false, the other all too collectivistic and therefore false as well. To the doctrine of knowledge by inference corresponds the opinion of Thomas Hobbes, according to which our fellow-feeling for others is in reality a feeling sorry for ourselves. Beholding his troubles we conclude that we, too, may one day be in the same predicament, and that inspires us with a sentiment which appears to be social, but is in reality selfish. It can easily be seen that the very possibility of sympathy is here denied. A husband could, on Hobbes's premises, not feel sympathy for his wife's pain in labor because he could not possibly imagine himself in childbed—a conclusion both absurd in itself and contrary to all experience. To the aprioristic doctrine corresponds the philosophy of such authors as Arthur Schopenhauer and Eduard von Hartmann. The latter speaks of an "essential identity" or "identity of being" between the sufferer and his sympathizing friend (*Phänomenologie des sittlichen Bewusstseins* [Berlin, 1924], pp. 611, 626), and this reveals the kernel of his explanation. The I and the you are both modifications of a common life; no wonder then that their sentiments are echoed and reciprocated. Whereas Hobbes denies the possibility of fellow-feeling in the proper sense of the word, Schopenhauer and Hartmann are blind to its problematic. Indeed, in a fashion they, too, deny its very possibility. "The occurrence of a feeling in some sort of supra-individual spirit or universal consciousness [or herd instinct], in which the two persons merely participate together, coalescing therein, as it were," Scheler rightly remarks (*Nature of Sympathy*, p. 65), "would not be fellow-feeling at all." Besides, if the I and the you are really, in the final analysis, identical, why then do we so often *not* feel sympathy for another's sorrow? Both theories are, as can be seen, reductionist. They argue the phenomenon of sympathy away. Even according to Schopenhauer and Hartmann, we do not really grieve for another, a stranger. Yet the salient fact is that in true fellow-feeling we *do* experience sorrow for another, even though he is a stranger, a complete stranger, another and alien self.

Neither the materialism of Hobbes, therefore, nor the mysticism of Schopenhauer and von Hartmann, can offer us a key to the understanding of sympathy. It is neither a phenomenon in the self-enclosed monad nor a phenomenon of the universal world soul; it is an aspect of *intersubjectivity*.

The step up from the knowledge of another self to sympathy with him, though, as we shall see, steep—a real transformation of our being—is yet not too difficult to comprehend. As we come to know him, we come to see the values and unvalues connected with him: we become aware of features in him which we like and features which we condemn. Just because he is not an object which can be treated objectively, we shall have a human reaction to his character traits, positive or negative, as the case may be. But out of this reaction, or, rather, chain of reactions, there will grow, there is bound to grow, a bond which will entail both love and hate.

The psychology of this process has been splendidly elucidated by Ernest Schachtel. The developing human, so he has most lucidly explained, goes from a condition in which he appreciates both objects and persons in accordance with the value which they have for him, to a condition in which he appreciates both objects and persons in accordance with the value which they have in themselves. Schachtel contrasts an autocentric and an allocentric attitude. The neonate, and even the small baby, is autocentric. By this fact he proves that he is still essentially animalic, for it is characteristic of animal perception that it fixes on whatever has meaning in connection with its own need organization, and on nothing beyond. The mother is at first simply a source of food, and a little later a general body servant. The decisive step is taken when she comes to be seen as a person in her own right, not only valuable for what she does for us, but valuable because she is what she is. When that step has been reached, allocentricity has (to some extent) replaced autocentricity. This is the "metamorphosis" which suggested the title of Schachtel's book. Perception has ceased to be animalic and become human. "Human perception is not only in the service of the question, addressed to the object, 'How can I use you or protect myself against you?' but—in allocentric perception—it also answers the question, 'Who or what are you who are part of this same world of which I am a part?' " (p. 222). Because of this shift from autocentricity to allocentricity man's world-view is incomparably richer than even that of the animal with the sharpest senses, and

> This richness is based on man's capacity temporarily to emancipate himself from being dominated and driven exclusively by the needs he shares with other animals (food, sex, care of the young, shelter, rest, etc.) and to perceive the world around him in its own right and not under the perspective of how it may be used to provide for these needs [p. 221].

The allocentric attitude, so we should note in passing, is at the root of man's highest achievements, science and art. To speak of the latter first: Zurbaran's *Oranges and Lemons* (in the Norton Simon collection) or Caravaggio's *Basket of Fruit* (in the Biblioteca Ambrosiana in Milan) are not food items, but things which shine with a beauty of their own; Velasquez' *Portrait of Juan de Pareja* (in The Metropolitan Museum of Art in New York) is not the picture of the painter's assistant, but that of a friend who is seen and appreciated for what he is. As far as science is concerned, it stands in sharp contrast to technology, even if these two branches of human enterprise interact and stimulate each other. Technology is utilitarian, and that means autocentric. Science strives to know reality as it is, and not as it is useful, and that means that it is allocentric.

The most important implication of allocentricity, however, is the fact that it can serve as a secure basis for human sympathy. "In the allocentric attitude, which is the foundation of allocentric perception," Schachtel writes (p. 226), enunciating another great truth, "there is an element of affirmation. Every act of allocentric perception has this affirmative quality which acknowledges the object of the act as existing in its own right." Perhaps we should distinguish here two forms of love: the one might be called possessive; the other, devoted. Possessive love, like the miser's love for his gold coin, is autocentric; devoted love, like the love of two true friends for each other, is allocentric. Rightly have several authors emphasized that the success of a marriage consists in the partners' ascent from mutual exploitation as sex objects to that high form of friendship in which Aristotle saw the very essence of the conjugal bond (see, e.g., W. R. D. Fairbairn, *An Object–Relations Theory of Personality* [New York, 1954], pp. 139, 140; see also Scheler, *Nature of Sympathy*, esp. pp. 25, 111, 170).

We have just spoken of the mutual attachment of husband and wife; earlier we spoke of the one-sided relationship of the child to its mother. Let us now, for completeness' sake, cast a brief glance at the corresponding relationship of the mother to her child. We again find the same duality. There is a possessive attitude, and there is an entirely different sentiment, the sentiment of maternal devotion. The two are often intermixed, as inseparable in practice as tea and milk once the cup has been stirred. But even here a maturation—a transition from autocentricity to allocentricity, from possessiveness, which is egoistic, to devotedness, which is altruistic—is laid on and has to be described as desirable from a human and ethical point of view. Where possessiveness is not overcome, and that happens all too often—who has not met, in fact or in realistic fiction, a mother to whom a daughter or a son is not much more than a personal convenience, indeed, a body servant?—we have a kind of arrested development. The initial promise inherent in the relationship has not been fulfilled. The mother, we may say, has not been properly socialized.

ABIDING LIMITATIONS TO FELLOW-FEELING

67. We have now virtually achieved the purpose of this introduction, which was to set the stage for a closer examination of the process of socialization.

It has a *terminus a quo*, autocentricity, and a *terminus ad quem*, allocentricity.
It is a continuum, one pole of which is animality and animal self-preference; the
other, humanity and humaneness, which means sociality and sympathy. All
that remains to be done within the framework of this section is to point out,
with the soberness which becomes the scientist, how difficult the movement
from that beginning to that consummation really is.

A sentimental attitude to the baby is a thoroughly life-promoting stance and
as such valuable or even invaluable, but it must be severely excluded from the
search for truth. Doting parents observe that the infant cries whenever they
cry, and they conclude that the little mite is showing them sympathy. Piaget
analyzes this phenomenon in *The Origins of Intelligence in Children* and comes
to a sobering conclusion. When the baby wails, he hears himself wailing, and
this hearing-himself-wailing then prolongs the period of wailing. It is the sound
as such which induces him to be still more sorry for himself: now, that sound
"as such" may in fact issue from another human being, but the baby himself
does not realize that; he cannot even realize it, for he is as yet wholly wrapped
up in autocentricity. "Just as the child comes to listen to the sound of his voice
instead of merely crying and thus inaugurates acquired circular reactions,"
Piaget writes,

> so also he listens to the voice of another and, inasmuch as the sounds heard
> are analogous to the sounds he himself makes, he can only perceive them by
> means of corresponding auditory–vocal schemata. The imitation of sounds,
> in the beginning, is thus only the confusion of one's own voice with that of
> another, coming from the fact that the voice of others is actively perceived
> . . . [pp. 87–88].

In another of his writings, *The Moral Judgment of the Child* (London & New
York, 1932), Piaget becomes involved in a discussion with one of his col-
leagues, and what he says in the course of it is highly instructive for the student
of human socialization. In an article entitled "Observations sur la compassion
et le sens de la justice chez l'enfant" (*Archives de Psychologie*, 21 [1928], 208–
14), Hélène Antipoff asserts that the child, on seeing pain inflicted on somebody
else, identifies with him and feels "vindictive joy" if the author of the hurt is
punished, i.e., himself hurt. She speaks of "an innate and instinctive moral
manifestation which, in order to develop, really requires neither preliminary
experience nor socialization among other children." Her conviction of the in-
nateness and instinctive character of this motion on the child's part cannot,
however, be very deep for she soon changes to a rather different interpretation.
"We have here," she says, "an elementary moral structure which the child seems
to possess very early." Very early is not from the beginning; what is innate and
instinctive is and must be present at birth. Piaget for his part insists that the
whole phenomenon, such as it is, is due to learning, to what we sociologists call
the internalization of norms.

> Nothing in the very interesting observations quoted by Mme Antipoff goes
> to show this innateness. She deals with observations on the behaviour of chil-
> dren between 3 and 9, and it is obvious that at the age of three, a child has
> already come under all sorts of adult influences such as can account for the

fact that its polarization is now . . . in terms of good and evil. The proof of this is that the child speaks; it says "serves him right" and "naughty boy," etc. How could it have learned these words without coming under the moral influence of the person who taught them to it, and without accepting at the same time a whole set of explicit or implicit commandments? . . . To our mind, when a child merely avenges some unfortunate . . . all we have is an extension of the vindictive tendency [*Moral Judgment*, pp. 228–29].

Unlike Piaget who is consistently factual, Cooley was inclined to develop a very optimistic view of man and especially of children, but even he was forced, by his first-hand life experience, to admit that sympathy is of slow growth. This is what he writes in *Human Nature and the Social Order*: "A child who is extremely sociable, bubbling over with joy in companionship, may yet show a total [*sic*] incomprehension of pain [on the part of others]. . . . While both of my children were extremely sociable, R. was not at all sympathetic in the sense of having quick insight into others' states of feeling" (p. 87).

Even in the later phases of life, when allocentricity has already won a few decisive battles against autocentricity and can be said to prevail, there still remain serious limitations to the sentiment of sympathy. Two deserve special mention here. (*a*) The sentiment may be impure. We may rejoice at another man's good fortune, but we may also feel a pang of envy, and such is the inner complication of man that he often experiences both emotions at the same time. Worse still: we may grieve at another's man's ill luck, but we may also gloat over his discomfiture, indeed, even over a genuine sorrow. We can see here very clearly that the social and psychological phenomenon of sympathy must not be confused with the ethical, especially not with the ethical in the positive acceptance of the term. (*b*) Fellow-feeling consists of two prongs—pitying and rejoicing-with—but these two are often not equally developed. It is the opinion of competent observers that pitying is more common than vicarious rejoicing, and though there are no statistics, there seems to be enough evidence to support this estimate. Scheler (*Nature of Sympathy*, p. 135) reminds us that in the German language the word *Mitleid* (pity) is a long-established term, whereas *Mitfreude* is merely a weak and comparatively artificial analogical formation. The situation is not really different in the English tongue as the awkward phrase "rejoicing-with" just used can amply prove. But, ethically speaking, our participation in a fellow-man's joy is a more valuable sentiment than our participation in his sorrow, for he who rejoices with a neighbor at his (the neighbor's) happiness has clearly overcome society's arch-enemy, envy. Painful and abiding limitations to sympathy are thus revealed.

Still, the main difficulty does not lie in this direction. It lies in the persistence of man's basic autocentric attitude. Before this is reduced, insofar as it is ever reduced, it undergoes a certain modification; one might even speak of a certain socialization, provided the term were correctly interpreted according to the specific use which is made of it here. The autocentricity of the baby is naïve, without guile, innocent, and that is the main reason why it is never taken amiss and always excused. The autocentricity of the developing child and of the developed adult, on the other hand, is part and parcel of a cunning life-policy, of a largely conscious strategy in the pursuit of individual ends, often at the expense of the interests of one's neighbors. When we meet a man and ask ourselves what advantages we can draw from this our new acquaintanceship, we act autocentrically, or more or less so. The great bulk of economic interaction is of this kind. Nothing is more revealing than the English linguistic usage which has substituted the word "hands" for the word "workers." The employer is not interested in his employees as persons; all he is interested in is their usable limbs. The Marxist critique of capitalism is twofold: it accuses this system of society of economic exploitation and of human estrangement. It must surely be asked which of these two weaknesses—which of these two curses—is worse, and it is by no means irrational to condemn the latter more than the former. Other cultures, like the feudal, were different. The very word "feudal" is philologically connected with such terms as "faith" and "fealty," and mutual devotedness was at least ideally demanded of the relationship between feu superior and feu inferior, *dominus* and *mannus*.

It would, however, be a mistake to assume that there could be societal arrangements which would make it possible to eradicate autocentricity altogether. Insofar as socialism held out such a hope, it was unduly optimistic; it was utopian. "Man lives always in the world of the objects-of-use, in the perspective of secondary autocentricity," Schachtel writes (*Metamorphosis*, p. 248), and we must once again agree with him. "He could not exist without this perspective. In providing for his needs, the objects-of-use perspective largely replaces the instinct-organization of the animals." Schachtel also says that "the autocentric view of objects and people is part of the human condition . . ." (p. 176), and this, too, is an unexceptionable statement. One of the most ambitious systems of ethics ever put forward, it will be generally agreed, is Kant's as presented in his *Critique of Practical Reason*. The core of this majestic work is the categorical imperative, and though this injunction is formulated in many different ways, perhaps the clearest wording of it is as follows: Act in such a way that you never treat your neighbor merely as a means, but always also as an end. This is one of the highest flights of human idealism, and yet it depicts the autocentric attitude as basic and the allocentric attitude as adventitious and therefore secondary. We are and remain self-centered; nature has made us so. But culture, which has a power of its own, manages to give us a second nature, and it is no less real than the first. The process of socialization is an uphill struggle, yet it is not impossible to get close to the peak.

1

The Socialization of the Individual

68. However great the possibilities of development hidden within him, the new-born human baby is to all intents and purposes an animal. The question arises, however, what kind of animal, for there are many essential distinctions which have to be drawn.

Perhaps the most important of these distinctions is that between creatures which have to remain for a while in the nest and those which are under no such necessity. Zoologists speak in the first case of nidicolous, and in the second case of nidifugous, species. The singing bird is nidicolous; so is the cat; so is the squirrel. Chicken and ducks, on the other hand, are nidifugous, and so are horses and bovines; so, above all, are the simians—as their bone structure proves, our nearest relatives in the animal kingdom.

But what about man? In which category does he belong? Even to raise this question is to recognize that he is the odd man out, that he does not fit anywhere into the established system of nature. For man is both nidifugous and nidicolous. He is therefore, from this important point of view, a contradiction in terms.

According to his physical structure, *Homo sapiens* is indeed nidifugous. For he belongs to the group of primates, and primates are born with fully developed sense organs and, more especially, with open eyes, and their limbs are from the very first day on capable of many modes of movement. And yet he is at birth totally helpless—not like the calf, which can literally stand on its own legs, but rather like the cat, which, as everybody knows, needs time in order to become able to fend for itself. We have here a striking conflict between structure and function. The necessary structure is there, but it cannot function in the way the structure by itself would suggest, until about a year of life has passed.

The uniqueness of man's neonatal condition is indeed striking. Everywhere else in nature structure and function are positively connected: structure is given to make functioning possible, functioning has an appropriate structure at its disposal. Only here is there a negative correlation: there is a structure, but it cannot lead to proper and appropriate functioning. The newborn calf or elephant or giraffe can use its legs immediately in order to follow the herd; man cannot, and yet his legs are reduced replicas of the grown-up's walking limbs, as they are in the case of the animals which we have mentioned.

But are we really confronted with an incompatibility of structure and function? Apparently, yes. But on a deeper consideration we are bound to see that appearances are deceptive, that the true conflict lies on another plane. For, surely, we must be reluctant to assume that nature, otherwise so precise in her arrangements, has at this point lost her grip and produced, as if by a blunder, a setup which does not work. Nature is not divided against herself. Behind the contradiction between the structural ability of the neonate to walk and his functional inability to do so, there hides, in fact, a clash between nature and culture.

What is to follow now is unavoidably conjectural, but it is the kind of conjecture which has both reason and experience on its side. Our argument in this context can start from one assured fact which will impart factualness to all we have to say. Observation proves that there can be no comparison between the newborn monkey, who is to all intents and purposes ready for the life of its species, and the newborn human, who is not. But observation also proves that such a comparison is entirely possible if we match the monkey, not with the newborn baby, the neonate, but with the infant twelve months old. It takes us humans roughly a year to reach the condition which baboons and chimpanzees (and other nidifugous species) have attained at the moment of entry into an independent existence. Our problem therefore shifts to the question why human development is relatively slower than animal; differently expressed: why humans must go through what is in effect an extrauterine period of gestation which their cousins among the simians need not endure because they achieve total maturation inside the womb. Yet differently expressed: Why are men born—zoologically speaking—premature?

If we search for an answer to this query, we are led, not to a law of nature, but to a deed of men. There is a good deal of disagreement as to the detail, but there is also a good deal of unanimity on the essential point. It is the upright stature, the upright gait, of man which has caused, and is causing, his premature ejection from the womb. The pain of childbirth and the notorious weakness of the spinal column are also effects of this cause—the pain of childbirth because the pelvis has altered its shape in response to the new bearing, the weakness of the spinal column because two extremities must now carry the bulk which was meant to be supported by four. Standing erect appears, therefore, to be an act by which the species *Homo sapiens* has stepped out of the animal kingdom. We have no need to magnify this act: originally it was perhaps no more than a primate's—a near simian's—attempt to see a little farther than before. And yet it had far-reaching consequences because it brought into prominence the great energy to which all culture, including all sociality, owes its existence—the will of man. By this signal deed, the laws of nature lost their absolute domination over our race and had to share it henceforth with our collective power of self-assertion and self-determination.

Man is and remains, therefore, naturally nidifugous, but culturally he is nidicolous; and it is obvious that the cultural fact is as potent as the natural. Portmann has rightly and aptly spoken of man as a "secondary nest-dweller" (*Fragmente*, p. 65). For the proper understanding of the process of socialization, it is vitally important to grasp with all due clarity what happens in the extrauterine fetal year, in the nest-dwelling period which culture has forced on our physis. A great potential error lies in wait at this point. It might be said, and it has been said, that in the stretch of time with which we are concerned man's abilities "mature." That is, of course, true, but it is by no means the whole truth. If maturation of native abilities were all that is happening, there would be little difference between men and animals, especially nidifugous animals. They, too, have to mature. A newborn rhinoceros or a newborn giraffe is indeed a small-scale replica of its sire or dam and so in a definite sense already a grown-up, but still there is some further maturation, and not only in the article of growth. What is so essentially different in the case of man is that *entirely new* species-specific, species-characteristic, traits appear in him in the crucial twelve-month after his birth. The rhinoceros and the giraffe, the monkey and the ape, develop what they bring with them from the womb; man acquires what he has not possessed before. He *is* not like other men, i.e., other human beings; he *becomes* like them; he is *made* similar to them, and that is very different from mere maturation. Maturation is a biological process; humanization an educational effort; the contrast between the two could not be clearer. It is natural for the sociologist, for the humanist, to insist on this point, but it is instructive and reassuring to see that a biologist and zoologist like Adolf Portmann takes exactly the same view (ibid.).

If proof be wanted for these assertions, a study of linguistic development can provide it. Man brings a larynx with him, an apparatus for the production of sounds, and he can howl and wail as soon as he arrives; in this respect he is exactly like the chimpanzee or the baboon. And his capacities in this regard mature. His lungs strengthen; the body becomes capable of pressing more air through the vocal cords; the whimper can change into a roar. But all this maturation would not give the infant human language. This appears only when he learns to imitate the sounds he hears around him, and this happens no earlier than the ninth or tenth month of life. At this point, the paths of men and animals, even highly intelligent animals, diverge. In an important paper entitled "La Conduite du petit chimpanzé et de l'enfant de l'homme" published in the *Journal Psychologique* (34 [1937], 494–532), N. Kohts has shown that the chimpanzee does not imitate or acquire the sounds which impinge upon him. He merely continues to vocalize as before. He does not advance from natural to cultural, i.e., subjectively meaningful, expression and communication. The speech which is the distinguishing mark of the species *Homo sapiens* does not come out of him; it is, on the contrary, laid into him. From about his first birthday onward, or a little later, he has in principle two kinds of utterance at his disposal: he can produce animalic sounds, and he will use this ability mainly to externalize bodily, emotional states; and he can formulate words and sentences, an acquired capacity with the aid of which he will clarify his thought and communicate meanings. He will have body language and mind language, and the two cannot possibly be regarded as the same thing.

Of course, even mind language, though entirely distinct from body language, will have to use the same physical apparatus as body language. The rational statement will be produced in the same larynx as the groan of pain and the cry of terror. And there is more: yet another physical apparatus is involved, besides that of sound production—the brain. But the brain is a somatic feature; though nature has favored man by giving him a heavier one than any other animal's, she has yet given brains to animals as well. We must therefore ask, in defense of the general philosophy on which the present work is based, whether the changes which occur in the extrauterine fetal year are indeed as radical as we have indicated, and whether, as far at any rate as the brain is concerned, there is, in fact, something new which appears, and not only a process of maturation.

Let us note first of all that even in this detail man stands in contrast both to the nidifugous species which are his kindred in the matter of structure, and to the nidicolous species with whom he agrees in the need for parental care. The brain of nidifugous animals at birth is already comparable in size and weight to what it will be at maturity; in the case of nidicolous animals the discrepancy is far greater. If the rate of increase is reduced to an index figure, it is 10 for the squirrel, a typically nidicolous variety; for the baboon it is only 2.2. In other words, the squirrel's brain becomes ten times as heavy in the course of its lifetime, that of the monkey only a little in excess of twice. For man, the figure is 4.3. He is in between. He is a unique case.

Coming now to a consideration of the totally evolved brain, we see the difference between man and the other primates in the following table which Portmann has elaborated (*Fragmente*, p. 77):

	Body weight (average)	Brain weight (average)
Baboon	12.5 kilogram	170 gram
Chimpanzee	61.0 ”	363 ”
Man	70.0 ”	1290 ”

The difference is certainly striking—but is it more than a numerical difference? Does all the dissimilarity between man and the animal merely come down to this: that he has a heavier brain to begin with, and that this brain gains somewhat more in weight than that of others as he grows up? And is the difference in the figures—be it the measurement on the scales, be it the index of increase in time—really so massive that we have the right to speak here of a difference in kind and not merely one of degree?

If the relative heaviness of the human brain were all that mattered, it would certainly be doubtful whether we could justifiably speak of an essential contrast between man and animal in this respect. But it is not all that matters. The true dissimilarity, the true contrast, lies once again, not in the area of structure, but in the area of function. The brain is a tool, both in the case of humans and in the case of other creatures—but *whose* tool is it? That is the decisive question. Both in the case of humans and in the case of other creatures it is a tool of life; but the word "life" covers two distinct realities as different as black and white. There is the somnambulist life of the beast and there is the knowing life of man; there is a life which is totally contained within nature and entirely in thrall to her laws, and there is a life which has set itself off from nature and is bending her to its own purposes. The neonate's life, like the life of other beings, is of the first kind; there is dim awareness but no conscious knowledge; there is a pursuit of vital satisfactions, but as yet no deliberate strategy and, above all, no discipline of the instincts. The grown-up's life, on the other hand, is characterized by at least a modicum of self-assertion against nature, including in this term the nature-given urges of the human animal himself. In the neonate, the brain is as yet master; later on it becomes a servant. The new element which enters in, under the influence of the social forces, is the creation of a human and social will, alongside, and often in opposition to, the will of the body. In Freudian language, it is the coming to man, and into man, of a superego whose directedness is different from that of the id. No brain, however massive, would ever of itself cause a creature to turn around and to face reality, and to conceive it as a field which has to be conquered and controlled.

The true importance of the growth of the brain, phylogenetic and ontogenetic, in the history of the race and in the history of the individual, lies, not only in its positive, but also in its negative, consequences, not only in the evolution and perfection of our central organ, but also in the involution and emaciation of our innate urges. Domination by instincts is one thing, self-determination by the will (working through the instrumentality of the brain) is quite another. The two possibilities are contradictory opposites: if the one waxes, the other wanes. They are such opposites first of all in the sense of abstract logic. Insofar as instincts (nature) steer man, his own will has to remain suspended; it would only be disturbing action and that to no purpose. Insofar as values (internalized norms) steer man, his instincts have to remain silent; they would often drive him in a different direction and have to be subdued if the set goals of action have to be realized. If nature had given *Homo sapiens* both true, i.e., imperative, instinct, and true, i.e., free, unconquerable, willing, she would have been like a man in an elevator who has pressed the up-button and the down-button at the same time. But it is not so in reality: to the extent that brain power increases, the power of the instincts declines (though never to the extent that they have not to be kept under control). Discussing the fact of cerebralization, Portmann (p. 74) speaks of a shifting of the center for important functions into the area of the cortex and describes the observable reduction of the instincts, the impoverishment of their influence, as a consequence and concomitant (see also p. 80).

Just how important the contrast is between the id and its assertion, on the one hand, and the ego and superego in their action, on the other, can be seen from a comparison between hymenopterous and human sociality. Bees and ants are in the grip of nature; what they do is what they have to do; they are ruled by their instincts. Men live within an area of freedom which, however partial and restricted it may be, is nonetheless real; they do what they have learned to do; they are led by their internalized norms and values. That this is indeed so can be seen not only on the macroscopic scale, in hill and hive as against human society (with this difference we are not concerned at the moment), but also on the microscopic scale, in individuals. The newly hatched bee or ant has hardly any possibility of further variation; when it learns (insofar as it does learn), it merely learns to do better what is preordained that it do. The newborn baby, on the other hand, has vast possibilities of later variation. The suggestion that it is a *tabula rasa* on which education may write any letters is indeed wrong; only the mind is such a *tabula rasa*, and in order to dominate, the will will have to assert itself, often painfully, against the body and its inherent animalic trends. But the possibility that this may happen, and the promise that it will happen, are the true distinguishing marks of the human neonate. His relatively heavy and complex brain is an earnest of this possibility, of this promise, but no more. It is social stimulation, it is human education, which initiate the decisive transformation and see to it that it is driven forward as far as it may be.

It will become obvious beyond the shadow of a doubt that we are speaking here with the voice of science and not in the accents of metaphysics when we observe the *modus operandi* of the limbs of the human baby and hold it against that of the limbs of a monkey or ape. Nature has ordained that the little baboon or chimpanzee use his hand-feet or feet-hands mainly for holding fast to the furry underside of its mother; in the case of the human infant, she leaves the use of his hands and feet up to him. The free play of the extremities, which gives the human neonate much richer opportunities than there are at the disposal of the newborn ape, Portmann says (p. 33), reminds us that our first condition must be seen, not only in negative terms, in terms of helplessness, but also in positive terms, in terms of perfectibility and freedom.

The human neonate is therefore not only a creature which can mature, but also a creature which will be revolutionized. A revolution is a radical change, literally a turning-upside-down. The term is entirely apt as a description of what occurs. Born a slave to his body, the human being becomes enough of a master over it to rank incomparably higher in the hierarchy of being than the cleverest and best-trained beast. A first proof that this steep ascent is succeeding is the appearance of insightful action, the beginning accompaniment of conduct by understanding and knowledge. Characteristically that happens at exactly the juncture at which language is acquired, the prime hallmark of human sociality—around the ninth or tenth month. But this point of time lies well beyond the period which is usually defined as neonatal.

THE MENTAL CONDITION OF THE NEONATE

69. One aspect of the radical revolution just spoken of which we all have to traverse on our way to humanization and socialization is the total transformation of our mental condition. Let us begin our analysis by a look at what we know best, the mentality of the grown-up person. This mentality is characterized by a number of decisive distinctions and confrontations; chief among them is the distinction between the self and the world of objects, be they animate or inanimate, things or persons. So sharp is this distinction that it is applied even to the self and its bodily husk with which materialistic philosophy and the submerged metaphysic of modern man tell us it is in a manner identical. There is no linguistic difference between the statement "I have two black suits" and the statement "I have two brown eyes." This is how we talk; this is how we think. When we say that the human mind is structured, we mean in the first place this constant contrasting of ego and it, including one's own organism, the Freudian id.

But the grown-up person not only sees the world in terms of distinct objects; he sees these objects as independent of each other and of himself. He apprehends them in their own forms, in their own sensible qualities, and in their own location in space. He knows full well that the things surrounding him, or, rather, a good many of them, have their uses and thereby a practical value for himself, but this use value is to him only one of their attributes and neither the exclusive nor the immediate center of his interest. Knowing an object is to the adult one thing, appropriating and exploiting it quite another. If we may borrow an expression from Immanuel Kant and use it in a rather un-Kantian signification, we may say that the grown-up person confronts a multitude of things-in-themselves.

In both these decisive respects, the mentality of the young infant is entirely different. He knows no objects; indeed, we cannot even say that he is aware of objects unless we use the word in a very reduced, dim, and dull sense. His conscious life, insofar as he has one, is totally concentrated on his own organism. There is merely a comprehensive tone of feeling, and nothing else. Heinz Werner, in his *Comparative Psychology of Mental Development* (Chicago, 1948; pp. 64, 65) speaks of "a mere state of feeling, a total sensation, in which object and subject are merged," and he quotes in this context William Stern's great classic, *Die Psychologie der frühen Kindheit*, to the effect that "All that we are fully justified in assuming for the mentality of the newborn child is a blurred state of consciousness in which sensorial and emotional phenomena are inseparably fused." In exactly the same vein, Schachtel asserts (*Metamorphosis*, p. 125), that an "exclusive emphasis on the felt sensation of the organism precedes any subject–object and within–without differentiation." In yet other words: the mind of the baby is a close prisoner of his own body. It is not outward looking like the grown-up's mind.

If the life-experience of the young baby is considered, this exclusive preoccupation with his own physical state is readily understood. In the fetal condition, in the maternal womb, from which he has only just emerged, all needs are supplied as soon as they arise. There is neither hunger nor thirst. But with an independent existence, there begins the constant alternation between tension and release which we all have to suffer and which we all can enjoy, and which to Freud appeared as the very hallmark of human life. This swinging to and fro between uneasiness or pain and satisfaction or happy satiety is, in its novelty, so intense an experience that it is no wonder if it blots out all other images, actual or potential. In a book written in the first place for sociologists, it is perhaps justifiable to emphasize that it blots out, not only the images of things, but also the images of fellow-humans. Because of its total preoccupation with a physical state, if for no other reason, the mind of the infant is essentially *a*social.

But the child does have his being within a setting of things and persons, and the day is bound to dawn when they begin to impinge on him, not only factually and objectively, but also subjectively and mentally. A vague awareness then springs up. But that awareness will be very different from the knowledge possessed by grown-up persons, and the difference will be, not merely one of degree (e.g., degree of clarity), as monists and materialists like to assert, but rather one of essence. The knowledge of the grown-up person is, as we have seen, bipolar: here am I; there is the object, material or social. The awareness of the infant, on the other hand, is monopolar. He sees everything exclusively in relation to himself. An object is not "that out there"; it is "that which comes toward me to make me feel good or bad." A thing is always a thing of use; a person is always a servant or a menace. The most important item in the nursling's life is, of course, the nipple, an object which is both thingly and personal.

In the first days of life it is seen, neither as constituting a thing, nor as belonging to a person. "The newborn child who nurses," writes Piaget (*Origins of Intelligence*, pp. 74, 37; see also p. 141),

> recognizes the nipple by the combination of sucking and swallowing reflexes without making the nipple a thing. . . . If, to the observer, the breast which the nursling is about to take is external to the child and constitutes an image separate from him, to the newborn child, on the contrary, there can only exist awareness of attitudes, of emotions, or sensations of hunger and of satisfaction. Neither sight nor hearing yet gives rise to perceptions independent of these general reactions. . . . So also a month-old child can recognize certain visual images without, however, really exteriorizing them. . . . Any subjective state can be recognized without being attributed to the action of objects independent of the ego.

If, then, the awakening consciousness sees objects at all, it sees them through an opaque medium, as it were, and that medium is the feeling tone of the organism. Because of this, it is much nearer to the vision of the world characteristic of the animal than to that of the grown-up human person. Just as the cradle or cot is to the baby, not a wooden or metal structure x inches high and y inches across, but "that in which I am going to nestle and feel comfortable," so the basket is to the dog not a receptacle woven of osier twigs n inches in diameter but "that in which I can curl up and feel content." The reason for this subjective similarity between small child and animal rests in an objective similarity. The small child has not, like the grown-up man, stepped out of nature and taken up a position over against her. He is still contained in the cadres of nature.

Another detail which proves that this is indeed so is the relatively dynamic character of the animal's and infant's view of the world, which contrasts most impressively with the relatively static character of the grown-up's *visus mundi*. To the animal or infant things do not appear inert or fixed, but active and motile: either they move toward him or he moves toward them. As far as dogs are concerned, it has been experimentally proved that they no longer regard their basket as their basket if the possibility of snuggling up in it has been removed. Similar tests have been made with children. If a baby of nine or ten months has found a handkerchief hidden under a pillow to its right, and that handkerchief is then moved, under his very eyes, to the left, he will still search for it to the right. For his knowledge (if the term may be used) is part and parcel of an action scheme, a process of action, and impressions which are not part and parcel of that stream are insignificant to him (see Schachtel, *Metamorphosis*, p. 257; Werner, *Comparative Psychology*, p. 61).

It is because of this close connection between impression and action, this quasi-organic relationship between organism and environment, that phantasy can play a very much larger part in the life of the infant than in that of the mature person. A mature person, when he thinks of a horse, has before him a very definite image; he knows that a horse has four legs, that it exists only in three or four colors, etc., etc., and he will demand that even a hobbyhorse should, to some extent, conform to these realities. Not so the infant. As everybody knows, he is as happy if he takes a simple stick between his legs and pretends to "ride" it as if he is presented with a meticulously correct replica of a real horse. (The hobbyhorses of our toy shops are, when the truth is told, made more for the grown-up buyer than for the infant user, and that is not impossible to understand, for it is he, the buyer, who has to be satisfied if he is to count out the money.) The reason for this indifference of the infant to the detail stems from the fact indicated just now: a toy horse is, to the child, not what looks like a horse, but what is usable for the purpose of riding. The rest is irrelevant to him. His whole idea of what is real and what is unreal is different from that of the adult. Riding on a toy horse, or on a simple stick, is real riding to him because his action is real; that the thing with the aid of which it is carried out is unreal in the adult's sense, i.e., not in accordance with certain sense impressions, matters to him but little. It is in all likelihood not even so that the child's imagination supplies the lacking features. The adult's certainly will, but then he is more attuned to distinct images and concepts and less to movement and action schemes. "The things of the child's world are created as much for his motor-affective activity as by objective stimuli," writes one who knows the infant psyche well. "The affective and motor behavior of the child impresses itself on the world of things and fashions it" (Werner, *Comparative Psychology*, p. 65).

In contrast, the world of the grown-up is a world of data—hard and fast data. From this point of view, the process of humanization and socialization involves a certain freezing of the objective world. Within the darkling stream of the proto-consciousness, vortices begin to form, then nodi, and finally definable facts which stand out like rocks in running water. Things begin to separate; persons receive a face. Behind the nipple there appears the breast, behind the breast the mother, and that not only as a body, but finally also as a person. What we have to underline in this context and for the purposes of this book is the fact that for a "natural" world view is substituted a more "artificial" one, for the concretely apprehended the abstractly defined, for the thing-in-action the thing-in-itself, as we called it a few pages back in defiance of the Kantian usage, but in a usage of the term which, we trust, is entirely clear within our argument.

It was unavoidable that this should happen. Without it, man could not have risen above nature and become her master; without it, too, men could not have developed a social mode of living, and these two developments were, from the beginning, laid on in the great scheme of things and had the forces of life behind them. But in any assessment of evolution it is essential not to forget the losses over the gains, even if most of us would agree that, compared with the gains, the losses are well-nigh insignificant. Insignificant they may be according to most yardsticks, yet they exist. What our race has lost in phylogenesis and what everyone of us loses in his ontogenesis is a certain directness in the contact with the surrounding world, an immediacy which it is impossible ever to regain. Between the action center and the action sphere there step the word, the concept, and the name. Words, concepts, and names, however, are artifacts. Their creation in phylogenesis and their acquisition in ontogenesis add to the world of nature a world of culture and make men denizens of the two realms, with all the consequences which this complication must unavoidably entail.

We do not need in this book to go into the problems which the interposition of language between our senses and reality has created for our physical knowledge. These problems have been the great theme of modern philosophy in general and of Logical Positivism in particular. But the complex of questions which we have just encountered presents itself on many levels and not least in the social sciences. Among the more philosophically-minded Marxists, Georg Lukács has asserted, above all in *Geschichte als Klassenbewusstsein*, that we can meet the truth only in practice and never in theory. Theory is based on concepts which are necessarily static; true life on the other hand is in a flow; it can never be adequately presented by, and grasped through, the medium of definitions or propositions which are in their very nature falsifications of reality. If this trouble is depicted as a specific weakness of capitalist society (because the upper class in that society fears the forward movement of history which will dispossess it and therefore prefers and propagates a static view of life), then the universal problem of reification, of the transmutation of the dynamic into the static, is misunderstood. The tendency toward reification, toward the freezing of life, appears, as Henri Bergson has convincingly shown in all his works, and more especially in *The Two Sources of Morality and Religion*, as early as the dawn of human evolution, and unavoidably so. In order to survive, man is forced to concentrate his attention on that part of reality which he can hope to conquer and to utilize, and this is in the first place the land, the static part of reality *par excellence*. His incipient intellect thus becomes attuned to that which is immobile, that which is inert, and the study of immobile and inert matter—mechanics, physics—will become its preferred pursuit. It is a fact not to be gainsaid that, throughout history, mankind has been more proficient in the study of dead matter than in the study of life, be it organic or social. The trouble brought up by Lukács does not therefore begin with the capitalist era; it is generically human.

It is indeed a kind of trouble; the tendency to prefer, *a limine*, static concepts to dynamic images, to see that which is in flow through eyes which are accommodated to that which is at rest, must falsify the perception and interpretation of reality, or at least aspects of it. But this is simply part of the price which man has to pay for his humanization. The progression from hominid to *Homo sapiens*, whatever its historical detail may have been, was assuredly based on the creation of subject-and-object relationships between him and matter, him and his surrounding world. Only in this fashion could he have become what he has in fact become, the master in the house. Only in this fashion could he have developed a mind. For the dynamic images which he discarded were dreamlike—not much more than a floating mist—while the static concepts which he acquired are crystalline and clear-cut. Only by stepping out of nature, by opening up a ditch between self and thing, by contemplating the abandoned frame of existence from another shore, could man have learned how to think. Not without reason is thinking also called reflection. Re-flection, however, is, as philologists explain, a swivelling around and bending, or looking, back.

This stepping out of nature, this replacement of dream-like images by crystalline and clear-cut concepts, is a process which every newborn child (we would even be entitled to write: every newborn hominid) must run through for himself. In this particular, Baer's assertion that ontogenesis is a repetition of phylogenesis, holds good beyond the area which the great biologist intended it to cover.

But if man would not have concrete ideas, or indeed ideas of any kind—would not have a mind at all—without withdrawing from the quasi-organic nexus within which nature holds both the animal and the animal-like neonate, he would, without this liberation, not have a social life either. A child would not even come to know his mother without clarifying and consolidating those impressions which he at first alone possesses, without combining "that which smells good and gives warmth, that which holds me and yields milk," etc., into one integrated person, and that basic process runs entirely parallel to—indeed, is identical with—the process of reification. Disjointed acts eventuating in a change of organic feeling tone cease to be merely disjointed acts; they grow together into an intuitive knowledge of being safe and cared for, and they are increasingly referred to *one* action center, one safety-giving and care-taking agent, a human person with a countenance and a being of her own.

Nobody will deny that there is a process of this kind. But the length to which it will go is a matter of contention. There is an old *bon mot*, which some may see in the light of a joke, but which to others indicates a truth; according to it, if there are two persons, Mr. Jones and Mr. Davis, there is in reality neither; there is only Mr. Davis' Mr. Jones and Mr. Jones's Mr. Davis. There is some justification to this adage, but not much. To consider the issue properly from a sociological point of view, we must pass from the dyadic relationship (mother–child, Jones–Davis) to the consideration of a multilateral set, a group. But as soon as we look at a triad—which is, of course, a much better model of society than a dyad—we see that the "reification" of the person advances exactly as far as the reification of things. If there is, in addition to Mr. Jones and Mr. Davis, a Mr. Griffith as well, there is not only Mr. Davis' Mr. Jones and Mr. Griffith's Mr. Jones, but also a Mr. Jones common to them both, and if there were no such objectified Mr. Jones, they could never converse about him. True, this common, objectified, Mr. Jones will fully coincide neither with Davis' nor with Griffith's idea of him, each of the latter two seeing features in Jones which the other does not; and on the features which they both see, they will often not be in full agreement. Yet there will be enough agreement to make conversation more than a talking at cross-purposes, and this is decisive. If there is to be any social life, it must be possible to *name* persons, and the name must be more than an empty and fictitious label. It must conjure up—it must describe—a true personality, just as a sound pattern annexed to an inanimate object must convey a largely realistic reference to it. The great importance attributed to names in primitive societies reflects a realization of the crucial role which names play in social intercourse.

To sum up: the dim world-awareness of the neonate turns into the increasingly distinct world-knowledge of the developing individual, and that through a process of fission. A unitary organic self-feeling breaks asunder into a subjective and an objective half, an apprehension of the ego as ego and of the objects as objects. These two foci are interconnected, both in their emergence and in their persistence. As Piaget has once again so felicitously expressed it: "Intellectual activity, departing from a relation of interdependence between organism and environment, or lack of differentiation between subject and object, progresses simultaneously in the conquest of things and reflection on itself, these two processes of inverse direction being correlative" (*Origins of Intelligence*, p. 19). But what is true of ego and it is true also of self and other. We shall see this in greater detail later on.

Here it is our chief task to explain the manner in which this whole development gets under way. Transitions are as a rule gradual, but we recognize their character best if we compare and contrast an earlier and a later condition; we can then see the essential change which takes place. The baby's focusing on an object brought into his field of vision and his following that object with his eyes when it is moved around appear *prima facie* as kindred, if not indeed as identical, events. But that is not really so. When an object is brought into the baby's field of vision, what happens is that his physical apparatus accommodates to it. The lens, for instance, will contract. But this is merely an automatic reflex, a reaction to a physical stimulus. When, on the other hand, the object is moved around and the baby follows it with his eyes, and especially when he moves his head in order to be able to follow it with his eyes, this is a voluntary action, an assertion of the self, of the personality; it is not merely a reflex or reaction of the body. To this action there corresponds a mental mode which can be circumscribed by the words "I want to see this thing!" Whereas the accommodation of the lens to the object is an event (in the proper, narrower meaning of the term), a happening, totally enclosed in the confines, and regulated by the laws, of nature, the movement of the head is a deed of a person, an assertion of his will. In this case, the action center, the will, manipulates part of the body, the neck muscles to be exact; it uses the organism as an instrument, it asserts itself against it. A subject-and-object relationship, or, rather, a set of such relationships, has emerged.

We mentioned earlier that thumb-sucking has been observed in the fetal state, and thumb-sucking is also an activity which most infants engage in when they emerge from the neonatal phase. Superficially the two phenomena appear to be identical, but appearances are deceptive. Thumb-sucking in the womb cannot be anything but a physical reaction of some kind; it can hardly be interpreted as a voluntary action. But thumb-sucking after the end of the first month of life or so is something entirely different. In the meantime the baby has experienced the pleasure of being fed at the breast and, naturally, it wishes to secure that pleasure as often as it may. But the breast is not available all the time; the child has to find a replacement for it, a second best, and it discovers it in the thumb. The thumb will do as a substitute for the nipple if the nipple is not forthcoming. What is so new to this second form of thumb-sucking in comparison with the first is that it is the result of experimentation, of a search for a solution; in other words: that it is not an automatic reaction but a voluntary action. As such it is no longer merely animalic, it is already, in a very definite sense of the word, essentially human. For what is it that man does, grown-up man, in all that he undertakes, but to experiment, to search for solutions of his life's problems?

In saying all this, we are not for one moment forgetting that it would be quite wrong to open up too wide a gap between the will to live manifested in the accommodation of the lens to an object within the field of vision, and the will to live manifested in the effort to follow the object in its movement across that field. To the biologist, to the medical man, the two phenomena may well appear to be the same thing; their ontology does not clamor with the same urgency for a distinction here as does that of the psychologist and the sociologist. But to the sociologist and the psychologist, the manipulation of the neck-muscles is an effect, not only of the will to live, but also of the will to *know*, and that is something else. The will to live in general (Henri Bergson's *élan vital*) is an objective datum of nature, but the specific will which can be characterized as a will to know is a subjective striving. We may, indeed we must, even go as far as to say that the will to know is laid on in, emerges from, and continues to be underlaid by, the basic will to be, but this takes nothing from the fact that it is a will which has separated itself out of the wider stream of being and become concentrated, concretized, individuated, in a human personality. It is with nature as it is with our mother: we owe her our existence, but as soon as we have come to birth, we assert our selfhood and in the end, more likely than not, we shall even turn against her.

Only a human self is capable of social relations. The formation of that self, now explained—a development which does not end with the ejection of the infant body from the maternal womb, but rather begins with it—is therefore the given starting point even for a study of socialization.

THE LACK OF SOCIALITY IN THE NEONATE

70. In the beginning, there is merely the body. At a second stage, there arises a self which dwells in that body, but is in no way identical with it. It is only during a third stage that the habit of sociality is ingrafted in that self. It tends to fill it out, but it does not send down its roots into the bodily substratum, which remains animalic and self-regarding.

One child psychologist, Boyd R. McCandless, has called the first relation of the infant to his environment "a megalomaniacal type of adjustment, in which the child seems to 'think' that he is the beginning and end of his universe . . ." ("Childhood Socialization," in *Handbook of Socialization Theory and Research*, ed. D. A. Goslin [Chicago, 1969], p. 798). Another, Ernest Schachtel, has spoken of a "narcissistic situation in which no object exists for the perceiver and all impinging objects tend to be experienced merely as states of the perceiver's comfort or discomfort, as 'vital sensations'" (*Metamorphosis*, p. 181). The two words used—"megalomania" and "narcissism"—are strong terms and contain an element of metaphor, even of hyperbole; yet they are entirely apt. For the small infant is in fact all wrapped up in himself. "The whole concept of self and others does not make sense at this earliest period," Schachtel writes in another place (p. 302), "and nothing corresponding to this concept exists for the small infant."

Statements of this kind are sure to run into heavy opposition. Even those who are realistic enough not to fall for the concept of an inborn instinct of gregariousness often tend to assume that there is at least a slight bent toward sociality. This opinion deserves the most serious consideration if, and insofar as, it is possible to adduce facts in support of it. One such fact, or fancied fact, is the infant's readiness to smile back if he is smiled at. Does this response to kindliness not betoken a spontaneous reaction to human approaches, and, since a smile is an undeniable sign of pleasure, an entirely positive reaction?

If this matter is studied soberly and without sentimentality, it must be stated, in deference to phenomenological realism, that there are several kinds of smiling which must be neatly distinguished. A smile may be a physical reaction, and it may be a cultural reaction. It may show that he who smiles is pleased with his own condition, or alternatively that he is pleased with somebody else. There is an egocentric and there is an alterocentric smile. The young infant's smile is a physical reflex, expressing contentedness with the state of the smiler's own physique; it is egocentric. The doting parent who is thrilled when his offspring in the cradle smiles back at him for the first time mistakes the facial expression for what it is not—something similar to the glad eye which he himself, an adult, gives to those he cherishes.

Smiling behavior has been observed in premature babies, and it has been inferred from this fact that it is present even before birth (see Eckhard H. Hess, "The Ethological Approach to Socialization," in *Early Experiences and the Processes of Socialization*, edd. Ronald A. Hoppe, G. Alexander Milton, and Edward C. Simmel [New York & London, 1970], p. 32). Whatever the value (or otherwise) of this inference, we are on safe ground when we refer to another fact often observed which points in a similar direction. Blind babies smile. Even their smile may, of course, be a positive, pleasure-born response to a human approach—for instance, through the instrumentality of the human voice—but it need not, and in many cases will not, be that. It may be, and it often will be, the externalization of an inner, organic state of well-being, not unlike the contented grunt of the pig which has eaten its fill.

Competent observers, such as C. W. Valentine and Jean Piaget, have shown that the smile is not, in the earliest phases of life, what it becomes later on, a sign of affection. It cannot be that, for the child will smile at things as well as at persons; indeed, as a rule, it will smile at things before it begins to smile at persons. In a research protocol concerning his infant son Laurent, Jean Piaget notes: "At O [years]; 2 [months] (19) [days] he did not smile at people a single time in a whole day; on the other hand, he smiled at all the familiar objects" (*Origins of Intelligence*, p. 73). In this factual, almost clinical, statement, the word "familiar" is the most important; it affords us the key to the understanding of the whole phenomenon and reveals with all desirable clarity that even smiling, to begin with, is autocentric and not allocentric.

We all are happy to some slight degree when we recognize a familiar face or figure or landscape or what-not; not without reason have the modern languages developed the standing phrase "the pleasure of recognition." Strictly speaking: infants do not have this pleasure; they cannot recognize simply because they do not yet cognize. But they have an entirely parallel experience, and one which is a good deal more intense than that of the adult. Schachtel (*Metamorphosis*, p. 148) has called this precursor of conscious recognition "resensation." As soon as the first period of somnolence, of being-asleep-while-awake, is over for the baby, as soon as sense impressions have received any shape at all, they can be "resensed," i.e., in a manner "recognized" as having occurred before. There is the toy dangling above the bassinet; there is the face which appears and re-appears above the cradle. Vaguely, the infant has the idea of having seen this before. This idea, this *déjà vu*, is, to the baby, a pleasurable occurrence. He feels that it is a kind of feat on his part. He has exercised one of his awakening abilities and been successful in his effort. It is well known that the child, when he begins to walk, likes to walk, not only and not mainly because he wants to get somewhere, but rather for the sake of walking. "A child who has just found himself able to walk," writes Erik Erikson in his *Childhood and Society* (New York, 1950; p. 235), "seems driven to repeat the act for the pure delight of functioning, and out of the need to master and perfect a newly initiated func-tion." The realization that he is able to stand on his legs and to put one foot in front of the other fills him with elation and thereby increases his self-confidence and his vital tone. It is the same with "resensation." Here, too, a dormant ability awakens, and its incipient utilization gives satisfaction to the infant, who likes to feel his own forces at work. Resensation thus is rewarding; it is, so to speak, its own reward. And, obviously, it is not as yet socially significant. For it makes very little difference whether what is resensed, or dimly recognized, is alive or dead, a person or a thing. Insofar as the mother's face or voice is likely to be the impression which is most frequently received, it is as a rule a human person who is most frequently the recipient of the smile. But this is purely accidental. Smiling, at this stage, is not an outward-directed sign.

Basically, that is to say, purely physiologically, considered, the early smile is merely a bodily reflex, and the mechanism of it may be set in motion by any pleasurable experience. In the beginning, it is entirely unspecialized. Later on, culture gets a hold on it and fills it with a social content. It becomes specialized, reserved, so to speak, for a social use. The grown-up person no longer smiles when he recognizes, or rather re-recognizes, a thing; he smiles when he recog-nizes a person and uses the same facial configuration for expressing his pleasure at any social encounter. But this cannot be called natural. The smile which we give formally when we hold out our right hand to a new acquaintance, and even the smile which moves across our features spontaneously when we are face to face with a sympathetic person, are the fruit of our education, one of the proofs that we have become cultured beings.

The case of laughter is, as we may point out in a brief, but perhaps instructive aside, rather similar. C. W. Valentine had this to say on it in his presidential address in 1930 to the Psychology Section of the British Academy for the Ad-vancement of Science: "The first clear laugh I noted in my children was that of B (whom I watched especially for laughter development) at the age of thirty-nine days—a laugh of delight at being put into position to take food. Several other observations showed that the getting of food or anticipation of it was the earliest cause of laughter, as Dearborn also noted in his daughter." And Valen-tine adds: "Yorkes noted that his chimpanzee would frequently laugh in re-sponse to favourite foods" (*Report* of the Ninety-Eighth Meeting, Bristol, 1930 [London, 1931], pp. 184, 185). Here again we see the total transformation of a physical reflex externalizing an internal condition into a cultural response to an outside stimulation, in most cases stimulation through the action of a fellow human being. Clearly, laughter, like the smile, can be allocentric as well as autocentric, but in early childhood days it is the latter.

But we must press on with our analysis, and the next step can best be introduced by another quotation from Piaget's research protocols. Referring once again to his infant son Laurent, he writes: "At 0 [years]; 3 [months] (6 and 7) [days] . . . , he manifests a certain astonishment and even anxiety in the presence of new objects which he would like to grasp . . . but smiles (or smiles only with his eyes) while taking familiar objects . . ." (*Origins of Intelligence*, p. 73). "Astonishment and even anxiety": the reverse side of the coin is revealed to us in these words. As his hours of somnolence decrease and his waking hours increase, as his dim awareness of the environment becomes less dim and draws closer to conscious knowledge, the infant is forced to make a distinction between what is familiar and therefore pleasurable, and what is unfamiliar and therefore potentially hostile and painful. Once the habit of sorting things out in this way is established, a new and higher level of existence is achieved.

This new and higher level of existence gives society and sociality a first chance to impinge upon the infant and become subjectively significant to him. Normally, in ordered conditions, the family, with its continued child-care acts, is a stable system and, therefore, as we say, "familiar." It carries entirely positive accents; it belongs to that part of the world which the child knows and therefore can feel "at home" in. In this way, the family—and that is to say, society—becomes a kind of protective enclosure which shields the self against dangers, real or imagined, and all the more threatening since many of them are unknown and merely apprehended. The school known as Neo-Freudian (and which could, with as much justification, be called un-Freudian) has laid the greatest possible emphasis on this fact; Harry Stack Sullivan's *Interpersonal Theory of Psychiatry* is particularly insistent in this respect. Sullivan goes as far as to suggest that suffering from a feeling of insecurity hurts the individual more than do the whips of bodily needs. This may be, this must be, an exaggeration, yet the opinion of Sullivan and his friends is in a large measure justified. The same theme had been worked, a hundred years or so before, by Auguste Comte. Both Comte and Sullivan remind us that the human infant, when he emerges from his mother's womb, is totally helpless; his anxieties must therefore be correspondingly great. If they are held at bay, if they are banished, if they are in fact replaced by a feeling of security and happiness, this is due to the mother physical and the mother social, the genetrix and the human race, the *grand être*, whom Comte wishes to see symbolized by an individual mother, Raphael's madonna with the bambino in her arms. If he were to face raw, stark-naked nature in all its brutality alone, the infant would soon be annihilated; he dimly senses that this is so. Life and all the values it has to offer are therefore a gift to him by other human beings, the mother in the first place (not only the birth-giving, but also the child-caring, mother), and the rest of humanity in the second place, those who have built houses and homes, who have taught us to till the fields and to domesticate cattle, and so on and so forth; in a word: those who have erected dikes against the miseries which threaten to flood us from without. By these considerations a highly positive, optimistic note is brought into the analysis of the ontogenesis of sociality. Sociality is accepted, so it is said, by the developing infant because it is his security, his salvation.

But everything in this world has its shadowy as well as its sunlit side; where there is profit, there must also be costs. The encounter of the developing self with the surrounding objects physical and social would be blissful if the physical objects were all servo-mechanisms and the social objects were all body servants of his majesty, the I. But they are not. Physical objects care nothing about the well-being of the infant; social objects, including even the most devoted mother, have interests, values, and, above all, a will of their own, and do not always fall in with the wishes of the ego. For this reason, the ego experiences the world— and even the security-giving world, the family and society—as resistance. Up to the third year of life, psychologists tell us (see Piaget, *The Language and Thought of the Child* [London, 1967], pp. 231–36), that which he desires is most real to the child. But from then on he has increasingly to recognize that that is most real which is endowed with an existence of its own—in other words, that which exists in and by its own right—and then the pleasant megalomaniacal, narcissistic, solipsistic dreams of babyhood are ended, and a more sober world view comes to prevail. As the Freudians would say: the reign of the pleasure principle is at an end and that of the reality principle begins.

The more sober world view which has to come to the individual and gathers into sharper focus around the age of three is, *inter alia*, a more social world view. True, the family and society remain what they had been before, protective enclosures which provide a pleasant feeling of security; but they reveal now, as it were, a new and less agreeable face: the infant has to learn that a shell which protects is also a shell which confines. Pressures are experienced by him, and they impinge on him from two directions. There are sideways pressures, which are exerted from neighbors, brothers and sisters, for instance, and downward pressures, which are exerted by a less tangible but even more irresistible power—the law, a term which we are using in this context in the widest possible connotation, which includes the informal laws of custom as well as the formalized norms of legislation. In other words: there is competition which painfully reduces security; and there is discipline which even more painfully reduces freedom. How the individual is brought to accept these heavy burdens is the great theme of any analysis of the process of socialization.

THE BEGINNINGS OF SOCIALITY

71. The truth which we have elaborated in the foregoing pages and to which we have to hold fast in our further exploration is the insight that, in the case of the species *Homo sapiens*, sociality is not a primary endowment but a secondary acquisition. This fact forces itself even on those who would like to uphold the opposite opinion, whether they wish to admit it or not. Thus Harriet Rheingold writes in an article entitled "The Social and Socializing Infant" (in *Handbook of Socialization Theory*, ed. Goslin, pp. 779–90) that "the human infant begins life as a social organism . . ." and that "the human infant is social by biological origin" (pp. 779, 780). Yet these delusionary assertions are immediately retracted. When the author comes down to the more concrete data, she indicates clearly enough that it is not the neonate who is social, but the circumstances into which he is propelled. "In summary," she writes (p. 781), not really summarizing as much as shifting her ground, "the human infant is born into a social environment; he can remain alive only in a social environment; and from birth he takes his place in that environment." All this is very true, but it does not prove that the newborn child himself is natively and naturally social; it proves only that he is entering a system of life which is inherently social and the pervasive sociality of which is bound to engulf him and to make a social being of him in the course of time.

"The cry of the infant is a social signal," Harriet Rheingold also writes (p. 783); "with the cry he communicates with the people in his environment." Wrong! We have the same confusion here between objective consequence and subjective intention which we encountered in our first volume when we considered the so-called warning cry (SOCIAL BOND I 81). So long as the child is still in the condition of somnolence, he cannot be said by any stretch of the imagination to send out signals or to communicate; he has as yet no conception of an addressee. Yet he cries straight away. Not a teleological approach is indicated here, but a strictly causal one. The neonate cries when his stomach pinches him or his intestine is full of wind, just as the dog yelps when his toe is trod on. He has no idea that his whine is to bring help. That help is, however, laid on in, and forthcoming from, a circle to which he does not as yet belong, that of grown-up, socialized men. But because help is in fact arriving from that quarter, and because he is in due course, in the course of awakening, becoming aware of it and its human character and characteristics, he is seeking and finding entry into its ranks.

The first step is, therefore, that the infant enters society, and the second step then that society enters the infant. But these words do not say enough. Society enters the infant, so we must hasten to add, and to emphasize, through his self-regard. "It is . . . possible," writes Harriet Rheingold (p. 782), and here we reject merely her hesitancy, "that the infant is responsive to people because they have become associated with the satisfactions resulting from certain caretaking operations." This is by no means only a possibility, it is the sober truth of the whole matter.

But it would be something of an exaggeration to say that the association, by the infant, of people with the satisfactions resulting from certain caretaking operations is the beginning of sociality. It is at best the beginning of that beginning. The onset of human sociality in the proper sense of the word has an inescapable negative presupposition without which no further step would be possible: namely, the baby's emergence from, and escape out of, animality. This relative liberation is achieved through a certain shift in the use of the native senses, for some of these senses bind us closely to animality while others allow us a good measure of freedom. The more the former prevail over the latter, the less human and social we still are; the more the latter prevail over the former, the more human and social we have become.

Smell and taste are the more animalic senses; hearing and sight the more humanizable ones; and touch is in between. There is no need to say much about the fact that dogs rely on their noses more than on their eyes, and humans on their eyes more than on their noses. Indeed, the sense of smell is largely decayed in *Homo sapiens*. We saw in the first volume that animal sociality, for instance, in the bee hive, but also in the monkey horde, is predominantly based on the odor of hive and herd. Insofar as animals have an "image" of their neighbors, it is not really an image in the proper sense of the word, a vision, but rather an olfactory one, the dim recognition that the organism encountered smells aright (or, should we say, stinks aright?). The experiences of smell and taste are in-dissolubly linked to—we might even assert, permeated by—feelings of pleasure and displeasure; they are signposts toward appetitions and avoidances. But what we see or hear does not affect us in the same way. We have a certain dis-tance from what we see and hear. Our critical faculties can come into play; so can our culturally developed sense of value and unvalue; so finally can our con-scious will. Not without reason do we say "I see" when we mean "I understand," or "I have apprehended a truth." Not without reason is cultural transmission based on the instrumentalities of eye and ear. We hear instruction or we see it in print. What, on the other hand, can smell and (physical) taste do for the transmission of culture?

By drawing this distinction between smell and taste, the permanently animal senses, on the one hand, and hearing or sight, the largely humanizable senses, on the other, we do not mean, of course, to set up an absolute distinction or clear-cut contrast between them. Our noses and palates can be educated; and we sometimes "see red" even as grown-ups, i.e., we sometimes react to visual impressions as the bull does to the red flag (or rather, to be precise, to the red flag when waved about). But even a relative difference remains a difference, and a shift between its terms may have far-reaching consequences. So it is in the case of the infant in the state of acculturation. Between the neonate's smell-ing and tasting the breast and the schoolboy's seeing or hearing his mother, there lies a whole revolution. It is in the first place a restructuring of the appa-ratus of cognition; it is in the second place, by unavoidable consequence, as it were, the initiation of a social mode of life.

The word "revolution," though strong, is hardly too strong in this context. In *The World of Man* (London, 1934; p. 132). Georg Walther Groddeck has sug-gested that the child takes cognizance of things and persons mainly with the aid of their odor, and he has added that the infant, small in stature and often held in the lap, is attuned above all to the smell of the lap, the legs, and the sexual and excretory organs. This may, or may not, be an exaggeration, but the salient point of the statement is well taken. Every one of us knows that the grown-up person does not normally recognize and identify others by their odor. The visual image has almost totally ousted the olfactory impression. If this is not a radical revolution, what is?

Particularly interesting in the present context is the case of the sense of hear-ing. Before the infant hears the words spoken to him as words, he hears them as sounds; differently expressed: before they are to him carriers of meaning, they are mere releasers of emotion. An angry sound, or rather, to be more exact, a harsh or shrill sound, makes him feel wretched; only later will he understand the rational expression of anger which is conveyed by the word. The infant child is therefore in the same category as the dog, as far as this particular is concerned, as he is indeed with regard to the predominance of the olfactory over the visual inlet of sense impressions. Thus, though the same physical mechanisms are involved, the same eardrum, for instance, infantile and adult—i.e., autocentric and allocentric, somatic and cultural or social—hearing are entirely different things. (We have spoken about this matter once before, in SOCIAL BOND I 79, and the reader should refer back to the more detailed explanation given there.)

It must surely be obvious that the facts just adduced make it totally inappropriate to speak of the presence of sociality in the neonate, its presence "by biological origin." For the core of sociality is communication; communication, however, is tied to words; and words cannot be learned before there is allocentric, i.e., cultural and social, hearing. We all know how excruciatingly difficult it is to convey to somebody else the content of an olfactory or gustatory experience. I know very well what my pain or my pleasure is like, what taste I have in my mouth or how a certain odor affects my nostrils, but how can I convincingly and half-way precisely inform another person about these feelings? As far as these sensations are concerned, we are indeed islands, each one of us. But it is not so with regard to things seen. They can be described with relative ease. I can perfectly well inform a neighbor about the extension of a physical object, its height and depth and length, while I am helpless when I wish him to realize—"to see"— the intensity of my toothache. True, the sense of sight and the auditory sense are present at birth, as are the sense of smell and the sense of (physical) taste, but only in an undeveloped form, and without their due development they could not become the media of communication, the carriers of a social life.

But if the infant is to turn into a social being, it is not sufficient that he learn how to put his humanizable senses above the permanently animalic ones and to humanize them, at least to some extent; he must liberate himself from animality in a second manner as well. The animal, as every zoologist and ethologist will agree, is confined to a closely circumscribed *nunc*. Not that we would have to deny recollections and anticipations altogether, but they are at best resensations and presensations, not knowledge of the past and future properly so called. Such knowledge is, however, a *sine qua non* of social interaction. If we are to know a person at all, we must know him or her over time. The appearances of the mother's face above the cradle must become a chain of appearances; the infant must realize that it is the same mother all the time. But even this is not enough. Social interaction presupposes, not only the knowledge of a person or persons, but in addition knowledge of his, her, or their modes of action. For only in this way shall we be able to attune our actions to theirs and to shape out of them a harmonized stream of conduct. "The biologic individual," writes George Herbert Mead in *Mind, Self, and Society* (Chicago, 1934; p. 351), "lives in an undifferentiated now; the social reflective individual takes this up into a flow of experience within which stands a fixed past and a more or less uncertain future."

The point which we have just been making is in a manner identical with the one which we made immediately before. Odors and physical tastes are very difficult to remember, if they can be memorized at all. At best we can say: I have smelled something like this, I have tasted something like this, before. A visual impression, on the other hand, with its sharp outlines remains and can be recalled. But what can be recalled best of all is the word, the concept. This is the true matter of memory; we remember by means of language. But language, as we have seen, presupposes allocentric, i.e., cultural–social hearing without which it cannot be acquired by the individual. Thus the essential widening of the temporal horizon is the effect of the very same process which humanizes the use of the physical–sensual apparatus and thereby prepares the socialization of man.

Nevertheless, this second point has an interest all its own, though not so much in our present context. We wish to notice it merely in passing. Both animals and men exist, objectively speaking, in a combined matrix of space and time; but animals exist in space rather than in time, and man exists equally both in space and in time. Indeed, insofar as he is immersed in the process of social interaction, he exists in time rather than in space. This is a theme of great philosophical importance which has been brought out above all by Henri Bergson, especially by his successful effort to show the difference between physical and human time (or duration). Physical time, as Bergson has explained, when it is conceptualized, cannot completely free itself from indebtedness to spatial conceptions; it is only duration which represents a flow in the proper sense of the word. We cannot, and shall not, dwell on this subject here, but we had to mention it in order to support and to deepen our assertion that the development of a sense of time flow, of duration, is an indispensable preliminary to the socialization of the individual.

The question how the liberation of the infant from the trammels of animality is brought about now arises. As always in these matters, two wrong styles of theorizing lie in wait at this point, one exaggerating the individualistic–materialistic, the other the sociologistic–educational aspect or alternative. The former (which we have already rejected) would see the whole process in terms of the maturation of the individual organism. It would teach that the full use of eyes and ears and the full activation of memory are capacities which unfold by themselves, carried only by the forces of nature, much as a plant unfolds its buds or ripens its fruit. The other would give all the credit, not to the individual organism and the forces of nature, but to the social environment and the forces of culture. It would tend to think of the infant as wax, i.e., passive, and of society as the seal, that is to say, a power to impress, to mold, and to make. The truth lies, in this case as in so many others, in the middle. The humanization and socialization of the person are cooperative processes, and the cooperation involved is both harmonious and antagonistic.

Let us concentrate for a moment on the first and simplest human relationship, that between mother and child. The child-care acts which the mother performs are only for a very short time lavished on an inert bundle of flesh and blood. Soon, surprisingly soon, that bundle proves that it is more than an animate object, that it is a subject, an action center, with a will of its own. However restricted the sense has to be in which we have to use the word in this context, the infant tries to *comprehend*. He strives to identify the source from which all the services come, and this striving awakens the capacities to see and to remember which are indeed naturally there, but which would remain dormant or even decay were it not for the mother's impact on the child, and the child's responding, yet self-generated, effort to know her. It is not one-sided stimulation which we have before us in this process; it is true interaction. Sociality does not grow in and on the infant; nor is it bestowed on him as a gift from without. It is the end product of a social process. Society is as self-created in every concrete instance, in ontogeny, as it must have been on the global scale, in phylogeny.

A very attenuated form of social instinctivism kindred to Harriet Rheingold's stance criticized above maintains that we have at least a native tendency to respond to the human face. We have indeed a native tendency to respond to stimulations, but social stimulations are, to begin with, in no privileged position. They acquire whatever extra attractiveness they have, compared to stimulations which originate in things and thingly events, only in the course of time. Just how this happens can best be explained by a number of quotations from Charles Horton Cooley's *Human Nature and the Social Order.* He is the best—the most convincing—witness we can call because he, too, had a bent toward organismic conceptions and with it a tendency to overestimate the sociability, even the kindliness, of man. Yet soberness forced him to acknowledge that the beginning of social responsiveness is not birth, but experience. "Such evidence as we have from the direct observation of children does not seem to me to substantiate the opinion that we have a definite instinctive sensibility to facial expression," he writes (p. 100).

> Persons and animals interest [the newborn] primarily because they offer a greater amount and variety of sensible stimulus than other objects. . . . The prestige [human beings] thus acquire over the child's mind is shared with such other stimulating phenomena as cars, engines, windmills, patches of sunlight, and bright-colored garments. . . . the early manifestations of sociability indicate less fellow feeling than the adult imagination likes to impute, but are expressions of a pleasure which persons excite chiefly because they offer such a variety of stimuli to sight, hearing, and touch . . . [pp. 323, 83].

The fact that they do offer such a variety of stimuli, more stimulating stimuli than dead objects have to offer, is a primary, not to be overestimated, reason why the awakening infant comes to attune himself to a social world, the world of men. "To conceive a kindly and approving companion," Cooley writes (p. 96), "is something that one involuntarily tries to do, in accordance with that instinctive hedonizing inseparable from all wholesome mental processes. . . ." All this is undoubtedly correct. Cooley merely exaggerates when he says: "I take it that the child has by heredity a generous capacity and need for social feeling . . ." (p. 86). No. He has merely a generous capacity and need for feeling (which is, in the final analysis, a need for feeling alive). The social experience gains the ascendancy over other experiences only later on because it normally has a good deal more to offer. And so, by "the time a child is a year old the social feeling that at first is indistinguishable from sensuous pleasure has become much specialized upon persons . . ." (p. 85).

One detail which is of great concern to the psychologist, but which is of importance for the sociologist as well, should not be missed at this point. From the mother come at all times two associated stimuli, one visual and one auditory. She smiles at the baby and she talks to him. We are calling these stimuli associated, and they are so in objective fact and for the matured subjective consciousness. But they are not so for the infant. He sees something, and that is one thing; and he hears something, and that is another thing. He has to learn how to combine these impressions. "The child tries, in a sense, to listen to the face and to look at the voice," Piaget explains (*Origins of Intelligence*, p. 87). But this trying, this stretching, this striving, brings him to develop a sociologically as well as psychologically supremely important capacity: the capacity to integrate. He learns to integrate his senses; he learns to integrate the world of objects mediated by these senses; he learns to integrate the impressions received from others and to see them as unitary persons; and, through all this, there is prepared in and for him the ability, destined to become very important later on, to see society as a system and not merely as a series or congeries of disconnected, at best juxtaposed, men or events.

We spoke earlier of the phenomenon of smiling, and we pointed out that the infant will smile as happily at things as he will at people. But there is this difference: that people will smile at him as well, and this initiates a number of pregnant developments. At first, to be sure, the smile is not received as a sign of love. Cooley, who was as good an observer of his own children as Valentine and Piaget, reports: "I observed both my children carefully to discover whether they smiled in response to a smile, and obtained negative results when they were under ten months old. A baby does not smile by imitation, but because he is pleased; and what pleases him in the first year of life is usually some rather obvious stimulus to the senses. If you wish a smile, you must earn it by acceptable exertion . . ." (*Human Nature*, p. 84). You have to contort your face, wriggle your ears, if you can, or put on some other performance for the benefit of the baby. But if you do that—and most human beings do—the message will finally get through to the child that he is being wooed, and that not only amusement but an all-round good will is offered to him. And this is the beginning of sociality. The feeling grows up in him whom sociological jargon likes to describe as the socializee that it is good to be in the society of men, and thus the "hedonizing inseparable from all wholesome mental processes," of which we heard Cooley speaking a little while ago, opens the door into the individual mind to the social and socializing forces. Fired by parental love, a general trust in human beings springs up, and once this has happened, the growing individual will be willing to embed himself in social life.

But, in this hard world, things are not so simple as that. The baby accepts society as a source of pleasure; he must also accept the less agreeable implications of social life. Self-regard lets sociality into the house, but that sociality must also give room to the self-regard of others. Erik Erikson, after discussing the creation of a sense of trust, speaks immediately of the "lasting need of the individual to have his will reaffirmed and delineated within an adult order of things which at the same time reaffirms and delineates the will of others" (*Childhood and Society*, p. 254), and herein lies the rub. Because of it, some students of early human life have seen socialization in terms of pain and shock rather than in terms of reassurance and pleasure. Thus McCandless, in his essay on "Childhood Socialization," asks (p. 798): "How is [the first] blissful stage . . . dissipated, as it must be?" and he answers:

> Through fear—fear [of the loss] of parental support, fear of the loss of love. The megalomaniac infant learns that not all is bliss in his world—he is threatened. The breast is not offered the instant it is wanted. Curiosity is not immediately rewarded by new stimulation. Thus the child learns that he is not the end-all and be-all of the universe. . . . This is the first step in learning that other people are important: they can give, but they can also take away, threatening life itself.

If, as we have pointed out, the recognition of the value of others to the self is the beginning of sociality, then so is the recognition of the claims of others against the self. You cannot accept only one side of a coin. Or, as the Germanic law expressed it, he who has taken the good drop, must take the bad drop as well.

We should not, however, understand the whole complicated process aright if we did not realize that even this shock, even this pain, redounds in the end to the advantage of the individual, even though he himself may never come to know it. It induces him to free himself from dependency. It is a strong confirmation of the basically dualistic approach of this book that dependency—the dependence of the infant from those who take care of him—is of two kinds: there is physical and instrumental dependency; and there is social and emotional dependency. The former is, like all facts, neither good nor bad; it is simply necessary. The latter, characteristically, can be either good or bad. It is good if and insofar as it creates a feeling of security which conquers anxiety and holds it at bay. It is bad if and insofar as it leads to a condition of passivity, of looking-to-others-for-all-one-needs. The latter alternative is a real danger. It is very well known that children, when they become able to walk, sometimes refuse to do so; they find it more commodious to be carried by their parents. But if the parents fall in with this wish, they "spoil" the child. He must accept the burden of walking, or else he will not become a full man. This illustration is archetypal. Innumerable similar acts of spoiling are possible and do occur. It is well-nigh unavoidable that the infant emerging from his pristine torpor should conceive the idea that society is a system of service laid on for his benefit, and that he should prefer to remain permanently embedded in this system. To the extent that he succeeds in this design, he blocks his own socialization. (To the extent that he succeeds, he is in fact, not merely not advancing, but even heading back toward, the fetal condition with its total absorption of the self in nature—the fact which induced Freud to formulate his theory of the death wish.) "The principal effect of this [wish to] return to embeddedness," says Schachtel, and he is correct, "is that the person does not become able to love and to encounter other people in their own right, but attempts to use them as providers of quasi-parental care and protection" (*Metamorphosis*, p. 75).

This danger and its most dire implication, a permanent infantilism of some sort, a mere semi-sociality, is avoided and averted if those in the child's ambit insist on due self-limitation on his part. The Benthamite principle that everybody should count for one and nobody for more than one, put forward by the great utilitarian philosopher as the basic maxim of a democratic society, is in reality of much wider importance and constitutes the guiding light of any sound educational effort. It normally succeeds, not so much because of the infant's factual dependence on the parent, who is also the prime educator, as is so often said in oversimplification, but because of the infant's attachment to and affection for the parent, which spring from that dependence but are essentially different from it—a subjective sentiment and not an objective fact. But by calling it a subjective sentiment we do not try to characterize it as, or to identify it with, love. Love, if the word is to have any precise meaning, is unselfish, but in the small child's attachment to, and even in his affection for, his parent or parents, there is still a large component of natural selfishness. Psychologists have proved (see Lucy Rau Ferguson, "Dependency Motivation in Socialization," in *Early Experiences and the Processes of Socialization*, edd. Hoppe et al., p. 73) that the peak of attachment to the mother coincides with the period when the infant shows the most intense fear reactions to strangers. He will therefore obey her commands partly, or even mainly, because the loss of her good will would deprive him of the most valuable protection he possesses against the manifold threats which, he well knows, or at least feels and apprehends, invest man, and especially the weak, on all sides.

The specific claims of society on the individual to be socialized are presented to him in the form of do's and don'ts, with the don'ts falling more heavily into the scales than the do's. This pressure on him to act in certain ways and not to act in others brings something entirely new into human life—something not provided for by the forces of nature, indeed, something which runs counter to the forces of nature. Sigmund Freud called it drive reduction. Nature has not anchored drives in our flesh and blood so that they should be frustrated; she has given them to us so that they should be fulfilled. Yet asserting them to the full would make all social life impossible. Drive reduction, drive frustration, is the price the human race has to pay for the blessings of society and culture.

For the individual, the social and socializing pressures are essentially a form of *discipline*. A homely, if perhaps crude, example is sphincter control, the control of bladder and bowel movements. Nature is interested only in elimination as such, the ridding of the organism of used-up and decayed materials. As far as nature is concerned, defecation and urination may happen anyhow, anytime, or anywhere; there is, as we have said, no permissible or impermissible right or wrong here. But society steps in to introduce a permissible and impermissible, a right and wrong; to introduce, in other words, discrimination. It is permissible and right to relieve the body at certain times and in certain places, impermissible and wrong to do so at other times and in other places. The physiological rhythm is decisive for the newborn infant; it has to yield later to an entirely different schedule, one laid down by society and culture.

When the process of socialization and acculturation is looked at from the collective rather than from the individual point of view, two terms present themselves for the purpose of description. Socialization is in the first place an imposition of *norms*. It is in the second place an inculcation of *values*. Norms may be prohibitions or commands; values, negative or positive. In the example which we have given, the norm imposed may be formulated by saying: you shall yield to the urges of your body only in the manner approved of by your fellow-men; the value involved is the value of cleanliness. Needless to say, values and norms are in the final analysis identical. Norms strive to realize values; values inspire and determine norms. How it is that values and norms arise, spread and prevail, gather authority and become the social bond of human groupings, is a problem which will be investigated, with all due care and completeness, in the third volume of the present work. Here, in the second, devoted to the socialization of the individual, the salient point to be retained is that they enter, at a crucial moment of man's career, into his life and into his self, to add a second nature, a social nature, to his being, which up till then had been no more than a purely physical, purely animalic, existence.

THE DEVELOPMENT OF SELFHOOD—A PRECONDITION OF SOCIALITY

72. The central fact of the last section—the fact that there is opposition between man's organismic drives, which crave unimpeded fulfillment, and man's enveloping culture, which does, and must, insist on drive reduction—has given rise to a widespread and persistent opinion which is less than correct: the opinion that the self and society are forever locked in combat. Scores of authors could be paraded here who have expressed this conviction in more or less extreme terms. Yet in reality the tension is not between the self and society, it is between nature and culture, and that is an entirely different thing. The tug-of-war rages, not between self and non-self, but rather in the ego itself. Each one of us is internally riven, belonging with his body to nature and with his mind to society. George Herbert Mead has expressed the essential truth in the following words:

> The content of the self is individual (selfish, therefore, or the source of selfishness), whereas the structure of the self is social—hence unselfish, or the basis of unselfishness. The relation between the rational or primarily social side of the self and its impulsive or emotional or primarily anti-social and individual side is such that the latter is, for the most part, controlled with respect to its behavioristic expressions by the former . . . [*Mind, Self, and Society*, p. 230, note].

The terms employed are perhaps not entirely clear, but the judgment conveyed is. By "the content of the self" Mead means, or ought to mean, the urges of the body which report themselves to the brain and to the mind and strive to dominate the whole human being, tending to make him a slave to the pleasure principle. By "the structure of the self" Mead means, or ought to mean, the discipline-accepting and discipline-instilling function of the mind, the will, which has become social and would like to see order under its own roof and under the wider canopy of society as well. Nineteen hundred years before Mead, St. Paul (Rom. 7:23) expressed the salient fact even more clearly and pungently. There is one law in my members, he had said, and another law in my mind, and they are fighting against each other.

This consideration, so much in line with universal human experience, yet at the same time so vigorously opposed by many, must necessarily be the chief topic of our further analyses. In his *Theory of Moral Sentiments*, Adam Smith has spoken of a man in our breast, of a monitor within, and the question is how he—our social self—comes to enter into us, for he is certainly not born with us. Insofar as he becomes the core of our personality, and more especially insofar as he, the carrier of Freud's reality principle, becomes capable of controlling the pleasure-addicted strivings of the flesh and blood, the strengthening of the self brings with it a strengthening, and not a weakening, of the social bond.

The simple fact of the matter is that an unfolded sociality of the kind which is characteristic of human coexistence, presupposes an unfolded personality, for only such a perfected personality is capable of participating in the mind-filled and meaning-filled give-and-take which is constantly being enacted among human beings. But an unfolded, perfected, personality is necessarily a conscious personality; and consciousness implies, for genetic reasons, necessarily and basically a consciousness of self. In a sense, therefore, which may superficially appear paradoxical, but which is in reality nothing of the kind, the awakening of the individual to self-knowledge is a *sine qua non*, not only of human sociality as such, but even of improved and improving sociality. It is, of course, true that a personality conscious of itself is also a personality conscious of its needs and of its interests, including the needs and interests which set it apart from, and make it opposed to, the needs and the interests of others. The self-knowing individual may become the self-willed individual in the negative sense of that term. But this only shows that the socialization of the individual will is the core phenomenon and the core necessity of all human existence. It is the *hic Rhodus, hic salta* of our whole species. The danger of which we are speaking is real enough. The awakening and sharpening self-aware mind may become merely an instrument for the more clever pursuit of selfish ends. But this takes nothing from the fact that an awakening and sharpening (and therefore of necessity self-aware) mind is also the precondition of socialized action in the human (as opposed, for instance, to the hymenopterous) sense of the word, the vessel, as it were, into which social contents have to be poured, and into which alone social contents can possibly be poured. In "order to cooperate," Piaget has very rightly written, "one must be conscious of one's ego and situate it in relation to thought in general. . . . Consciousness of self is therefore both a product and a condition of cooperation" (*Moral Judgment*, pp. 87, 400).

The statement of Piaget's just quoted has, however, two separable parts which are not linked by any inner logic or necessity, and of which the one may well be accepted or rejected without the other. It is possible to agree that consciousness of self is a condition of cooperation in the specifically human sense of the word and to deny at the same time that it is its product. Or, to turn the matter around, it is possible to assert that consciousness of self is a product, a consequence, of the recognition of one's own organism and not of interaction with other human beings. The psychologist Koffka, for instance, has suggested that it begins, at any rate, with a definition of the boundaries of the body. Mead, on the other hand, has decidedly, almost violently, condemned this idea. He calls it necessary

> to utter a warning against the easy assumption that experiences originating from under the skin provide an inner world within which in some obscure manner reflection may arise, and against the assumption that the body of the individual as a perceptual object provides a center to which experiences may be attached, thus creating a private and psychical field that has in it the germ of representation and so of reflection.

"Neither a colic nor a stubbed toe," he goes on to say,

> can give birth to reflection, nor do pleasures or pains, emotions or moods, constitute inner psychical contents, inevitably referred to a self, thus forming an inner world within which autochthonous thought can spring up. Reflection . . . involves two attitudes at least: one of indicating a novel feature of the object which gives rise to conflicting impulses (analysis); and the other of so organizing the reaction toward the object, thus perceived, that one indicates the reaction to himself as he might to another (representation). The direct activities out of which thought grows are social acts, and presumably find their earliest expression in primitive social responses [*Mind, Self, and Society*, p. 357].

The truth in this debate lies with George Herbert Mead. This can be proved, but the proof is unfortunately bound to come up against considerable resistance. Every society has its specific subconscious metaphysic, and that of our own is consistently materialistic. There is a universal tendency to identify the self with the body, and though even the simple sentence "I have a body" puts a negative on this idea, since it makes the body appear as a possession of the ego and hence separate from the ego, this tendency continues to assert itself and to predominate. Yet a deeper psychology can show, and must insist, that consciousness of the body is not necessarily consciousness of the self. An animal or a baby is often conscious of its body; it feels pleasure, it feels pain; but it does not, in Mead's phrase, refer these experiences to a self. It does not refer them to anybody or anything; it simply experiences them. If we were to express this fact in sophisticated language, we would have to lend to the animal, or to the baby, the words, not "I hurt," but "it hurts." Referring everything to a self has become so settled a habit with grown-up man that he must necessarily find it difficult to understand that the sentence "I hurt" or "I have a body" presupposes considerable mental maturity. This is nevertheless the case. The word "I" is a concept. Neither the animal nor the small baby is capable of conceptualization. It has to receive this capacity, along with so much else, along especially with human language, from society.

It is often asserted that the higher animals have self-consciousness, but when statements of this kind are more closely examined, it usually appears that what is meant is the fact that they have "personality" in the sense of individuality, that they are not all alike but are each endowed with a character of his own. George Schaller, for instance, in his field report entitled *The Year of the Gorilla* (Chicago, 1967) consistently treats his apish friends as "personalities" in this sense, going so far as to ascribe to one ("Mrs. V.") "a gaunt, ascetic mien" (p. 202). And yet he is forced to write, coming much closer to the sober truth: "Animals frequently do resemble man in their emotional and instinctive behaviour, although, unlike man, they are perhaps not consciously aware of their own thought processes" (p. 173). They certainly are like man in their instinctive behavior; they certainly are comparable to him in their emotional behavior; but they are as certainly unlike man and not comparable to him in the article of self-knowledge.

Let us raise at this point the truly searching and decisive question whether animals or small babies are capable of conceiving even the unity of their bodies, the integration of their organisms; in other words: whether they are capable of seeing themselves as physical wholes. We are calling this query decisive as well as truly searching because an idea of the body as a unity would seem to be, according to the materialistic world view itself, a necessary precondition to the development of the conception of a unitary self. A. E. Parr has devoted deep thought to this problem (see esp. "On Self-Recognition and Social Reaction in Relation to Biomechanics," *Ecology*, 18 [1937], 321ff.). He comes to the conclusion that many difficulties block the animal's way even to this insight. Some of them cannot touch themselves; others cannot see themselves as wholes. "There are, of course, mirrors in nature and an animal may occasionally chance upon his reflection"—so we can sum up this outstanding biologist's analysis (according to a personal communication)—

> yet he lacks the powers of deduction to realize that the reflection is a counterpart of himself. This relative ignorance of self has its social implications. Having no adequate concept of his own body, an animal can have no clear conviction that his associates are of his kind. He does not consciously recognize his companions or even his offspring as being "birds of a feather"; his mate may be only a foreign object that has a special allure.

We should note these social implications, for they are deeply significant; but in the present context we must notice even more the concomitant psychological implications. Animals, including those which rank very high in the scale of being, have at best a rudimentary sense of their physical selves; such a rudimentary image, however, cannot be a sufficient basis for the much more intellectualized concept of a total, psychical as well as physical, self, for that *consciousness* of self which is the inescapable precondition of participation in a communal life permeated with mentality and meaning.

A human neonate, a small baby, cannot see himself as a whole; he cannot, therefore, have any conception of the unity of his body; and even less can he have a native knowledge of his own integrated self. How, then, does he acquire a knowledge of his body? The true answer to this question lies, not in the direction of materialism, but, as we have seen Mead insisting, in the direction of sociality. Even our knowledge of our own bodies is an outcome of social life.

Close observation for which, among others, the great psychologist J. M. Baldwin has been responsible (see his *Social and Ethical Interpretations in Mental Development*; New York, 1897), has shown that the infant is at first without sense of subjectivity and consciousness of self. We can still see this in the somewhat older child, the child who begins to speak. As everybody knows, he is apt to say, not "I am hungry," but "Billy is hungry." He places himself in the same category as others and indeed as observed objects. The discovery of the self, and more especially the discovery of one's own body, is a reflection, an aftereffect, of the discovery of other selves and their respective bodies. The child perceives the mother's lips, and he sees them move; he will then try to move his own lips and succeed in doing so, and from this activity comes the knowledge that he has lips of the same kind his mother has. We are not arguing here for a theory of imitation à la Tarde, least of all for an instinctivist theory of this kind. The child imitates only in an objective sense of the word, not in a subjective sense. He does not intend to imitate, and what appears objectively as imitation is even less a bodily reflex or a natural response. What he does do is to try out his own body to find out whether he can achieve what he has observed others performing. The point is important for we have to recognize that there is cooperation, on nearly equal terms, between grown-up and infant, socializer and socializee. Granted that the grown-up, the socializer, acts as a model of a kind, the acquisition of a sense of one's own body is yet a genuine achievement of the child's, the result of an effort on his part. The acquisition of self-knowledge in the more than somatic sense of the word, that is to say, the acquisition of a knowledge of the self as an action center, proceeds in a parallel fashion. The baby does what he sees others doing; he joyfully learns that he can perform what he sees others performing; and from this experience grows his sense of selfhood, of being a doer of deeds. Once he has come to realize that he is an ego like others, once the stage of subjectivity has been reached, the "projective" condition (as Baldwin calls it) gives way to the "ejective." Having ascribed to himself the properties of others, the growing child begins to ascribe to others the properties he knows to be his own. Projection and ejection, awareness of others and consciousness of self, are in this way interconnected; they constitute, according to Baldwin, man's whole personal life. What we have to underline is that, in this give-and-take, projection and ejection may indeed be equally strong, but they are not equally primal. The question which is earlier, the chicken or the egg, is normally unanswerable, but in this case it can be answered. The chicken is before the egg. Projection comes before ejection; the ascription of the properties of others to the self comes before the ascription of the properties of the self to others. True, the development of a self-knowing ego, which is so important a precondition of socialization, is, as we have emphasized, an achievement of the child's; yet it is the response of that child to a social situation, to the existence of others. In the absence of their stimulating, provoking, influence, the dominant capacity for self-conceptualization would not be evoked and evolved. A mere, sheer animal existence would continue, and there would be nothing which could possibly be humanized and, in the human meaning of the term, socialized.

A small point of detail is worth mentioning before we move on. The young child is more interested in people than in things because people are active and he feels challenged to indulge in the same kind of activity. But he is not equally interested in all human beings. He is decidedly more interested in grown-ups than in age-mates. The reason for this preference is hardly mysterious. The grown-up is more powerful than the contemporary, hence more fascinating, hence more worthy to be taken as a model. In this respect, Tarde is undoubtedly right: imitation goes *a superioribus ad inferiores*. The social situation is indeed a primary reality, but so is the lack of sociality on the part of the new human being who enters into it. He is not interested in his neighbors because they are of his species; his interest is not social; it is experiential. The consciousness of self does not spring from a consciousness of kind; it is the aftereffect of preoccupation with what is very different from the self, much bigger, much more massive—indeed, to the awakening weakling, monstrous.

The primacy of the social situation can also be seen, a little later, in the primacy of the word over the physical image. Here again the scholarly observer is likely to be at loggerheads with current opinion. Current opinion, in thrall to the conviction that what is bodily is always more basic than what is social, assumes that there is first a cluster of sense impressions and then a word is affixed to it to serve as a convenient label. In reality, it is the other way round. There is first, not a cluster of sense impressions, but merely a congeries of them. There is a chaotic flux of impressions with no vortices within it. It is the word, provided by society, which offers the childish mind a rallying point, a *point d'appui*. "The popular notion of learning to speak," writes Cooley in *Social Organization* (p. 69),

> is that the child first has the idea and then gets from others a sound to use in communicating it; but a closer study shows that this is hardly true even of the simplest ideas, and is nearly the reverse of truth as regards developed thought. In that the word usually goes before, leading and kindling the idea—we should not have the latter if we did not have the word first.

But what is true of other words is true of the word "I" as well. As soon as it comes to the developing child, it gives him strong help in connecting, conflating, and consolidating the self-ideas which he has seriatim assembled. In this way, not only do others give to the socializee the rudiments of self-knowledge by revealing to him the parts of the body which are at first merely objectively, but not yet subjectively, his own, they also give him the perfection of that knowledge by offering him, in the word, a prime means of assemblage and integration—a unitary, all-comprising name for a unitary, all-comprising self.

We have so far represented the discovery of one's own body and the discovery of one's own self as parallel processes, and so they are, but only up to a point, and the time has come now to consider the differences. In order to know one's own body, it is sufficient to remain on the surface. A body is after all a physical object which can be seen and touched. But in order to know one's own self, it is necessary to penetrate through the surface and to enter into the hidden places of the heart and mind. Following Baldwin, we have said that a sense of selfhood grows in the child when he sees others acting and attempts to act in the manner they do; he then achieves the realization that he, too, is an action center. This is self-knowledge of a kind, but not complete—not essential—self-knowledge. If self-knowledge is to become complete and essential, a knowledge of one's *intentions* and *motives* has to be achieved. But the small child, like the animal, knows nothing of intentions and motives. His mode of behavior is unproblematic to him. It is geared to his natural drives. It always thrusts outward; it is unreflective. A change can come only when there is re-flection, a bending back and looking into the antecedents, the *psychic* antecedents, of one's deeds.

One "is struck to see how unconscious of itself and how little inclined to introspection is the egocentric thought of very young children . . . ," Piaget writes in *The Moral Judgment of the Child* (p. 187), and in *Judgment and Reasoning in the Child* (Chapter 4) he has gone even more fully into the matter. A change takes place only when the child becomes an object to himself, or, better, when he makes himself an object to himself. But why should he do so? There is a world of difference between following the springs of action and considering the springs of action. The former is natural and connected with a reward, the release of tension. The latter is unnatural and worrisome. If the old adage ignorance is bliss applies anywhere, it is here. The discovery of one's intentions and motives is the end of innocence. It is the final parting from the natural life and the irrevocable entry into humanity and culture—humanity and culture in all their greatness, but also in all their problematic and all their pain.

Yet the child has hardly any choice. He is confronted with others; he has to try to understand those others—to understand them in their intentions and their motives. If they were only his compliant servants, all would be different. He could then issue commands dictated by his physical needs and be punctiliously obeyed. But life is not like that. The self opening up to the world experiences resistance and must ask why there is this resistance and how it may be overcome. It is impossible to be a human being and to live in a circle of human beings without developing a vital strategy. But strategic planning presupposes a knowledge of the terrain, and that terrain is a field of personal selves with personal wishes, personal intentions, personal motives. Thus the child discovers the psyche and its operations. And once he has entered into the inner life of others, it is only a relatively small step (though still a momentous one) to entering into his own psyche, to learning to identify his own personal wishes, personal intentions, and personal motives.

The technical term which George Herbert Mead has coined to describe this mechanism is "role-taking." In his encounter with others, the child learns how to see himself through the eyes of those others. He imaginatively takes their roles—that is to say, identifies for a moment with them—though at first only for the purposes of exploration and experimentation, and this is enough to teach him how to see himself as an object. By stepping, as it were, into the shoes of his neighbors, he has become another man even to himself, he has in a manner reduplicated—split into a knower and one-to-be-known. In this way, perfect and essential self-knowledge comes to be initiated. If we may express all this in the language of ancient philosophy, we may say that the infant is to begin with a closed universe, but that his neighbors proffer an Archimedean point from which the seemingly impossible feat of seeing this universe from without (while yet remaining within) can be achieved. Even this deepest self-knowledge is thus possible only in and through society. There "has to be a social process going on in order that there may be individuals," Mead writes.

The process out of which the self arises is a social process which implies interaction of individuals in the group, implies the pre-existence of the group. . . . when the whole social process of experience and behavior is brought within the experience of any one of the separate individuals implicated therein, . . . the individual becomes self-conscious and has a mind . . . [*Mind, Self, and Society,* pp. 89, 164, 134].

More recently, Leonard S. Cottrell has summed up the same basic idea very clearly by calling it "the proposition that the self emerges and is perceived by the individual only through the responses of reference others whose roles he takes toward his own acts," and has further expressed himself in the following words: "The self, as a person perceives and knows it, is . . . experienced by the person only through his taking the role of his reference others in responding to himself. The being he knows therefore lives in the responses of others externally present and/or internalized." In a word: "self is a reflexive product of social interaction" ("Interpersonal Interaction and the Development of the Self," in *Handbook of Socialization Theory,* ed. Goslin, pp. 552, 565, 548).

What the child discovers in his fellow-men, be they parents, siblings, or strangers, is, however, not only their intentions and their motives, but also their *judgments*, and more especially their judgments of him. The distinction of right and wrong, so alien to nature, so central to social life, enters into him through their strictures on his conduct. Now, these strictures on his conduct may be of two kinds: they may be dictated by the convenience, the interests, the resentments, of those with whom he interacts, or they may be inspired by certain principles which bear in them the character of objectivity and which present themselves with the claim of being a law for everyone: "A decent person does not do this"; "This is not done." In other words, these strictures may be rooted in selfishness, and they may be rooted in sociality. Insofar as they are rooted in selfishness, they will increase the child's own self-regard and evoke a stance of defense and counteraggression. The sociological theories which base themselves on individualism and atomism, from the Sophists via Hobbes down to Homans, see only this kind of social interaction and social experience. An orderly and pacified social life arises, in their opinion, if, and only if, an equilibrium of the contending selfishness is reached. But such an attitude overlooks the penetration of the social norms into the individual self, and indeed, into the depths of the individual self. The atomists are blind to the most potent strand within the social bond, not to say to the social bond iself. There is no safeguard to sociality which can be compared to, or praised above, the successful internalization of objective norms. The Kantian ethic with its categorical imperative, demanding that we should act in such a manner that the mode of our action could be a law for everyone, is not only a product of abstract speculation; it is also the upshot of concrete observation. It certainly needs further, more consistent, application in practical life; it is, however, realized in every deed we do in obedience to an internalized objective norm (in contradistinction to what we do in deference to superior power and brutal pressure). Now Kant believed that the demands of the categorical imperative, of consistent ethics, regularly run counter to the native inclinations of natural man; he was inclined to define as moral that which we would rather avoid doing. Even in this he was correct if by natural man we mean the human animal as it comes raw from the mother's womb. But then he is not only no moral man, he is as yet no man at all; he is as yet no human self. That human self arises through self-knowledge; self-knowledge in turn arises through the observation of other selves if that observation is turned around (re-flected) and takes in one's own ego. But the observation of other selves not only reveals their personal intentions and motives; it also reveals the existence of an objective code whose implementation by each and all creates and underpins that framework of order which we call society.

It is an unfortunate necessity, a weakness of our minds mirrored in and mediated by our languages, that we cannot speak of concomitant processes other than by taking up first the one and then the other, and thus creating the impression that they are not really concomitant but successive after all. The theologian is in the same quandary; he must discuss the Father first and the Son afterward, even though he has to teach that they are coequal and coeval. Here we are challenged to realize that the self and society are also coequal and coeval; that they are, in Cooley's graphic phrase, twin-born. (Insofar as one twin leaves the womb before the other, even this splendid formulation is still imperfect, above all too weak.) What precedes sociality is not the self properly so called; it is merely the self-void body, the organic shell. The self arises through the experience of a social life, of "social objects" as Freud called them, of other selves, as we might more soberly say, who are at the same time asserting their own interests and presenting and enforcing the claims of society. We can in theory separate a mother's or father's or sibling's or neighbor's deed inspired by his self-regard from one which is informed by his sociality; in practice we cannot —and the child in particular cannot—undergo the experience of the one without being exposed to the experience of the other. We might as well try to see the wharp of a texture without seeing the woof or the woof without seeing the wharp, if the whole cloth is before our eyes.

It is possible, of course, in certain extraordinary circumstances (we are sorely tempted to write: among foolish people) that a child is presented with only part of the picture. It is possible where certain unrealistic principles of pedagogy are pursued that the educators keep from him the norms on which the house of society rests, the limitations on the part of the individual on which society has to insist in order to enable all to live together and to cooperate in peace. But such a situation will be pathogenic as well as pathological. And, characteristically—we have to emphasize this strongly in a section devoted to showing that the development of selfhood is a precondition to the development of sociality—it is not only the sociality of the child which will not be attained, but his selfhood as well. He will become a deviant. He will be less than a normal self, for normal is only the self which conforms to the basic norms.

The close interconnection which exists between the actions done by persons in the child's environment out of self-regard and the actions which they perform as agents of social control can also be recognized if we look, not at the broad canvas of social life, but at one single strand in it, if we concentrate on one unit of action, one single move. It has become a commonplace among sociologists that behind every such action, every such move, there are two indispensable springs. The one is known as motivational orientation, the other as value orientation, or, even better, as normative orientation. I am hungry; I crave bread; I act in order to procure some. My physis—my empty stomach—provides the motivational orientation, and some would see it as a sufficient condition of the ensuing conduct. But it is not, by itself, sufficient. For I crave bread, which my society has taught me to value; I do not crave grubs which are highly valued in Australia's primitive communities. Purely physiologically, witchetty worms would be as sustaining an item of diet for me as wheaten rolls would be for the inhabitants of Arnhem Land, but my appetite is not aroused by them; I feel no orientation toward them. Still, as far as motivational orientation is concerned, culture can only concretize and modify the overall orientation (here, that toward food); it cannot act on its own.

A number of authors have, for very good reasons, pointed out that not all the needs of the self are bodily needs and that therefore even motivational orientation must not be defined in purely somatic and materialistic terms. There is a need for friendship; there is a need for beauty. No organs of our physis are involved; these are immaterial, spiritual, needs, and yet they generate motivational orientations. The argument has its force, and we would not deny it. Yet, in the final analysis, all motivational orientations are grounded in our physical existence. Friendship and beauty are, at least in a wider sense, life-sustaining, life-enhancing, values. When we crave them, when we pursue them, we do not have to face drive reduction. We would therefore add them to the number of natural desires. If they are satisfied, the sum total of our pleasures is increased.

But it is different with normative orientation. This is not given in and by nature; it is entirely created by man, and, above all, it involves drive reduction, places limitations on our natural urges and desires, and therefore causes, not pleasure, but pain. In order to provide myself with bread, I can pursue any number of techniques. I can, for instance, steal it or rob it; I can also buy it and pay for it. It is a normative orientation which determines me to buy and pay rather than to steal or rob. The bought loaf is physically no more life-sustaining than a stolen one; in paying for it, I obey the behest of society rather than the command of nature. Yet, entering the shop, having a loaf wrapped, and handing over the money, is *one* action, or chain of actions, apprehended by the observing child as one. And so normative orientation is learned at the same time as motivational orientation, *uno actu*, as the ancient philosophers would have said. True, the raw material of normative orientation, as it were, the physical craving, hunger and lust, pre-exists; it is given in and with the organism; but only as a dark urge. Conscious action—and that alone can count as truly human conduct, conduct characteristic of the species *Homo sapiens*—conscious action is (if we disregard the case of deviancy, of crime) always motivated by an internalized desire for law-abidingness as well as by a basically nature-given drive for need satisfaction. We conclude therefore that the child is socialized, not only because he experiences the whole broad stream of social action and interaction, but also because he contemplates and comprehends many disparate pieces of action and interaction, many disparate deeds. In each one of them self-regard and sociality are fused, and presented in fusion. In fusion also they are apprehended and internalized by the child.

So strong is the inrush of normative elements into the mind of the child that they ultimately take root within him and coexist and contend within him with natural appetitions, with motivational orientations. After having seen others respect property, after having been told, "you must not steal," he comes to say to himself: "I, too, must respect property, I must not steal." Schematically we may perhaps distinguish three phases, or at least three strands, in that process: there is, first, the observation of norm-abiding behavior in those around us; there is, afterward, the presentation, by significant others, our educators in the widest sense of the word, of the norms in more or less abstract terms; and there is finally the internalization of the norms, their merger with the action principle of one's own action center. As Leonard Cottrell has expressed it, showing that the development of a self-critical and self-disciplining attitude in the self is merely a prolongation of, and of the same nature as, the self-conceptualization of the self: "we can perceive, evaluate, and otherwise react to ourselves only through the acts of others who respond or have responded in the past to us, and whose role we have taken for ourselves as objects." But the time comes when "the origins of the 'other' part of the self–other system are no longer identifiable and the person appears to experience a truly self–self dialogue and is convinced he experiences a self without the mediation of some other" (p. 559). Just how this last-named mental condition is reached will have to be investigated in a later context (Section 79). Here we have to point out that what we can simply call the moralization of the mind, the moralization of the self, is once again a strengthening, and not a weakening, of the person through the influence of the social environment. It is correct, of course, that self-judgment induces hesitancy in action, and that guilt feelings reduce the vital tone, that they are, as some would say, psychologically wasteful, costs without profit. In a utilitarian balance sheet of pleasure and pain, gain and loss, they certainly weigh in the scales of pain and loss. But they show a different face when they are seen in the context of a dynamics of the personality. Hesitancy is, or at least can be, a preliminary to normatively correct conduct; so can guilt feelings. Arising from normatively incorrect conduct in the past, they may, they are even likely to, lead to normatively correct conduct in the future. Both bid to strengthen the will of man, and as the will is the core of man, of the specifically *human* being, they simply strengthen man, the human self, the human personality. Where they fail to achieve this consummation, the person involved becomes weaker, not only as a social creature, but concomitantly also as an ego, a self-controlling and self-controlled man. The individual who sits in judgment over his own behavior and applies social norms to it is in this way on a higher plane than the individual who does not do so—on a higher plane, both as a self or a soul, and as a member of a body social.

On the foregoing pages, we have presented a rather optimistic view of the relations between self and society suggesting that they normally tend toward harmony and not toward conflict, and in this particular we have followed, as on so many other points, the tradition which started with Cooley, prolonged itself in Mead, and is still very much with us. Yet optimism is essentially a mood and not a principle of scientific investigation, and we have to consider up to what point it is justified or justifiable. An harmonious interplay of self and society is indeed laid on as a grand possibility in the scheme of things, and often it does come to fruition; but there is no guarantee that this happy consummation will always be reached. Cooley took the view that selfhood and sociality develop together and that the mind is therefore as social as it is self-regarding. With this opinion he was on safe ground. But where he was at fault was in his treatment of the influence of the body and bodily urges on the relationship between the individual and the community. He did not give this problem much attention; indeed, he hardly regarded it as a problem at all. The following quotation shows how he felt in the matter: The "social interests prevail in conscience over the sensual because they are the major force; that is, they are, on the whole, so much more numerous, vivid, and persistent, that they determine the general system of thought, of which conscience is the fullest expression" (*Human Nature*, p. 378). Is this much more than wishful thinking? Is the idea of giving away a luscious pear or forgoing the enjoyment of a succulent steak more vivid and persistent than the natural appetite of consuming them? In another passage (p. 55), Cooley admits that the importance of the involuntary forces must not be overlooked, but he insists at the same time that they must not be seen as "antithetical to choice—as if the captain were expected to work the ship all alone, or in opposition to the crew, instead of using them as subordinate agents." Perhaps the involuntary forces, that is to say, our somatic appetitions, our greeds and lusts, are not antithetical to choice as such: we remain free to accept or to reject their bidding; we are to that extent true captains of our boat. But they are antithetical to self-denying choices; they are an ever rebellious, and not an ever obedient, crew. Cooley speaks of conscience, mind, and thought, but man is not only conscience, mind, and thought. He is also flesh and blood; he is also greedy and lustful. What the sociologist, as a student of reality, is interested in, is *human action*, and that is never more than some kind of compromise between voluntary and involuntary forces, the demands of self-indulgence and the claims of sociality, superego and id.

There are obviously two convictions in Cooley's mind and in the minds of his followers, both of which are unexceptionable if taken in isolation; but they must not be taken in isolation because, in this hard world of conflicts and contradictions, they are bound to clash. The one we have already encountered; it is to the effect that selfhood and sociality are not likely to be at loggerheads because they begin, unfold, strengthen, and perfect themselves together and *pari passu.* The other concerns the animal world, including man's physical organism, and asserts that the behavior of animals and physical organisms must not be adjudged either morally good or morally bad because there is no choice in the matter and they are, and have to be, simply what they are. There is no sense in calling the patellar reflex either good or bad; it simply happens; we might as well call the laws of gravitation ethical or unethical. But the problem which Cooley failed to see, and to which an entire overly optimistic tradition is blind, is the *combination* of body and mind, the encasement of a socializable and normally highly socialized mind in a body which is incapable of socialization. Maybe the social interests prevail *in conscience* over the sensual; maybe they determine the general system of *thought*. That is not the salient question. The salient question is whether they prevail in, and determine, the general system of *conduct*, and that cannot realistically be asserted. Who has not felt the power of the words which Ovid has put into the mouth of Medea: *Video meliora proboque, deteriora sequor*—"I see what is morally better and approve of it, but I do what is worse." When Cooley says (*Social Organization*, p. 32) that in human relations "mankind realizes itself," he greatly oversimplifies the facts. In human relations mankind realizes its cultural and spiritual possibilities, but it can do so only at the price of a constant combat with its own actualities, which are animalic, self-preferring, non-moral, and, therefore, all too often antisocial.

In an aside which is obviously ill considered and must not be held too much against him, Cooley has made the curious statement that "Kindliness seems to exist primarily as an animal instinct . . ." (*Human Nature*, p. 158). This is, to be blunt, nothing but unqualified nonsense. The counterthrust, in the history of the human sciences, came in Sigmund Freud's concept of a destructive or death instinct. This, too—decidedly not one of Freud's more happy inspirations—is an idea which has little to do with reality. Destructive, death-dealing urges do, of course, exist, but we must not conceive of them in terms of a primary instinct like libido, the urge to mate, with which Freud coordinated them. What we do see in nature is basically a positive, not a negative, tendency, the will to be; that certainly is laid deeply into life; and in certain circumstances it cannot reach its aim without the annihilation of other lives. A lion, made as he is, cannot survive without killing gazelles or calves. But the predator who devours his prey feels neither pity nor hatred for it; he simply devours it. Pity and hate are not, as Cooley or Freud suggests, qualities of animal existence. Perhaps they are prefigured and preformed there, but in a concretized and recognizable form they are exclusively human. In humans they develop with and in the mind and, purely on the mental level, they have an equal initial chance of unfolding and maturing. But positive and negative sentiments have that equal chance *merely* on the mental level, not on the level of conduct. It is easy for a hungry man to give his mental assent to the proposition that he should share his last crust of bread with another man equally famished, but it is difficult for him actually to share it. His stomach, his whole body, will cry out against such a self-denying action. The spirit indeed is willing, says the Gospel, but the flesh is weak. That is what Cooley forgot, and what a realistic analysis of the origins and limitations of sociality must not overlook.

The delusionary pessimism which Freud propagated can serve as a useful correction against the delusionary optimism peddled by Cooley. Unjustified in itself, it is apt to make us think and thereby helps to restore the balance. The Neo-Freudians (Freudians only in name and no longer in fact), especially those of America, enveloped by the same optimistic atmosphere which also produced Cooley and his school, have thrown the so-called death instinct out of the window. They were right, in principle, but their reaction to Freud's hardheadedness has gone too far. It is true that there is no death instinct properly so-called; it is also true that negative sentiments, such as envy and hate, arise only (as Karen Horney, Harry Stack Sullivan, and Franz Alexander have demonstrated) from the frustration of life instincts; but it is quite wrong to conclude, as many have done, and as too many have—with catastrophic results—attempted to show in therapy and education, that the removal of frustrations will produce the pacific and kindly man. The removal of those frustrations which are mandated by the basic social norms, the minimal norms of human coexistence, produces, not the pacific and kindly, but the asocial and selfish personality. This has been proved only too often, and he is a blind doctrinaire who does not want to see it. The sad, but hard, fact of the matter is that social life is impossible without co-ordinating norms, and that coordinating norms in turn are impossible to im-plement without drive reduction, without some taming of the animal within us. There is no conflict between the self and society, but there is an abiding tension between the bodily appetites and social discipline, and it is none the less real for being normally latent and covert. In this war between nature and culture, culture has no more desirable ally than the human self, centered, as it is, in the human will. But that will must be truly human; it must have been informed and perfected by educational influences in the widest sense of the word, and if this has not happened, if it has remained the servant of beastly greeds and lusts, there will indeed be a hostile encounter between the individual and society which may lead to the degradation and destruction of them both.

THE ROLE OF CONFLICT IN THE DEVELOPMENT OF SOCIALITY

73. Connected with the weakness of the Cooley position and the Cooley tradi-tion which we have just considered is another and kindred one: a tendency to underestimate the role of conflict in the development of selfhood and, hence, of sociality. There are indeed, as we shall see, passages in Cooley's works in which he appears to acknowledge the centrality of conflict in these processes, but they are more in the nature of occasional asides and hardly belong to the core of his thinking. "Where there is a little common interest and activity," he writes in *Social Organization* (p. 26), "kindness grows like weeds on the roadside." We need not and should not frontally attack this assertion; if we did, we should be as guilty of allowing a mood of pessimism some influence on our analysis as he is of giving in to, and following up, a mood of optimism. But we should insist that the proposition quoted cannot be the truth and the whole truth unless we connect it with another which contrapuntally belongs to it—the proposition that even where there is much common interest and activity, clashes are sure to occur in no small number. Social life is both cooperation and conflict; it is, as Sumner has so graphically expressed it, *antagonistic* cooperation. Antagonism, however, plays a particularly effective role in the evolution of the self, includ-ing the socialized self, and any inclination to close one's eyes to the great part it plays must necessarily warp the picture. In *The Language and Thought of the Child* (p. 65), Piaget writes: "It may well be through quarrelling that children first come to feel the need for making themselves understood." This observa-tion, which has all the great child psychologist's experience to back it up, is deeply revealing. The need to make oneself understood is a real need, not to say, the social need κατ' ἐξοχήν; it is a need which is basic to cooperation and, hence, entirely positive and constructive in its effects. Yet it stems from conflict as much as it does from cooperation and is genetically not unconnected with what is destructive and negative in social life.

Already Cooley's basic simile, the simile of the looking-glass self, is somewhat problematical in this respect. We know ourselves because we see ourselves reflected in a mirror, and that mirror is the mind of our neighbors. Take them away, and not only they disappear, but we do so as well, because there is now nothing to reveal and define us. Basically this way of looking at the matter is correct. Psychologists who are much closer to the facts than Cooley was assert the same. Thus Piaget clearly and quite consistently upholds the opinion that we can hardly get any distinct view of ourselves except by placing ourselves at the standpoint of someone else, and, according to Sullivan, the self is being formed by "the reflections of our personality that we have encountered mirrored in those with whom we deal" (cited in Martin Birnbach, *Neo-Freudian Social Philosophy* [Stanford, Calif., 1962], p. 65). Yet a mirror is something passive; it will reflect our image, and any image, without demur; we cannot conflict with it. Our fellow-men are not of this kind. Self-recognition comes through looking at ourselves through the eyes of others; so far Cooley is correct. It is indeed comparable to beholding a picture in a glass; but it is a far, far more complex, and, above all, a far, far less pacific, process.

We have emphasized already that the definition of the ego by the alter is parallel to the definition of the living self by the lifeless environment. Just as we know our ego because we can contrast it with other egos, so we know our ego because we can contrast it with our physical environment. As the concepts of self and other are functions of each other, so are the concepts of self and things. But even things are not experienced as entirely passive. The looking glass, in its essential service, that of reflecting our outlines, is hardly a characteristic representative of our physical setting. For that setting is experienced primarily as *resistance*—resistance to our wishes. A much better representative of it than the looking glass is the wall which blocks our way. The child comes to know it because he will run his forehead against it and feel pain. Still, things can after all be manipulated; we can learn how to go around them. People are different. They resist us not simply by being there, but also by asserting a will contrary to our own. It is our combat with them which teaches us that we are selves of our own, and not simply their being there, their existence as convenient looking glasses.

Coming to much more simple and sober aspects of the matter: it must surely be a great question whether the infant's cooperative relation to his mother does more for the origin and strengthening of his ego concept than his conflict relation with his siblings. As far as the mother is concerned, the care she lavishes on the baby is accepted by him in a matter-of-fact way; there is little to stimulate his ego feeling as long as this blissful state of affairs lasts. In a symbiotic relation, under a fusion of lives, the independence of the associates will hardly spring to mind. It will spring to mind, however, as soon as a rift appears, that is to say, as soon as one partner does not get from the other what he craves. If the relation between mother and child were an isolated and exclusive one, the child would be, and remain, a mere dependent on his stronger half. But it is not isolated and exclusive. The mother is normally concerned about more children than one; she also has obligations toward her husband and others; she therefore must divide her attention and her time. It is precisely in the unavoidable and enforced interstices between child-care acts that the child feels most vividly that he is an independent self with interests of his own. It is the shouting for attention, not the reception of it, which helps him to achieve that integration of the self and that self-knowledge and self-determination which is characteristic of the normal personality. Parsons writes in one of his shorter papers: "only when the *need for love* has been established as the paramount *goal* of the personality can we say that there is a genuine ego present" ("Social Structure and Personality Development," p. 178). This is true, but it needs to be more fully formulated. We should speak of a *felt* need for love, not simply of a need for love, and we should remember that a need is felt only when it is not immediately satisfied. Parsons' proposition, like that of Cooley considered a little while ago, needs completion through a contrapuntal opposite. If he puts the emphasis on the need for love, we can write with equal justification: "Only when the *need for self-assertion* has been established as the paramount *goal* of the personality can we say that there is a genuine ego present."

We may appeal at this point to common experience. There are cases in which the relation between mother and child is too close, and too closed to the outside —cases which the common sense of humanity has characterized and condemned as "monkey love." The consequences of such over-mothering are well known. They are, above all, a deficiency in self-integration and self-reliance and may branch out into such disorders as homosexuality. Mother love is a good thing; but, according to an old adage, there can be too much of a good thing. The developing personality owes as much to the limitation of parental services as to their provision. Man is normally born into a competitive situation. It is this situation, with the need it establishes for him to look out for himself and to assert his interests, which gives the infant his ego, his very self.

It is very instructive in this discussion to go back from Cooley's finished texts, which present a far-too-rosy view of self-development and socialization and owe to this optimism a good deal of their appeal and their success, to his primary observations, for instance, to those of his raw materials which are contained in his article "A Study of the Early Use of Self-Words by a Child" (*The Psychological Review*, 15, No. 6 [November 1908], 339–57; repr. in *Sociological Theory and Social Research* [New York, 1969], pp. 229–47). Here we read: "Second month, 11th day, B cries for her bottle, and cried in apparent anger when it is taken away from her." Shortly afterward: "3–1. B, two months old, already cries to be taken up, or in protest against being laid down, also for her bottle." In connection with the latter information, Cooley jots down a remark which is surely realistic:

> This and some of the following observations are given as possible manifestations of an early sense of appropriation, such as later underlies the use of self-words. Those cases where the thing appropriated is not a material object but the attentions of other people are especially pertinent. They seem to be the beginnings of that desire for control over others, for social power, which plays so large a part in the mature self [*Sociological Theory and Social Research*, p. 233].

It would be tedious to parade here the numerous passages which point in the same direction and which all go to show that selfhood and self-knowledge spring from the assertion of the self *against* his associates and not, or far less, from the services rendered, from the love shown, by these associates to the self. Only a few may be given, to put the matter into higher relief. Under 10th month, 16th day, we read: "She [the baby observed] has put forth will, has intended and achieved, and her look shows the sense of power." Under 15th month, 17th day: "*B* is vigorously appropriative; screams when she is not allowed her own way. . . ." Same month, 24th day: "*B* seems to be jealous, or at least fretfully appropriative, of other people. . . . She will not let any one else touch her mother when the latter is holding her, but will grunt complainingly and push the offender away. . . . She expresses the idea 'mine' very clearly." Such observations continue all the way; for instance: "26–16. *R* [a brother] was threatening to take away a necklace. She almost screamed: 'Dat mine.' Speaking of her dress she said: 'That's *my* dress; that's *mine*; that's *baby's*, all in the same sentence." "26–17. Saying 'My book' with great emphasis, at times almost a scream, when threatened with dispossession by *R*" (pp. 234, 235, 246).

Such observations induce Cooley—whenever he remembers them—to take an attitude toward the process of socialization and its inherent difficulties and limitations which is soberly realistic and agrees well with the tenor of the present analysis. The following quotations will show how true this is:

Watching her [baby B's] use of the first person, I was at once struck with the fact that she employed it almost wholly in a possessive sense, and that, too, when in an aggressive, self-assertive mood. . . . self-feeling . . . appears to be associated chiefly with ideas of the exercise of power . . . ideas that emphasize the antithesis between the mind and the rest of the world. The first definite thoughts that a child associates with self-feeling are probably those of his earliest endeavors to control visible objects. . . . Then he attempts to control the actions of the persons about him, and so his circle of power and of self-feeling widens without interruption to the most complex objects of mature ambition [*Human Nature*, pp. 190, 177].

In proportion to their energy men will always seek power. It is, perhaps, the deepest of instincts, resting directly on the primary need for self-expression. [There is] a tendency in all of us to abuse power when not under definite legal or moral control. . . . the self-assertive passions . . . I believe . . . are fierce, inextinguishable, indispensable [*Social Organization*, pp. 251, 261, 35].

Most realistic, because most aware of the great part conflict plays in the development of both the individual and the social self is the following passage from *Human Nature and the Social Order* (p. 174): "perhaps the best way to realize the naïve meaning of 'I' is to listen to the talk of children playing together, especially if they do not agree very well."

"Especially if they do not agree very well." The choice of words in this formulation is highly characteristic. Why did Cooley—the same Cooley who, as an observer, had to state that self-feeling in children is associated with "grasping, tugging, and screaming" (ibid., p. 191)—why did he not write: "especially if they quarrel, if they are at each other's throats"? The answer is surely obvious:

because he did not like the facts which he yet saw all too clearly spread out before him. There is a deep conflict between Cooley the observer and Cooley the theoretician. There are two passages from his pen which, when juxtaposed, show this with all desirable clarity. Under 23rd month, 19th day, Cooley the observer notes: " 'My' might be used at first as a mere exclamation associated with controversy." But under 25th month, 13th day, we read: "I never heard her use 'my' in altercation" (*Sociological Theory and Social Research*, pp. 239, 244). These two statements—unless we draw a distinction between controversy and altercation which would be impermissible hair-splitting—are in flagrant opposition to each other. The latter is characteristic of the entry of wishful thinking into the process of theory construction and hence is to be resisted and rejected. Another witness of the same persistent tendency toward falsification is also the following entry (on p. 245): "26–1. 'I won't.' Said reflectively, not controversially, this morning when asked to come up stairs." Not controversially! Little Miss B. refuses to do what she is bidden. She puts her will against that of her elders. To call this very definite utterance a "reflective" one is surely the height of artificiality.

But the last-quoted jotting has an addendum which allows us to look deeper into Cooley's mind and to get down to the root of his errors. "26–1. 'I won't.' Said reflectively, not controversially, this morning when asked to come up stairs. (An echo from other children?)" Cooley obviously assumes that a child learns self-assertion, assertion of his own will in defense of his own convenience, in the same way as he learns self-restriction and self-sacrifice. He notes under 23rd month, 21st day: "I have little doubt that *B* uses 'I' with a sense of appropriative feeling which she has perceived to accompany its use by other children," and again under the 23rd day: " 'Give it to me' is associated in her mind with appropriative activities observed in others" (p. 239). Such perception, such observation, such association, is not, however, necessary to create appropriative feelings and appropriative activities, for these are laid on and laid down in bodily appetitions and are as natural as the sucking of the mother's milk. Perhaps Cooley's clearest utterance on this point is the following jotting which undertakes to reply to the question how the subjective meaning of "I" is grasped. Cooley writes (p. 231): "My answer is that the child gradually comes to notice the indications of self-feeling (the emphasis, the appropriative actions, etc.) accompanying the use of 'I,' 'me' and 'my' by others. These indications awaken his own self-feeling, already existing in an inarticulate form." The very last words—"already existing in an inarticulate form"—certainly show an approach to the truth, but Cooley immediately veers away from it again by laying the emphasis once more on the child's learning even self-feeling from others. "He sympathizes with them," he writes (meaning by "them" the "indications of self-feeling"), "and reproduces them in his own use of these words." It is thus, we are expected to believe, that they "come to stand for a *self-assertive feeling or attitude*, for self-will and appropriation." As if a child would need instruction in self-preference! Yet Cooley's worst mistake is to assume that the conditions and chances of development are equal for both selfish and social, even altruistic, attitudes. This is surely profoundly delusionary. Selfishness is natural because it has a somatic foundation, the pleasure-craving body; sociality is not. "Take the greed of gain, for example, . . ." Cooley writes in *Social Organization* (pp. 36, 37).

> It is immoral . . . only when it is without adequate control from sympathy, when the self realized is a narrow self. . . . Those who dwell preponderantly on the selfish aspect of human nature and flout as sentimentalism the "altruistic" conception of it, make their chief error in failing to see that our self itself is altruistic. . . . The improvement of society does not call for any essential change in human nature, but, chiefly, for a larger and higher application of its familiar impulses.

Who would not wish that it were so? But a wish is not a fact. The fact of the matter is that the self is, and can be, altruistic only to the extent that "human nature" is changed from an instinctive-animalic into a cultural "nature," a "nature" denying its own instinctiveness and animality, and if this is not "an essential change," what is? We must counter Cooley's attack on those who underline the naturalness of self-preference by writing, in variation of his own words: "Those who dwell preponderantly upon the social and altruistic aspects of human nature and flout as cynicism the 'egoistic' conception of it, make their chief error in failing to see that our body itself is egoistic"—that body which we can indeed control, but never shed.

Cooley's whole lack of realism can be seen best in two contexts. One is his discussion of sports; the other, his utopian musing on the future of commerce and industry. Sports, he tells us (pp. 34, 35), produce the team spirit, and are thereby one of the most effective socializing influences at work in the world. Needless to say, he is correct, but he forgets, or at any rate underestimates, two important aspects of sportive activities. The one is the fact that the friendship between the teammates is matched by their enmity to the team's adversaries. In fact, the positive-constructive team relationship among the insiders is merely a corollary, a consequence, of the negative-competitive conflict relationship to the outsiders. Besides—and this, too, is significant—even the most vivid team spirit does not entirely dissolve the mutual competition among the teammates. However united the front which they appear to offer on the sports field, there is always a good deal of juggling for position and personal advantage inside their own ranks. Everybody wishes to be the star. If the phenomenon of sport is to be brought into the whole discussion, it must be brought in properly, with all its sides, positive and negative, and not only partially, through one facet of it which happens to suit a theoretical position.

As far as industry and commerce are concerned, Cooley admits that today "there is a lack of that higher discipline which prints the good of the whole upon the heart of the member," but who is to follow him when he suggests that "the desire for separate power or distinction" will one day be "lost in the overruling sense of common humanity"? This is sheer utopianism, and utopian also are such sentiments and sentences as the following: "Human nature desires the good, when it once perceives it. . . ." "One of the most obvious [!] things about selfishness is the unhappiness of it. . . ." "One is never more human, and as a rule never happier, than when he is sacrificing his narrow and merely private interest to the higher call of the congenial group" (ibid., pp. 352, 350, 88, 191,

38). Is the soldier never happier than when he advances into a hail of bullets in defense of his country? Is the citizen never happier than when he pays his annual income tax? Is there ever going to be a time when the sacrifice of life or even of purchasing power will be anything but a sacrifice? Socialization produces marvels, for the soldier will die and the citizens will pay, but not because they like to die or to pay, merely because they accept the negative implications of sociality, its inherent discipline, along with the positive ones, above all, personal security from harm.

So pervasive is Cooley's delusionary view of socialization that it taints even his best and most realistic concept, that of the primary group. It is in the primary group, the nursery, the family circle, the play group at the corner, he tells us, that we all have been, and are being, socialized, and he is correct. And equally close to reality is a sentence such as the following:

> It is not to be supposed that the unity of the primary group is one of mere harmony and love. It is always a differentiated and usually a competitive unity, admitting of self-assertion and various appropriative passions; but these passions are socialized by sympathy, and come, or tend to come, under the discipline of a common spirit [p. 23].

But were there nothing but sympathy to rely on, for instance, in a nursery full of children, the unity of the group would not last very long; there would be too many black eyes and bleeding noses. What enables the process of socialization to proceed, and to do its job, in circumstances such as these is surely the presence of some authoritative figure, some appointed peacemaker and peacekeeper, a mother or a nurse, who sees to it that every child gets his fair chance; even the biggest bully may at times be a healthy influence if he secures some semblance of order within a gang. In a word: there must be *social control*, and social control, however internalized, needs some external enforcement, indeed, *permanent* external enforcement, actual or potential, actual or threatening—unless indeed we are concerned with a circle of saints. But saints are not the normal subject matter of the science of sociology.

In one of his early papers, "A Study of the Early Use of Self-Words by a Child," Cooley raises the question "In what sense is 'I' a social conception?"; and he replies: "The answer to this is apparently something as follows: 'I' is social in that the very essence of it is the assertion of self-will in a social medium of which the speaker is conscious" (*Sociological Theory and Social Research*, p. 232). This statement is unexceptionable, and Cooley should have stuck to it. Primarily and permanently social, social in the full sense of the word, is merely man's situation, his medium; his self is always to some extent a center of self-assertion, even if that extent is normally being reduced to a considerable degree by social and socializing forces. But if self-assertion is and remains the core of the self, conflict as well as cooperation must be acknowledged to be of the essence of social life, including the introduction to that life, the process of socialization.

These criticisms of Cooley are not, of course, meant to diminish his stature; we are all his disciples, and his strengths in any case far outnumber his weaknesses. We have used him only as a convenient example of a widespread and ever present intellectual, or, rather, ideological, tendency which must be held at bay if man is ever to achieve a realistic knowledge of his own social nature. That he stood not alone in his delusions can be seen from a side glance at George Herbert Mead. In an important footnote (*Mind, Self, and Society*, p. 224) Mead severely criticizes Cooley and separates himself from him, accusing Cooley of a bent toward solipsism. This is *prima facie* a strange accusation to bring against one who was *ex professo* a sociologist, yet Mead has strong ammunition to support his charge. He obviously thinks of passages like the following: "So far as the study of immediate social relations is concerned the personal idea is the real person. That is to say, it is in this alone that one man exists for another. . . . My association with you evidently consists in the relation between my idea of you and the rest of my mind" (*Human Nature*, pp. 118–19; see also p. 315). Mead followed Cooley in many things, but into this excessive idealism he refused to follow him. He readily admits—even more, he underlines—the kinship between Cooley and himself: "Even for Cooley the self presupposes experience, and experience is a process within which selves arise; but," he goes on to say,

> since that process is for him primarily internal and individual rather than external and social, he is committed in his psychology to a subjectivistic and idealistic, rather than an objectivistic and naturalistic, metaphysical position. . . . [For him] society has really no existence except in the individual's mind, and the concept of the self as in any sense intrinsically social is [merely] a product of imagination.

As can be seen, Mead lays claim to superior realism, and such superior realism should surely include a more down-to-earth attitude toward conflict as well. There are one or two passages in which a relatively sober attitude on Mead's part seems to be indicated, but they do not amount to very much. He states (p. 234), for instance, that significant communication may arise, not only out of cooperative, but also out of antagonistic, conduct, but the matter is not further pursued. Later (pp. 304, 305) he comes for a moment—but, alas, again only for a moment—close to the insight which the present work seeks to convey. "Human individuals," he says there, "realize or become aware of themselves as such, almost more easily and readily in terms of the social attitudes connected or associated with . . . 'hostile' impulses . . . than they do in terms of any other. . . ." This is certainly true. But why the hesitation? Why the restriction "almost"? This word is totally uncalled-for at this point. Another context (p. 358) includes the comment that

> the conception of social conduct . . . must not be confined to mutual reactions of individuals whose conduct accepts, conserves, and serves the others. . . . the instincts or impulses of hostility and flight . . . play most important rôles. . . . Nor is it amiss to point out that in the evolution of animal forms within the life-process the hunter and the hunted, the eater and the eaten, are as closely interwoven as are the mother and the child or the individuals of the two sexes.

The trouble with this passage is that it refers to animal life, not to human. When Mead writes that, "For the purposes of social conduct, the tiger is as much a part of the jungle society as the buffalo or the deer," he is speaking literally, not metaphorically. Yet human society is also a kind of jungle, and is often, not undeservedly, described as such; in human society, too, there are hunters and hunted, there are chains of conflict which both create and limit social integration. But this fact is not duly appreciated by Mead (and all too many others); it is played down and well-nigh denied.

Where Mead speaks directly of conflict among human beings (see p. 303), he immediately tries to take the sting out of the facts. He asserts that "Historical conflicts start, as a rule, with a community which is socially pretty highly organized," and adds that "a wider social organization is usually the result. . . ." We have here two arguments which, both of them, endeavor to change black into white. To take the second first: Is it really an advantage if wars take place between vast alliances rather than between small countries, or labor conflicts between unions of millions of members rather than between small craft guilds? Is there a gain in sociality if there is a gathering-in of hostile forces, a ganging-up? But more serious than the second argument is the first. Conflict, Mead implies, presupposes sociality. That is true. People who have nothing in common cannot and will not conflict. But the point is that, once again, the antithesis is as correct as the thesis: if conflict presupposes sociality, sociality on its part presupposes conflict. What Mead seems to dismiss is the Hobbist problem— the basic problem of the coexistence of self-preferring, only partially socialized, individuals, and of the ordering and pacification of that coexistence—and he who dismisses that problem cannot claim to be a realistic sociologist.

In the end, Mead drifts into the very same sort of delusion as Cooley, even though he claims, as we have seen, that his is an objectivistic and naturalistic position. Social processes, he maintains (p. 258),

> are such that they carry with them neighborliness and, in so far as we have co-operative activity, assistance to those in trouble and in suffering. The fundamental attitude of helping the other person who is down, who finds himself in sickness or other misfortune, belongs to the very structure of the individuals in a human community. It can be found even under conditions where there is the opposing attitude of complete hostility, as in giving assistance to the wounded enemy in the midst of a battle.

Mead is not conscious of the great and tragic difference between a human and a humane society. Human societies are not necessarily humane. There is indeed assistance to the wounded in battle (though normally after battle rather than in battle), but it does not come from the enemy. It comes from a neutral body, the Red Cross, which had to be created precisely because hostile armies do *not*, in fact, spontaneously look after each others' casualties, however atrocious their suffering, as Henri Dunant, the founder of the Red Cross, observed during the Battle of Solferino.

A perusal of Dunant's report of that dreadful carnage would have sobered Mead considerably. The distress of the great humanitarian breaks through, for instance, in the passage where he talks about a charge of the cavalry. The horses, he writes, were more human than their riders (*Eine Erinnerung an Solferino* [Basel, 1863], p. 25). Yet there are also stories of kindness and compassion (passim). But why were some of the soldiers prepared to aid the wounded, even in the enemy camp? The answer is clear: because there were norms to that effect, customs and usages of warfare, which they had internalized and which were recalled to their memory before the engagement by their commanders (see p. 45). Those who were not under such constraints, the peasants of the surrounding countryside, showed neither kindness nor compassion. They stripped the dying of their possessions, pulling the shoes off their swollen feet, and buried some of those still living with the dead, eager to be rid of their imposed chores (pp. 37, 41; see also pp. 53, 54, 91, 92).

Mead's lack of realism reaches its climax (*Mind, Self, and Society*, p. 272) when he writes: "An illustration [of neighborliness] is that of the good Samaritan. . . . It is a response which we all make in a certain sense to everybody." "In a certain sense" is a restriction of some kind, but otherwise Mead's statement is extreme. "All" are Good Samaritans to "everybody"? The Gospel is more realistic. In the parable told in Luke (10:30–37), a priest and a Levite pass the helpless and stricken man and make no charitable response, leaving him to his fate. Their hardness of heart is at least as dramatic as the kindness of the stranger who later appears on the scene. Cases of this kind—passers-by refusing assistance to the victim of a traffic accident, for instance—are brought up by the newspapers over and over again. No, the Good Samaritan is not Mr. Everyman. He is held up by Jesus as a shining example of what man *should* be, not as a sober illustration of what man *is*.

In the final analysis, all these misinterpretations of the process of personality formation and personality socialization are due to the mishandling of the basic tenet of empiricism, the *tabula rasa* concept, the conviction that man is an empty blackboard which will accept any characters, the word "altruism" for instance as readily as the word "egoism." Sound in itself, the *tabula rasa* concept must be properly defined and delimited if it is to be a reliable truth. What precisely, so we musk ask, is a *tabula rasa*? Is it man or is it man's mind? Too many people are prepared to equate these two concepts; Cooley and Mead certainly were. But then man's most tangible part, his body, is disregarded, and that will not do. The body, however, is not a *tabula rasa*. It is the very opposite. It comes from the hands of nature with appetites, drives, preferences, and so on, all fully spelled out, with tendencies which are simply given *ab initio* and which indeed can be controlled or even suppressed, but never changed by "writing on them" as one can on a blackboard, or on the mind. A hard test of these assertions is the observation of those societies in which great and consistent care is taken that no self-preference be introduced into the children's selves. We are thinking here of such social experiments as the communal living of the Hutterian Brothers or the Israeli kibbutzim. In such settings, if anywhere, would have to be found conflict-free nurseries and play groups and classrooms, but they are not to be found even there. "Our data on early childhood," says Melford E. Spiro in his well-documented study *The Children of the Kibbutz* (Cambridge, Mass., 1958; pp. 375–76),

> suggest—with respect to private possessions at any rate—that the child is no *tabula rasa*, who, depending on his cultural environment, is equally amenable to private or collective property arrangements. On the contrary, the data suggest that the child's early motivations are strongly directed toward private own-

ership, an orientation from which he is only gradually weaned by effective cultural techniques.

Self-preference, therefore, is a primary fact even in a society which has placed a ban on self-preference and has secured far-reaching obedience to that ban on the part of the adult population.

Among the Hutterites, the sibling relationship is surrounded by a strong emotional halo. So much so that the members of these sectarian settlements "often prefer to marry siblings of their own siblings' spouses"—two brothers, for instance, marrying two sisters, or a brother and sister marrying a sister and brother (John W. Bennett, *Hutterian Brethren* [Stanford, Calif., 1967], p. 126). Furthermore, "Hutterian child-training methods . . . are completely lacking in one feature commonly found in Gentile systems: the encouragement of competition between the children." Thus there is "a thoroughly egalitarian atmosphere, where differences in skill and intelligence are minimized." And yet! Bennett has to state that "Sibling rivalry is prevalent among the small children . . ." and has to be dealt with "firmly." Nobody has introduced it into this setting, but it is there all the same because a tendency toward it is born with every child, Hutterian or not. This sibling rivalry, this self-preference, shows itself in particular in a tendency toward exclusive private property, which runs counter to all that is sacred to Hutterian brethren. "The ideology of communal property is so pervasive," our informant writes, "that queries assuming an ideology of ownership are not clearly understood, and when understood, are avoided." Nevertheless, he has to concede, "there is a last-ditch sphere of personal autonomy that centers around articles deliberately acquired by one person and used by him only," "a basic acquisitive residue" (pp. 128, 127, 171, 172). What else can we infer from this information but that this communistic society is not in every respect radically different from others and that the personalities being formed within its ambit owe something of their selfhood to conflict with siblings and neighbors?

In the Israeli kibbutzim, the situation is no different. We have already quoted Spiro's overall conclusion. Here are a few of his detailed observations: "The desire to live in the kibbutz entails the acceptance of its most important and characteristic feature—collective ownership. . . . Food, toys, clothing—all belong to the group." Yet the toys are public property more in theory than in practice. "There is abundant evidence," Spiro writes, "in all but the very youngest children, that the preschool children do perceive certain objects as belonging to them." He then gives a list of examples in which the natural use of "mine" and "thine," and indeed the stressed and stressful use of these words, is evidenced. For instance: "The nurse passes out water-colors for painting. When Tsvi gets his colors, he sings repeatedly: 'This is *mine*, this is *mine*'" (*Children of the Kibbutz*, pp. 373, 374). Leaving then the two-to-four-year-olds, Spiro goes on to say:

> Concern with private property is strong, among at least some of the older children as well. In the Transitional Class, for example, two girls not only esteem material possessions, but they are highly envious of the possessions of others, becoming agitated should another child have a "nicer" dress, blouse, or hair

ribbon. One day . . . one of these girls changed blouses four times because she felt that another's was prettier than hers. Similar attitudes are to be found in the grade school, especially among the younger children. Their few private possessions—books, marbles, wristwatches—are jealously retained as their own. They are strongly assertive of their property rights, according to their teacher, insisting that an object "is mine," should another child wish to take it. Some are envious of another's possessions, resenting the fact that another has something which they do not have [p. 374].

Later on, this competitiveness, this possessiveness, this self-preferring, wanes. "Although the desire for possessions looms large in the responses of the younger children," Spiro reports (p. 375), "it is negligible in the responses of the adult sabras. . . . the sabra attitude to private property would suggest that the kibbutz value of collective ownership has been successfully transmitted from the founding to the second generation." What this success of education shows is, not that there is to begin with a *tabula rasa*, but only that even the strongest innate features, including the strongest innate antisocial features, can be subdued by social influences. In childhood, however, and, hence, in the process of personality formation, in the process of forming personalities capable of entering fully into social intercourse, they must inevitably play their part. Conflict, therefore, cannot be left out of the account; indeed, it can hardly be even thought away.

The finally successful conquest of conflict over personal possessions in these experimental societies does not, however, imply an equally successful eradication of competitiveness in general. On the contrary. As Spiro shows, competitiveness penetrates into the last nook and cranny of these would-be egalitarian and communal structures. He writes (p. 402):

Kibbutz children must compete with their peers for the love of their nurse; they must compete with their siblings for the love of their parents; and they must compete with their peers for the use of toys and other play objects in the children's house. Hence we would not only expect the sabra desire for esteem to be strong, but we would assume it to entail competitive elements. Turning to the data, we find that the sabras do in fact have a strong need for approval and esteem, and that it does entail, for some of them at least, strong competitive elements. This need can be traced continuously from the children in the nurseries to the adult sabras in the kibbutz.

Let us now draw the necessary conclusion from our discussion. If the term "human nature" is taken in its proper sense, in the meaning of the native or animal nature of man, in contradistinction to his acquired and cultural "nature" (which is really a non-nature), then competitiveness is indeed part of it, and it will be present, as an impurity, as a nuisance, as a danger, even in societies which have firmly set their faces against it. In the process of growing up, before the educational effort has fully done its work, it must necessarily assert itself; there is no remedy for it. "All evidence points to the same conclusion," Spiro says (p. 92): "sibling rivalry (and its concomitant symptoms) is not only found in the kibbutz, but is very intense." What then can we expect in cultures which are not trying with might and main to be communities in the fullest sense of the term, and among human beings who are not siblings held together by the bonds of the family? Those who would see society well integrated and permeated by as brotherly a spirit as the imperfection of all things human permits must be glad and grateful that, by the perfecting and even individualizing of the personality, a ground is prepared in which the seeds of sociality can be sown and in which they can develop and bear their fruit.

BEING SOCIAL AND SEEMING SOCIAL

74. There is yet a third widespread error, besides the underestimation of the body's influence on human conduct and the underestimation of the role of conflict in the process of socialization, and we must deal with it. It consists in the overestimation of truthfulness in social life. We may once again use Cooley as the object of demonstration and target of criticism, but the misconceptions which he at times displays can be found as early as the eighteenth century and belong to the inner substance of the optimistic—or rather overly optimistic—liberal tradition. The whole of Adam Smith's classic work *An Inquiry Into the Nature and Causes of the Wealth of Nations* rests on the comfortable conviction that "honesty is the best policy." Reduced to its barest bones, this philosophy maintains that every human being constantly aims at the maximization of his happiness, and that he cannot possibly achieve this natural aim if he does not secure the complete good will of his neighbors; but in order to secure the complete good will of his neighbors he has to serve them to the best of his ability, for social life is a tit-for-tat, a sustained exchange of goods and services. This social philosophy, present in every phase of the development of the economic and social sciences, fancies itself particularly realistic. It insists that its starting point—man's indwelling drive for felicity—is unimpugnable, and that its conclusion—the definition of society as an equilibrium system counterbalancing all personal egotisms—is scientific (Newtonian) in the strictest sense of the word. Yet the delusionary character is so obvious that it could be discovered by any child. If it does not seem obvious to anybody and everybody, if it is at least not abandoned and shed, but carried forward from generation to generation, the reason is that it has all the power of wishful thinking to back it up.

Whatever one's creed, whether one is a utilitarian or not, it is correct to say that every man aims at the maximization of his happiness; it is also true that the volume of happiness he achieves will partially—even very largely—depend on the degree of good will which his neighbors will entertain toward him. But is it equally true that, in order to secure that good will, it is necessary to serve one's neighbors? Is it not amply sufficient to *appear* to serve them? Such phrases as *veritas vincit*, the truth will out, the truth will prevail, etc., have been bandied about a good deal, but what evidence is there that in fact truth is stronger than deception, and that deception does not, more often than one would expect, prove the stronger in the end?

Adam Smith was, above all, an economist, though he was a moral philosopher as well, and in the economic sphere it is doubly and trebly true that truth does not prevail of itself; that, in commercial dealings, deception is ever present and often prevailing. Perhaps his adage that honesty is the best policy was less erroneous in his own day than it is at present. In small, still precapitalist, towns, such as his own Kirkaldy, or even his own Glasgow, tradesmen were very well known to and by their customers and had to watch their step. A reputation, once lost, was not easy to recover. This, to be sure, was a healthy hindrance to excessive cheating. But since then the market place, and, indeed, the whole of society, has become anonymous. Few now deal with opposite numbers whom they know. Worse still, with general "progress," the technique of deception has progressed as well, and it has become increasingly difficult to distinguish between justified and unjustified claims. A society which, like capitalism, is a mechanism kept moving by the spring of private and personal interest, and which has a tendency to allow unlimited freedom to that interest, is almost bound to generate unfair practices on a large scale. A short side glance at commercial law will amply confirm what we are saying. At first it was thought sufficient to operate with the *caveat emptor* principle: let the buyer beware. He can be relied on sooner or later to recognize the frauds tried on him by his suppliers and to punish them by withdrawing their custom from them, forcing them, if they persist in their evil doings, out of the market. But it was found in the end that the *caveat emptor* principle is too weak to guarantee even a minimum of honest dealing. Even countries with a long and lively attachment to liberal ideas were forced to change over, at least in part, to the truth-in-advertising principle, and to enact statutes based on it. The mutual supervision of the citizens, on which Adam Smith had pinned his high hopes, will work well enough if everybody is at all times fully informed about everything. But such full information does not exist under capitalist conditions and is perhaps impossible in all societies.

When Charles Cooley took up the subject which Adam Smith had handled in his day, five generations had come and gone, and the relations between human beings (and not only in the economic sphere) had become much more distant and anonymous. The village atmosphere which had characterized even the towns of the late-eighteenth century had perished for the bulk of the population. Salesmanship had become an art, and the activity was anything but moral. No wonder, therefore, Cooley could write in his first book, *Human Nature and the Social Order*: "Probably a close and candid consideration of the matter would lead to the conclusion that every one is something of an impostor, that we all pose more or less, under the impulse to produce a desired impression upon others" (p. 352). But on the very next page an attempt is made to mitigate this hard, but realistic, judgment. "In general it may be said," Cooley writes there, "that imposture is of considerable but always secondary importance. . . ." Of secondary importance! Books which try honestly to say what the author sees, such as Erving Goffman's study *The Presentation of Self in Everyday Life*, tell a different story.

In his second book, *Social Organization*, optimism had so far penetrated into, and come to pervade, Cooley's thinking, that he could write: "Truth is a kind of justice, and wherever there is identification of oneself with the life of the group it is fostered, and lying tends to be felt as mean and impolitic" (p. 182). Lying is certainly felt to be mean for we have, all of us, imbibed enough of the moral code which society tries to introduce into us and anchor in us to realize that it is wrong. But is it also felt to be impolitic? Surely not. To assert that it is widely judged to be impolitic is a serious sign of blindness. Cooley is certainly right when he maintains that "Truth or good faith toward other members of a fellowship is . . . a universal human ideal" (p. 39), but it is an ideal honored more in the breach than in the observance. Even the law does not overstrain its demands for truthfulness; in its deep knowledge of man it realizes that a policy of deception is so strongly seductive (not to say, necessary) a tool where vital interests are concerned that it would be useless to proscribe it, at least in stressful situations. The criminal whose guilt can well be proved is yet allowed to plead "not guilty" before his judges, and he is not considered to add further to his criminality by thus perpetrating a conscious lie.

Just how far Cooley's error could go (and the error of his fellow-travelers, who are many) can be seen from the following brief quotation: "in diplomacy, for instance, there is a growing belief that it pays to be simple and honest." Cooley was simple and honest, and so are those who feel like him. But diplomacy would not be diplomacy—indeed, it would not be needed—if simplicity and honesty could be brought to prevail. It is no less ridiculous to assert that "where a social whole exists it may be as painful to do wrong as to suffer it . . ." or that "the golden rule"—the rule that we should do to others as we would be done by—"springs directly from human nature" (pp. 185, 42, 40).

It is sometimes a helpful intellectual exercise to take things and turn them upside down for a moment, and then to consider what we can learn from the unusual aspect they offer. (G. K. Chesterton was a past master of this technique and achieved at times impressive results with it.) Cooley quotes, in *Social Organization* (p. 44), an author who has this to say on games: "Your deepest desire is to beat the other boy, not merely to seem to beat him." This is true, of course, and it is true, not only in the context of boys and their games, but also of men and their serious contests. But can this correct observation be inverted? Can it be said that "your deepest desire is to aid the next man, not merely to seem to aid him"? If this could in fact be said, the condition of the human race would be very different from what it is—indeed, we need not hesitate to assert, far better than it now is, than it has ever been, and than it is likely to be in times to come. The reason is rather obvious. If you beat your competitor, you are rewarded in various ways—in money if the competition is economic, in prestige, if it is societal, by a feeling of triumph and superiority in every case. But if you aid your neighbor, you have as a rule to undergo a sacrifice, in money, in time, in effort, and this sacrifice will not be acceptable to natural man; we can expect it only from moralized man. But moralized man and social man must not be equated. It is precisely Cooley's error to assume that they coincide. Socialized man is at best semi-moralized man, man moralized up to a moderate standard of law-abidingness. Those few who need no urging to accept sacrifices for the sake of their fellows have ever been a small contingent, not to say a kind of miracle. We call them saints.

If it is true, as this book maintains, that sociality is acquired, not inherited, then it will be acquired in the partial form in which it is observed and experienced by the developing infant. Entering into a social system in which everybody maximizes his personal advantage while trying to minimize his burdens, he will take this state of things for granted, especially since he will find out that it is at best orally condemned, but in reality operated and accepted as legitimate on all hands. As the old proverb has it, in Rome you do as the Romans do.

But, in this context, we should remember yet another proverb (also, as it happens, of Roman connection): *mundus vult decipi*—the world wishes to be deceived. The child is met by a mother, and other educators and instructors, who have a definite idea of what he ought to be: he ought to be considerate, kind, loving, and so on. A mode of conduct is in this way suggested to him, and insofar as it is not natural to him (and little of it is) he will sham it, especially as he will find out that such play-acting brings rewards. The whole duality and duplicity of the process of socialization comes out in this fact; dualism once again stares us in the face. We adjust to the social life which we come to experience and which is held up to us as a model in two ways: on the one hand, by internalizing and operating its norms; on the other, by internalizing and manipulating them. Insofar as we internalize them and implement them in action, we become true social beings; insofar as we internalize them and use them in a self-centered life policy, we remain creatures in which the basic animalic will to survive, at the expense of all others if necessary, has remained paramount and has only dressed itself up in a social garb. The latter possibility, or, rather, reality, is all too often underestimated in the image of man entertained by sociologists, many of whom wish man to be more social than he actually is.

Criticizing, in his contemporaries, the tendency upon which we have just touched, and which we earlier called the Cooley tradition, a recent writer, Eugene Weinstein, has asserted that generally "people are assumed to develop purposes consonant with the requirements of the social system in which they find themselves . . ." ("The Development of Interpersonal Competence," in *Handbook of Socialization Theory*, ed. Goslin, p. 753). This assumption is in fact present in so prestigious a sociologist as Talcott Parsons. But, as Weinstein aptly remarks,

> life is not quite like that. Normative scripts . . . are far from complete, and often are tangential to issues of central concern to us. Nor is role reciprocity automatic; it may well be the product of extensive and quite subtle negotiations with others whose purposes are not complementary to ours. Acquiring the interpersonal skills necessary to engage in such negotiations is central to the socialization process. In a very real sense it *is* socialization. For, if the process is defined as equipping individuals to function as participating members of society, no set of skills (except the prerequisite linguistic ones) is as essential to participating in society as the skills enabling people to get others to think, feel, or do what they want them to [ibid.].

Weinstein also writes—not only expressing his own opinion but echoing that of William J. Goode, whose article "Norm Commitment and Conformity to Role-Status Obligations" (*American Journal of Sociology*, 66, No. 3 [November 1960], 246–58) points in the same direction—that "Learning what role prescriptions and proscriptions are and how they are met in expressive behavior is fundamental in the development of interpersonal tactics. There is . . . substantial room to maneuver within . . . normatively given boundaries" ("Development of Interpersonal Competence," p. 765)—room to maneuver which the spontaneous human drive of self-preservation and self-preference is not likely to leave unused.

A profound insight is expressed in these words. It remains true that socialization, in the sense of social education, introduces sociality into the individual and weans him from the consistent and instinctual self-preference with which he is born, but it is equally true that the same process teaches him how to look after his own advantage in the circle of his fellows and therefore creates a new and by no means less insidious form of egotism in his mind. This secondary form of egotism is distinguished from the first inborn-instinctual one by the greatly enlarged role which *rationality* plays in it. It is, so to speak, less innocent; it is a cunning life policy, and those who pursue it cannot plead that they do not know what they are doing. The crude self-preference displayed by children has something charming about it, even though it is, from a moral point of view, at least in its effect, no less regrettable than the self-preference characteristic of adults. It is direct, unashamed, and, above all, guileless. But as soon as reason develops, a clever strategy tends to be elaborated, and its guiding idea is what economists describe as the economic principle or principle of rationality: always to get what one craves for the minimum of outlay, or to secure, for a given investment, the maximum return. It is by no means an accident that we fall at this point into commercial language. The human intellect is above all a calculator, and it calculates in terms of investment and profit, not only when it becomes active in the sphere of the market of goods, but also when it becomes active in society, which can, to some extent, be considered as an exchange, a marketing of mutual services. To the extent that this is so, a social theory like that of Homans is correct; it only overlooks that the extent is limited, even though it may be rather large.

As theorizing observers and as manufacturers of concepts, we are certainly entitled to contrast the innocent pursuit of self-interest by the child (manifested, for instance, in the phenomenon which is vulgarly known as cupboard-love) with the shrewd pursuit of self-interest by the adult, but we should realize that in life there is an early and an easy transition from the one to the other. Even the small child knows how to manipulate his parents, and a formula sometimes heard is: he knows instinctively how to get what he wants. If we speak of the really small child, the child before the development of reason has properly gotten under way, this mode of expression is misleading. He does not know how to get what he wants, and there is no instinctual life policy in pursuit of self-preference. But there is an instinctual, i.e., body-based, general urge toward self-preference which can serve as a starting point and as a feeding taproot of such a life policy; its locus is indeed the mind but its characteristic is to make the mind, with its reasoning powers, subservient to the body—to what Freud called the pleasure principle of the id. Self-sacrifice has no such starting point and no such feeding underground taproot.

In the interpersonal tactics of which we speak and which penetrate human relations as air does all empty spaces, the withholding and the manipulation of information play a prime part. The task which human reason sets itself is to seem as social as possible without actually being more social than is absolutely necessary, and so mutual deception is a deeply laid trait of social life. Only the totally naïve and the totally sanctified will eschew it. It is traditional to say that socialization consists in the learning of social roles; the simile used is that of the stage. It is an analogy which is helpful and justified, but it is ambiguous and should be explored in both its implications. The one is that we learn to "play our part" in social life; differently expressed, but remaining in the same frame of reference: that we learn to fulfill our functions and to do our duties in social life. This is as it were the social, as opposed to the selfish, aspect of the simile. But it has a selfish, in the sense of antisocial, implication as well. It also conveys the fact that we are constantly play-acting, that we habitually play comedy in front of each other, that we do not say what is really in our minds and hearts, that we wear masks. And it is in the second sense that the comparison of society and stage is utilized by an important and insightful subschool of sociology, or, to be more concrete, of symbolic interactionism of which we may take Erving Goffman as a good example. His main treatise, already mentioned in passing, is called *The Presentation of Self in Everyday Life*, but its German version has an even more pungent title. Re-translated it reads: we, all of us, play theater.

An author like Goffman, who sets out to map the scene and to round out the picture of reality which he undertakes to sketch, has, of course, a great deal of detail to present. We need not follow him into that detail. Suffice it to say that role playing may be of three factually and, above all, morally, rather different sorts. (*a*) The role may completely absorb and, so to speak, swallow up the actor. In this case the person, the actor, puts nothing of himself, of his true private self, into his conduct, but functions purely and exclusively as a public figure. An example of this kind is any role which is fully formalized. Ritualism leads to this condition. Many Eastern courts, like that of classical China, could be adduced here as convincing illustrations. Such action series and action systems represent the social maximum, but not the social optimum. What we get is not really a play but a puppet show the main characteristic of which is its mechanical nature. Where every move is prescribed and the prescription punctiliously carried out, it is as if a clockwork were running off, and not a process of human interaction. (*b*) The role may have been accepted by the actor, but is being acted out by him in his own manner. The play in this case develops not in accordance with a prepared and imposed script, but yet in a meaningful, harmonious, and life-serving manner. To remain with the instance of a royal court: the king then behaves, not like an enthroned puppet, but like a human being in the fullest sense of the word who simply happens to occupy his exalted position and knows what to do in order to do it justice, according to the old adage: kingly is who kingly does. This is certainly not the social maximum, but it is decidedly the social optimum, for here the role playing has the most precious quality of spontaneity. (An action is spontaneous, according to the *Concise Oxford Dictionary of Current English*, if it is "gracefully natural and unconstrained.") The individual is left his freedom, indeed, his true self, but that self has taken up and domiciled within its own core the role, the part, the function, which life has allotted to him. (*c*) The prescribed role may not be totally or even partially accepted by the actor; he may only pretend to play it, in reality playing his own game. In sociological jargon: he may try to define the situation on the stage, to substitute his own subjective definition for the objective definition, the agreed definition of it, which he covertly sets aside and cunningly hollows out. If a courtier is not in fact a servant of the king, but a fortune hunter who merely wishes to promote his own interest, to acquire power, or to accumulate riches, we see on the stage, not puppets and not persons, but merely masks. The difference from the second case is obvious for there the actor is a recognizable person, though a successfully socialized one. Socialization has, in this happy contingency, done no harm to his personhood. The difference from the first case is less obvious but by no means less real. For in the third case there is nothing mechanical in the actor's action. The energy by which that action or action system is carried out is real enough, but it grows, not out of an oversocialized, nor yet of a rightly socialized, but of an undersocialized self. What we have before us is the social minimum. Here only the form of the play is social; its substance is not. What we see is in essence a dogfight, a contest of egotisms for the prizes of life.

Setting aside the first case, which is not of central importance in modern societies in which formalization and ritualization (although tendencies of this kind exist) have not gone to any length, we are left with the second and the third as paradigms of real and observable conduct in the contemporary world. Real and observable indeed they are, yet in the purity in which we have described them they are rarely, if ever, observable and real. We find them constantly, but only in interpenetration. The simile of the tea and the milk after the cup has been stirred springs to mind once again. What we have paraded in the last paragraph is essentially a set of ideal types in the sense of Max Weber, definitions gained by artificially isolating one strand observable in real life and exaggerating its characteristics so that its essence may become clearly visible. What is decisive for a study of socialization is the fact that education is an attempt to lead the individual from condition c to condition b, from the natural pursuit of self-interest even in and through the social role, to the spontaneous fulfillment of the social role even in spite of the temptations offered by self-interest. In practice, even the spontaneous role-player will serve his own interest if it can legitimately be done (for instance, by satisfying his vanity or simply by enjoying the knowledge of having done a job well), while even one who consistently shams and shifts will be unable to prevent the penetration of some social norms into his inner self altogether.

As will have become obvious, it is impossible to discuss the whole subject of being social *versus* seeming social without bringing in, involuntarily rather than voluntarily, a moralistic undertone. Every human being has his tactics and his strategy in life, yet these very words can hardly be used without evoking and associating with them such terms as "misrepresentation" or "deception," that is, terms heavily laden with disapproval—"dyslogistic" terms, as Jeremy Bentham used to call them. We should not, and we shall not, enter into an ethical discussion properly so called here; it is not our avocation. The point of view of the moral philosopher is different from that of the sociologist, for the moral philosopher is concerned with the Ought, the sociologist with the Is—with society as it actually functions, not with society in an imaginable, but not realized, ideal condition. Keeping closely to the facts, then: observable people condemn a cunning life policy more in others than they do in themselves. It is true that they know full well that they themselves are play-acting, and some uneasiness, some stirring of conscience, is felt, now and then by everybody. The knowledge of the prescribed norms is laid so deeply into normally educated man that he cannot help holding them against his actual conduct and acknowledging to himself that he is following them but partially and deviating from them whenever it can be done without incurring consequences unpleasant to himself. For this reason most people have a feeling on and off—it was called "consciousness of sin" in earlier days—that everybody else around is more moral than they themselves. But how much influence such considerations and such feelings have on overt action is, and must remain, a moot question. Optimists will say: much; pessimists, misanthropes: little. But even the greatest of optimists, if he knows ongoing social processes as the sociologist ought to know them, will have to acknowledge that social life is permeated with self-promoting policies and that there are as many nodi of such policies as there are participating human beings.

Goffman, in developing his analysis, his comparison of society with the theater, makes a distinction between front stage and backstage, between what the spectators can see and what goes on behind the scenes. His illustration is a small hotel in the Shetland Isles. There is a sharp contrast between the deference shown to a guest in the dining room and the contempt shown for him in the kitchen. The waiter's remarks to the cook would scandalize the diner if he could hear them. While the moralist who hides in all of us will condemn such duplicity, the sociologist will also have to draw attention to the fact that in societies as they are, among men as they are, such antisocial outbursts have a positive function to fulfill. A waiter's work is to some extent humiliating; his ego easily develops inferiority feelings; he will have a strong and understandable desire to abreact or overcompensate them; the pungent remarks about the guests will therefore make him feel better and re-establish his self-image; and they will in the end help him to continue with his service. If men were what they might be, all this would not be necessary; but they are not what they ought to be; they are what they are. And least of all can we expect high ethical standards on the part of those who are yet in the process of social education.

The distinction of a front stage and a backstage, of the limelight and the behind-the-scenes, will, however, be most useful for our investigation if we take it beyond the limit to which Goffman has driven it and apply it, not to the relation of two groups, like a superordinated and a subordinated one, but to the relation of individual and society. If we so apply it, we see that the most important backstage of society is the internal life of the individual. Only his social actions are observable; his individual considerations and motives are not. They may be guessed at, they may be inferred, but they are certainly not known, and this is one of the facts as highly important for sociology as it is for life. If men were mind-readers, everything would be different from what it is; but they are not, and that is good. Man—so much is surely clear, and no science of society is needed to prove it—needs, in order to function, a sphere of privacy into which others cannot penetrate. But what is more private, and what more central and essential to the minimal sphere of privacy, than man's own mind? The process of socialization which introduces norms and values into the inner citadel of man must do its work without destroying a last refuge of selfhood and liberty, for in the survival of an ultimate element of selfhood and liberty roots that spontaneity of human action without which, as we have seen, social interaction would not be more than a puppet show or a clockwork. But if such a last refuge, such an ultimate element of personal independence remains, it is unavoidable—given the fact that the human action center is tied to a self-preferring body—that it should also be the center of a personal life policy. To grudge man the possibility of developing and following such a life policy would be tantamount to denying him his claim to manhood. Whatever the attitude of moral philosophers, mankind at large—socialized humanity—has not grudged, indeed has granted it, and granted it fully and freely. Normal growing-up, therefore, normal socialization, unavoidably develops in the socializee an adaptation to social life under which he learns not only how to serve, but also how to hold his own, to manipulate and to exploit—how to *seem* social as well as how to *be* social. A supreme proof of this fact is the candid confessions of so many saints. The greatest among them have always insisted that they are the greatest sinners. They knew—and, in contrast to others, acknowledged—that even the highest sanctity, like the most successful socialization, can never totally overwhelm the natural self-regard of men.

In his excellent essay "The Development of Interpersonal Competence," Eugene Weinstein has written that "all children start out as Machiavelles (although some are better at it than others). Much of early socialization is directed at repressing these tendencies. The learning of role boundaries and the internalization of moral standards are the means by which natural Machiavellianism is curbed" (p. 770). This is entirely true. Care must only be taken—so we can say in summing up—that two facts are not forgotten. A tendency curbed is not a tendency eradicated; it is a tendency weakened but still in existence; and to the natural Machiavellianism of the first days comes in the end its rational after-form—one might almost say the art form of Machiavellianism—in the adult person who has learned how to get the best out of the *contrat social*, to give least and to receive most.

There remains, in the present context, but one more error which we have to drive out, and, once again, Charles Cooley may serve us as a Shying Sally. Is it sufficient, if the give-and-take of society is to function optimally, that the process of socialization—the internalization of norms and values—penetrate the individual consciousness of the associated individuals, or do external safeguards remain necessary even where social education is widely successful? In other words: can a merely subjective sociality subsist without an objective prop? More practically expressed: would a society whose members have developed a spirit of law-abidingness still need a police force? Cooley says no, but it is impossible to follow him in this respect. "What *we* think," he writes, and the italics are his own (*Human Nature*, p. 366), "must, in one form or another, be the arbiter of right and wrong, so far as there can be any. Other tests become valid only in so far as conscience adopts them." To what conclusion this subjectivism, which is also an optimism, leads can be seen from the following passage: "any external authority can work morally upon us only through conscience . . ." (p. 414). This is untrue. External authority can work upon us also through *constraint*, and the effects of this constraint are moralizing, at least for society at large, even if they do the individual no moral good unless they also attain his conscience. This will not always be the case, but often it will be. Social pressures are needed, in the final analysis, for three reasons: first, to guarantee the peace and quiet of the inclusive society by removing, if necessary, the criminal whose conscience is but insufficiently socialized and moralized; secondly, to educate the oncoming generation whose law-abidingness has (as we shall see later on) to be brought about with the help of outer constraints before it can rest squarely on inner conscience; and, thirdly and lastly, but by no means least importantly, to serve as an ultimate defense of the smooth functioning of social life, in case the self-restraint of normal citizens should happen to fail. This danger is real; not only the so-called criminal element, but anybody and everybody, is apt to stumble and fall because, as we have seen, particularly in this section, socialization is, even at its best, merely a partial reconstitution, a limited metamorphosis, of natural man. Cooley himself realized this at times: "our higher nature has but an imperfect and transient mastery over our lower . . . ," he writes in *Social Organization* (p. 52). And in *Human Nature and the Social Order* he says (pp. 422–23): "there is . . . no such thing as the absence of restraint, in the sense of social limitations. . . . A freedom consisting in the removal of limiting conditions is inconceivable." There is a passage in the former book (p. 373) which reveals both his insight and his mistake: "the individual cut off from that scaffolding of suggestion that the aspiration of the race has gradually prepared for him is sure to be lawless and sensual. . . ." This is true, but a "scaffolding of suggestion" alone cannot be strong enough to curb lawlessness and sensuality. Where education fails, and nowhere is it a full success, enforcement must supply what pure pleading cannot provide.

SOMATIC ORDER AND SOCIAL SYSTEM: THEIR MUTUAL SUPPORT

75. We have insisted all along that between body and sociality, the somatic order and the social system, there is mutual antagonism. As G. C. Williams has shown, in his important and strictly scientific book *Adaptation and Natural Selection* (Princeton, 1966), nature has created an instinct of self-preservation which carries within it a natural tendency toward self-preference; she has not created an instinct for the preservation of the species. (The sex urge is indeed a drive subserving the propagation, and thus ultimately also the preservation, of the species, but it is significant that nature has secured the fulfillment of this function by instilling in man, not a direct desire to defend conspecifics, but merely a craving to procure for himself the entirely self-centered pleasure connected with the sex act.) This does not mean that there is no will on the part of society to survive; it means only that that will is not instinctual, not inborn, not in the narrower sense of the word natural, but developed in and by culture and resting on the realization of the values of social life. The social habit runs counter to the somatic order in that it is based on, and has to insist on, drive reduction.

But the relation of somatic order and social system is more complex. While there is mutual antagonism, there is also mutual support. What is to follow now is in no way a retreat from the fundamental theses of this book, but, on the contrary—as will be seen presently—an additional development and defense of their essential assertions.

Somatic order and social order form a whole; that whole is broken in itself, and yet it functions as an integrated totality. That is the basic problem of sociality. It can never be completely solved, but it never threatens the survival of the common life either. The continuation of the common life alone proves that there is mutual support of the two constitutive orders, at least to some extent. But the term "mutual" as used in this connection must be correctly interpreted if the truth is to come out. The support given to the social system by the somatic order is entirely different—different in kind—from the support given to the somatic order by the social system.

The somatic order helps the social system merely on the level of material needs, on the bread-and-butter level, so to speak. The means of subsistence which the members of a society require for survival are provided under an impetus which is entirely natural. Everybody works in order to secure food *for himself*. Of course, the resulting production is a support of society, but, strictly speaking, only a support of its human material, not of society as such. It does not strengthen social integration in the specifically human meaning of the term, however much it may do for economic integration, technical cooperation, and so on. Indeed, the most important phenomenon pervading the sphere of production and ever underpinning and promoting its efficiency—competition—is antisocial in its bearings, for it sets man against man. True, cooperative forms of food-getting spring up spontaneously, and there is at all times cooperation as well as competition. An Eskimo will not eat of a caribou he has brought in before he has divided it up among his fellow-villagers. But under such apparent sociality there hides quite obviously essential and real self-concern. Cooperation, sharing, here is merely an insurance against threatening future dearth. The hunter gives away part of what he has secured, so that he may, at the appropriate time, receive part of what his neighbors have acquired. This is so manifest that it need hardly be elaborated on. The idea that society will one day be so organized that everybody will work merely to serve his fellow-men, or merely to serve the social whole, belongs to the most utopian aspects of utopian socialism. Communal systems have proved unworkable when the spring of self-interest is paralyzed. It is characteristic that practically the only basic form of social interaction which the science of economics knows is the exchange relationship. (One of its early protagonists, Richard Whateley, therefore suggested that it best be labeled catallactics—the science of exchanges.) But people engage in exchanges, in truck and barter and buying and selling, only if, and because, each participant *himself* profits in the transaction. After all we have said the reader will know what we mean when we call economic life, in Kant's graphic phrase, the sphere of unsociable sociality *par excellence*.

To look now at the other side of the coin: the social system helps the somatic order, not on the level of material needs, but on the level of organization. This formulation shows how important, in the case of man, the social norms are to the survival even of the individual. Order and organization are correlative, not to say, synonymous, terms. The social norms, by organizing the life of man, give his existence a basic pattern, a firm outline, without which he could hardly carry on for very long. Without it, he would sooner or later become the victim of anomie, and anomie is a prime cause of suicide, as Emile Durkheim—whose lead we are going to follow for a while—has classically shown.

The human body, like any other organism, has a whole series of somatic needs; some observers present a long list, others but a short one, but all agree that we are confronted by a multiplicity. The question therefore arises, how these many needs are coordinated. Where nature reigns supreme, they are co-ordinated by physical mechanisms; the word mechanism can here be taken in a rather narrow sense. "These [nature-given] instincts," says Wilfred Trotter in *Instincts of the Herd in Peace and War* (London, 1916; p. 47), "cannot be supposed at all frequently to conflict amongst themselves. . . . When the cir-cumstances are appropriate for the yielding to one, the others automatically fall into the background, and the governing impulse is absolute master." The ref-erence to automatic functioning, to a cut-off mechanism, must perhaps be taken with a small grain of salt; cows allowed into a meadow of lush alfalfa grass in the spring may overeat instead of stopping when their hunger is already stilled, yet by and large Trotter's assertion can stand. Normally, cattle will stop grazing when their need for food has diminished so much through food intake that it is no longer superior in intensity to their need to rest. Common human experience, too, proves that Trotter is right. However hungry we may be, a great fright will, for the moment, suspend our hunger; intense hunger will suspend, again for a moment, the sex urge; when the sex mechanisms are set in motion, interest in food will be reduced almost to the vanishing point, to assert itself again only when this interest is satisfied, and so on. As far as nature-given instincts are concerned, the somatic order alone is sufficient to prevent disorganization and thereby to ensure the satisfaction of all needs in due succession and proportion, and, in the end effect, the healthy functioning of the entire system.

But we have spoken of extreme cases, and they are not of everyday occur-rence. It is only a shocking fright which will suspend our hunger, and only a ravenous hunger which will interrupt our sexual urge. Before imperative com-mands of this kind are sent from the sensual centers to the control posts in the brain, all our desires are in some state of activity, not to say, equally aroused, and we must deliberate what we shall do. To quote a crude example: a man who has enough money in his pocket to buy a good meal or to acquire the ser-vices of a prostitute, must, as our language formulates it, "make up his mind." His *mind*: the formulation is correct. The body will not direct him. There are, of course, materialists who will insist that, in the final analysis, it is after all the body, especially the inner secretion, which will steer the will. But such an assertion, which would imply a consistent determinism, is entirely metaphysical, entirely unprovable, however much it may be dressed up in the glad rags of scientism. Even if instinctual urges do more than confront a man with a di-lemma, even if we assume that they permeate his will and its operation, that will cannot be regarded as totally passive and powerless. It is against our con-stant and convincing experience to maintain that we are helpless drifters blown about by the winds of physical desire, and that we have no influence at all on what we do.

Normally, then, man must decide about the future direction of his conduct. The cases in which nature will do it for him—in other words, the cases in which nature will do for him what she does for animals—are so extraordinary and so rare that we may leave them out of the account. Man therefore needs a compass to steer by, and that compass is provided by culture. It is the order of values—what earlier philosophers called the *ordo amoris*—instilled in him by education which will suggest to him what to pursue and what to reject or postpone or even suppress. The Puritan with a pound or a dollar in his pocket would know very well what not to do and what to do with it. He would not waste it on "bawbees," on "riotous living," but save it with the ultimate aim of "saving" himself. In such decisions (which were common at one time, so common indeed as to make possible the creation of a capitalist society, i.e., a society based on money-saving), we see the far-reaching freedom of man, for the self-denier does more than to cast the decisive vote in a contest between two alluring pleasures, the pleasures of the palate and the pleasures of the venereal appetite. He rejects *all* animalic cravings for the sake of purely psychic satisfactions which the animal does not know and which nature has not mandated, but which have their origin and their locus entirely in the mind.

The memory of an old conceit (hardly more than a joke of the schools) arises here before the inner eye: the figure of Buridan's ass. In a discussion of the all-pervasiveness and all-powerfulness of the laws of nature, it was asserted that a donkey placed between two bales of hay, both equally large, both equally sweet-smelling, in fact, both equal in every respect, would have to starve to death, for he would be drawn with equal intensity to both the right and the left and so be unable to make the life-saving move. The basic proposition behind this seemingly meaningless problem is worth discussing even now. The scientific answer to it is not only that Buridan's ass would in practice survive because in nature, in opposition to the controlled laboratory, equally potent sources of attraction are unimaginable and one would be sure to have the edge over the other; it is also that the animal would posit displacement actions (see SOCIAL BOND I 13) which would alter its position and thus break the deadlock. A robin motivated to flee because it feels threatened, but also motivated to stand its ground because it instinctually wishes to defend its territory, will begin to scratch the ground or to pick up particles of food. Energy will have been mobilized in its body, but it cannot come out either in the way of fight or in the way of flight; it must therefore come out in some third way. In the same manner, Buridan's ass cannot turn to the left because it is equally attracted to the right, and vice versa; but in its frustration it may, for instance, paw the ground, and then its position vis-à-vis the two bales of hay will automatically change, making one move more appropriate than the other. Our point is that the mechanism of nature will ultimately solve the difficulty. It is not necessary to ascribe to the donkey either mind or will.

Man, in a similar dilemma, will be able to decide freely which side to turn to. He, too, will be torn hither and thither if two modes of action attract him with equal strength, but, unlike the animal, he can objectify the situation, i.e., place it clearly before himself. He can then rise above it. He can say, and he will say, "I must do something, be it even by painfully prizing myself free from the ties which hold me captive, be it even by sacrificing one desirable object which powerfully appeals to me." Placed in the quandary of Buridan's ass, man will be able to prove that he is more than an ass, more than any animal, more than any purely natural creature; that he is truly man, that is to say, is a being with the privilege of self-determination. That privilege does not destroy ordering, however, for in the individual who has gone through the process of socialization, the will, though still free, has become instructed; it has come to know what to a person like himself should appear worthy to be loved and what fit to be rejected. It is true that displacement phenomena appear in human beings, too. An example sometimes given is a young person in an examination. There may be a desire to flee, but there will also be a countermanding desire to stay and to get it over with. In this quandary, he or she will probably break out in a cold sweat; if it is a he rather than a she, he may also ejaculate semen. Such cases have been observed. But, characteristically, these phenomena are, strictly speaking, reactions and not actions properly so called; they are comparable to yawning or sneezing, and not to decisions of the will. In a moral dilemma, or even in a simple dilemma of valuation—shall I buy a pear rather than an apple?—the will, guided by the internalized order of preferences, will help to make up the mind and thus release the liberating move.

We have said all this in order to show that man, unlike the animal, cannot function with the somatic system alone and needs the social system to give him direction in his vital efforts. If he has not internalized an *ordo amoris*, he will be like a zigzagging drunkard or a rudderless boat, unable to operate and unfit for life. No wonder that anomie leads to suicide. Don Juan figures are cases in point. Pursuing only one goal (success with women) but neglecting others (for instance, the need for the stability which monogamous marriage can give), they are particularly liable to end in self-destruction, as Durkheim has been able to demonstrate.

But Durkheim's main assertion is not only that we require a guide, or else we become disoriented and incapable of vital action. He sees the problem in much more garish colors. Not only are there many desires competing with each other, creating the need for decisions which are not determined—which are not, so to speak, spared—by a natural, somatic order of values given *a priori*, but these desires tend to be greeds, insatiable, each of them, and thereby all the more difficult, nay, naturally impossible, to reconcile. We admitted earlier that animals may, on occasions, overeat. But they do not, and they cannot, make gluttony a life policy and gorge themselves until obesity induces heart failure and cuts them off. Man can, and here and there does. Society is his salvation, not only because it tells him which gratification to pursue first and which later, but also because it sets a limit to *all* his physical gratifications and inculcates a life-preserving discipline.

In sum: if to survive is the overriding end of the somatic order of things, it needs the social order as an indispensable supplement. The process of socialization is placed before the equipollent necessity to develop man's will and at the same time to develop man's willingness not always to assert that will, or at least not to assert it in certain directions. The animal's and the young child's operations are all directed outward; their natural aim is to get control of things. The grown-up person's operations are, some of them, directed outward, but, some of them, also directed inward; the aim of the latter (an aim, not natural, but socio-cultural) is to get control of the self, especially the physical self. Only if and when a self-imposed subjective discipline comes to blend into the objective order of things and fills up, by its norms, the gaps which have been left by nature or arisen in natural ordering is there a firm pattern of life the processes of which can run smoothly and reliably and guarantee that stability without which a creature like man is sooner or later going to be undone.

THE ROLE OF LANGUAGE IN THE DEVELOPMENT OF SOCIALITY

76. We have now considered both the natural starting point and the necessary ends of the process of socialization and are therefore free to turn our attention to some of the details. Among them, the role of language occupies a high rank. Concluding backward from the main use we make throughout our lives of our vocal cords, popular opinion believes that nature has given us our apparatus of speech so that we may be able to communicate with our fellow-men. This naïve finalism is totally erroneous. But equally erroneous is the more refined finalism which maintains that the voice is, in some way, "ordered to" linguistic communication (as Aquinas would have expressed it). The voice is not antecedently or naturally ordered to that end. It may perhaps be seen in this light in the framework of a theological world view, but this is an entirely different matter. Scientifically speaking: it is man himself who has made meaningful cultured language out of meaningless animal vocalization. The achievement is his. Nature has given only the potentiality, no more. The creativity has come from man.

In nature, the voice is an instrument, not of communication or message-bearing, but for the externalization of internal states entirely confined to the individual, such as fear or pain. The cry of terror and the groan of distress play their part in the economy of the individual organism. They relieve some of the anxiety or mitigate to a certain extent the experience of suffering. It may perhaps be said that they are directed outward, but they are not addressed to anybody. The case of the vocal sex invitation, though apparently social, is in reality not very different. The robin sings or displays his red breast to the hen which he woos because the chemistry of his inner secretion has set in motion a certain mechanism which dilates his throat muscles and swells his feathery chest. And so far as the female is concerned, she does not, properly speaking, receive a message (though, in our careless modes of expression, we sometimes put it that way). There is (if she responds) merely a release of corresponding secretions and the activation of corresponding mechanisms on her part. There is no mutual understanding or communication.

What we have just pointed out can be expressed in the idiom of sociology by saying that language is essentially not a physical phenomenon, but a social institution, which means that it is developed, as are all social institutions, in a social process and laid into the individual by a sustained educational effort. Still, the natural bases of voice utilization play their part even in the evolution of cultural language, and that part is a largely positive, a helpful, one. All social institutions place limitations on our behavior; all are forms of discipline. Language is no different from the rest. We "have" to say: there is no bread; we are not "allowed" to say: there ain't no bread. Yet these linguistic limitations, this specific discipline, sits very lightly on us. We do not chafe under it as we do under do's and don'ts contained in the social codes. The relief which we get when we express ourselves—externalize our inner states—is so considerable that the observation of the prescribed forms is not experienced as a high price to pay. Linguistic development, even in the narrower, the socio-cultural, sense of the word, is therefore not significantly inhibited by self-regard. Indeed, it may well receive support and furtherance from that quarter.

Still, Mead is entirely correct when he asserts that speech has "a long road . . . to travel from the situation where there is nothing but vocal cries over to the situation in which significant symbols are utilized" (*Mind, Self, and Society*, p. 67). But the change is not only long and drawn out; it is not really a continuum; there is a radical break somewhere in it. It occurs at the point where a sound pattern contracts a meaning—a meaning which can spring from mind to mind. Where does that meaning come from? An individualistic age such as ours is inclined to assume that it arises within the individual by a sort of spontaneous generation. But that is not so; indeed, it is hardly possible even to imagine how it could be. Communicable meanings can only be received in and from a process of communication already functioning, already going on. They wash into the individuals (plural), that is to say, both into the speaker and into the listener, from the outside; subjective language presupposes objective language. We appear to be involved here in a vicious circle. Society seems impossible without language, but language seems impossible without society. The answer to this conundrum must be that they can only develop *pari passu*. If such a statement is judged unsatisfactory, if a more articulated ontology is demanded, we have no choice, in view of the facts, but to assert that social life is ontologically prior to linguistic expression, that it is more true to say that language is the child of society than it is to say that society is the child of language. We cannot hesitate when asked to identify the chicken and the egg.

The reason why we have to make this decision lies in the fact that even individual, entirely internal, thought, thought which is not yet expressed, is a kind of conversation. When I think, I am both listener and speaker, and there is a verbal give-and-take, even though, materially, there are only brain waves, but no sound waves. Cooley has spoken well of the "interlocutory character of thought" (*Human Nature*, p. 360; see also p. 92), and Mead considers it as a matter of course that "the very process of thinking is . . . simply an inner conversation that goes on . . ." (*Mind, Self, and Society*, p. 141). A long chain of observers from Plato to Goethe and Thoreau have drawn attention to this truth, but anybody will recognize it who will care to observe his own thought processes. When we think, we talk to ourselves; we discuss matters of interest with ourselves. We can do this only after we have learned to talk to others, to carry on discussions with others. "As far as a parrot is concerned," writes Mead (p.

67), and nowhere does he seem nearer to the heart of the matter than in such formulations, "its 'speech' means nothing, but where one significantly says something with his own vocal process he is saying it to himself as well as to everybody else within reach of his voice." What is peculiar to the situation in which significant symbols are utilized, in contradistinction to the one where there is nothing but vocal cries, is "that the individual responds to his own stimulus in the same way as other people respond. Then the stimulus becomes significant; then one is saying something." Mead supports his analysis by a simple example. He writes:

> You ask somebody to bring a visitor a chair. You arouse the tendency to get the chair in the other, but if he is slow to act you get the chair yourself. The response to the vocal gesture is [in this case] the doing of a certain thing, and you arouse that same tendency [as in your interlocutor also] in yourself. You are always replying to yourself, just as other people reply. You assume that in some degree there must be identity in the reply. It is action on a common basis [ibid.].

That common basis is the common life in society. The upshot of this whole discussion is that the internal use of words in thought (which might be called self-conversation) is contingent upon, and secondary to, the external use of words in conversation. Personal use follows upon social use. The suggestion of an individualistic bias that we ourselves and on our own might be able to develop meaningful mental and vocal symbols on the basis of some process of cerebral maturation is doubly unrealistic: first, because such internally developed symbols would be no bridge to others; and, secondly, because we would be unable to perform unaided a feat of such magnitude. Both these circumstances, both these facts, force us to the conclusion that meaningful language is a gift of society to us.

There is, then, natural vocalization, but there is no such thing as natural speech; lungs, larynx, and vocal cords are inherited along with the brain parts which control their use, but language is acquired. To many, this will be entirely obvious, and they may criticize us for spending so much time on the subject. But he who knows how many prejudices are in circulation, how often there is talk of animal languages, or at least of the animals' supposed capacity for the learning of languages, will agree that the foregoing paragraphs of this section were necessary if error is to be kept at bay.

What we have said already gives us the *terminus a quo* and the *terminus ad quem* in the process by which human language is acquired. The *terminus a quo* is the production of meaningless sounds (sounds which merely externalize internal organic states); the *terminus ad quem*, the use of meaningful language (language which formulates and communicates mind contents and is therefore fully social even within the individual's mind). Between these two poles there is interpolated a transitional stage in which social language is used non-socially, as it is, for instance, in soliloquies. The assertion that there is this intermediary condition may sound, at first hearing, like an artificial argument in support of the general thesis of this book: namely, that sociality is not present at birth and has to be created by a slow and difficult educational effort. But child psychology has amply demonstrated that there is indeed, in each typical life, such a stage when a social institution is used non-socially because its user is not yet fully socialized.

Between the ages of three months and one year, the infant produces a large number of sounds—cooing, gurgling, whining, groaning, and the like—which are difficult to interpret and carry no recognizable message, and this period has therefore been called the "babbling stage." The term is objectionable insofar as it one-sidedly emphasizes the disabilities of the child while it does not do justice to the great abilities present at the time. The child cannot as yet speak any language, but he is still capable of learning to speak all languages. Learning means in this case basically and essentially imitation. The capacity to imitate is undoubtedly present in the infant from the moment of birth, but it has to be activated by social influences if it is to become effective. We have to distinguish a pre-imitative and an imitative phase, the latter beginning roughly at the age of eight months (see Willard W. Hartup and Brian Coates, "The Role of Imitation in Childhood Socialization," in *Early Experiences and the Processes of Socialization*, edd. Hoppe et al., p. 118). During the earlier period the child merely duplicates the sounds which impinge upon him; if somebody else within earshot cries, he will cry too. Those responses of other people are repeated by him at the time which are already in his own repertoire, but no others. It is only during the later period that there is assimilation of something new (and of that assimilation animals appear incapable). Models are accepted, and there is a striving to perform what they are performing, e.g., to formulate words and to form sentences. In the first phase, it is as if a button were pressed to initiate the production of sound. Hartup and Coates speak of a "reflexive matching" of the behavior of others. But to developments of the second phase there is little, if any, reflexive or mechanical side. There is a true human effort, both on the part of the child imitating and of the grown-ups trying to induce imitation. In a word: there is genuine learning. Of course, this learning, as must be emphasized, is at the same time also unlearning, in the sense of a loss of earlier (but indistinct) capacities. As is well known, the Chinese has a sound intermediate between the English speaker's "l" and "r" which an English or American infant can be brought to produce, while a Chinese one can quite early acquire the ability to produce the English "r" or "l" in a precise and univocal manner. In the respective grown-ups this elasticity is gone. Try as he may, the adult Chinese speaking English cannot clearly pronounce either "play" or "pray," and the native of an English-speaking country has the corresponding opposite inability clearly to say something carrying the sound intermediate between "r" and "l," "pray" and "play." Scottish or American infants are free to roll or not to roll their "r's." But full-grown Americans cannot do so, while full-grown Scots can. The matter is instructive because it shows very impressively what we have repeatedly emphasized: namely, that nature provides indefinite potentialities but no more, while only culture provides definite human institutions as every language and every word is one. For their acquisition a double price has to be paid: the one we have just mentioned; it is the loss of all-round openness. A second language is (do we not all know it?) far more difficult to acquire than the first. The other is the limitation, the discipline to which we have to submit. We become tied to certain sound-patterns; worse still, we become slaves to certain rules of word sequence and sentence construction, to grammar, which is a proper code of law. Yet our gain is much larger than both our losses put together. We can make ourselves understood; we learn to command the services of others. Vico hit upon a deep insight which we would do well to ponder when he recognized that the imperative is the root of all linguistic forms, both on the phylogenetic and the ontogenetic level.

The use of the imperative, addressed to a fellow-human, a mother, for instance, is already in a sense a fully social use; nevertheless, the semi-socialized child will, as we have indicated, employ the words taught him by society also in a consistently, exclusively, self-regarding way. A boy who, when hammering away with a wooden gavel at a wooden block, says "Billy hit" strives only to make his hitting motion less difficult or more effective; he is not saying anything to anybody; indeed, he has not even reached the condition envisaged in Mead's analysis quoted above, under which human beings split themselves, as it were, and are at the same time talkers and (their only) listeners; as yet the body is in command and language is merely one of its tools. If we may once again borrow Ernest Schachtel's terminology, the mode of speech of our hypothetical Billy is not, like the grown-up's language, which is meant for the interlocutor, allocentric, but autocentric.

The autocentricity of such speech is noticeable, not only in monologues, where it is not surprising, but also in dialogues, or, rather, apparent dialogues. In his very thorough study *The Language and Thought of the Child*, Jean Piaget notes that when a young child has tried to describe an object to a listener, and the listener asks a question because in his judgment he has not received sufficient information, the child will often simply repeat his original words, i.e., do what one should *not* do to communicate, and that effectively. Speaking means to him making statements; it does not yet mean conversation. The objective situation enfolding speaker and listener is indeed social, but the subjective use of the medium of language is not yet so. The child does not bother to tell his vis-à-vis what he already knows; he is too much taken up with himself to think this necessary. Certain experiments were carried out by the great child psychologist in order to gain a deeper understanding of this curious phenomenon. Stories were told to a child, and he was asked to hand them on to another child, but the retelling was not, as a rule, successful. The main reason for this was in every case not the child's simplicity or any other of his natural limitations, but his lack of sociality. "The explainer," Piaget reports (p. 101), "always gave us the impression of talking to himself, without bothering about the other child. Very rarely did he succeed in placing himself at the latter's point of view." "Conversation between children," he concludes, is

> not sufficient at first to take the speakers out of their ego-centrism, because each child, whether he is trying to explain his own thoughts or to understand those of others, is shut up in his own point of view. . . . the words spoken are not thought of from the point of view of the person spoken to, and the latter, instead of taking them at their face value, selects them according to his own interest, and distorts them in favour of previously formed conceptions [pp. 99, 98].

In other words: apparent dialogue between children is, as a rule, what dialogue among grown-ups is only in very exceptional and quickly corrected cases, a talking at cross-purposes.

Students of language are in the habit of drawing a distinction between internal and external language, and so do mature people whether they are scholars or not. Young children, on the other hand, do not know this contrast. As Werner and Kaplan point out in *Symbol Formation* (New York 1963; p. 328), among them "the distinction between inner and external speech is relatively slight, speech for the self and speech for the other are little differentiated from one another. In the older child and in the normal adult . . . the differentiation between speech for the self and speech for others becomes progressively more marked." It is because of the lack of differentiation between thought-in-words and speech-in-words that "the child up to an age, as yet undetermined but probably somewhere about seven, is incapable of keeping to himself the thoughts which enter his mind. He says everything. He has no verbal continence" (Piaget, *Language and Thought*, p. 38). Verbal incontinence, the tendency to say out loud what one silently thinks, is known to occur in grown-ups too, especially in the elderly, but there it is a sign of mental decay. We see once again the vast difference between the non-social youngster and the socialized man; what is normal in the one is abnormal in the other.

Why does the infant under one year of age, before socialization has started in earnest, use the vocal organs which nature has given him and the words which he owes to society? Piaget gives us a very clear answer:

> The child does not in the first instance communicate with his fellow-beings in order to share thoughts and reflexions; he does so in order to play. . . . many remarks are made by children in an interrogative form without being in any way questions addressed to anyone. The proof of this is that the child does not listen to the answer, and does not even expect it. He supplies it himself. This happens frequently between the ages of 3 and 5 [pp. 27, 29–30].

Because of these facts, Piaget enters between egocentric and socialized speech an intermediate form which he calls "collective monologue" and which he rightly connects with egocentricity rather than with sociality. The term "collective monologue" is ill chosen; what is meant is monologue before others, monologue in a social setting. The pungent essayist Alfred Polgar once called a coffeehouse a place where people go because they want to have company while they are alone. The same quip might be used here, and we have introduced it because it draws our attention to an important fact. The coffeehouse atmosphere is experienced as stimulating, but it does not lead to social contacts. In the same way, the presence of the mother suits the infant, he feels secure, he feels relaxed, and therefore he begins to prattle. But he does not engage in conversation. "The child loves to know that he is near his mother. . . . What he says . . . is enveloped with the feeling of a presence . . . ," Piaget explains (p. 243). "But, on the other hand, one cannot but be struck by the soliloquistic character of these same remarks. . . . He does not ask himself whether she is listening or not. He speaks for himself just as an adult does when he speaks within himself."

Observation has shown that talk before mothers is more autocentric than talk before age-mates (p. 245), and the reason for this probably is that mothers are always taken for granted, while play-fellows are not. Yet the young child will soliloquize even in the circle of contemporaries. If this happens, and if all the infants present give tongue at the same time, then we have indeed something which might justifiably be called collective monologizing (though not "collective monologue"). Then the characteristics of what Piaget calls collective monologue come out clearly—words are thrown out at random and where they fall matters little to the speakers (p. 20; see also p. 18). The "general characteristic of monologues of this category is that the words have no social function," Piaget declares (p. 16), and we must add that they do not have that function, that purpose and effect of communication, because he who pronounces them is as yet no social being.

Needless to say, as general socialization advances, so does the social use of language. Psychologists, bent upon numerical precision, have elaborated an index which shows in detail how progress in this direction is made. In our context, the initial situation is most important, and with regard to it, Piaget writes: "It . . . is immediately evident in observing children of one to two years, that, in the beginnings of speech, only a few definite requests or commands may be considered as truly spoken to another, all other utterances are a soliloquy in the course of which the child speaks as much to himself as to those around him" (p. 256). Requests or commands are, of course, social in the sense that they are addressed to others, but that sociality is more formal than real. They lack reciprocity: they imply that the addressee is, not a *socius*, but a servant. They are thus evidence of autocentricity, not allocentricity. Piaget calculates for a boy of three that egocentric speech, even in the narrower sense of the word, accounts for over 70% of the total of his spontaneous speech (ibid.). In the case of two subjects of six-and-a-half years, it is still nearly half that total. Sociality is clearly of very slow growth! It is only between seven and eight years of age that egocentric talk loses some of its importance (pp. 37, 41; see also p. 257). If quarreling is taken for the object of investigation, it is seen that there is a slow change-over from "primitive" to "genuine" argument. Primitive argument merely pits point of view against point of view without indication of reasons or motives. It begins at about age five or five-and-a-half. Genuine argument is characterized by the giving of explanations for, and justifications of, the position adopted and defended. It does not appear until the age of seven or seven-and-a-half is reached (p. 70). It alone is truly social; what is called primitive argument is still too close to "dual monologue" to deserve the epithet. It is yet basically, if no longer entirely, autocentric.

We are, however, at present less interested in the timetable than in the mode of the great metamorphosis of language and must ask, not when, but how, the change occurs. And here we shall do well to adduce yet another statement from Piaget's pen, partly in order to show that we have him with us in our analysis, partly because it helps us to advance from the facts which he so efficiently reveals to more theoretical considerations. He writes: "At a minimum, to communicate adequately the child must learn to regard the world from the point of view of others" (1926 ed.; p. 165). This sentence, though in the nature of an incidental remark, links Piaget at once to George Herbert Mead whose general explication of socialization, somewhat developed and modified, constitutes the intellectual basis of the present work.

In the final analysis, the whole matter is supremely simple. Vocalization turns into language, monologue into dialogue, autocentricity into allocentricity, when a speaker begins to ask: Is my utterance being received by others, is it a message understood? (Pure self-regard will soon induce him to raise that query, for his requests can only be met and his commands carried out if they are grasped by those to whom they are transmitted.) The change-over takes place, then, when the speaker assumes, in addition to his own role, the role of the listener. This is clearly a specific instance of the general assertion of George Herbert Mead's according to which socialization is achieved, and a reflected self-image developed, through the assumption of other people's roles, especially through looking at oneself through their eyes. But listening to ourselves with other men's ears is at least as important as looking at ourselves with their eyes and probably more so. No wonder that Mead has placed particular emphasis on the contribution made by language to the process of socialization.

Bracketing together, and for good reasons, visual and vocal signs, Mead formulates his basic conviction as follows:

> The importance . . . of the vocal stimulus lies in this fact that the individual can hear what he says and in hearing what he says is tending to respond as the other person responds. . . . We are, especially through the use of the social gestures, continually arousing in ourselves those responses which we call out in other persons, so that we are taking the attitudes of other persons into our own conduct. The critical importance of language in the development of human experience lies in this fact that the stimulus is one that can react upon the speaking individual as it reacts upon the other [*Mind, Self, and Society*, pp. 69, 70].

Language appears in this passage as the door through which the common denominator, which links man with man, enters into a self. But Mead drives the analysis even deeper. Not only are the means of communication with others developed in us in this way, but even the mind itself, the human person's personal mind, which, as we have seen, is the subsoil in which alone sociality can be anchored. "To the extent that the [human] animal can take the attitude of the other and utilize that attitude for the control of his own conduct," Mead writes (pp. 191–92),

> we have what is termed mind; and that is the only apparatus involved in the appearance of mind. I know of no way in which intelligence or mind could arise or could have arisen, other than through the internalization by the individual of social processes of experience and behavior, that is, through this internalization of the conversation of significant gestures, as made possible by the individual's taking the attitudes of other individuals toward himself and toward what is being thought about. And if mind or thought has arisen in this way, then there neither can be nor could have been any mind or thought without language; and the early stages of the development of language must have been prior to the development of mind or thought.

These remarkable sentences convey an essential truth covering both phylogenesis ("could have arisen," i.e., in the history of our species) and ontogenesis ("could arise," i.e., now, in the case of incoming individuals); yet care must be taken to interpret the reference to the priority of language correctly. Phylo-genetically it can only be thought of as a logical or systemic, and not as a tem-poral, priority. There can have been no language before thought, just as there can have been no language or thought before social integration. All three must have developed each other, and that *pari passu*. But ontogenetically the case is different, as we have already pointed out. Language is in the infant's social set-ting before it is in him. In him there is, to start with, only babbling. It is through the transmutation of babbling into language that mind, thought, and sociality, all three, come into being in the individual.

Because language is in the infant's social setting before it enters into him, and because it enters into him with all its definitions of words and rules of syntax, individuals can understand each other. We have discussed this matter already in dealing with the knowledge of other selves, and may refer the reader back to what we said there (see above, pp. 20–26). Here, where we mean to bring this analysis to a close, we have only to draw the final conclusions from our insights. They involve the very nature of the social sciences and more particularly of sociology. There have always been two basic trends within that discipline: one tending to see society from the outside, as nature is seen, and has to be seen, by the natural sciences; the other tending to grasp it from the inside, considering it as the work of men and therefore as penetrable by the human intellect—pen-etrable to a depth to which nature, which men have not made, cannot be pen-etrated. The former tradition is totally alien to the attitude which is at the root of the present work, all of which is a polemic against it. No more need be said about it at this point. But understanding *ab intra* has to be discussed for a mo-ment here. Max Weber has called for it. Men, he pointed out, have intentions. These intentions we may and must grasp. Their acts have meaning and, again, this meaning we may and must comprehend. But meaning was to Max Weber in the first place, not to say exclusively, meaning to the intending or actual ac-tor, and in this he laid himself open to serious criticism. As the present author has shown in *The Fundamental Forms of Social Thought*, Weber was a captive of his own individualism and individualistic prejudice. If intention is the crucial element to be understood, how can anybody except the actor know it since it is locked up within him? Weber postulates a gap between alter and ego which makes his whole concept of understanding, and of an understanding sociology, rather doubtful. Yet our analysis of language has enabled us to rescue it and to give it a firmer basis. Language is not only a means of communication; it is also a model of communication, indeed, a model of all human cooperation in the broadest sense of the term. The meanings of words not only are meanings to a speaker; they are meanings common to him and to his neighbors. They are the bridge between the two, as well as the bridge which the scholarly observer can utilize. Words are socially defined; but also socially defined are the social situations in which interacting individuals find themselves. The social definition of the social situation is a bridge of the same kind as a shared language. This bridge exists, and can be crossed, even when and where no single syllable is spoken. It, too, is a common denominator which makes understanding possible. It is therefore the social definition of a situation of interaction which an under-

standing sociology should try to get into focus, and not only the private intentions of one of the participating persons.

George Herbert Mead was close to this insight. The fundamental thesis of
Mind, Self, and Society is that meaning is, properly speaking, always meaning
within a social matrix, not meaning within an individual mind. "Meaning arises
and lies within the field of the relation between the gesture of a given human
organism and the subsequent behavior of this organism as indicated to another
human organism by that gesture," we read (pp. 75–76). "If that gesture does
so indicate to another organism the subsequent (or resultant) behavior of the
given organism, then it has meaning. In other words, the relationship between a
given stimulus—as a gesture—and the later phases of the social act of which
it is an early (if not the initial) phase constitutes the field within which meaning
originates and exists." Introduction into that field can be described as the very
essence of the process of socialization; it is the social initiation κατ' ἐξοχήν.

Individualistic thinking à la Weber appeared to Mead as less than rational.
He writes:

> It is absurd to look at the mind simply from the standpoint of the individual
> human organism; for, although it has its focus there, it is essentially a social
> phenomenon. . . . We must regard mind . . . as arising and developing within
> the social process, within the empirical matrix of social interactions. We must,
> that is, get an inner individual experience from the standpoint of social acts
> which include the experiences of separate individuals in a social context where-
> in those individuals interact [p. 133].

And again: "The self is not so much a substance as a process in which the
conversation of gestures has been internalized within an organic form. This
process does not exist for itself, but is simply a phase of the whole social organization of which the individual is a part" (p. 178).

This is well put. Yet a danger lies hidden in Mead's argument and, not surprisingly, it is an inclination toward the error opposite to the one of which Max
Weber was the victim. If Weber was an excessive individualist, Mead talks at
times—fortunately very rarely—as if he were an excessive collectivist or or-
ganicist. Thus he writes in a footnote (p. 164): "The relation of individual
organisms to the social whole of which they are members is analogous to the
relation of the individual cells of a multi-cellular organism to the organism as
a whole." Mead cannot really mean this; his whole style of thinking forbids it.
At the very most he could compare the individual to a cell which has been ingrafted and has grown into the body social, but that would strain the basic
metaphor beyond endurance. Surely, it is precisely Mead's conviction, as it is
of the present writer, that man is not genetically social, but socialized through
education, and any mode of expression which obfuscates this basic insight is to
be rejected. Mead may have wavered, but he did not finally fall. We see this
best from the way in which he handled that adjunct of organicism, social instinctivism. In another footnote (p. 139) he incidentally mentions the "gre-
garious instinct" and asserts that it belongs to man along with the reproductive
and parental urge. But at the end of his investigation he describes the supposed
"herding instinct" as "debatable," and writes that the "vagueness and lack of

definition of this group of impulses have led many to use this instinct to explain phenomena of social conduct that lie on an entirely different level of behavior" (p. 349). This is far too weak a rebuttal of an opinion which would tend to make nonsense of Mead's whole basic conviction that man is social, not because nature has made him so, but because he has been integrated into the ongoing process of cultural life, but it is a rebuttal all the same. Nobody has yet been foolish enough to suggest that language—the specific topic of the present section—is inherited. If it is not, then the strongest of presumptions must be that all other social institutions, and indeed sociality itself, are also acquired, as Mead has always insisted throughout his work.

THE TIMETABLE OF SOCIALIZATION

77. In the immediately preceding section we lightly touched upon a subject which needs a little more attention, though it is perhaps only of secondary interest to the sociologist: the timetable of socialization. We saw that the age of seven marks a sharp change linguistically; before that time, talk is largely autocentric, and even argument is more formal than real; after it, talk is largely allocentric, and argument becomes a meaningful exchange of mutually related utterances, i.e., true conversation. But the age limit of seven is decisive even beyond the linguistic field. Piaget says very simply and directly: "There is . . . no real social life between children of less than 7 or 8 years" (*Language and Thought*, p. 40). One great justification of this judgment is the fact that it is only between seven and eight years of age that a desire manifests itself to work with others. Before the age of five children generally prefer to work alone, and thereafter there is a slow and tardy change-over to collaboration, but it remains for quite a while confined to play and does not affect work more properly so called.

It might be argued at this point that play *is* the work of children, and there is undoubtedly something in this statement. But play in the wider sense of the word has to be subdivided into two categories: play in the narrower sense of the word, and game. When children play, their roles are not strictly coordinated; they do not stick to a definite part; they change in a quick, often mercurial, fashion from one line to another. The game is essentially different. The roles are integrated; everyone has a definite part allotted to him; he has to perform within the cadres of a team. (Team relationships exist then, not only with those who fight on the same side, but even with the temporary adversaries.) There are rules; there are duties; there is a specific meaning to a game which is absent from play. A game is to some extent a model of society; play is not. Abandonment of the play stage and entry into the game stage is, therefore, a good indicator of the arrival of socialization.

One traditional fashion of characterizing this progress is to say that, before the age of seven or so, the child's mind is still "primitive." Comparisons between the child and the primitive are found in many parts of the literature; to give but one example, we may refer to A. F. Chamberlain's *The Child: A Study in the Evolution of Man* (London, 1901), a work with whose tenor many agree.

Even Piaget writes in one of his works (*Moral Judgment,* p. 340): "the adult who is under the dominion of unilateral respect for the 'Elders' and for tradition is really behaving like a child." If this statement is taken in its narrowest meaning, it might perhaps pass muster; but if it is meant to hint that there is a more general similarity between the infantile and the savage mind, it has to be resisted.

It is true that children and primitives have that much in common that both think in terms of images, not of concepts, and nobody will deny the importance of this fact. But the sociologist must at once emphasize that there is the sharpest possible contrast between the two because the primitive's thought is profoundly social, whereas the child's is not. The great transformation which occurs at seven-plus can be seen in two details, both of which are of supreme importance and thrown into particularly high relief by a comparison between the infant and the so-called backward races. One of these aspects belongs to the field of epistemology; the other, to the field of ethics.

So far as epistemology is concerned, the young child has no idea of the social whole as such. This has been well explained by Mikel Dufrenne in his fine book *La Personnalité de base* (p. 292):

> What exercises a decisive influence on the child is the conduct of the adult in relation to him; the child is not aware [*sensible*] of the social as such, he is aware [only] of interpersonal relations. . . . Even when he play-acts or "poses" in front of a public, he experiences the presence of others in terms of individuals rather than of a group; his horizon is limited to singular presences and the social as such is revealed to him only little by little, even though it never ceases to affect him through the agency of his parents.

Many authors have insisted (among the classics, for instance, Alfred Fouillée) that we cannot properly speak of a society where its members do not carry a conception of it in their minds. If this element in the definition of sociality is accepted—and a good deal speaks in favor of its acceptance—the child under seven is not social. But the primitive is, indeed, supremely so. So real is the reality of society to him that he considers himself and his associates as incarnations of the same stream of life. All Jews were sons of Adam, all MacDonalds offsprings of Donald, all O'Keefes had Keefe as their ultimate progenitor. Figures like Adam, Donald, and Keefe are the pictorial equivalents of an abstract idea of society which the modern infant acquires only at the age of seven or thereabouts.

The ethical difference between child mentality and primitive mentality, and between those still under and those already over seven years of age, consists in the absence of any idea of collective responsibility on the part of the youngest age-group. This is but logical, for how could a boy or girl under seven conceive of collective responsibility if he or she has no concept of society, of social integration, of the unity of a social whole? Piaget fully acknowledges the fact. During "this stage," he avers, "the child is essentially egocentric. . . . There can therefore be no question of collective responsibility" (*Moral Judgment,* p. 249). In another passage he expresses himself even more energetically. There is, he says of the idea of coresponsibility and collective punishment, not "the least trace" of it in the young child (p. 234). It is not so in the case of the somewhat older schoolboy or schoolgirl. If the teacher decides to keep a class in, by way of punishment, for an additional hour, this may be resented as punishment, but the infliction of it on a whole group is not resented. Indeed, it may well be preferred to more individualized forms of disciplining. Even stronger, however, is the contrast between the child and the primitive. Because of the close-knit character of the clan or tribe, the conception and conviction of its unity in merit and guilt—and more especially the attribution of merit or guilt on the part of a member to the body social as a whole—is an integral part of its collective unconscious. "In Adam's fall, we sinned all," as an old hymn expresses it. Wherever we look in the primitive world, we find evidences of this moral collectivism, and, as a rule, much more than mere traces of it. Hence the child under seven and the primitive as yet untouched by modern individualism are totally opposed to each other in this particular. Indeed, it is obvious that, as far as responsibility is concerned, the child under seven is close to sophisticated modern man and by no means to the "savage."

There is yet a third aspect to this evolution: namely, the waning of prelogical and the waxing strong of logical and formalized thinking; and this restructuring of the organization and operation of the mind also fits into the time schedule which we have presented. There is undoubtedly a definite social side to this great transformation, for we cannot possibly think logically or formalistically before the grip of exclusive subjectivity on us is broken. Logico-formal thinking is objective thinking, and the objectivation of our thinking is due to our entry into social life; more specifically: to our learning to see ourselves through the eyes of others and thereby to making our egos objects to ourselves. But the development of which we are speaking here is a consequence of socialization, not an ingredient in it, and we therefore have to postpone the consideration of it until later. The topic will be considered again in Section 80.

THE SETTING OF SOCIALIZATION

78. Of more consequence to the sociologist than the timetable of socialization is the shift in the setting of it which the progression of the child from infancy through later childhood to beginning maturity entails. Traditionally a rather simplistic conception of this matter has prevailed and probably still prevails. The setting of socialization, so we are told, is "the primary group." The term is Cooley's, and he has explained its meaning in the following sentences:

> By primary groups I mean those characterized by intimate face-to-face association and coöperation. . . . The most important spheres of this intimate association and coöperation . . . are the family, the play-group of children, and the neighborhood or community group of elders. . . . Primary groups are primary in the sense that they give the individual his earliest and completest experience of social unity. . . . they are fundamental in forming the social nature and ideals of the individual [*Social Organization*, pp. 23, 24, 26–27, 23].

A generation or more divide Charles Cooley from Abram Kardiner; they were also different because the one, Cooley, was more of a sociologist than a psychologist, the other, Kardiner, more a psychologist than a sociologist. Yet the concept of the primary group is central to the thinking of both these great students of man. To give but one relevant passage from Abram Kardiner's pen: "The family," he writes (Abram Kardiner and Lionel Ovesey, *The Mark of Oppression* [New York, 1951], p. 381), "is the locus of personality formation, and hence the most reliable avenue for the transmission of culture." Still somewhat Darwinist in general background, the so-called Neo-Freudians, of whom Kardiner was one, maintain, and for the best reasons in the world, that primary forms of life, including, above all, the family, were selected in the great process of testing which we call history because of their utility, their subservience to the needs and interests of both the individual and the species. No other institutions could have formed a type of human being better adjusted to coexistence with others and integration into society—a fact which stands out with all desirable clarity in the deep social problematic, the widespread mental instability and incidence of criminality, in cultures which allow primary groups to decay and dissolve.

There are thus few concepts in either psychology or sociology which have found more willing acceptance and more universal application than this, and rightly so. The assertion that man becomes man in the warmth of the narrow circle thus defined is so realistic, so obviously true, that there can be no basic disagreement with the fundamental intuition behind the term. Yet "primary group," however true and realistic the conception as such may be, is a somewhat vague idea which must be further concretized and analyzed if it is to be useful in the attempt to understand the process of socialization. Properly speaking, primary group is merely a middle term. There is a wider social reality behind it (behind the family, for instance), and there are narrower human relationships within it which must not be overlooked if error is to be avoided.

The child is normally born into the primary group known as the family, and the family provides the earliest human environment within which his personal character begins to form. Yet at first it is not the family as a whole which acts on him, but one particularly close member of it, the mother. The first human experience of the infant, especially the neonate, is not, strictly speaking, social (which normally means multilateral), but dyadic. True, society at large determines the form of the family and thus the function of the mother as well, yet the mother in the opening stages is a biotic rather than a social agent, and, for some months at any rate, a personality, an individuality, a unique self rather than a social functionary. The relationship to the child, especially the child still at the breast, is also less than fully social because the element of discipline, of compulsion, of duty, is absent from it. The mother is a servant, not an equal, and that fact must give the baby an entirely positive idea of social life; social life appears in the rosy dawn, the golden age of each one of us, as a source of benefits, sunshine without shadow. An attitude of vital trust is thus laid on and built up which is, as many have strongly emphasized, an indispensable presupposition to the introduction of restrictions, of prohibitions, into individual life. A bitter drop falls into the cup as soon as that happens; but there is so much initial sweetness to this cup that the child continues to drink from it.

Of course, the original dyadic relationship between mother and child is only an element in the stream of social life, and the social life enveloping it must penetrate it just as any porous substance is penetrated by the surrounding fluid. Social life is social control, and social control is asserted first by and through the mother. We may think here, for instance, of the elementary demands of cleanliness, a high human value, of bladder control and bowel control. The servant thus becomes the master. Tamotsu Shibutani has well characterized the situation as it develops. He writes (*Society and Personality* [Englewood Cliffs, N.J., 1961], pp. 508–509):

> Since an infant is unable to exercise self-control, he attempts to consummate his impulses immediately. There is no ability to delay gratification, to accept frustration, or to cope with limiting or dangerous circumstances. These adjustments are made for the child by his mother or someone else who is responsible for his care. Each child is egocentric, but not autonomous. He is highly dependent upon someone else for survival, for the accomplishment of essential adjustments which he subsequently controls for himself, and compliance with the demands of others arises initially from this dependency. Tenderness and provision for one's needs are gratifying, and a child cannot afford to alienate the source. Direction is introduced into his life from the outside.

While the introduction of direction, i.e., of social control, into the child's life brings his relation to the mother more into line with other (standard) human relationships, there remains for a time an important difference from normal sociality; namely, the absence of power on the child's part—power to resist. "Although a child is confronted from the beginning with demands that he curb his impulses, he continues to strive for immediate gratification," Shibutani writes.

> Long before his sense of personal identity is established, he struggles for autonomy. Initially he resists parental control in an attempt to realize his biological impulses. Later he learns to temper his outbursts, but he still strives to reserve an area in which he can make his own decisions. At this point there is no self-control as such, only compliance with the demands of people recognized as capable of enforcing them. Parents are not equal partners in the process of socialization; the norms that they impose constitute external conditions to which the child must adjust [p. 509].

The operative words in this last sentence are "*external* conditions" and "*must* adjust." As long as social control is mediated by the mother, with others being merely her adjuncts, the child's life is heteronomous. This heteronomy, however, lasts a good deal longer. It continues when the primacy of the dyadic relationship is over, and the socializee becomes part of a group, for instance, a nursery full of children. As we have to distinguish two phases in the nearly exclusive mother–child nexus—namely, a phase of pure support and a phase of support-*cum*-discipline—so we have to distinguish two formations in the morphology of primary groups—namely, a heteronomous and an autonomous variety. This distinction coincides to a large extent, though by no means fully, and certainly not by definition, with the distinction between a play stage and a game stage. The nursery group is a primary group in Cooley's sense of the word, but he should have made it clear that it is a *heteronomous* primary group. (He comes close to the truth where he speaks, in *Social Organization* [p. 49], of the need to provide "enough judicious supervision to ensure the ascendency of good play traditions.") Without the presence of a peace-keeping and regulating authority, there would be a guarantee neither of minimal harmony nor yet of minimal cooperation; play would probably dissolve into conflicts over toys and into play "groups" of one. As Shibutani expresses it, using psychoanalytic terminology: "in the absence of adequate authority figures the superego does not develop, and the child's object relations remain at the narcissistic level" (*Society and Personality*, p. 551). Altogether different is the autonomous group, of which the game offers a characteristic instance. Here we meet for the first time a true model—a replica on a reduced scale—of archetypal sociality. Game groups are their own legislators. The rules of the game, both the norms of cooperation and the norms of conflict control and conflict resolution, are set by the group itself. It is true that they too are often introduced from the outside. Football players play football according to traditional, not self-created, principles. But this is not a case of heteronomy, just as social life at large is not. The objective rules of the game are collectively as well as subjectively accepted by the players by dint of their autonomy; more simply expressed: because they *wish* to accept them. If a football game follows the book, this is, on a small scale, no different from the great process of the reception of Roman law by the Germanic peoples when they, in freedom and spontaneity, decided, on their entry into the capitalist–individualist era of history, that the Roman law would suit them, and when they informally, but yet bindingly, resolved to live by its norms. That there is indeed full autonomy can be seen from the fact (which is of even greater vital importance in practice than in theory) that the interpretation of the received rules remains with the recipients. Rules are little in the abstract; they are everything in their concretized form. He who concretizes them is he who truly legislates, for it is he who pours them into a shape in which they can come to dominate, to determine, reality.

If we may schematize a little, we may say, then, in summing up, that there are four phases, as far as the setting of socialization is concerned: two dyadic, two characterized, like normal social life, by multiplicity, by a criss-crossing of human relationships. The conclusion of the process of socialization, the final emergence of the fully socialized individual, can only be achieved in the transition from the penultimate to the ultimate phase, from retreating heteronomy to advancing autonomy. It is then that "internalization of norms" is brought about which, to analysts like Emile Durkheim and Talcott Parsons, appeared as the center of both the social order and individual existence. The individual meets society at the moment of birth, but he *merges* with it only when he internalizes its norms. Only then does he cease to be an object of society and become a social subject, a true *socius*, a personality with both selfhood and sociality at his core.

THE INTERNALIZATION OF NORMS

79. In one of the most important books of the century, *The Two Sources of Morality and Religion*, Henri Bergson has asserted, and, to the satisfaction of many of us, proved, that the role played in nature by instinct is played within culture by habit. Hymenopterous societies and human societies are distinguished by the fact that the former are systems underlaid by necessity with only a fringe of freedom, while the latter are systems underlaid by freedom with only a fringe of necessity. But freedom without order is anarchy; it cannot endure. If it is to endure, it must bring forth form-giving, order-ensuring, institutions. Human societies fulfill this condition of survival by developing systems of habit. Habits bind and yet do not coerce. They make possible a life which grants both freedom and order.

If this is indeed so—and all the arguments and facts brought together in the present investigation go to show that Bergson's theory is basically correct —the core of the process of socialization, and more especially of its final stage, the internalization of norms, must be the learning of certain habits. It is hardly possible to entertain any doubts on this score, but there are many possible misconceptions which must be held at bay. One of them is to the effect that habits form through the simple repetition of the act concerned. Certainly, some habits form in this way, but by no means all, and assuredly not the most important ones from the sociological point of view. The baby in the cradle wishes to be comfortable; he will wriggle around until he has found a position which suits him. He will continue to maneuver himself into that position, and so the habit of lying in a certain way will come into existence. But psychologists have warned us that there is very often a difference between the process of learning and the learned process (see Dunlap, *Habits*, pp. 7, 34, 35). To give a crude but instructive example, let us think of toilet training. Not to urinate or to defecate except at certain times and in certain places is also a habit, and its implementation is helped by its continued observation, by regularly not releasing bowel and bladder contents any time and in any way, but only in the culturally approved manner. But to *learn* this habit, repetition is not enough. This habit is the effect, the fruit, of learning, but not its cause and not its method. Three elements are normally at the root of habit formation (see ibid., pp. 160, 161): the desire to learn, the resolve to persist in the repetition of the act concerned, and the visualization of the end result. None of these is present in the process of toilet training. When it starts (and it is only of this initial moment that we are speaking at present), the child is too young to visualize and to appreciate the end result (cleanliness), and if he desires anything, it is not the acquisition of an unpleasant body discipline and the repetition of self-repression; it is, on the contrary, to relieve himself whenever his organism suggests that he do so.

There is this great difference between learning to lie comfortably in the cot and learning to control one's sphincters: the one is natural and pleasant, the other cultural (which means non-natural, not to say unnatural) and unpleasant. In Freudian language: the one is dominated by the pleasure principle, the other by the reality principle; the one is commanded by the id and the other by the superego. (As for the ego, it is, of course, as yet too young to be of any great help. Piaget asserts that "there is nothing that allows us to affirm the existence of . . . norms in the pre-social behaviour occurring before the appearance of language" [*Moral Judgment*, p. 405]. No matter when toilet training begins, however late that may be, it is impossible to imagine that self-control is already so far advanced at the time that bowel and bladder control may come to be self-imposed and willingly or rationally accepted.) In the case of conduct which runs counter to organic tendencies, both the desire to learn and the resolve to persist in the repetition of the act concerned must be supplied from the outside; they are not in the child. The same applies to the visualization of the end result; the value of cleanliness must be explained, recommended, instilled. In a word: where cultural norms are concerned, and the norms to be acquired in the process of socialization are cultural norms, *pressure* has to enter the process of habit formation or it will come to naught. Conformity has to be enforced, however little our anti-authoritarian age may like the idea. It is not habit *per se* which civilizes man, it is custom, that is to say, socialized habit, habit approved of and insisted on by the community. If Bergson somewhat underplays this fact, he commits an error similar to Cooley's, and for the same reason: an insufficient awareness of the beastliness of the id.

However, it is precisely Bergson, who, through his earlier, more philosophical, writings, can help us to understand how a normative, that is to say, disciplinary, element can enter into the chains of human action. In *Matière et mémoire* and *Evolution créatrice*, he has shown that time means one thing in the realm of nature and quite another in the life of society. Nature, strictly speaking, does not know duration. It is at every moment a system of interconnected simultaneities, a fact which, for instance, is clearly seen in the possibility of describing the astronomical system in terms of simultaneous equations. In human society there is always a flow; trying to describe it in terms of simultaneous equations is tantamount to transmuting the dynamic into the static and falsifying the picture by freezing life out of it. The baby, too, is caught in a framework of simultaneity. To stay with our illustration: intestinal conditions call for relief; the sphincters are opened, and the bowels are voided. There is no delay; everything happens at once. Education, however, introduces delay and this means much more than might be expected. It means that the child is entering the confines, the system, of human time. L. K. Frank has analyzed the great change so well (*Society as the Patient* [New Brunswick, N.J., 1948], pp. 340–43): whereas there was before a physical stimulus A and a physical response N, there is now a physical stimulus A with intermediate links B, C, and D, etc. (e.g., repairing to the toilet) leading only ultimately to the physical event N. But B, C, D, etc., are not, and in any case need not be, physical in nature. They are cultural, disciplining, humanizing. A and N are simply factual, natural in the precise meaning of the terms. B, C, D, however, are pieces of conduct demanded of the individual and backed by social pressures. With regard to them there can be a right or wrong: they can be described in terms of do and do not, ought to and must not. "A time perspective has been imposed upon events which thereby assume an altered meaning. . . . The infant is coerced into surrendering his physiological autonomy to the control of the duly sanctioned culture patterns that are now imposed upon him" (pp. 342, 340, 341).

"Imposed," "coerced": clearly, it is the pressure in the background which thrusts the cultural norms upon and into the infant to be socialized. Therefore, to understand the internalization of norms, it is above all necessary to understand the nature and variety of social pressure. Typologically, it would seem that it falls into three categories, which might be called objective, authoritarian, and egalitarian pressure, respectively. Objective pressure consists in the presentation to the child of an established system of order which he, the relative outsider, the would-be nonconformist, cannot hope to escape and which simply overawes him. Traditionally, there has been talk of a "cake of custom" to indicate that the various do's and don'ts appear to form a phalanx in which each one is supported by all. But in this "cake" there are not only regularities of socially approved and supported habits; there are also regularities of nature. Understandably, the child cannot distinguish between the physical inescapability of the change of day and night and the merely conventional "necessity" of clock time (an accidental legacy to us from Babylonian culture). He will experience it all as *one* set of norms. The educational policies of Rousseau and Kant recommended that this objective pressure should become the be-all and end-all of pedagogy. Such human norms as were indispensable should be presented to the pupil in the light of "categorical" imperatives, as near necessities not much different from the necessity revealed by the law of gravitation according to which heavy objects "must" fall toward the center of the earth.

What Rousseau and Kant wished to achieve by this educational technique was the avoidance of the use of the second type of pressure, the pressure which we have called authoritarian. It might also be labeled vertical pressure, for its distinguishing mark is that it is exerted by a more highly placed person on one more lowly placed. Authoritarian or vertical pressure produces, if successful, a condition of heteronomy. The object of it has to live by a law not his own. This is the reason why Kant rejected and Rousseau abominated it. They wished for the free man, and even the free child, in a free society. While it is impossible not to sympathize with this high ideal, it is equally impossible not to declare it unrealistic. Apart from everything else, the objective pressure on which the two great liberal philosophers wished to rely has to be concretized, broken down into concrete norms, if it is to help in character-building; it also must be formulated, rationalized, for in its original, inchoate form it is hardly more than an all-round dark feeling of awe. For these two purposes, however, educators are needed, and they cannot be without personal authority. It was all very well for Rousseau to write the novel *Emile* in which a successful tutor is depicted who is anti-authoritarian in theory and non-authoritarian in practice. If he had tried his hand at education instead of sending his offspring to the foundling hospital, as he did, he would have found his task a little more difficult, or rather a lot more daunting, than Emile's self-effacing companion–friend, Jean Jacques.

What Kant was ready to accept, and what Rousseau was, if somewhat reluctantly, prepared to tolerate, was the third kind of pressure, the pressure which we have called egalitarian. It might also be described as horizontal pressure, for it is exerted by equals, neighbors upon neighbors, sideways as it were. It can come into play when and where men stand on the same level; it is characteristic of societies which have given themselves to the principle of autonomy, individual and collective. A positive attitude to this mutual surveillance is all the easier to entertain as it is often no more than a subsidiary safeguard of sociality, almost a power behind the scenes, hardly visible upon the stage of life. But in this book we are not speaking of men already socialized, we are speaking of those yet to be socialized, and so far as they are concerned, egalitarian pressure alone is insufficient to achieve the aim of education, the humanization and socialization of the person. This judgment—undoubtedly a hard and, therefore, unpopular one—is not the expendable result of an anti-humanistic attitude, of a jaundiced view of human nature, but the necessary conclusion from sober and scientific observation. Child psychology has proved that a period of heteronomous morality must precede the stage of moral autonomy, and that the latter can never be reached unless the former is passed through. We can once again avail ourselves in this context of the results of Jean Piaget's deep-delving studies. They are all the more convincing since he is obviously still imbued with the spirit of his Genevan fellow-citizen Jean Jacques and would have liked nothing better than to play down the role of authoritarian, vertical, pressure. Instead the facts force him to admit its indispensability. The "earliest forms assumed by a child's sense of duty," he writes (*Moral Judgment*, p. 105), "are essentially heteronomous forms." This is assuredly no accident. It is grounded in the basic fact of all sociology: namely, that the child is not social by native equipment.

But first to the topic of objective pressure. We have already pointed out that its power stems from the fact that there is a network of order in which the inescapable necessities of nature and the established, but not really inescapable, rules of society are woven together into one fabric in which the warp strongly supports the woof. There is, however, yet another reason why the child should so willingly submit to the constituted order of life which confronts him: besides the regularities of nature and those of society the texture of which we are speaking also contains the habits which he himself has developed and which he would not have developed and perpetuated if they had not suited him. This is a strand which is often not given the credit which it deserves. Because of its presence, the web of order is not totally alien to the infant who gets caught in it. His submission is not just total submission to alien determinations; it is also submission to self-generated patterns and, thus, submission to one's own past and to one's own will. Still, in the mixture, alien determinations greatly outnumber the self-generated patterns, and it remains true that the human animal agrees to bow its head before the dictates of the circumstances which confront him when he arrives because in his impotence he feels almost annihilated before their majesty and might.

Unable to analyze, to distinguish, self-imposed, socially imposed, and nature-imposed rules and regulations, the child experiences reality as a closed system of interdependent and mutually supportive elements; because this is the impression he receives, he believes that it is also self-maintaining. If there is a breach of the rules, there will be a spontaneous, indeed, an automatic, reaction which will bring things back to their former state. Every deviation from the set conditions is like the touching of one side of a pair of scales: there will be a swinging up and down of the sides until in the end the equilibrium is re-established and the cross-beam is again horizontal. A first, still shadowy, but already definable, kind of ethic thus forms in the child's mind: crime automatically generates its own corrective, for the concatenation of the two is mechanical. Speaking of youngsters up to the age of seven or eight, Piaget declares that "it seems quite natural to the child that a fault should automatically bring about its own punishment" (p. 255). There is a definite idea of justice here. We can call it justice immanent in things; we could also call it a Newtonian justice, one that obeys the laws of the lever and is itself, like the lever's law, a law of nature.

We have called this justice, but it must be conceded at once that the term is admissible in this context only if it is very widely, not to say very vaguely, defined. The normal grown-up in contemporary society would probably deny it the name. Indeed, he is likely to be shocked by the manner in which the child imagines that it operates. If a small child is asked who has committed a greater sin, he who has inadvertently broken two cups or he who has deliberately broken one cup, he will invariably say: the former. Caught in mechanistic, that is to say, non-human conceptions, he considers only the external result, not the internal motive. The guiltlessness of a person who, by ill chance, has caused an accident weighs with him as little as the guilt of another who has meant to cause harm. He who has followed our text can hardly be surprised. The child up to seven years of age is hardly social; he has not as yet acquired an assured knowledge of other selves. How then could he possibly appreciate motives which are hidden in the very depths of those selves? Small children, Piaget tells us, see punishment as retribution. They "do not attempt to understand the psychological context; deeds and punishments are for them simply so much material to be brought into some sort of balance, and this kind of moral mechanics, this materialism of retributive justice, . . . makes them insensible to the human side of the problem" (p. 266). The quotation, needless to say, conveys the truth exactly as it is, but perhaps it inverts the chain of causation. The moral mechanics of the child's mind may indeed help to make him insensible to the human side of crime and its attendant guilt, but this is a feedback effect, consequence rather than cause; it is, on the contrary, because the child is, to begin with, insensible to the human side of human conduct and its motivation, and perceives only its material surface, that he develops a moral mechanics in his mind which, if it generates a concept of justice there at all, provides only a very primitive and problematic version of it.

One point is interesting in this connection and should be mentioned because of its wider bearings: the fact that the child judges his own conduct exactly as he does that of others. He knows his own motives and cannot help knowing them, but they do not seem to him particularly significant. He is, Piaget tells us (p. 187), "far more interested in the result than in the motivation of his own actions." This may seem surprising but, once again, we have to say that he who has read this book from the beginning should not be surprised. As the knowledge of one's own self is dependent upon, and a consequence of, the knowledge of other selves, it cannot operate before that knowledge of other selves is sufficiently advanced to stimulate a reflective consideration, a self-knowledge, of oneself. Of course, once attention is drawn to the importance of motivation, and especially to the presence of attenuating or excusing circumstances—such as

the absence of evil intentions in cases where outer circumstances seem to indicate a wrongful act, whereas in reality there has merely been a simple accident
—the greater ease with which one's own ego is explored will begin to tell. Children are at that stage inclined to demand stricter punishment for others than
they consider just in relation to themselves. They know their own excuses better
than the excuses possibly at the disposal of their neighbors. Piaget states this
fact (p. 180) and stops there. He might well have mentioned, too, that the demand of stricter punishment for others and of milder treatment for themselves
is also another evidence of their long-surviving egocentricity. Ideas of justice are
simply quite rudimentary up to, say, the end of the first decade of life.

Rudimentary they may be, but that does not mean that they are without function, and that means, without value. We must consider the mechanistic ethics,
the ethical automatism, of the young boy or girl from two points of view: *ex
ante* and *ex post*. If we look at this half-morality which refuses to take note of
the inner motive and judges exclusively by the outer result, from the point of
view of the adult, it hardly appears as an acceptable morality at all. In practice
it would be bound to lead, at least now and then, to the punishment of the
guiltless and the scot-free escape of the guilty. But quite apart from the fact
that even the law is still largely based on an overvaluation of outer evidence
and an undervaluation of hidden motivations, we must see the child's ethics
dynamically, i.e., as a stage, and indeed as a necessary stage, in the development
toward a fuller and truer ethic. Perhaps we are not going too far if we say that
it is precisely the chief weakness—the automatism—of these early ethical conceptions which helps better ones to emerge and to establish themselves. In the
unconscious there remains, surviving from the early days of awestruck submission to the established system of order, a dim but definite and effective
feeling that crime is invariably followed by due retribution; this cannot but be
helpful in the life of both society and the individual. Rational considerations,
such as statistical proof that only too many in fact escape condign punishment,
will sooner or later weaken that feeling, which underpins law-abidingness, but
it is doubtful whether it will ever be totally obliterated.

In any case, whether it be possible or impossible ultimately to obliterate the
feeling that each crime has its price which is sooner or later sure to be exacted,
it is certain that that feeling will be present, and will operate powerfully, in the
next phase of development, which we have called the stage of heteronomy. On
its threshold, a double concretization will take place; the child will be presented
with a set of definite rules and with a definite set of people who command and
enforce these rules. The rules will be regarded as absolutely binding, as categorical imperatives. From "the moment that the child begins to imitate the
rules of others," Piaget writes (pp. 45–46), "he regards the rules . . . as sacred
and untouchable; he refuses to alter these rules [for instance, in the case of a
game] and claims that any modification, even if accepted by general opinion,
would be wrong." Indeed, Piaget calls "the respect felt by little children for
the commands given them by adults" a "mystical attitude" (p. 56).

But if there is such a "mystical attitude," such an unquestioning submission
of the child to the rules presented to him, what then about the basic thesis of
this whole work according to which human beings are not born social, but have

to be made social? Is not acceptance of law proof that law-abidingness is natural and even inborn? By no means. Closer inspection destroys any impression of this kind which a mere fleeting glance at the facts might possibly create. First of all, even in the case of the infant, the idea that guilt automatically generates condign punishment, is a result, a precipitate, of social life. Piaget's systematic observations of the infant psyche leave us no doubt on that score. From the first day, he explains, "the child is influenced by his parents. He is subjected from his cradle to a multiplicity of regulations, and even before language he becomes conscious of certain obligations. . . . Belief in immanent justice originates . . . in a transference to things of feelings acquired under the influence of adult constraint" (pp. 2, 260; see also p. 258).

But this proof that the acceptance of imposed rules does not argue a native basis for law-abidingness falls short of being conclusive and immediately convincing even though it is, objectively speaking, entirely sound. Doubts can be cast because it is almost impossible to separate with any finality what is inherited and what is acquired. It may be suggested that the willing reception by the young child of rules presented to him may only look like an acquired attitude, whereas it is in reality an inherited stance, and even Piaget's scholarly authority may be far from sufficient to invalidate this opinion which is sure to be accoutered in all the glad rags of "science." We need heavier artillery at this point; it is at our disposal, and its fire power is superior to any possible counterargument.

If it is impossible to decide by simple observation whether the inception of the belief that the existing laws of life are binding and self-enforcing or self-avenging is owing to inheritance or experience, no doubts can attach to the lessons which we can learn by watching children's behavior, for this is, comparatively speaking, an open book. But that behavior is, even after rules have been presented and duly accepted, still decidedly egocentric. We have made a distinction between play (which is egocentric) and game (which is, in principle, social), but, of course, there is a broad belt of transition between the two. During that transitional stage, which can teach us a good deal, the rules of the game are already given, but they are handled in the willful manner which is characteristic of mere play. "With regard to the rules of games," Piaget writes, and he adduces another great authority, William Stern, in support of his position,

> the beginnings of children's games are characterized by long periods of egocentrism. The child is dominated . . . by a whole set of rules and examples that are imposed upon him from outside. But unable as he is . . . to place himself on a level of equality with regard to his seniors, he utilizes for his own ends, unaware even of his own isolation, all that he has succeeded in grasping of the social realities that surround him. . . . But though he imitates what he observes, and believes in perfect good faith that he is playing like the others, the child thinks of nothing at first but of utilizing these new acquisitions for himself. He plays in an individualistic manner with material that is social. Such is egocentrism [p. 27].

We have, however, at this point, an even stronger argument which we can throw into the battle. The lowest kind of social relationship is, without a doubt,

that of conflict, the social situation in which the participants are to each other
no more than adversaries to be defeated, but the child, up to, say, seven years
of age, is incapable of even that much meaningful interaction with others. It
is well known that boys and girls in that developmental stage often pronounce,
as the facit of a game: I have won and you have won, too, a sheer impossibility.
Sharply expressed: the interactors are to each other not even adversaries. The
rules are known and they ordain at a minimum what criteria decide about good
success or ill success, but they are not applied as the contest would demand.
The fact is that the children do not compete, but each one pursues his own
amusement (pp. 16, 31, 32, 52). What we have before us is comparable to
the "collective monologue" (see above, p. 102), but not something which is akin
to meaningful conversation or any other genuinely social interaction.

It is only between the ages of seven and eight that there appears what can
justifiably be described as cooperation (the term, of course, including that
antagonistic cooperation which is of the essence of most games). The children
now know that only one can carry off the prize; they also know that a combat
is not fair unless some antecedent norms are attended to; and they even begin
to have an inkling of the fact that disobedience to these norms leads to anarchy.
Yet even then the basis of law-abidingness is not yet laid. For at that time, there
is still no general consensus concerning the exact rules to be followed: inquiries
show that discrepant ideas are held with regard to what is right and what is
wrong. What Piaget calls, with a most appropriate word, the "codification of
rules" is only achieved in the age group of the eleven- or twelve-year-olds (see
Moral Judgment, p. 17).

They, however, have crossed a Rubicon. They are already socialized persons,
and that means that they have internalized the do's and don'ts, the established
regularities and regulations, of the society in which they have grown up. These
no longer grip them merely from without, but control them—to some extent at
any rate—also from within. The "simulation of sociality" (Piaget's phrase, p.
62) is at an end; true sociality has begun. Therefore rules and laws appear to
them in an entirely new light. Two changes are of crucial importance: first, the
governing norms are largely stripped of their mystical halo. They are respected
because they are useful and reasonable, not because they emanate from a center
of willing which is experienced as superordinated, overwhelming, and irresistible. They may be changed if utility and reason appear to demand it. But
they may be changed only because the authority behind them is no longer an
objective, socio-cosmic order, but a society consisting of coordinated individuals; differently expressed: the authority behind them is the *consensus* of these
individuals. This is the second, and the truly decisive, point. After full socialization there rules autonomy, not heteronomy as before. The rules of social life are
now understood as folkways, the generally accepted and shared ways in which
a folk—a population—normally and normfully acts (p. 57).

If the foregoing argument is surveyed as a whole, if it is realized that so far
in the history of mankind autonomy has followed upon heteronomy, true upon
imposed law-abidingness, freedom with sociality upon constraint, then the idea
may easily get about that a reform of social education is due or overdue. Why
force the child through the painful channels of heteronomy, why not habituate

him straight away to the final condition which establishes freedom at the same time as order? All the many attempts at non-authoritarian education now under way root in such a conception which, since the French Revolution, has been endemic in Western societies. The matter is truly momentous, but it is also simple. Passage through heteronomy, as we may formulate our thesis, is a *sine qua non* of autonomy. There are all too many who, given to wishful thinking on the human condition—on what can here rightly be called human nature—believe that early discipline is both unnecessary and harmful. Even Piaget, a remote disciple of Rousseau's, inclines in this direction, and, most reluctantly, we have to part company with him at this point.

In certain contexts, Piaget makes large concessions to the point of view to be upheld here. Thus he writes (p. 364): "The spirit of discipline, it must be agreed, constitutes the starting-point of all moral life. There must be, not only a certain regularity of behaviour, but rules, and rules clothed with sufficient authority. No one will seriously deny that this is the price to be paid for the development of personality." But he runs into a great dilemma, the necessity (as he sees it) of choosing between two of his masters, Pierre Bovet and Emile Durkheim: "Either respect is directed to the group and results from the pressure exercised by the group upon the individual or else it is directed to individuals and is the outcome of the relations of individuals amongst themselves. The first of these theses is upheld by Durkheim, the second by M. Bovet" (p. 95). In this quandary, Piaget would rather follow Bovet than Durkheim; he would prefer to think that "all the moral sentiments are rooted in the respect felt by individuals for each other . . ." (p. 102). Indeed, he goes even further. He throws a dark light on constraint and accuses it, at least by implication, of retarding, not promoting, socialization. "Constraint," he asserts (p. 53), "is always the ally of childish egocentrism." And again: "social constraint does not really suffice to 'socialize' the child but accentuates its egocentrism" (p. 350).

These are strong statements. The latter of them is no doubt an exaggeration. There is nothing in Piaget's own analyses which would lend support to the assertion that social constraint—and we must note that Piaget speaks of *social* constraint, not constraint by odd individuals—*accentuates*, i.e., increases, egocentrism. As to the former statement to the effect that constraint is an "ally" of childish egocentrism, it is ambiguous. It can mean that the two are historically associated, elements of the same developmental phase. If understood in this sense, it is entirely correct. But it can also mean that they are allies like two countries who fight on the same side during a war, allies who would sustain and preserve each other, and there is at least a hint of this conception about Piaget's words. But if this is his opinion, he is wrong. The truth is that heteronomy prepares the way for autonomy, authority for reciprocity. Piaget realizes that this conviction "may be" justified. He writes (p. 366): "It may be, of course, that only those who have gone through the external discipline imposed by a master will be capable later on of any inner discipline. This is the commonly accepted view. . . ." (It is, so we may interject, the view of common sense as well as of common acceptance.) And elsewhere: "adult authority . . . perhaps . . . constitutes a necessary moment in the moral evolution of the child . . ." (p. 319). Why say "perhaps"? Why the hesitation? Piaget would fain be rid of the whole dilemma. Though he brings it up, he wants nothing more than to lay it to rest. "The question may, of course, be raised," he writes (p. 324), "whether such realities [as the autonomous morality of equality] could ever develop without a preliminary stage, during which the child's conscience is moulded by his unilateral respect for the adult. As this cannot be put to the test by experiment, it is idle to argue the point."

It is decidedly *not* idle to argue the point; indeed, it is necessary to come to a decision. Perhaps the matter cannot be put to the test by experiment, but it can certainly be judged in the light of experience. Experience, however, proves, and that with all desirable clarity, that no system of social pacification can endure without at least subsidiary organs of law enforcement. We may, in this context, refer to the analyses contained in our first volume, above all to the eye-opening consequences of police strikes. We may and must refer to the insights of one of sociology's greatest luminaries, Giambattista Vico, whose light far outshines even that of Emile Durkheim. What he shows is that where obedience to the indispensable minimal norms of human coexistence is guaranteed by all in general, it is guaranteed by nobody in particular; social control then decays; individual egoism is liberated; and society's compass begins to point in the direction of barbarism. This sounds harsh in human ears and doubly harsh in the ears of those who, like Bovet and Piaget, are Rousseauans, libertarians, liberals. But for scholarship wishful thinking is a poison which has to be avoided at all cost. The truth must prevail, however unpleasant it may be. The upsurge of egotism and criminality, especially juvenile, in recent years and more particularly the spread of drug addiction, is proof, on a broad front, of what is bound to happen when the enforcement, if need be by strong measures, of the social codes is allowed to weaken. We would say, then, that heteronomy is not only a passing stage of personal evolution, but an abiding need even in the case of the adult—that an element of it must remain even where and when the process of the internalization of norms has run its course, for there is no human being who would be beyond the danger of corruption, even if he has been thoroughly moralized.

It is always best to controvert a prestigious author with the help of arguments which he himself has put forward. We are able to do this here and to pit Piaget against Piaget. "Mutual respect," he writes (p. 90), "is, in a sense, the state of equilibrium towards which unilateral respect is tending when differences between child and adult, younger and older are becoming effaced. . . . It can even be maintained that mutual respect and cooperation are never completely realized." And again (p. 402): "Arising from the ties of authority and unilateral respect, the relations of constraint . . . characterize most of the features of society as it exists. . . . Defined by equality and mutual respect, the relations of cooperation, on the contrary, constitute an equilibrial limit rather than a static [i.e., reliable or viable] system." This is only too true. Like all things human, the internalization of norms is a process which invariably and unavoidably falls short of perfection. It is amazing how much it can achieve, especially in close-knit societies, but it cannot turn men into angels. The presence and the power of the body alone (which is forever in thrall to the pleasure principle) constitutes a permanent threat to the morality, indeed, the sociality, of human action and makes strong defense works necessary if the inbeating floods are not to submerge the land.

The considerations which we have just concluded also give us a clue to the correct definition of the fully socialized and moralized man. In principle, he is the man who will obey the established socio-moral norms spontaneously, out of his own free will, without having to be coerced in any way by external, punitive sanctions, actual or threatened. Justin Aronfreed expresses himself in this sense: "We might consider an act to be internalized to the extent that its maintenance has become independent of external outcomes—that is, to the extent that its reinforcing consequences are internally mediated, without the support of external events such as reward or punishment" (*Conduct and Conscience: The Socialization of Internalized Control Over Behavior* [New York & London, 1968], p. 18). Yet elsewhere Aronfreed formulates his definition a little differently. "Behavior becomes internalized," he says there (p. 49), "when its elicitation . . . shows some independence of its external outcomes." Clearly, the second wording is more cautious, more restrictive, than the first; the word "some" makes a good deal of difference. The fact of the matter is that we need two definitions of internalized norm-abiding conduct and of the norm-abiding man: one ideal-typical (and Aronfreed's first passage would seem to provide it), and one realistic (and Aronfreed's second passage comes close to that more sober version). As can be seen, we are still arguing against Piaget here (and, incidentally, we have Aronfreed on our side; see esp. his pp. 263, 265). "Internalization," Aronfreed correctly insists (p. 18), "would certainly not be synonymous with socialization, since much of a child's socially acquired behavior remains heavily dependent on its immediate external consequences." The observational basis of such a statement is unimpugnable; but why restrict it to the child? The adult person, too, lives in a world in which sanctions are likely to follow upon norm-breaking conduct, sanctions whose occasional infliction helps to keep everybody within the confines of the law. We would therefore modify Aronfreed's first definition and concretize his second by saying: we might consider a socially approved action pattern to be internalized to the extent that its maintenance has become independent of any concrete external outcome and remains dependent only on the submerged and subconsciously effective social pressure permeating the entire social environment. Of that latter, entirely general, social pressure nobody is entirely free, and of it nobody can be freed if his conduct is not to decline into asociality.

This effort to provide a realistic definition of norm-abidingness and of normal norm-abiding man has brought us up against the problem of punishment, and we must say a word about it. Since this volume is concerned neither with the techniques of education nor with the implications of criminal law, we may restrict ourselves to a statement of principles. By definition, punishment is an evil, for it consists in the infliction of pain or at least in the refusal or withdrawal of good, but this decides nothing about its desirability and/or necessity. It means only that it should be systematically minimized. What then is the minimal amount of punishment which is needed in the process of socialization properly so called—i.e., the process of social education—and in that prolonged process of socialization which must go on all through life in order to forestall backsliding into egocentricity and possibly animality? It is, clearly, an amount sufficient to maintain that respect for the order of law, the order of life, which sustains, and is essential to, even the norm-abidingness of the normal norm-abiding man —an amount sufficient to generate and to keep in being a *general climate* of norm-abidingness. This statement is unavoidably very vague; it will have to be made more concrete in a future volume in which the system of social sanctions will be discussed. But it is not so vague as to make it impossible for us to enunciate here a supremely important maxim: punishment should never concentrate exclusively on the reform of the actual norm-breaker and should always consider the potential norm-breaker as well. In other words: it should always be social *pressure*. Needless to say, a painful problem arises here: reform would seem to demand a mild, social pressure, a strict penal system. But this is a difficulty (alas, an excruciating one) which cannot be further followed at this point.

What we have to do, now, is to link our assertions concerning punishment with the analyses which we presented earlier. This is easy. As there are two types of norm-setting, heteronomy and autonomy, so there are two types of norm enforcement, retribution and restoration. Heteronomy is linked to retribution, both temporally and logically, whereas autonomy is linked to restoration. This division of punishment into restitutive and retributive is classical, and present, for instance, in a fully unfolded form, in Durkheim. Piaget complicates the picture somewhat, but his distinctions come in the end to the same. He divides retributive punishment into expiatory punishment and punishment due to reciprocity. With this somewhat hairsplitting effort we do not have to preoccupy ourselves, but we have to emphasize that, up to the age of seven or so, children think of punishment mainly as expiation, an attitude which is connected with their idea that the socio-cosmic order is sacred; after the age of seven they tend more toward punishment by reciprocity. Between seven and, say, ten, the demands of equity are not yet fully attended to; there is still more attention to formal equality than to the hidden concrete circumstances of the culprit (so that, for instance, attenuating conditions are not yet duly and fully taken into account). It is only upon entering adolescence that children begin to feel about punishment as the most fair-minded adults do. "The little ones prefer the most severe [punishment] so as to emphasize the necessity of punishment itself," Piaget writes (*Moral Judgment*, p. 225; see also pp. 199, 208, 216, 217); "the other [i.e., older] children are more in favour of the measures of reciprocity which simply serve to make the transgressor feel that the bond of solidarity has been broken and that things must be put right again."

It is unavoidable that the problem which plagued us before arises again, and again demands our attention. Just as it has been said that autonomy can totally displace heteronomy, that no superordinated guarantor of order is needed among adult men (a proposition rejected in this book, as the reader will recall), so it is being said that restitution can totally displace retribution—retribution to which the ugly name of vengeance is sometimes given in these discussions. Perhaps it will be the best strategy to distinguish here two questions and to consider them one after the other. The first is this: Does restitution in fact, in the observable world, totally drive out retribution? The second runs: Should restitution ideally drive out retribution? Should a society which can justly lay claim to the adjective good be satisfied if the state of things before a wrongful disturbance is restored; in other words: should it forgo the use of punishment in the proper sense of the term altogether? Let us see.

The answer to the first query is easy. In the world of hard facts there are hardly acts of punishment, let alone penal systems, which do not contain an element of expiation alongside the effort to restore a disturbed situation to normalcy. Piaget admits it, at least half-and-half, in distinguishing two types of reaction with regard to punishment, the first considering at least a modicum of retribution a moral necessity, the other not. The first, Piaget admits, "favoured as it is by certain types of family life and social relationships, survives at all ages and is even to be found in many adults" (p. 199). The mode of expression used here is very delicate, and we have to make it a little cruder in order to bring out its implications. The necessity of punishment, we are surely given to understand in this passage, is not acknowledged by the true humanitarian. "Distributive justice," he says elsewhere, "is the most fundamental form of justice itself" (p. 316). Retributive justice, then, is at most a second best and at worst a form of sadism.

In this context, Piaget criticizes, not only Durkheim with whom he is in conflict all the time, but even Bovet with whom, as we have seen, he expressed his agreement before. In Durkheim's view, society—social pressure, or, to be even more precise, collective pressure—is the source of all morality. The "relation between two individuals is insufficient to explain the genesis of any of the facts of duty. When, therefore, one individual respects another, he does so only in so far as the other is invested with social authority" (p. 382). Durkheim is thinking particularly of the schoolmaster. In *L'Education sociale*, he accepts the necessity of school punishments as a means of reasserting the influence of the wellspring of all order and harmony; differently expressed: of personal responsibility and morality. This is too "sociologistic" for Piaget, and he feels himself closer to Bovet. What Bovet teaches is that the infant respects at first only his parents; then he transfers this sentiment to adults in general, later to older children, and finally even to his contemporaries. Punishment is thus basically the pressure of individuals on individuals; "all forms of respect would, in so far as they were sources of moral obligation, derive from unilateral respect . . ." (p. 389). As can be seen, Bovet is far more individualistic–nominalistic than Durkheim: it is not the collectivity but the superordinated person who is the source of authority and, therefore, in case of need, the appointed wielder of the rod. But it is obvious that the difference between Durkheim and Bovet is small. It is hairsplitting and useless to ask if the father acts as a representative of the collectivity or as an independent individual agent; both roles are united in him and indissolubly fused. When we see a brass candlestick, we do not say either that it is tin rather than copper or copper rather than tin; we say that it is both. The child who has his behind smacked is surely not going to ask whether his father has thrashed him as a person or as a functionary. Piaget moves for a moment close to this insight, but veers away from it in the end: the earliest of all rules, he says (p. 383), are accepted, "not because they are current in the social group" but "because they are imposed upon him by [individual] grown-ups who are both attractive and formidable."

The relative closeness of Bovet to Durkheim displeases Piaget. Bovet's individualism is sympathetic to him but not his authoritarianism. The egalitarian in Piaget revolts. "According to M. Bovet," he writes (p. 391), "mutual respect, having been derived from unilateral respect, remains in a sense identical with it or, at any rate, is still based upon it. In our view, mutual respect, being involved in a different system of equilibria, deserves to be distinguished from the unilateral variety." It certainly deserves so to be distinguished from a logical point of view: pressure sideways is different from pressure from above. But this definitional acrisy is for Piaget more than a *jeu d'esprit*. Deriving from Rousseau, he revives not only Rousseau's semi-religious belief in the healthiness of social equilibrium, but also his fond assumption that, given such an equilibrium, law enforcement is unnecessary and, indeed, reprehensible. His aim is not to point out that the one is different from the other, but to recommend the one and to disrecommend the other. We can see the substructure of Piaget's thought in one particular passage (p. 387), where he says that there is a "quasi physical element of fear which plays a part in unilateral respect" and a "purely moral fear of falling in the esteem of the respected person" which plays a part in reciprocal respect. "The need to be respected thus balances that of respecting. . . ." Equilibration without the threat of painful punishment will do the trick.

Alas, it will not! Are we to assume that the child who has as yet not been fully socialized, or the adult criminal in whose case socialization has failed, will agree to curb his self-regarding urges, rooted as they are in his very flesh and blood, simply because he may lose the "respect" of his neighbors? What utopianism it is to believe this! So far as fully socialized persons are concerned (if there are such), social pressure becomes irrelevant: then both pressure sideways and pressure from above are irrelevant. Conscience alone—the man or monitor within, as Adam Smith called that voice in his *Theory of Moral Sentiments*—will guarantee law-abidingness. But it must be added at once that no man is proof against corruption. Is not everyone bidden to pray daily: Lead us not into temptation? It is precisely the law-abiding man who knows best that both pressures—that sideways relied on by Bovet, and that from above insisted on by Durkheim—are forever indispensable.

Once again, we are happy to be able to defeat Piaget in his more idealistic by Piaget in his more realistic mood. "We grant, of course," he says (p. 391), and he grants in fact all we would wish him to grant, "that in point of fact traces of unilateral respect and of inter-individual constraint are to be found everywhere. . . . mutual respect is never to be found pure and unadulterated, but is only an ideal form of equilibrium towards which unilateral respect is guided as the inequalities of age and of social authority tend to disappear." This "ideal [of law-abidingness] independent of any real command" (p. 392) may indeed be a point toward which some of us are moving, but it is like the point of intersection between two rail lines which meet only in infinity.

Even more clearly does Piaget write elsewhere: "From a purely legal point of view, punishment is perhaps necessary for the defence of society . . ." (p.

339). The "perhaps" is once again a profoundly unjustified addition, and what is the "purely legal" point of view? Is it not simply the social point of view, the view of all those who wish to see society coherent and ordered? Would law have arisen if it were not needed? And is not the criminal law more desperately needed (as Durkheim always maintained) than the civil, simply because the judgments of the civil courts would be nothing more than humble appeals to the lawbreaker if the power of the criminal courts, with their attendant enforcement officers, were not there to give them authority and inescapability?

It is from this point of view that the whole phenomenon of punishment has to be approached. In approaching it, it is by no means unnecessary to repeat that punishment beyond a certain, historically variable degree is socially destructive, not socially constructive, i.e., leading to the weakening rather than the tightening of the social bond. Such excessive penalization is nowhere meant in the disquisitions which we now follow.

Due retribution, first of all, soothes the wounded feelings of the persons hurt. Say, a man has been killed; his widow and orphans would lose all confidence in the fairness of the social system under which they live if there were no due process against the killer and, in case of culpability, due punishment. From them this negative feeling would, as a secondary development, spread outward to the rest of society, and law-abidingness in general would be reduced. (Léon Bourget's novel *Le Disciple* is a moving illustration of this fact.) It does no good to say that even a bereaved widow and orphaned children should forgive. Forgiveness is a resplendent virtue, and the Gospel rightly recommends and exalts it. But forgiveness is a heroic virtue, and society as we know it expects heroism of nobody; indeed, it would be vain to expect it of all and sundry, since the common run of men has not reached the height of self-control and of self-sacrifice which would be required. In a world of ordinary men and women —men and women whose law-abidingness needs continued support, even if it has reached a level which is normally sufficient for all practical purposes—the punishment of crime, the ever-renewed proof that crime does not pay, is an indispensable ingredient in the process of socialization to which even the already socialized have to be subjected, and which is, quite simply, the life process of society.

Vengeance and retribution are not the same for yet another reason: vengeance looks to the past and retribution to the future. Vengeance is part and parcel of the abreaction of the hatred which a crime has generated; its inherent danger is the evocation of counter vengeance and so the starting of a chain reaction which may or even must destroy society. It has happened in history and none too rarely. Vengeance is thus not social pressure toward law-abidingness, but retribution is. Retribution is educational. In it, the private party is not involved; the whole of society asserts itself. And it asserts itself because it wishes to see peace and order secure.

Sociologically speaking: the call for a society without a penal system, a society in which restitution has totally ousted retribution, is the outgrowth of a faulty social theory. It assumes that a society consists only of individuals, and that therefore lawbreaking hurts individuals only. But this is not so. In addition to the individuals, there is the social whole, and we can, nay must, assert its reality,

even if we should take care not to sink too deeply into a reifying, realistic ontology, e.g., organicism. In addition to the individuals damnified, there is the
defied and therefore damnified society, and punishment at all levels is merely
its self-assertion, the assertion of its will to live, which cannot be rightly denied
to it, as it cannot be denied to any individual.

Many writers consider the terms "punishment" and "sanction" as synonymous, even though the term punishment refers more to him who receives correction than to him who inflicts it, while the term sanction has the latter more
in view than the former. There are, however, others (see, for instance, Parsons'
"Social Structure and Personality Development," p. 183) who define sanction
more widely and include in its meaning reward as well as punishment. This
brings us to a new problem. The expression "reward and punishment," the
bracketing together of these two conceptions, is one of the most widely current
standing phrases in the English language and indicates a deep-laid association
of ideas. We should ask then whether the reward of norm-abiding conduct is
also a means of socialization, alongside the punishment of norm-defying action,
and, if so, whether it has the same role to play in the economy of the educational process.

The rewarding of norm-abiding conduct is undoubtedly also a means of socialization, but, in the nature of things, it can never play the same role in the
economy of the educational process as the punishment of norm-defying action.
There are two reasons for this sad fact, one economic, the other psychological.
If every norm-abiding action were to be rewarded, *every* action in a well-
integrated society would have to be rewarded, and there would not be the necessary means to continue paying such premiums. Besides, the law known to
economists as the diminishing utility of value would come into play. Foolish
families which represent helping with the domestic chores not as normal duties
of the children but as special efforts on their part which must be specially paid
for, for instance by the distribution of candy, inevitably find that the children
continually tend to raise their price. The reason for this is explained in economic
theory: a second glass of beer is never as highly valued as the first, a third glass
as the second, and so on. Rewarding ordinary conduct, or the element of norm-
abidingness contained in it, is therefore a self-defeating policy. Reward has
necessarily to be reserved for extraordinary achievement. This is what the
human race has always known. There are no medals for the fulfillment of
soldierly duties; there are medals only for signal acts of heroism. When, toward
the end of the Second World War, the German government started a wider distribution of the Iron Cross, that famous and formerly much-coveted decoration
soon fell into disrepute.

There is, however, a social theory which tends to argue that reward is much
more important than would appear at first sight and than is suggested here. It
is asserted that every law-abiding action is in fact rewarded, because it is
matched by another—the corresponding—law-abiding action on the side of
one's partner. If I peacefully give my money to a salesgirl, I am rewarded by
the peacefulness of her surrender of the bought article. No doubt, things may
be construed in this fashion, and a certain truth content need not be denied to
this construction. But such truth as there is is purely formal. The theory of

which we are speaking is part and parcel of the mechanistic tradition according to which the core of social life is the equilibration of individual pushes and pulls, such as the push of the buyer and the pull of the seller, and every social action a contract in which equivalent is exchanged for equivalent. Some social actions, indeed, many social actions, are such contracts, but law- and norm-abidingness is not created by them but rather presupposed by them. It is in reality not so that the contracting parties give peace and security to each other; peace and security are given to them both by the superordinated social system which comprises them and which they merely implement in relation to each other. This implementation may be construed as an exchange of equivalents, but it is never experienced as such; public order and peacefulness are taken for granted. A reward which is not felt as a reward is not really a reward.

If this is true of the dealings among adults, it is much more true of the dealings between adults and children, socializers and socializees. It is most unrealistic to think that children could be induced to regard the peaceful continuation of family life as an adequate reward for the effort at self-discipline which is being demanded of them; it is even more unrealistic to fancy that they will spontaneously consider it in this light. The tit-for-tat theory of social life is, in addition to other weaknesses, far too rationalistic. It assumes that social intercourse is a chain of bargains. It is not necessary to be a Pareto in order to know that the bulk of social behavior is, as he calls it, non-logical, i.e., non-rational. Greed in actual life is controlled by fear, the fear of punishment. When a mother says to a naughty child: if you do that again, I shall not love you any more, she is threatening him with evil and not protesting the falsification of an exchange relationship. By evil we mean here positive evil, pain, and the expectation of that—of punishment—is the norm-forming as well as norm-instilling, norm-internalizing energy. "Social roles," so one observer has correctly and wisely written, "unlike other learned behavior patterns, very likely are performed not because they are rewarding but because they are mandatory" (Spiro, "Social Systems, Personality, Functional Analysis," p. 102).

In what has immediately gone before, we have already changed over to the second point which we have to make in this context; it is not economic, but psychological. It is simply that punishment is incomparably more effective than reward. A particularly careful analysis of this matter is contained in Justin Aronfreed's *Conduct and Conscience: The Socialization of Internalized Control over Behavior*. In principle, this author admits, both punishment and reward are at the disposal of the agent of socialization. "Two processes," he writes (p. 170), "interact in . . . aversive learning [i.e., learning to avoid what is socially harmful]. The first process is the . . . conditioning of anxiety of either external cues or the intrinsic stimulus correlates of behavior. The second process is the reinforcement of [alternative, socially not harmful] behavior which is instrumental to the reduction of anxiety." But though the two are, in principle, usable, the one can, in practice, be used to much more purpose than the other. "The evidence for the suppressive effect of observed punishment is more impressive than the evidence for the facilitative effect of observed reward," we read in one place (p. 189), and in another (p. 195) we are told: "The findings of . . . recent experiments . . . provide evidence that the effectiveness of internalized suppres-

sion [of socially harmful conduct] is a function of the intensity of anxiety which
is discriminately associated with punished or prohibited behavior."

As is unavoidable, Aronfreed finds himself in this context willy-nilly drawn
into a polemic against those "social and educational philosophers which imply
that punishment is undesirable," and he mentions one particular adversary by
name, B. F. Skinner, whose writings are very popular because they fall in with
those philosophies which today appear to be part and parcel of the unconscious
metaphysic of the age. Needless to say, excessive and unmotivated punishment
may be a traumatic experience which will disturb, upset, and repel rather than
socialize the child, but in this case, as in all others, the abuse of a thing says
nothing against its appropriate and reasonable use. "Limitations on the use of
punishment should not prevent us from recognizing the massive contribution
that it makes to the internalized control of conduct," Aronfreed writes (p. 62).
He shows that a good deal of the Skinnerian doctrine is derived from experiments with animals whose mode of response is all too readily transferred to
humans—experiments, moreover, many of which are quite unrealistic because
the animals investigated "were placed in essentially insoluble learning situations." No wonder that such guinea pigs show nothing but frustration! Where,
however, more reasonable paradigms were used, "it soon became apparent
that punishment learning"—true learning—"could be effective," even among
animals. Aronfreed then surveys recent experimental work with children and
finds his general attitude (which is also the attitude of the present writer) fully
confirmed. Indeed, he claims to have common consent on his—on our—side
(see esp. p. 56). We cannot go into the detail here, significant though it is.
It was proved, for instance, that socially acceptable choices are more easily
achieved through conditioning which uses reward and punishment rather than
reward and no reward; which uses punishment alone rather than reward alone;
and so on, and so forth. The upshot of it all is summed up by Aronfreed in the
following two sentences:

> Positive reinforcement alone would probably not be sufficient . . . to produce
> modifications of behavior which are completely discrepant with the child's
> initial motivational dispositions, for example, in situations where the child
> must learn that no . . . aggressive act is permissible. . . . These constraints on
> the applicability of positive reinforcement make it necessary to assume that
> many internalized forms of conduct could never be acquired without contin-
> gencies which introduce punishment and aversive control over the child's
> behavior [pp. 61, 62].

In reporting on the experimental work done (p. 62), Aronfreed writes that
"these paradigms have demonstrated quite clearly the adaptiveness and stability of both the external and internalized control over behavior which can be
induced by punishment." In this statement, the term, or the fact, of "stability"
is of special importance (as need not be circumstantially proved). Social life
can only function successfully if the socializing lessons which the child learns
stick. On this point, our psychologist says very clearly "that conditioned aversive stimuli maintain independent value more easily than do conditioned positive
stimuli when they are removed from the conditions under which their value was

acquired" (p. 27). This point, too, is, once again, amply supported by experimental as well as experiential evidence, and, once again, we cannot go into the detail here. But it is easily available in the literature of psychology.

It is sometimes alleged that surrounding a child with love (in the jargon of modern psychology, intensive nurturance) is helpful to socialization because it will give a positive value, in the eyes of the child, to everything the loving person does. That person will become a model to the child; imitation will socialize him. Aronfreed, with his great knowledge of the observational and experimental work done in the field, makes two important points in this connection. The first is that the influence of imitation should not be overestimated; a child may act like his supposed model, not because he imitates him, but because they both are in the grip of the same social pressures.

> An increase in objective similarity of behavior between child and socializing agent does not require us to suppose that the child is learning through imitation. . . . A child's behavior will frequently be similar to the observed behavior of another person . . . because it is under the established constraints of cues in the child's social environment, rather than because the other person's behavior serves as a model for changes in the child's behavioral repertoire [p. 91].

This consideration brings us back to the power of social control, but the second point which Aronfreed makes underlines the importance of that power even more. "A number of theorists have proposed," he writes,

> that the child's early experience of nurturance and affection establishes the positive affective value of the attributes of its social models and thus fosters its generalized disposition to reproduce the attributes in its own behavior. . . . Some of the evidence from [later] studies suggests [however] that the disposition of children to reproduce the behavior or judgments of another person is more sensitive to continuity or withdrawal of the level of nurturance to which they have become adapted than it is to the sheer amount of nurturance that they have received from the person.

This insight is even more clearly expressed on the next page, and we take the liberty of italicizing a few words in order to give yet more clarity to it: "It is much more plausible to attribute this effect of nurturance to the salience or contrast of withdrawal of affection *as a component of punishment,* and to a consequent increment in the intensity of the child's anxiety, than it is to assume that nurturance somehow lends positive value . . . to a model's . . . behavior" (pp. 88, 89, 90). What this means is simply that a child surrounded by love is easier to control and to educate because it is easier to put him under pressure; he has more to lose. "Withdrawal of love or the threat of it," says Boyd R. McCandless in "Childhood Socialization," "is the paradigm or vehicle for psychological punishment, and seems to be almost uncannily effective as a socializing agent . . ." (p. 801). Not the love shown, but the desire to keep that love, is the helper of the process of socialization. This may be a very hard and unpleasant insight, but it is a true insight all the same; and if it is calmly considered, it is by no means surprising, for without the threat of sanctions against overly egoistic conduct, the natural tendency toward such conduct cannot possibly be curbed.

What we have suggested in the last paragraph is that the relation between parental affection and parental correction is a positive, not a negative, one. Far from excluding each other, they must go together. As the Bible has it: "He that loveth his son frequently chastiseth him" (Eccles. 30:1). Since parental affection has deep cultural and even (remotely) natural foundations, it may be taken for granted in the case of every normal family, and it creates, in the lap of that family, a climate of community, a feeling of security and warmth, for the sake of which all members are willing to accept hardships, such as the burden of discipline and even the sanctions which back it up. Moderate and motivated chastisement will not, in the judgment of the child, shatter that feeling, even though it may throw a temporary shadow over it. This, then, is the function of parental love in the economy of the process of socialization: that it creates a willingness to accept self-limitation and to suffer the penal consequences which follow transient breakdowns in that self-limitation on the part of the child. Parental love unconnected with a readiness to put pressure on the yet unformed personality under its care to obey the social codes and to inflict sanctions when need arises has no function in that economy. It will lead to the educational failure known popularly as a spoiled child. While "a minimally nurturant base for social attachment" and even "a substantial degree of attachment to nurturant socializing agents" are "a prerequisite of the child's effective internalization of aversive control over its conduct," Aronfreed writes (pp. 310, 309), "a highly [i.e., overly] nurturant climate of rearing may curtail a child's internalization of control."

From the point of view of the child, correction, whether it consists in the infliction of pain, or merely in the withdrawal of privileges, must necessarily appear as an unvalue, something which one would rather avoid than face. Yet it would be wrong not to recognize that there is at least an edge of positive value to that unvalue, and that the child is in most cases quite clearly aware of it. A failure to punish where punishment is due is all too often interpreted by the child as a lack of concern for him. The parent who does not intervene when a prohibited act has been committed is seen as disinterested and indifferent, and this kind of "love" may in fact lead to an estrangement from the loved object (see Shibutani, *Society and Personality*, p. 555). Besides, appropriate (not excessive) correction is often regarded as a price which is paid for an illicit indulgence, and as a means for restoring—repacifying—a disturbed relationship. To "accept . . . punishments constitutes the most natural form of reparation," writes Piaget in *The Moral Judgment of the Child* (p. 322). "The pain inflicted thus seems to reestablish the relations that had momentarily been interrupted. . . ." The slate is clean again; the shadow is lifted from the common life.

If the failure to keep up sufficient social pressure is thus damaging both to society and to the child to be introduced into society, its removal altogether and even more its replacement by a policy of indiscriminate rewarding are bound to have catastrophic consequences. Psychiatrists are agreed that the results of excessive frustration are no greater and no more deplorable than the results of too great indulgence (see Klein, *Envy and Gratitude*, p. 15). The child who is not constrained to internalize a modicum, a minimum, of social norms is, in principle and in practice, in the condition of anomie, and anomie is, as Durkheim has classically shown, an inability to operate in the cadres of society and thus, not surprisingly, a frequent cause of suicide. Durkheim's analysis (see esp. *Suicide*, trans. John A. Spaulding and George Simpson [London, 1952], pp. 241–360) is too well known to need repeating here. But perhaps we should emphasize that his convictions agreed entirely with an observer of very different complexion, Sigmund Freud. Freud writes of the id that it is "a chaos, a cauldron of seething excitement," and his opinion can be summarized by saying that "the blind strivings for gratification of the id would doom it to annihilation" if it were not saved by a systematic "denial of instinctual satisfactions," by "privation" (see Birnbach, *Neo-Freudian Social Philosophy*, pp. 17, 22).

There is yet one more factor operative in the process of socialization which we have to study: the role performed in it by the intellect, the human *ratio*. We have left it to the end because we want to indicate, by placing it there, that it plays only an auxiliary part—which does not mean that its contribution is negligible. If it were true, as Bentham and other rationalists maintained, that every human action is preceded by the casting up of a balance sheet of probable cost and gain, everything would be different; refinement of the mathematical *ratio* would then be the core of social education. But we have already rejected this interpretation of the springs of human action as an unrealistic construct. The opposite opinion, held by Pareto and other partisans of an essentially zoological concept of man, according to which we act first and think of reasons only afterward, appears closer to the facts. Yet it must surely be somewhat modified. It is true that actions flowing from men's individual and collective habit systems are as little reflective—as little subjected to preliminary calculation—as actions flowing from their somatic drives or instincts. Yet these habit systems carry within them certain regularities—indeed, we may go so far as to say, certain principles—which can be formulated, explored, and explained, and to do just this was the essential task which Socrates, that fountainhead of Western philosophizing, wished to impose on human thought. We all speak our native tongues without, initially, consciously knowing their rules; yet a grammar may be extracted from living language, and if we internalize it, we shall speak better, more clearly, and more correctly than before. So it is with the principles of social living. They may be epitomized, and if they are thus formulated, they are much easier to teach. They can then be lodged, not only in the habit system, but also in the mind and the memory, of the young; and that is by no means a small thing.

Furthermore, although social pressure remains the true guarantor of norm-abiding action, it may itself be, to some extent, rationalized. Preaching to the unconverted is not very effective, but preaching to the converted often is. A child already largely socialized may as positively respond to a word of guidance as to a threat of punishment, indeed, more so. As one psychologist has lucidly explained:

> Anxiety arousal may be necessary for efficient rule learning, but after sufficient training in rule observation, the anxiety component plays a less important role. . . . Once a rule has been learned, it may function to produce inhibition [of norm-defying conduct] with little or no accompanying anxiety. . . . As the child increases in age, the relative contributions of emotional and cognitive components to response inhibition will shift. With younger children, response

inhibition will be most successfully achieved by a reliance on physical punishment techniques which stress the production of anxiety. With older children,
punishment techniques which diminish the role of anxiety and stress the role
of verbal control of motor behavior, through the appeal to general rules, will
be more effective [Ross D. Parke, "The Role of Punishment in the Socialization Process," in *Early Experiences and the Processes of Socialization*, edd.
Hoppe et al., p. 98].

Basically, then, socialization works with and by the emotions, especially the
emotion of anxiety, but it may use the cognitive capacities of man to good purpose (see Aronfreed, *Conduct and Conscience*, pp. 71ff.). Correction, if the
administration of it is accompanied by a verbal appeal, is far more effective than
if it is inflicted without explanation. Even in the latter case the child concerned
may well know why he is being punished or threatened with punishment, but
bringing the reason for it out in the open will yet help, at any rate, *pro futuro*.
When a rationale is given, a knowledge of the commands and prohibitions contained in the social codes is built up, and knowledge is the factor which constitutes the difference between human education and animal training. The
mechanical element is taken out of the process of socialization; it is, as it were,
humanized.

This raises the question whether instruction alone—in other words: simple
appeal to the intellect—is not all that is needed in the process of socialization, a
belief which is fairly widespread in the contemporary world. But a decidedly
negative answer has to be returned to the question thus raised. There are, above
all, two reasons why a purely intellectualist approach to social education cannot
succeed. The first has to do with the timetable of socialization. Clear comprehension of the rationale behind the specific do's and don'ts which constitute the
reigning folkways is not possible before a certain—a considerable—degree of
mental maturity is reached. Then, however, it is too late thoroughly to transform
the personality from a nearly animalic to a properly cultural condition. Good
habits—individual habits in harmony with collective customs—have to be inculcated before their deeper justification can be explained to the child (see
ibid., esp. p. 29). The second reason concerns the powerlessness of the pure
intellect. Psychological investigations have shown that children, when asked,
reveal a perfectly good verbal knowledge of moral rules, e.g., the rule that lying
is to be avoided, and yet would never regard these rules as in practice binding
on them (see H. Hartshorne and M. A. May, *Studies in the Nature of Character.
I. Studies in Deceit*; New York, 1928). Here, incidentally, lies the weakness of
all rationalist ethics: that of Kant's categorical imperative, for instance. To say
that an imperative is "categorical" is little or nothing; it must be *felt* to be categorical—that is much or even everything. Reason can support the social pressures generated in and ruling over social life; it can in no way supplant them.

There is, however, yet another contribution which the refinement of reason
can make to the socialization of the individual and thereby to the smooth functioning of social life. The matured intellect has two great capacities which may
be brought to bear, even by the individual, on the social prescriptions and proscriptions which come to meet him: discrimination and generalization. He who
knows how to make distinctions will also know how to distinguish the licit from

the illicit. Because the social codes are the products of growth, i.e., of a sub-rational process, and because the instilling of these codes in the personality is the consequence of habituation, i.e., again of a subrational process, its injunctions are never clearly defined. The guidance they give is certainly definite, but it is not—at any rate, not at the edges—always univocal. Theft is known to be forbidden, but is this or that concrete action really theft? Even the law, the most carefully developed and clearly formulated of the social codes, is often puzzled; the code of custom necessarily leads to much more puzzlement. The sharper the judgment of a person, the easier it will be for him to lay such puzzlement to rest; in other words: to obey the commands of custom as they should be obeyed.

But generalization is even more important than discrimination. It helps not only with the application, but also with the completion, of social discipline. The child who has come to know that stealing candy is forbidden also knows, if he is normally intelligent, that stealing sugarplums is equally forbidden, and that the sanction which represses the one misdemeanor will equally be brought to bear if the other is committed. "The child's acquisition of concepts enables it to place actions which are overtly very different into the same class, for example in terms of their common intentions or consequences," says Aronfreed (ibid., p. 69; see also Piaget, *Moral Judgment*, p. 166). But this means that norm-abidingness is not limited to the area, always very restricted, of individual life-experience, and that it spreads out, from the actually encountered to the potentially encounterable. There is thus a tendency toward all-round sociality, and it is carried by the intellect as well as by experience and emotion. Yet it remains true that the role played by the *ratio* is merely auxiliary and secondary. We can rationally generalize what we already know, but what we have to know in order to generalize it—in this case the social and moral norm—is taken, not from speculation, but from life.

If the Socratic conviction is accepted that a life consciously lived is superior to a life but naïvely experienced, reason can be said to contribute to the perfection of human sociality. Yet however perfect that sociality may be, it remains (as we have already pointed out) exposed to dangers, simply because the individual is at all times subject to the temptation to prefer the satisfaction of his animalic drives to obedient fulfillment of disciplinary norms. Most of the crises in the relations of individual and society arise from contingencies in personal life-histories and have not, therefore, to be considered in this work; they are raw material for biographers, not sociologists. There is, however, at least one such crisis which is collective rather than individual and must therefore be investigated here: the so-called teen-age crisis, the rebelliousness characteristic of some societies, such as our own, of the immediate sub-adult. Since it is obviously connected with physical maturation, more particularly the maturation of the sexual apparatus, it is often considered as falling into the area of physiology rather than into that of sociology. This is, however, an erroneous approach. The problems involved stem, not from physical maturation as such, but from the complications it creates in the relationship between inborn drives and induced disciplines.

There are, first of all, several factors which have nothing whatsoever to do with somatic conditions, but are purely social in character. Chief among them is a shift in the setting of socialization: the family is joined, and to some extent replaced, by the peer group, the playmates in the street, the fellow-scholars in the school, and so on. The peer group, however, is a society very different in structure from the family, and this is bound to have serious consequences. While the family is in all typical cases strongly, not to say strictly, integrated, the peer group is usually rather loose-textured. Not that pressures are absent; far from it; they may in fact be rather demanding. But the ruling norms are more elastic, if for no other reason than that they are less sharply formulated. "The activities of adolescents have a normative structure . . . that differs from the normative structures of childhood in being less explicit and, contrasted to parents, lacking clearly designated persons of superior status who are the examplars, proponents, and sanctioning agents of the moral code," writes Ernest Q. Campbell ("Adolescent Socialization," in *Handbook of Socialization Theory*, ed. Goslin, p. 843). No wonder, then, that the growing boy or girl is apt to feel more at ease in this setting than in the family circle, which is comparatively restrictive.

The peer group is, furthermore, not only a society of mutual interaction, but also a society of mutual support: it is given, not only to innocuous enterprises like common amusements, but also to the more serious business of defending common or parallel interests. If the process of socialization has not yet been concluded—and how could it be at the age of fourteen or fifteen?—there will still be considerable resistance to the demands of the social codes, and this resistance will be increased if the resister feels himself surrounded by others in similar situations and with similar complaints. While the child acts—however self-centeredly—within the cadres of the order which he finds, the adolescent begins to see that order from the outside, as it were, and reacts critically to it. He will ask whether all the do's, and especially the don'ts, of established society are really necessary and often conclude, aided and abetted by his contemporaries, that they are not.

This conviction will be greatly strengthened by the discovery, made at this time of life, that many of the norms presented to and pressed upon the young are not in fact obeyed by the adults who, hypocritically, preach them. The widespread idealism of youth has its roots in this fact. Is it not possible, is it not indeed easy, to be better than one's elders? Unavoidably—and need we hesitate to say, deservedly?—there will be a serious loss of prestige on the part of the agents of socialization who will appear in the light of policemen who themselves commit crimes. What is particularly apt to happen (though societies differ greatly in this respect) is the spread of a hedonistic life policy among the teen-age groups: why forgo pleasures forbidden by those who themselves surreptitiously indulge in them?

One of the reasons why there are considerable differences between societies in this respect lies in the fact that they are subject to very dissimilar rates of change. Cultures of great stability, action systems which are largely repetitive, give a comparative advantage to the old; provided the technique remains the same, he who has plowed the soil thirty times does it better than he who has done it only once or who attempts it for the first time. In such conditions, the prestige of the adults will be high, the rebelliousness of the sub-adults low. We may think of classical Chinese society as an apt illustration. Where, however, a culture is rather dynamic, where the action system undergoes rapid change, for instance, through technical advances, there the young have a comparative advantage over the old. To have been trained thirty years ago means to be old-fashioned; to have been trained one year ago, to be up-to-date. In such conditions, the prestige of the adults will be low, the rebelliousness of the sub-adults high. Technical strength is not moral strength; the transfer of a feeling of superiority owing to some technical know-how to the moral field is illicit; yet it will take place. The late- and post-capitalist West is laboring under this situation, and the troubles which have recently plagued it, such as widespread drug addiction among teen-agers, have one of their roots in the generally unsettled—"progressive"—state of their economies.

Rebelliousness may, however, be due, not only to a feeling of strength, but also to a feeling of weakness. He who has a strong challenge to face and does not know that he will be able to meet it will be on edge and, therefore, easily disgruntled and rebellious. Nothing is easier to understand from a simple human point of view than this. The sub-adult knows that he will have to make a place for himself in adult society and the prospect may well daunt him, especially in strongly competitive societies. Now dynamical societies are, as a rule, also competitive societies. One of the reasons, and by no means the least, for their dynamism lies in the fact that competition squeezes the last ounce of effort out of their people. We have therefore a curious concatenation of tendencies: while the young are feeling confident (because they are modern), they are at the same time also feeling anxious (because they have not yet proved to themselves that they will make good). "As the . . . child comes into the status of an adolescent, the level of his socially stimulated anxiety becomes higher, for the pressure upon him . . . for attainment . . . becomes greater," writes Allison Davis, who has studied this factor very closely ("Socialization and Adolescent Personality," in *Readings in Social Psychology*, edd. Theodore M. Newcomb and Eugene L. Hartley [New York, 1947], p. 146); "to win prestige in the larger society, the individual is willing to bear a certain level of anxiety. . . . Anxiety leads to striving because only thus can anxiety be reduced to a tolerable level" (pp. 150, 146). Yet striving, while tending to reduce inner tensions, also increases them. The young person in competitive societies is thus caught in a vicious circle which cannot but intensify his unhappiness with the world around.

Into this already very trying mental condition breaks the activation of the sexual interest as a further aggravating factor. The child of seven or eight is not bothered by the traditional ban on pre- and extramarital sex satisfactions; the young person of seventeen or eighteen unavoidably is. Unlike other animal species, *Homo sapiens* has no special rutting season, with suspension of the mating appetite at other times; the pressure is on without interruption. Hence the need arises to dampen this fire all along life's way (see Portmann, *Fragmente*, pp. 81–82). But more has to be achieved in the process of education than simply that drive reduction on the necessity of which even Sigmund Freud has always insisted. Crude, animalic sex rests on a greed for physical excitement and physical pleasure which is not inherently social, which is, indeed, grossly egoistical, and which may lead to a life policy in which the partner is considered merely as a means toward selfish enjoyment and not as an end in himself, a person to be loved. What Gladwin and Sarason say of one society is true of all: "Even the most passionate Trukese lover is acting in a manner which is self-centered" (Gladwin, p. 283), and, "It appears that both men and women view or approach sexual activity in a rather self-centered (narcissistic) way in which the pleasures that might accrue to the partner are somewhat incidental" (Sarason, p. 233; see Thomas Gladwin and S. B. Sarason, *Truk: Man in Paradise*; New York, 1953). We cannot go out of our way here to investigate how animal lust is metamorphosed into human love; not simply social control, but what might be called higher education is involved. But social control *is* involved, too, and it is indeed the *sine qua non* of that higher education, that finer humanization of which we are speaking. Unless society manages to convince the teen-ager that the sexual instinct *is*, to start with, purely beastly, and that it *has to be* tamed, like all inborn beastliness, he will, with a most important part of his being, remain in thrall to animality. Thus the battle for the control of animal propensities has to be fought out on a new front after the activation of the sex instinct. Indeed, it has to be refought then along the whole front, for the sexual mores are apt to appear as symbolic of society's all-round endeavor to clamp restrictions on the individual, to cripple his private life. This reopening of the contest leads to particularly sharp clashes, for the teen-age boy or girl has a personal power of self-assertion which is far higher than that of even an abnormally stubborn child.

But high as this personal power of self-assertion is, it is not (if past experience is something to judge by) high enough to block, in all normal cases, the perfection of the process of socialization. "Teen-age culture," so an expert has written (Campbell, "Adolescent Socialization," p. 840), "is institutionalized 'playing at' serious forms of deviance. . . ." It is a phase of experimentation, of the testing of the powers of social control, of trying to find out how far individual freedom may be extended, how tolerant or intolerant society really is. The outcome of it all has always been a final peacemaking. Exceptions, numerous and painful, confirm the rule that even the recalcitrant youngster turns ultimately into a norm-abiding adult.

This final peacemaking is all the less surprising since many elements in the order of values characteristic of youth cultures are contained in the order of values of the frame society, i.e., of adult society, as well. Ernest Campbell freely uses the term "adolescent society" and implies therefore that it is, in a sense, a society apart from society at large. Yet he writes: "I will not want my use of the term to connote a subversive system nor one necessarily inappropriate to preparation for adult life. . . . Its distinctions in comparison to adult society are typically those of relative emphasis, and when it is subversive or substitutive of adult values, these 'adult values' most typically represent what *some* adults want *some* of the time" (p. 837). Other observers are less optimistic. Thus James S. Coleman writes in his careful study, *The Adolescent Society* (New York, 1961; p. 9): "our society has within its midst a set of small teen-age societies, which focus teen-age interests and attitudes on things far removed from adult responsibilities, and which may develop standards that lead away from those goals established by the larger society." These words echo the concern, the apprehensions, necessarily arising in highly dynamical societies ("our" society is twentieth-century American society), and bring out a need, on the part of adult society, to make an effort to anchor its values, by educational means, more deeply in the minds of the oncoming generation—an effort which, under the influence of overly optimistic concepts of man, or perhaps simply out of a certain lack of will power and energy, is not, it appears, forthcoming. Lawlessness is certainly spreading in permissive societies; the dangers are real. Yet a sharp distinction has to be made between the decay of a certain traditional system of social control, and social control itself. The decay of a certain traditional system of social control has, wherever it has occurred in history, and that has been often, led to the impression that social control as such is decaying. In reality there often occurred an upsurge of new values, new demands of society on the individual, new disciplines. Of course, it is not impossible in the nature of things that an older type of norm-abidingness may undergo involution without a newer version's evolving and taking its place; what has not happened in the past may yet happen in the future. With that dire contingency we plan to deal in the concluding volume of the present work. Our task in this volume was to follow man from childhood to adulthood, from an animal existence to perfected sociality, which is also perfected humanity, and that task we hope now to have fulfilled.

RETARDANTS OF SOCIALIZATION: COMPETITION AND ENVY

80. Resistance to socialization is entirely natural: the organism, equipped by nature with powerful drives, the satisfaction of which promises considerable pleasure, is understandably reluctant to accept limitations and curbs. Of this fact we need say no more. But there are also retardants of socialization which stem, not only from the physical constitution of man, but also from his social circumstances, and the most important of them must be considered; it is the involvement of the individual in a competitive situation and the sentiment of envy which results from it. This sentiment is both universal and intense, as anyone has to admit who is prepared to face the facts. Aeschylus surely drew on a deep knowledge of human nature when he wrote in his *Oresteia*:

> Not many men, the proverb saith,
> Can love a friend who fortune prospereth
> Unenvying; and about the envious brain
> Cold poison clings and doubles all the pain
> Life brings him. His own woundings he must nurse
> And feels another's gladness like a curse
> [*Agamemnon*, trans. Gilbert Murray (London, 1952), p. 69].

Kant, too, in his *Metaphysik der Sitten*, expressed the conviction that "the tendency to envy is inherent in the nature of man" (see Sämtliche Werke III, ed. Karl Vorländer [Leipzig, 1922], p. 316). More recently, Helmut Schoeck has subjected this whole phenomenon to intense study and he, too, judges that envy "is a part of man's basic equipment." Envy, he writes, "is ineluctable, implacable and irreconcilable, is irritated by the slightest differences, is independent of the degree of inequality, appears in its worst form in social proximity or among near relatives, provides the dynamic for every social revolution, yet cannot of itself produce any kind of coherent revolutionary programme" (*Envy*, pp. 147, 247). Clearly, envy is a power to be reckoned with.

So important to the human race is the sentiment which we are considering that two sacred traditions place it, symbolically as it were, near the origin of society: the Hebrew, with its story of Abel and Cain, and the Roman, with its story of Romulus and Remus. In the life of the individual, too, it appears very early, almost as early as it can appear. "Jealousy," Piaget tells us (*Moral Judgment*, p. 317), "appears extremely early in babies: infants of 8 to 12 months often give signs of violent rage when they see another child seated on their mother's knees, or when a toy is taken from them and given to another child." Its incidence and intensity has been carefully studied by David M. Levy. This investigator used experimental methods. He gave children amputation dolls, i.e., dolls from which limbs could be wrenched in fits of anger, and placed them in psychological situations in which jealousy and envy would be experienced and abreacted by attacks on the celluloid symbols of the jealousy-arousing, envied competitors. Levy was greatly surprised by the frequency of overt outbreaks in presumably normal families (*Studies in Sibling Rivalry* [New York, 1937], pp. 9, 10, 11). Of 70 families of nursery school children, 35% showed the presence of ill will stemming from rivalry by the occurrence of such aggressive acts as hitting; of 844 other families, 30% evinced similar phenomena. The observed responses therefore appear to Levy "essentially normal" (p. 11). So frequent were the attacks on the dolls on which the anger of the jealous and envious youngsters was wreaked that the laboratory soon was forced to use clay babies instead of celluloid ones; the stock of the latter was quickly exhausted and could not immediately be restored (p. 21, note).

In line with the frequent incidence of the outbreaks was their high intensity. "In play situations constructed to release the feelings of children in a sibling rivalry experience," Levy writes (p. 72), "essentially similar patterns of activity appear that represent dynamic principles of behavior. The child's response to the mother–baby combination, when hostile, is felt chiefly as an urge to destroy, by immediate primitive release of feeling in the form of biting, crushing and tearing." A systematic survey of the manifestations shows, in addition to violent destruction (i.e., primitive murder), simple murder, torturing, maiming, hurting, causing "accidental" falls, and putting the toy away without attacking it (p. 16). A certain progression in cruelty was clearly observed in Levy's laboratory: "With increasing . . . activity, more primitive forms are revealed" (p. 31). After such comparatively harmless actions as dropping the doll, there follow less harmless ones: slapping, throwing, and the like, and finally tearing apart and crushing (p. 32).

> The mounting of hostility once it is initiated may explode into fury (wild attack on all objects). It may spread beyond the [play] material, requiring more of the same type of object (e.g., insisting on more baby dolls to attack). It may end in many repetitions of the primitive forms. . . . In several cases after demolition of the baby, the child ran around the room shouting in an exultant manner. This activity represented apparently satisfaction of victory—success-

ful completion of an impulse. At the same time, it appeared like a defiant gesture . . . [pp. 70, 64].

"A defiant gesture." Defiance of what? Defiance of whom? Clearly, of social control and its enforcing agents. "Checks to this impulse are already manifest at the three and four year levels. They operate typically in the initial phase of the act, either blocking it or allowing only its partial release" (p. 72). Characteristically, children who had had conflicts with siblings in real life showed less overt aggressivity in the experimental setting than children who were seemingly well adjusted to living with brothers or sisters (p. 27). This is an apparent paradox, but not a real one; children who had gone through conflicts had developed inner inhibitions, much as an organism develops antibodies after a bout with some infectious disease; the others simply gave free rein to their aggressiveness. But the efficacy of social control not only showed itself before, it also showed itself after, the hostile outbreaks. Levy records self-punishing actions and self-justificatory explanations—attempts to restore the situation and to redeem oneself. Such *ex post facto* corrections of illicit conduct had, however, sometimes the effect that, after a while, the illicit conduct recommenced. "Restoring the baby often starts a new line of hostile attacks," Levy states, and he speaks quite generally of an "inefficacy of the self-punishing behavior as a check on further hostility" (pp. 58, 54).

It goes without saying that sibling rivalry may also be the cause of psychopathic developments. An older child, for instance, feeling or fancying itself neglected in favor of a younger one, may return to baby talk in order to improve its own position in the competitive field. Such phenomena, technically known as regression, show once again how important envy is in the context of the process of socialization.

To those of us who consider the peace and harmony of society as so obvious a desideratum that even a value-free sociology cannot possibly gainsay it, the facts revealed by the analysis of sibling rivalry and envy generally must be disturbing, not to say distressing. Yet Helmut Schoeck takes a different tack. His opinion is that envy plays a positive and not a negative role in social life, that it is a help rather than a hindrance to social control. The "roots of social control," he says in his clearest statement (*Envy*, p. 176), "lie in the desire for equality and justice, or in other words the envious impulse, and . . . without them human society as we know it is barely conceivable." Earlier he had written: "Envy is a drive which lies at the core of man's life as a social being, and which occurs as soon as two individuals become capable of mutual comparison. . . . If we were not constantly obliged to take account of other men's envy of the extra pleasure that accrues to us as we begin to deviate from a social norm, 'social control' could not function" (p. 1). And again:

The mutual and spontaneous supervision exercised by human beings over each other—in other words, social control—owes its effectiveness to the envy latent in all of us. If we were quite incapable of envy and, more important, if we were also convinced that our behaviour would not be envied by anyone, that mutual, tentative exploration of the threshold of social tolerance—a constant social process upon which the predictability of social life depends—would never occur. Without envy there could be no social group of any size [p. 87].

It is not necessary to deny that there is a modicum of truth in these sentences. If we, for instance, mobilize the public prosecutor against an official who has taken bribes, a deep-digging analysis of our motives may well reveal that we have acted, in part, as we did because we envied the corrupt person his newly gained wealth. In part, but only in part. It is surely wrong to assert, as Schoeck does, that envy is the mainstay of law-and-order–defending conduct. The present work attempts to base sociology on a view of human nature entirely free from delusion; but it insists, and has to insist, that human culture generates springs of action different from those genetically transmitted to us. Not only envy (an inborn and negative trait), but also love of law and order, of social harmony (an acquired and entirely positive feature), induce us to force social control on others and (even more importantly) to submit to it ourselves. Not only is Schoeck's attitude anthropologically and anthroposophically incorrect, it has problematic implications for social theory and social practice which it is important to bring to light.

As far as social theory is concerned, Schoeck ranges himself, by what he says, on the side of those who regard society as a multiplicity and not a unity—the individualists and nominalists. It would be wrong to go to the opposite extreme and to assert that society is a unity rather than a multiplicity, for instance a quasi-organism, that it must be seen, in Durkheim's phrase, as an object (*une chose*). But the more moderate organicists are surely right when they maintain that the social norms, though originating in the actions of individuals and remaining dependent on individuals for their enforcement, gain an existence of their own and become realities. What men—even envious men—press upon their neighbors are *objective* rules of conduct; they make themselves servants of a law *under* which they live and act and have their being. That law (in the widest sense of the word) enters the developing child and becomes anchored in him, thus creating a condition of intersubjectivity which individualism and nominalism are too blind to discover. But insofar as an objective law becomes anchored in the individuals, insofar as law-abidingness becomes a value for them to the preservation of which they personally commit themselves, the need for envy as a support of social control and societal coherence disappears.

Still more unfortunate are the practical implications of Schoeck's opinion that envy is a necessary prop of the social system. If he were right, the total eradication of this sentiment could never become the aim of social education. He may, to be sure, be correct when he considers that such a total eradication of jealousy in all human beings is impossible; but that is not the issue. The question is whether the un-envious man should be an object and an ideal of pedagogy, and this is what we would assert against Helmut Schoeck. It is possible to eradicate envy *in toto*; it has happened in the case of some men. And it is possible to eradicate it *in parte*, to mitigate it; it has happened and is happening in some, or even many, men. When and where it happens, there emerges, not only the socialized individual, but also the guardian of sociality—the man who defends sociality for its own sake, for social (and not for selfish) reasons.

The fully socialized man feels guilty when he has offended against any of the norms contained in one of the social codes (and these norms include the ninth and tenth commandments, thou shalt not covet thy neighbor's wife and thy neighbor's goods). He feels in this way because he has internalized the norms concerned and compares in his mind what he has done with what he well knows he should have been doing. A bad conscience is in this way entirely internal to and in the moralized person. But it is not in this way that Schoeck conceives it. Where he discusses Paul Tournier's book, *Guilt and Grace* (p. 267), he identifies "sense of guilt" and "fear of the rest of the world's envy"; in other words: he places the fulcrum of a bad conscience outside the person, moralized or otherwise. As can be seen, his analysis underestimates the effect of the process of socialization, which is an *internalization* of norms, and underestimates the depth to which the individual is permeated by, and the degree to which he is possessed by, the social forces.

The truth is that envy (the social consequence of native individual self-preference) is as conquerable as any other selfish trait. Among the passages known to, but significantly not quoted by, Helmut Schoeck is one from *The Conversations of Dr. Johnson* (ed. Raymond Postgate [New York, 1930], p. 209) which expresses the facts in a very straightforward and convincing manner. "We are all envious naturally; but by checking envy, we get the better of it," the great sage writes. "So we are all thieves naturally; a child always tries to get what it wants the nearest way; by good instruction and good habits this is cured, till a man has not even an inclination to seize what is another's; has no struggle with himself about it." This is indeed so, and because it is so we conclude that the complex of sentiments known as jealousy and envy, inherent in and arising from the inescapable competitiveness connected with all social life, is but a retardant of socialization, albeit a powerful one, and neither a peremptory bar to it on the level of individual, nor yet, paradoxically, a support of it on the level of social, life.

In a specific context of his account (p. 193), Schoeck quotes one of Johnson's later emulators, H. L. Mencken: "In the face of another man's good fortune I am as inert as a curb broker before Johann Sebastian Bach. It gives me neither pleasure nor distress" (*The Vintage Mencken*, ed. Alastair Cooke [New York, 1956], p. 75). Is this conquest of jealousy, so we must ask in conclusion, the highest a successful process of socialization can achieve? Surely not. The eradication of the sentiment, however total, is and remains a negative achievement. But it has a positive counterpart as well. It is known to psychologists as identification. Schoeck notes (p. 220) that, in the United States, "mass media have apparently discovered an insatiable demand for pictures of the grand life led by the few." Why do those below love to watch those above them in the social scale during their leisure time? To stir up their ill will? To irritate themselves? Hardly. They gaze at the fabulous wonderland on the screen because beholding it gives them enjoyment, positive pleasure. This enjoyment, this pleasure, is technically called vicarious participation. In the case of a cinema crowd or a home viewer, such identification with people in enviable (yet not actually envied) situations is, of course, but shadowy and weak (though undoubtedly psychologically real). But there are societies—or, rather, communities—in which the operation of the very same mental mechanism is powerful and effective. Has he who reads these lines not sometimes rejoiced at a piece of good fortune which has come to one of his friends? Has he not felt the happiness of a near one as if it were his own? Such is the metamorphosis brought about by the social forces that natural envy can be transmuted into, and replaced by, sympathetic fellow-feeling, indeed, by a we-experience, in which the distance between the potential envier and his enviable neighbor is annihilated— dissolved, as it were, into thin air.

CONSEQUENCES OF THE DEVELOPMENT OF SOCIALITY

81. At the end of an effort, it is useful to ask what it has achieved. In the assumption, then, that the course of socialization is successfully completed (which means that a normal, not a maximal, degree of sociality has been developed in an individual), what has been done for the individual concerned? In what ways does it leave him different from or better than he was before?

The answer, in the most general terms, is that it has unfolded his human potentialities. These potentialities must be there *ab initio*; they must be given by nature. Both *Homo sapiens* and Hymenoptera operate within networks of social relationships, but whereas *Homo sapiens* draws great personal benefit from his cooperation with others insofar as the mind is concerned, Hymenoptera do not. They die, as they are born, somnolent creatures, not to say, mindless machines. This difference is basically physical or organic. The "ants and bees have brains but they have not anything that answers to the cortex," Mead writes (*Mind, Self, and Society*, p. 236).

> The individual members of even the most advanced invertebrate societies do not possess sufficient physiological capacities for developing minds or selves, consciousness or intelligence, out of their social relations and interactions with one another; and hence these societies cannot attain either the degree of complexity which would be presupposed by the emergence of minds and selves within them, or the further degree of complexity which would be possible only if minds and selves had emerged or arisen within them. Only the individual members of human societies possess the required physiological capacities for such social development of minds and selves; and hence only human societies are able to reach the level of complexity, in their structure and organization, which becomes possible as a result of the emergence of minds and selves in their individual members [ibid., note].

Mead is, of course, entirely correct when he speaks of a superiority, on the part of man, in physiological capacities, but we cannot leave the matter there. We must ask wherein this superiority consists. It consists, essentially, not in actually better, but in potentially better, equipment, in the possibility of making wider use of what nature has provided. If only actual, purely physical equipment is considered, it appears that man is in some respects inferior to the other phyla: he has neither the acute eye of the hawk, nor the delicate ear of the gazelle, nor yet the fine nose of the dog. And that actual, purely physical inferiority, insofar as it exists, is permanent; no degree of training, however intense and however prolonged, will enable man to see as well as the hawk or hear as well as the gazelle or smell as well as the dog. The perfectibility of man's performance—even his sensual performance—lies, not in his structures, but in his functioning. It lies, not in his senses, but in what he can *do* with his senses. He can use them for the creation of an objectivized world view, the view of a world from which he is detached and which stands over against him. He can use them, in Freudian terms, for opening up a cleft between the ego and the id, the subject and the object, reason and reality—which means that he can use them for stepping out of nature and turning himself from *homo*, a kind of animal, into *Homo sapiens*, a creature that has left animality behind.

What the student of socialization and its consequences needs at this point is an adequate understanding of man's sensual equipment, and for that he has to go to the psychologist. We must therefore entrust ourselves for a while to writers such as Ernest Schachtel whose great book *Metamorphosis* we have encountered before, and who can, once again, be of assistance. Schachtel distinguishes between two types of senses, the (relatively) autocentric and the (relatively) allocentric ones: those which would leave man enclosed in his own self and narrow setting, in his *Umwelt*, and those which can help him to free himself from this confinement and to achieve an existence of his own relatively loosened from natural constraints—an existence which enables him to gain an objectivized view of the *Welt*. Thermal sense, taste, and smell are predominantly autocentric; sight and hearing are (at first potentially and later actually) predominantly allocentric; touch is in between. "If we examine such senses as taste, smell, proprioception, or the thermal sense," Schachtel writes (p. 87),

> then we discover that they are closer to the objectless primitive sensory organization which registers degrees and qualities of well-being or ill-being than to the objectifying organization of the more highly developed human senses. . . . The experience of seeing [on the other hand] is predominantly one of seeing independently existing objects, an environment structured into a variety of objects which are related to each other and to the perceiver.

Schachtel calls the autocentric senses "feeling-bounded" (p. 90), and we may complete his terminology and contrastment by describing the allocentric senses as "knowledge-giving." This brings out the salient point. The senses popularly (and correctly) called the lower ones place us close to the animal with its "objectless primitive sensory organization which registers degrees and qualities of well-being or ill-being," while the senses popularly (and correctly) called the higher ones reveal to us "independently existing objects, an environment structured into a variety of objects related to each other and to the perceiver"—in other words, give us knowledge, make us into men. Or, to use once again Freudian terminology: the lower, autocentric senses are the instruments of the pleasure principle, while the higher, allocentric ones are the tools of the reality principle, the tools of our human ego, not the instruments of our animalic id.

It is quite clear, from what has just been said, that higher development (which includes socialization) consists in a shift from reliance on the lower to emphasis on the higher senses—in other words, in a restructuring of the sensual system—and in this, phylogenesis and ontogenesis for once agree.

> Ontogenetically and phylogenetically, when life begins it does not have an object world but proceeds only in degrees of well-being or ill-being, in degrees of nervous excitation, which, although often caused by agents of the environment, is not referred to the environment by the organism or probably does not

even show, in the earliest stages, bodily localization. These excitations evoke reactive movements, but they do not lead to the perception of objects. . . . In the most primitive linkage between organism and environment, then, "perception" consists not of the perception of an environment but of changes in excitation. The neonate probably feels these mainly, but not entirely, as varying degrees of comfort and discomfort. In contrast to this, adult man's perception shows the highest degree of objectification. In his perceptual experience he encounters a world of objects among which he moves and which he is able to perceive at any time during his waking hours, relatively independent of what momentary biological needs drive him and what temporary moods dominate him [pp. 86, 87].

What Ernest Schachtel explains in these sentences belongs to the safest possessions of traditional and tested epistemology. As early as the seventeenth century, René Descartes had written:

During our early days, our mind was so closely identified with the body that the only ideas it entertained were those with the aid of which it perceived what affected the body; such ideas were not even connected with any reference to the outside world, but merely registered the pain when something untoward happened to the body or the pleasure when it was something agreeable. At a later stage, when the body succeeded in securing a benefit or escaping a hurt, the mind domiciled in it began to realize that what is desired or what is eschewed exists on the outside [*Principes de la philosophie*, edd. Charles Adam and Paul Tannery, Oeuvres de Descartes x (Paris, 1964), pp. 58, 59; free and shortened translation].

Lest we (or Ernest Schachtel) be accused of drawing an oversimplifying distinction, let us add, before moving on, that there may be an autocentric—"feeling-bounded"—use of the eyes, just as there may be an allocentric—"knowledge-giving"—use of the nose. "Autocentric functioning of sight takes place in the newborn and predominates for a considerable period of time in infancy . . . ," Schachtel states (*Metamorphosis*, p. 105), and we may add that allocentric functioning of smell takes place in the grown-up and reaches, in some at least, considerable efficiency. We must also distinguish shades of autocentricity and allocentricity in the use of the same organ. "The perception of color, by itself, does not permit objectification, while the perception of form does," Schachtel explains. "Colors are not only and usually not even primarily 'recognized' but they are *felt* as exciting and soothing, dissonant or harmonious, clamorous or tranquil, vivid or calm, joyous or somber, warm or cool, disturbing and distracting or conducive to concentration and tranquillity." In contrast, form perception and form recognition are, comparatively speaking, detached or neutral in quality (pp. 108, 109).

These last considerations lead us to the threshold of another topic. From objectification comes objectivity, or at least the capacity for it. While our more autocentric senses serve, and to some extent preserve, our subjection to physical pleasure and pain and thus to animality (remember here what Bentham calls the pleasures of the palate and the pleasures of the venereal appetite), our more allocentric senses, and our unfoldment of them in the course of social life, not only give us far-reaching independence from nature, but even prepare our domination over nature, for they, and they alone, enable us to take the stance of independent observer, of scientist and technologist, the stance of men who know what they see and learn how to manipulate what can be manipulated. But before we more closely concern ourselves with this further gain arising from socialization, we must yet explore a little more fully the sociality and socialization of our specifically humanizable senses.

In what has gone before, we have emphasized, and surely with sufficient energy, that in the beginning *all* the senses, including sight, are only *potentially* and not actually knowledge-giving and in this sense truly human, and thus there arises the question why and how this potentiality is transmuted into actuality, why and how the great promise is fulfilled. At this crucial point we encounter the fact which the sociologist has to stress above all others—the primacy of social experience in the process which forms the human mind and, indeed, all culture. Nature would never do it and could never do it. For a purely natural creature—be it an animal or be it a human organism—is enclosed in a nexus, or, rather, a network, of stimuli and responses, impacts and reactions, and there is neither a reason for, nor a mechanism of, escape. Here, if anywhere, we behold a system of interdetermination such as the disciples of Newtonianism have ever and again postulated. But man is caught in the coils of this mechanism only with his body, and he belongs as well to another system in which freedoms are possible, indeed fundamental. There is the freedom to know; there is the freedom to assert one's will; there is the freedom to subjugate nature; and there is, last but not least, the freedom to discipline oneself. There is, as Kant would have expressed it, not only phenomenal, but also noumenal, man. Noumenal man, however, is the product of social life.

Social life begins, schematically speaking, with the relationship between mother and child, and this relationship is, in many senses of the word, the inception of all humanization, including the objectification and knowledge of the surrounding world. But it is no more than an inception. "The infant, at first, is not capable of distinguishing between himself and whatever persons or objects of his environment come sufficiently close to him to affect him," Schachtel writes (pp. 301–302). Even "the mother's breast is not, at first, part of 'another person'; it belongs to the undifferentiated little world of the infant, is part of his 'own cosmic entity,' as Sullivan puts it" in "Conceptions of Modern Psychiatry" (*Psychiatry*, 3, No. 1 [February 1940], 15). Of course, as soon as the neonate turns into an infant, there is a change. Feeling the mother's body is not proprioception, and a vague, dreamlike apprehension of another organism, another object, takes place. But this experience, such as it is, is not really knowledge-giving and, hence, not decisively humanizing. Indeed, the whole specific character of the mother–child relationship excludes the possibility of developing personal independence from the environment and, with it, the formation of an objectivized view of it. For the mother is essentially the infant's servant. She does what he wills and needs, and is not, for that reason, experienced as a resister. But it is only the experience of resistance which stimulates and establishes the conviction that there is a duality of self and other, will and will—a first and basic duality which is later joined by another modeled on it, the duality of self and thing, will and world.

Of that independence-giving, ego-forming, and objective-knowledge–preparing experience, of that resistance of alter to ego, there is plenty in the nursery, in what Cooley has called the primary group. Brothers and sisters are not servants of the self, they are in all normal cases typical resisters; and it is through meeting them and contending with them that the self apprehends and comprehends the existence of other selves as well as his own. We are keeping then, as the reader already knows, to Cooley's classical theory of the looking-glass self, though we would place the stress on the element of conflict rather than on that of simple coexistence. We spoke of all this in Section 73 and need not repeat what we said there. We would only add that the mother, too, might act as resister at this later stage and even replace brothers and sisters where such are lacking. She, too, may refuse to continue as the self's servant and assert herself against the erstwhile nursling. But if she does so, she plays a second role, not her first and natural one, but her additional and cultural one—not her role as wet nurse and caretaker, but her role as civilizer and educator, which is a very different task.

Inside the primary groups of which we are speaking, there exists a socially controlled situation; it is almost impossible to imagine a nursery or a kindergarten in which there is no adult supervisor to ensure peace and organize cooperative play. But as soon as there is cooperation, another stage in socialization supervenes. Children learn to recognize and to understand the roles of others; they make these roles the objects of their knowledge and thereby objectify even their own role—which means as well their own selves. This is the fact on which George Herbert Mead has placed the strongest stress, and his analysis has to be seen together with that of Cooley, as its complement and not as its competitor. We would say that they refer respectively to different phases (which may, however, be telescoped, at least to some extent): the formation of the (looking-glass) self logically precedes the imaginative taking of the roles of others of which Mead rightly makes so much. "The self," he writes (*Mind, Self, and Society*, p. 335), "arises in the development of the behavior of the social form that is capable of taking the attitude of others involved in the same co-operative activity. The pre-condition of such behavior is the development of the nervous system which enables the individual to take the attitude of the others." This is entirely true, but taking the attitude of others and thereby objectifying their role and one's own has not only physico-organic but experiential presuppositions. It cannot take place unless the fission between self and other has already occurred. Mead's stage can only be attained after Cooley's is successfully gone through. But Cooley's stage, properly understood, is not yet one of social integration; it is still one of interindividual explication. We see again that conflict is at the root of cooperation for it is conflict which creates the ego and the alter who can take cognizance of each others' and their own respective roles and thereby become capable of coordinating their activities into an interactive whole.

But the ability to perceive objects and even the actual perception of them are not yet sufficient to establish that integrated *visus mundi* which is the hallmark of fully unfolded *Homo sapiens*. For there are far too many objects to be seen. The danger is that they may move in and out of the mind without structuring themselves and leaving a permanent content behind. It is necessary that there be more or less systematic selection, that, as we expressed it in *The Sociology of Knowledge* (London, 1958; see esp. p. 108), some of the materials of knowledge should be elevated to the rank of true objects of knowledge. We spoke, in the last paragraphs, of objectification and objects, and that was necessary for the sake of the clarity of the account. The term "objectification" was certainly correct, the word "object" was somewhat less appropriate. When we speak of objects of knowledge, we may mean things which pass momentarily over the screen of our mind, or we may mean things which become permanently established there; when we speak of knowledge, we may mean transient attention to them or we may mean a secure knowing hold on them. Only a principle of selection can give us objects, and knowledge of them, in the second, the fuller, sense. The principle of selection, however, is the order of values which our society provides us with; we become lastingly aware only of those materials of knowledge on which our society has taught us to place a positive value accent. We can perhaps further clarify what we wish to explain here by using the terms, familiar to philosophers, of percept and concept. Percepts—that which we see with our senses—are the things which pass through (Latin: *per*) our minds; concepts—that which we define in our intellects—are those fewer things which our minds can be said to *con*tain. Since we pointed all this out in considerable detail in *The Sociology of Knowledge*, we shall not pursue the topic any further here. But we had to bring it up in the present context because we are trying, at present, to show what socialization means. By giving us an order of values and thereby reducing the sensuous manifold to manageable proportions, it enables us, not only to perceive, but even to conceive of, our objective world.

Needless to say, learning how to perceive and learning how to conceive are separate processes merely in the scholar's mind. In reality, the two abilities are acquired *uno actu*, or nearly so, for the impact of society on the developing mentality is one great comprehensive wave, carrying in it or with it all that culture has to give.

In the society in which, and against which, the present book is being written, there is so much inherent individualism and materialism, so deep a conviction that the human body means much, sociality and culture little, that we must support our position, however briefly, by a side glance at strictly scientific work in the field. D. O. Hebb's study *The Organization of Behavior* is based on up-to-date physiology; it is scientific in the technical sense of the term. Yet even he regrets the current idea that we see simply by dint of inborn mechanisms; seeing has to be learned. "The perception of simple objects seems so simple and direct," he writes, "that [apparently] it cannot be complex and the result of a long-drawn-out learning process. But . . . the learning process *is* necessary. . . . I propose that the human capacity for recognizing patterns without eyemovement is possible only as the result of an intensive and prolonged visual training that goes on . . . over a period of 12 to 16 years at least" (pp. 48, 46). Crucial in this context is the *identification* of objects—the very purpose, for a thinking being, of the act of vision. A "figure is perceived as having identity when it is seen immediately as similar to some figures and dissimilar to others . . ." (p. 26). This, Hebb has found in his experimental work, is impossible without training. Shibutani, too, reports about some experiments which show the importance of learning—cultural learning—for the physical act of perception, or, rather, the total act of perception, in which physical and cultural elements are deeply merged, as far as mature man is concerned. A room was constructed with a sloping floor and a rear wall receding toward the left and other special features which would tend to make objects in the room appear distorted. A married woman seeing her husband and a stranger in that room reported that the stranger appeared to her changed in shape and size, but asserted at the same time that she saw her husband undistorted. Repetitions of the experiment yielded the same result. Such investigations, Shibutani tells us (*Society and Personality*, p. 588), "reveal that what is perceived depends upon interpersonal relations to a far greater extent than had been suspected."

One other experiment which should be mentioned here because it links the phenomenon of the socialization of perception with the value-guided selectivity of attention on which the sociology of knowledge insists concerns distance vision. In the case of two persons having (physically) equally acute eyes, one may, on occasion, see better than the other: namely, if the one values the objects in the field of vision more highly than does the other. He will perceive them more quickly, more clearly, and at a measurably greater distance than his associate (or control) who has not learned to consider them as particularly value-laden (see A. Irving Hallowell, "Cultural Factors in the Structuralization of Perception," in *Social Psychology at the Crossroads,* edd. John H. Rohrer and Muzafer Sherif [New York, 1951], pp. 164, 165; see also p. 191).

We see: just as observational and experimental work bears out the assertion that the functioning of the senses is deeply influenced by the socio-cultural factor, so it confirms the basic thesis of the sociology of knowledge. Schachtel, who has no knowledge of such writers as Scheler or Karl Mannheim, yet shares, without realizing it, their decisive opinion. He distinguishes simple attention from focal attention and, where he does so, he quotes from William James (*Principles of Psychology* [New York, 1950], I 402): "My experience is what I agree to attend to." (He might as well have quoted from James's next sentence: "Only those items which I notice shape my mind—without selective interest, experience is an utter chaos.") What I agree to is, of course, what my society has taught me to see in a positive light, to value; hence, the value structure of society internalized in me determines what I shall experience. Schachtel also writes, and thereby comes very close to the classical formulations of the sociology of knowledge: "What is not focally perceived is not in full awareness. What is not accessible to focal awareness for reason of man's limited horizon remains unknown to him." And elsewhere: "attentive perception reveals object aspects qualitatively and quantitatively different from those yielded by inattentive, peripheral, and background conceptions." In this context Schachtel also gives it as his opinion that development leads the infant increasingly from a nearly animalic to a fully cultural experiencing of reality. It leads from "the predominance of the experience of impinging stimuli as disturbing the homeostatic state of comfortable embeddedness" to the "perception of objects and object qualities," and this great shift is "closely linked with the development of attention" (*Metamorphosis*, pp. 251, note; 254, 137). The perfection of attention, however, is focal attention; focusing, on its part, is selection—selection of the object to be focused on; and selection applies an order of values. As can be seen, the whole of the sociology of knowledge is contained in Schachtel's psychological analysis, simply because the observed facts have led him to the very same results the sociologists of knowledge have reached by more speculative paths.

Another science which is basically descriptive and hence undeniably close to the facts is social anthropology, and it, too, supports our thesis that our mental capacities are society's, and not only nature's, gifts to us. In his essay "Cultural Factors in the Structuralization of Perception," A. Irving Hallowell writes the following sentences which confirm both the socialization of the human senses and the determination of the human world view by the imposition, on the individual, of a socially elaborated and transmitted order of values:

> cultural variables are inevitably constituents of human perception. . . . once viewed in its total behavioral context, perception cannot be isolated from action, that is, from motivated and goal-directed behavior. Consequently, the perceptual field of the organism must be structuralized in a manner that bears a direct relation to its activities, no matter what these may be. . . . Since the human being makes his personal adjustments with reference to the attributes of a particular socio-cultural system, his basic perceptual processes will, in part, be influenced by the "cultural set" imposed by his group membership. . . . The fact that the human organism becomes selectively sensitized to certain arrays of stimuli rather than others is most certainly a function of the individual's membership in one cultural group, rather than another, whatever other factors may be involved. . . . Culture patterns considered as traditional instrumentalities of human existence function as selective agencies in the emergence of the kind of behavioral environment in which a group of human beings carry on their activities. Consequently the psychological field in which human behavior takes place is always culturally constituted, in part, and man's responses are never reducible in their entirety to stimuli derived from an "objective" or surrounding world, in the physical or geographic sense [pp. 166, 168, 167].

The human use of man's animal senses is powerfully promoted by one particular social institution—or, as we perhaps should say in the present context, by one particular gift of society to the individual—namely, language. According to prevailing prejudice, we first see objects with our physical eyes, and then we append to them labels, words to describe them, which are always secondary. In fact, however, it is to some extent, not to say largely, the other way around. Words come to us from surrounding society, and they tell us what we should look for and see. They open our eyes. They help us (a) in the objectification and fixation of our experience, and (b) in the selection of objects to be made permanent elements in our world view. Language teaches us both how to separate and how to integrate, how to discriminate and how to combine disjointed percepts into unitary concepts. Words are our guide to knowledge. The fashionable trend in philosophy which deplores the interposition of language between our senses and reality forgets that without this medium we should have no minds at all. It is true, of course, and in this respect the critics of language have their point, that words are not neutral—value-free—instruments of thought, but value-laden and, hence, unscientific. But they are so only because they emerge from life and retroactively play a helpful part in life. Hallowell (pp. 174, 175) gives us a clear example illustrating the way they operate. Some primitive societies carefully distinguish between cross cousins (for a male, mother's brother's daughter or father's sister's daughter) and parallel cousins (for a male, mother's sister's daughter or father's brother's daughter). The former are allowed to marry one another; the latter, not. These two categories are given different names. The word used for cross cousins has the overt meaning, or at least the covert undertone, "sweetheart," while the word used for parallel cousin is devoid of such suggestions and comes closer to our "sister" or "lady," denoting a need to be sexually disinterested. This makes social control, the maintenance of the marriage pattern at the base of these societies, much easier. But what interests us here above all else is the fact that these words tend to steer perception, to determine how a girl is seen and what is seen in her. Those who live under this discipline will notice a "sweetheart's" sexual attractiveness, her sexual characteristics, much more quickly, much more fully, and much more vividly than the corresponding features in a young woman differently described.

Together with the other mental capacities of which nature provides merely the physical structures, but society the human, i.e., real, functioning, we also receive the gift of memory properly so called. There is indeed a kind of memory of the body coming to us at times unexpectedly and uncalled-for, for instance, the vague resurfacing, when we taste a certain taste or smell a certain smell, of earlier occasions of the same or similar experience, but this is no more than a dreamlike feeling and does not, by itself, yield a definite image. It would be better to speak of this phenomenon, with Schachtel (*Metamorphosis*, p. 159), as passive resensing rather than as active memory, the core of which is the ability of voluntary recall. Memory, as we usually understand it, has, in addition to its physical substratum, three presuppositions, all socio-cultural. There must be, first of all, at least the rudiments of a personality. We recognize how true this is when we learn that our earliest memories are placed in about the fourth year of life. As long as the concept of I has not developed, the small child (just like the animal) is oriented toward the present and the future, not toward the past. There must be a recognition of the self as an ongoing and abiding process, before the events of yesterday and yesteryear can become significant. A second presupposition is that ascendancy of the humanizable over the more animalic senses on which so much else depends too. "Allocentric perceptions in sight and hearing lend themselves much more readily to voluntary recall than perceptions in the autocentric sense modalities," Schachtel states (p. 162), and we all know how true this is. We are habitually quite good at conjuring up again the image of a church we have seen or the sound of singing we have heard in it, but bad at realizing once more the smell of the incense to which we were exposed there. Words, however, are even more easily retained than sights and sounds, and so language is a third (socio-cultural) presupposition of an effective memory. No doubt, memory has its apparatus in the brain, but only through social influences does it go beyond the ability to resense and become the ability to recall.

One of the most outstanding works grappling with the phenomena of memory is Marcel Proust's incomparable artistic achievement *A la Recherche du temps perdu*. A mood of sadness lies over its pages because of the realization that our nostalgia for the things past can never be completely sated and overcome: what recollection offers us is always comparatively pale, comparatively lifeless. Yet what is loss from one point of view is gain from another. A creature who can recall the past is even more securely out of the clutches of nature than a creature who can merely see it in objective terms; he has, as it were, stepped back one yard further. But there is another important point that we have to notice here: memory is not only a help to objectivation, or even a more advanced form of it; it is also a guide to objectivity. We act in heat, we recollect in (at least relative) coolness. The stepping out of nature, and back from it, is followed by a turning around and facing it—facing it in a conquering mood. There is an easy transition from knowing (*savoir*) to ruling (*pouvoir*): as St. Thomas Aquinas would have expressed it, liberation from nature is "ordered to" domination over nature. From thought springs scientific and technological thought, and both stem from man's socialization, the latter even more than the former, more than simple and unsophisticated thought.

Here again we find that the growing ascendancy of the allocentric over the autocentric senses and the development of language are of crucial importance; they prepare objectivity, if they do not indeed half-and-half achieve it. The "sensations of hearing and seeing as such are indifferent, as far as their relation to pleasure and displeasure goes," writes Schachtel (*Metamorphosis*, p. 91), "quite in contrast to tasting and smelling, where the sensation itself is pleasant or unpleasant." As far as language is concerned, it is and must be intersubjective: How could it otherwise be a bridge between man and man? But if it is and must be intersubjective, it is and must be semi-objective. If I say "dog" and you say "'dog," our personal meanings may only partially coincide; I may be thinking of a Great Dane and you of a Pekingese. Yet there must be enough agreement between us to make a conversation possible, and that means that the sound pattern "dog" must have an objective reference, in addition to whatever subjective connotation it may carry for different people. Mead makes this point very strongly, and his statements may almost be called classical: when we use words, "We put ourselves in the attitude of all, and that which we all see is that which is expressed in universal terms . . ." (*Mind, Self, and Society*, p. 331). But since thinking is couched in, and proceeds with the aid of, words, i.e., universal terms, it, too, is necessarily semi-objective; objectivity is an implication, a reflex, a product of sociality. "Thinking always implies a symbol which will call out the same response in another that it calls out in the thinker. Such a symbol is a universal of discourse; it is universal in its character. . . . Our symbols are all universal. You cannot say anything that is absolutely particular; anything you say that has any meaning at all is universal" (pp. 147, 146). ("Anything you say" includes, of course, anything you say to yourself; like so many others, Mead defines thought as a conversation with oneself.) He draws, out of these considerations, one of his most crucial concepts, the concept of the generalized other, which we might transcribe, for our own purposes here, as the concept of the objectivized self. Linking this, his crowning term, with his preparatory analysis, the insight that we become selves by enacting, in imagination, the role sets of others insofar as we are the objects of their thought and action (see above, p. 64), he writes as follows:

> The very universality and impersonality of thought and reason is . . . the result of the given individual taking the attitudes of others toward himself, and of his finally crystallizing all these particular attitudes into a single attitude or standpoint which may be called that of the "generalized other." . . . The self is universal, it identifies itself with a universal "me" [pp. 90, 331].

In this way, ordinary discourse—because of its sociality—prepares scientific discourse. The ego which, in and through the use of language (the basic institution of society), identifies itself with a universal me is also an ego which disengages itself with some finality from its own id; it overcomes the organism-based pleasure principle and climbs to the level at which implementation of the reality principle—more simply expressed: rationality—becomes possible. What Freud calls the reality principle, the principle of rationality, implies two things: a seeing of the world which is not distorted by organic drives, i.e., a seeing which is objective in the sense of factual and clear, and the possibility of using the world for purposes which are not imposed by the organism but freely decided upon by the ego, purposes which may indeed include richer satisfactions (but then willingly granted ones) for the id, but which may just as well concern the realization of ideal schemes.

The thesis which we are arguing here—namely, that the scientific mode of thought arises from our social mode of existence, not from any refinement of our physical apparatus—gains powerful support from a study of the development of logical thinking. Only socialized man knows how to think logically: logic appears in mental phenomena at exactly the time when true sociality shows itself, between seven and eight years of age (see Piaget, *Language and Thought*, pp. 64, 70–71). Piaget distinguishes egocentric and communicable logic (p. 46), but only the latter—logic functioning within a social framework—deserves the name. True, egocentric logic, the "logic" of the child, may sometimes come to the same conclusions as logic properly so called, but its method is the very opposite of sound ratiocination; it is a method of hit and miss. "The mind leaps from premise to conclusion at a single bound, without stopping on the way. . . . Little value is attached to proving, or even checking, propositions" (p. 47). Given the self-enclosedness of the child, why should he not rely on intuition, and why should he bother about proof if intuition gives him complete conviction? Everything is different in the case of the person who has learned to live, communicate, and interact with others. He cannot expect these others to perform the same impetuous bounds forward as he, and he must be ready to prove his propositions if others are to be convinced. "Ego-centrism," says Piaget (p. 238), is "obedient to the self's good pleasure and not to the dictates of impersonal logic. . . . only the habits of discussion and social life will lead to the logical point of view. . . ." In this way, we owe methodical deduction, that indispensable tool of science, to sociality.

Connected with the child's innocence of formal logic is his lack of interest in causal analysis and causal exploration (which brings induction prominently into the discussion here). This lack of interest is, first of all, a fact. Piaget noted, and later analyzed, the questions of two children, called for short Lev and Pie, during a certain space of time, and showed that of Lev's 224 questions only two were attempts to find causal explanations; of Pie's 173 questions, none. This may at first appear somewhat surprising, but the surprise vanishes when the child's lack of sociality is taken into account. The autocentric child sees the world as a coherent whole; he is less interested in the detail and consequently also in what concrete facts may be the causes or the effects of others. Indeed, it is not too much to assert that he does not distinguish cause and effect at all. As everything appears connected with everything else, the child fails to grasp the whole problem and the whole task of causal analysis. It is for the same reason that children have no concept of chance. Since everything is connected with everything else, they feel that there will be some reason somewhere for the appearance of anything or everything; as far as the reason for some concrete phenomenon is concerned, they simply could not care less. Piaget speaks of a "subjective synthesis" which contrasts with an objective synthesis presupposing analysis; he speaks of a "syncretistic perception" which simply "excludes analysis" (pp. 140, 132).

All this changes when objectivation (and that is to say, socialization) supervenes. We encounter the same temporal threshold as before: "precausality tends to disappear at the same age as ego-centrism, viz., between 7 and 8" (p. 237). Even a close watch on children's language reveals the great transformation which takes place at this juncture. A youngster of six or even of seven will connect two sentences in an account by the copula "and" or "and then," while one of seven or eight will strive to bring in the words "because" or "since" if he can. The talk of smaller children is fact-stating, not causally explanatory. This "factual way of talking," Piaget states (p. 119), "is unadapted to causality. . . ." The "child lays stress on the events themselves rather than on the relations of time (order) or cause which unite them. . . ." The "feeling of relations remains ego-centric, and therefore incommunicable and practically unconscious" (pp. 107, 117). But socialization brings the need to communicate; the need to communicate in turn brings the desire to explain and hence to explain logically and causally. In "order to argue, demonstrations and logical relations etc. have to be made explicit, all of which runs counter to the ego-centrism of the child under 7. . . . the more the ego is made the centre of interests, the less will the mind be able to depersonalize its thought . . . ," writes Piaget (pp. 71, 237). We can complete his and our argument by turning this last statement around. The more the ego is made the locus of sociality, we can say, the less difficult it will be for the mind to operate in terms of objectivity, logic, causality, and science. "It is in ego-centric thought that we give rein to our imagination. When we think socially, we are far more obedient to the 'imperative of truth' " (p. 124).

"The imperative of truth"—with this powerful term we come to a kind of climax in our exploration. Among the many gifts which socialization gives to man, the concept of truth is, from many points of view, the most valuable. The infant does not possess it; it comes to the individual from those around him. It would not seem necessary to call in expert witnesses to support our analysis in this respect (though expert witnesses are, of course, available, great child psychologists like William Stern and Jean Piaget; see the latter's *Moral Judgment*, esp. pp. 143, 144, 160–63). There are two equally good reasons why the infant does not have, and cannot have, a concept of truth. The first is that he has, to begin with, no world view consisting of determinate objects. If truth is, in the medieval philosophers' language, an *adaequatio rei et intellectus*, i.e., the establishment of an agreement between thing and thought, then it is unavailable as long as things (quiddities) have not emerged from the inbeating waves of sensation. But just as important as this first, epistemological, reason is the second, which is ethical. The infant, egocentric as he is, has no idea of obligation. But truth, or, rather, truthfulness, is above all an obligation we owe to our fellow-men. As long as they do not count, as long as they appear merely as servo-organisms to the self, the infant does not feel that he owes them anything and consequently that he owes them the truth. Why should he not romance? Social control has no grip on him and so he drifts in any direction his fancy suggests to him. "Naturally inclined as he is to think about himself rather than about others, the child does not see the full significance of deceit. . . . For the need to speak the truth and even to seek it for oneself is only conceivable in so far as the individual thinks and acts as one of society . . ." (ibid., pp. 143, 160).

Some important classics of sociology, such as Auguste Comte, have maintained that there is a causal connection between truth in the epistemological and truth (or truthfulness) in the ethical sense of the word; as we conceive the former, that is to say, as we elaborate a scientific image of reality, we also lay the basis for the latter, a strict sticking to the truth in our relations with other men. If there is such a concatenation at all, it is a very brittle one. Machiavelli was more realistic when he suggested that the good politician knows the facts and cleanses his own mind of delusions, but at the same time tries to fill the minds of his adversaries with as many misconceptions as he can lodge there, for this is the way to defeat them in contest and conflict, when the time for it comes. Still, most men, unlike most Machiavellian politicians, are and remain reasonably truthful in their dealings with their fellow-men; but this virtue arises, not as a reflex of objectivation, of the evolution of a scientific world view, *per se*, but from an educational effort instituted and maintained *ad hoc* by the agents of socialization.

This brings us back to the great subject of the internalization of norms and values with which we have dealt at length and which we do not need to reopen. But here, where we have undertaken to discuss, not what society demands of us (truthfulness is essentially such a demand), but, on the contrary, what it has given to us, we must still consider two further gifts which we receive: the gift of sympathy and the gift of conscience. It might be said that sympathy and conscience, too, are demands on us, that we are required to show sympathy and to act in good conscience. But the very words which we have just used prove that more is involved than duty; we are speaking, not of the duty to *show* sympathy, but of the capacity to *feel* sympathy, and not of the duty to *act* in good conscience, but of the capacity to be *moved* by it. These two capacities belong to the great metamorphosis of the inner man, his transformation from an animalic organism into a cultural personality.

A critical reader of these pages may well be inclined to ask how sympathy can be fittted into the framework of an analysis which starts from the basic fact of natural self-preference and insists on it at every turn. But it must be remembered that self-preference, rooted in the instinct of self-preservation, dominates only the human body and not the human mind. Provided the self-preferential urgings of the body can be held at bay, and that is entirely possible for the will which is master in its own house, there is no reason why sympathetic feelings should not spring up within the mind.

We have just said: sympathetic *feelings*. Sympathy is an emotion and as such it is closely connected with bodily states. When our sympathy is aroused, our heart may beat faster or feel constricted, our pulse may quicken or falter, and so on, and so forth. Does this not indicate that sympathy is basically a somatic phenomenon or at least soma-based? By no means. Sympathy has somatic correlates, the bodily apparatus is involved in it, but the salient question is *how* and *by what* the body is mobilized. We are "moved," but what is it which moves us? It is a mental experience: the experience of witnessing, and participating in, the joy or the sorrow of another human being. Even unsophisticated observation proves that it is quite easy for a purely mental experience to affect the body, for instance, the circulation. When somebody criticizes or insults us, we blush or redden, even if our whole physique has been at rest and in no way exposed to appropriate stimuli. It is our mind, acting through the brain, which is the ultimate cause of the dilation of our blood vessels (and it makes no difference whatsoever that science has been unable to explain just how this happens or can happen).

Because sympathy is not a physical, but a mental, phenomenon, we cannot expect it in full bloom within the animal realm. (It must be remembered here that we are speaking at present of fellow-feeling between unconnected strangers, not, for instance, of parental love and its over-spillings; maternal solicitude is indeed a body-based and generally animalic emotion; but this is an entirely different matter.) Those who feel constrained, by their underlying materialism, to try to argue away the difference between man and beast have carried out all sorts of experiments in order to show the presence of a more than vestigial element of sympathy even in beasts, for instance, in rats. Justin Aronfreed has subjected these experiments to a very close scrutiny and come to the conclusion that they do not prove what they set out to prove. "A concept of altruism cannot properly be applied to the findings of those experiments in which animals merely have been shown to perform actions which relieve the distress of another animal," he writes.

> It appears almost invariably that the behavior is reinforced by explicit rewards . . . or is a cooperative effort to produce a mutually beneficial set of outcomes for both self and other. . . . The experiments are carried out under conditions where the performing animal might well experience the observed distress cues as having the value of aversive events which impinge directly upon itself. . . . The results of these experiments do not permit the inference that the animals are behaving sympathetically [*Conduct and Conscience*, pp. 150, 141].

We are meeting here once more (and, luckily, for the last time in these pages) the unfortunate tendency to conclude from certain outer similarities to definite inner identities, an entirely illicit procedure. Artistic sensibilities, for instance, have been attributed to animals, just as sympathetic ones have been credited to them. But what has emerged when truly scientific methods have been applied? A good example is the singing of mice. "Post mortem examination of such performers," writes Perry Scholes in his *Oxford Companion to Music* (London, 1950; p. 1128), "has disclosed the disappointing fact that they do not, like . . . the humans, sing out of the joy or sorrow of their heart, but merely out of an inflammation of their respiratory organs, their song being, in fact, merely an accidentally artistic wheeze."

In the assumption, then, that sympathy properly so called is a specifically human and a specifically mental phenomenon, how can its appearance be explained? We have already pointed out, in our Introduction, in sketching the framework of our investigation, that the assumption of a communal mind, dwelling both in the object of sympathy and in him who feels it (the theory of Schopenhauer and Eduard von Hartmann) is too unprovable and unproved to command assent. There remain therefore two approaches, both of which have the facts on their side and which we must try to reconcile. The one (true in itself but insufficient as an explanation) is subjectivistic and individualistic; the other, which lays bare the real roots of all fellow-feeling, operates with the concept of intersubjectivity.

The more subjectivistic and individualistic approach argues that the child finds and observes sympathy in the social setting in which he grows up. He himself experiences innumerable times the benefits which it yields. Yet gladly receiving sympathy does not, by itself, induce a young person gladly to give it. (This, too, has been demonstrated by experiment; see Aronfreed, *Conduct and Conscience*, p. 157.) But he finds and observes something else: the fact that sympathetic emotion, as well as the altruistic conduct to which it often leads, is strongly approved of in the environment. In technical language: it is reinforced by social approval. No wonder, therefore, if it grows. Aronfreed speaks of "selective contingent reinforcement of external outcomes which are associated with the relief of another person's distress" and explains that "the reinforcing outcomes of sympathetic behavior may take the form of approval, affection, or other direct social rewards for the child." So far, then, sympathy appears to be something bought and is therefore no true spontaneous sympathy, i.e., no sympathy coming from the inner core of man. But a process of internalization soon takes place. "These types of outcomes can produce an attachment of potentially reinforcing affective value to the intrinsic correlates of the child's sympathetic behavior, so that the maintenance of the behavior is no longer entirely dependent on either its observable consequences for others or its direct consequences for the child" (p. 151). Reward appears in this light merely an educational tool, a crutch, a walking school which the youngster has to use for a while but which he is going to discard, and which he would be ashamed to use again after he has come to man's estate.

No doubt, these passages point to an essential element in the ontogenesis of sympathetic emotion. Unless its tender shoots are fostered by society at large, and more especially by the agents of socialization, they will come to nothing. Yet the great slogan of selective reinforcement is not sufficient to explain the development of which we are speaking. True, not only may reward drop off, but the very expectation of reward, and the emotion of sympathy may come to be seen as a value in itself, something which ought to exist for its own sake. But if there were nothing but personal advantage at the very root of sympathy, it would not be able fully to unfold, not even to the limited extent to which we can see it at work in everyday society. There must be, and there is, a second inception of it: the experience of a *common* joy or a *common* sorrow. Aronfreed touches on this all-important aspect, but far too lightly: "Certain kinds of pleasurable events may be directly experienced simultaneously by both the child and another person," he writes in passing (p. 118), "and may thus occur in close contiguity with the other person's expressive cues of positive affect, with the result that the child's own affectivity becomes conditioned to the expressive cues." These words point in the right direction. Eric Erikson comes even closer to the core when he speaks, in connection with the mother–child relationship, of "an emotional pooling" (*Childhood and Society*, p. 207). If two persons experience common emotion (we need not think of mother and child here—any two persons), neither do they remain locked up in themselves so that they can only *infer* the other's joy or sorrow, nor is there *one* mind which would have the same content. No, there is *sharing*, an intersubjective condition, which leaves to each ego his own peculiar way of experiencing the event and yet links them together in an entirely real way. There is a stream of consciousness encompassing both, and each one is a vortex in that stream; and because each one is a vortex in that encompassing stream, there can be, and there is, genuine communication even of emotions between them, and, as a consequence, sympathy in the fullest sense of the word. Joy and sorrow enter into each mind much as a common word or a common custom will; there is then mutual understanding. Sympathy is a form of that understanding as is linguistic conversation, except that it involves another, a deeper, layer of being than mere verbal contact.

To sum up: sympathy arises from shared experiencing, from common emotions. When we speak of common emotion, we stress two aspects. First, that it is common, that is, a real, objective link which can lead to a real, subjective link; and, second, that it is emotion. Were there nothing in and to the ontogenesis of sympathy except selective reinforcement, reinforcement by means of reward, egocentrism could not be completely overcome. An element of calculation, a prudential element, would remain—the feeling that sympathy pays. But that would stain sympathy and limit it. Pure and full sympathy, such as Beethoven celebrated it in his Ninth Symphony, can arise only from a common life.

On a more sober level we may point out that our explanation of the rise of sympathy is in the tradition of George Herbert Mead, though we are going well beyond him because he was not overly interested in the subject of emotion. Given an inclusive society, the individuals within it learn to appreciate each others' roles in the common life, and this fact has three implications, an epistemic, an ethical, and an emotional one. Through it we come, first of all, to know others and even ourselves; we then learn to expect that others will perform their parts and realize that we are obligated to fulfill our own; and finally we grow into so much intersubjectivity that the affective conditions of others become our own, that we can genuinely sympathize with them. Needless to say, these three aspects are more distinguishable in the observer's intellect than in ongoing life; there they are irretrievably intermixed. The more we truly know others, the more likely we are to feel with them; but the more we feel with them, the more likely we are truly to know them. Social life is, in itself and in its impact on the individual, one unbroken whole.

Sympathy is the perfection of sociality in outward relations; conscience is its perfection in the inner self. But though sympathy operates *in foro externo* and conscience *in foro interno*, and though there is an obvious contrast between the two, their genesis is largely parallel. We can take our analysis once again through roughly the same stages as before.

Needless to say, animals do not experience pangs of conscience, but merely pangs of fear when they have transgressed a rule imposed on them. A dog who has had house-training will, when he has fouled the floor, show signs of distress, but this distress does not stem from any idea or even feeling that he has done wrong, but only from the anticipation that he will be whipped. Animals cannot distinguish the Is from the Ought; humans can and do. The English language masks this difference because one word—the word "training"—is equally applicable to humans and beasts. But other languages bring out the contrast and are, in this detail, more precise. Animal training is in German *Domptur* and in French *dressage*, while the bringing up of children is *Erziehung* and *éducation*. *Domptur* and *dressage* do not lead to the formation of conscience; *Erziehung* and *éducation* do.

Even human infants may be, and are, subjected to that purely mechanistic training which the French call *dressage* and the Germans *Domptur*, but the salient point in our context is that so long as there is no more than such breaking-in, there is no development of conscience, and hence no true humanization. This can only get under way when the child has begun to have some inkling of the difference between right and wrong, and this is entirely received from society. Only in society is there a contrast between that which is and that which ought to be; nature is all Is. Now, in establishing this duality in the child's mind and in inducing him to choose right over wrong, the infliction of punishment and the granting of rewards play a great and constructive role and to that extent there is a parallel to animal taming and training. But what the animal cannot learn and the young human can is self-criticism, and that is the beginning of what, in the fullness of time, becomes conscience.

In American literature (which stands, in this particular, in sharp contrast to American practice), the role of punishment in the prehistory and protohistory of individual conscience is energetically stressed. Justin Aronfreed, for instance, whose work—let us recall—is entitled *Conduct and Conscience*, has pointed out and emphasized that from punishment comes anxiety, from anxiety comes the desire for anxiety reduction, from the desire for anxiety reduction, self-criticism, and from self-criticism, and the habit of it, conscience. There is, so we are told, a constant process of internalization. At first, the concatenation between misbehavior and correction is learned and lodged in the child's memory, and good conduct stems merely from the desire to avoid the pain of correction; then such feelings as shame and guilt spring up, and these are stages on the way which finally leads to conscience, an entirely internal voice whose operation is unconnected with any external sanction. Here are a few apposite quotations: "When a child has had sufficient exposure to punishment for a particular act of transgression, it will begin to experience anxiety in anticipation of punishment. . . . The motivation for the child's internalized reactions to transgressions is a function of the intensity of anxiety which is mobilized by the intrinsic correlates of a committed transgression" (pp. 217, 214, 215). Self-criticism—the experience and the confession of guilt—is developed because it has anxiety-reducing effects. "The learning of self-criticism" is "controlled by anxiety-reduction" (p. 222). But "a reaction such as self-criticism, which reproduces components of external punishment, can be acquired and maintained by children in response to their own transgressions." If this happens, the battle of conscience-building is won. It *is* normally won: "The child's evaluation of conduct does generally take on an increasingly moral character in the course of development" (pp. 226, 247).

There is no need to quarrel with this analysis; it is manifestly realistic. Yet we must be clear about the climax of the process. Aronfreed defines conscience (perhaps a little clumsily, but all the same clearly) as "those areas of conduct where social experience has attached substantial affective value to the child's cognitive representation and evaluation of its own behavior" (p. 6), and asserts that "the acquisition of conscience can best be conceptualized as a continuous representation of social experience" (p. 256). The terms "cognitive [i.e., mental] representation" and "social experience," then, are the building stones of this concept of conscience. This leaves us essentially with the traditional image of a "monitor within" (cognitive representation) who tells us spontaneously of the criticisms from without which, in the case of transgression, we would incur (social experience). But this is not the highest form of conscience which we can imagine; there is still a duality left—the duality between the Is and the Ought, the social norm and the individual will, except that the contest between the two is shifted from the police court, as it were, to the *forum internum*, the inner self. But in the perfectly socialized man the Ought would have totally vanquished and absorbed the Is, and though this can happen only on the mental plane, it can be imagined to happen there; in the totally socialized man, there would be no need for a continued cognitive representation of social experience, for the norms of society would have entered into and filled out the individual will. In other words, in the perfectly socialized man, self and society would coincide. He would not have to be told—even by an inner voice—what to do and what to avoid; no warning finger would have to be raised before his face; he would unhesitatingly and spontaneously act as he should. Henri Bergson has defined the saint as the person whose will is merely the mold through which the divine will flows into the world (*The Two Sources of Morality and Religion*, paperback ed. [Garden City, N.Y., n. d.]; see esp. p. 232), and he has Scripture on his side. "I live, now not I," cries St. Paul, "but Christ liveth in me" (Gal. 2:20), and Christ himself prayed: "My Father, not as I will, but as Thou wilt" (Matt. 26:39). We need a parallel concept of the ideal man in

sociology, too. According to Aronfreed, conscience is a moral urge which operates within *consciousness*, and that is where, in the vast majority of cases, it
does indeed operate; but then we are still in the presence of sub-ideal man. In
the case of ideal man, the social norm has rooted itself not only in his knowledge, thought, and valuation, but also in his action center, in his *will* (which is
much more). True—let us admit it without reservation—this is only what
Plato called a "vision in the sky" and Kant an "idea," a concept from the
borderline between the observable and the merely imaginable. But we have
studied, in these pages, the process of socialization and the direction of its
thrust, and it behooves us in conclusion to say where its end point must lie,
even if we know that, because of man's inherent limitations, it can hardly be
attained.

An issue which has been discussed in many contexts and at many levels is
the relationship between the interests of the individual and the interests of society. Are they in harmony or are they in conflict? Do they coincide or do they
cut across each other? Two manifestly different answers are possible, one optimistic and one apparently pessimistic. The Leibnitzian tradition has asserted
that what is good for society is good for the individual as well, and vice versa.
Even man's self-regard leads, through a "divine chemistry," to benefits for all.
The Durkheimian tradition, on the other hand, considerably more sober and
considerably more scientific, has maintained that what is good for society,
namely social discipline, is, to say the least, restrictive for the individual, hence
as burdensome and unwelcome as any other yoke. In the light of our analysis,
this whole contrast collapses. What is good for society, namely social discipline,
is restrictive, burdensome, and unwelcome only for man's animal body, but not
for man in his totality. True, strict limits are set to physical indulgences and
this is painful, but the pain involved is but a small price to pay for the joys of
cultural life which are bought with it. The individual gains very greatly, even
as an individual. Society gives him security, and not only against attacks from
without. It also gives him security against destructive influences from within.
This precisely is the optimistic implication of Durkheim's analysis: that he is
able to show that a creature no longer controlled by instinct but left to his own
devices, a creature pushed and pulled in many different directions at once by
the uncoordinated lusts dwelling in his flesh, is likely to fall a victim to anomie,
to chaos, to self-destruction. Anomie is normlessness. The person who has internalized society's norms is safe; the life-preserving order and stability—the
ἄγραφοι νόμοι, as the ancients called them, the laws written on the heart—
make him so. But his is not only the great blessing of safety; his is also the even
greater blessing of justifiable self-respect. The individual who has truly identified with society, who has made society's values totally his own, has himself
become a value second to none.

SOCIAL HABIT AND PHYSICAL APPARATUS

82. Human action, as we have seen all along, is rarely entirely instinctive, but
it is also rarely entirely free. In principle, we possess freedom, but we cannot,

in practice, apply it all the time. "An incontinent exercise of choice wears people out . . . ," says Cooley in *Human Nature and the Social Order* (p. 70), and he is certainly correct. We must, and we do, combine self-determination with stability and order, and we achieve this (as Bergson has shown in *The Two Sources of Morality and Religion*) by developing, internalizing, and submitting to, habits. "It is no great exaggeration to say that living is for the most part learning, and that the remainder of life is merely the carrying on in practice what has previously been learned," writes the psychologist Knight Dunlap (*Habits*, p. 3), and a sociologist who belongs to the cultural school will wholeheartedly agree with him. "If we limit the term 'learn' somewhat narrowly," Dunlap continues, "we can truthfully say that a definite process of learning is the formation of a *habit*; and conversely, a habit is a way of living that has been learned. . . . Habits, in their totality, make up the character of the individual; that is, they *are* the individual, as he appears to other people." As he *appears* to other people, Dunlap writes; we have to add: as he *interacts* with other people, for this is the aspect with which the sociologist is primarily concerned.

In his introduction to the more recent editions of Dunlap's great book, Irwin Lubin has emphasized that one of the master's main convictions was the insight that "conditioning is always embedded in a cognitive or symbolic matrix" (p. xi), and Dunlap himself asserts (p. 6) that even "the seemingly merely manual, pedal or vocal habits are fundamentally mental." Yet it is impossible to deny that habits have a somatic side as well; they must somehow be incorporated into the brain for otherwise they would not endure and recur. It is impossible to imagine them as entirely free-floating, and we must therefore venture on an excursion into physiology if we want to give a comprehensive account of human conduct in society.

What we have rejected, in the immediately preceding paragraph, is the position classically formulated by René Descartes, according to whom there is an absolute contrast between animals and men. Animals to him are automata, they are moved by their machines, and if they know any psychism at all, it is merely a nervous mechanism; whereas man is mind, and the nervous mechanism which he possesses is at the command of the mind and moved by it. We cannot today see things quite in this light; Cartesian idealism appears to most of us exaggerated. Yet an exaggerated materialism which would deny the difference between animal and man and reduce human psychism, in the manner of Moleschott and Vogt, to a sweating of the brain, is equally unacceptable or even more so. What we have to do is to re-establish the dichotomy asserted by Descartes (which certainly exists) with the help of physiological analysis—to show that though both humans and beasts have and are machines, mechanism means in the one case something very different from what it means in the other. The contrast between the animal and man rests *inter alia* on the contrast between their respective brains.

The crucial fact of the matter is that animals (especially the lower ones) are very largely mechanical reactors, their reactions operated by their lower brain parts, whereas men are not, because they are in possession of a cerebral cortex which is the organ of psychism and the seat of will. There is indeed, even in man, a corporeal side to thinking and willing, but there is also a mental side to the cortical apparatus which constitutes part of his physical equipment. The cortex is the highest bodily endowment on his part and sets him off from all the lower creation. We cannot hope to unravel the knots which present themselves here, unless several essential truths are recognized and remembered. (*a*) The fact that some animals, too, have a cortex, or, rather, the rudiments of one, does not disprove the uniqueness of man. The uniqueness of man rests on the fact that in him the cortex is *dominant*, and not simply present and/or operative. Once again we see that a difference in degree amounts to a difference in kind. (*b*) The fact that mental life is as indissolubly connected with a physical organ as the obverse of a coin is with the converse does not mean that mental life is subordinated to the physical organ. Why should it be? It is merely materialistic prejudice to suggest that it is. If there is a pair of scales with two sides to it, what entitles the investigator to assert, and to assert apodictically, that the one necessarily has more pull than the other? (*c*) It makes no difference to our investigation that we cannot fully understand, or even hope to understand, how thought and brain cooperate. There is in this area an outer limit to our exploration at which we come up against mystery, and it is right and meet to say: *ignoramus, ignorabimus.* Yet there are many essential insights which lie entirely within our grasp, and we can achieve assured truths even if the ultimate answer eludes us and always will.

After these precautionary remarks, let us try, as best we can, to get the facts clear, such as technical physiology has come to know them. "The further one goes down the scale of animals," writes Paul Chauchard in *The Brain* (p. 31),

the less important becomes the cerebral cortex; psychic functions, which are increasingly limited, are then taken care of by the lower centers—the central gray nuclei [which constitute the hypothalamus] or even the mesencephalon. . . . The great difference between the animal brain and the human brain is that the animal has a rich innate supply of instincts that establish for him his normal conduct—instincts that depend chiefly on the hypothalamus. It has relatively little to learn. On the contrary, in man the hypothalamus is smaller and no longer commands truly instinctive kinds of behavior, but simple physiological processes. In man, everything is taken care of on the level of his habits. . . . A rat whose adrenal gland has been removed knows enough to choose the salt water that will prevent it from dying solely because of the sensitivity of its hypothalamus to the disequilibrium of its inner environment. Man has lost this instinct and creates gastronomy in order to be able to eat when not hungry. The animal has a sexual instinct that imposes upon it, in an innate way, the most complex kinds of behavior during courtship. In man, though a sexual need exists, the conditions of its exercise—even the notion of a partner of the opposite sex—are entirely acquired. Man is no longer the prey of instinct but becomes the slave of social customs which, grafted on to needs, have replaced instincts. He can therefore be free only by reflection, which, taking into account his real needs and his nature, will make him invent satisfactory kinds of behavior. This will be the role of the prefrontal functions [pp. 128, 129].

As can be seen, even a study of the brain reveals both the similarity and the contrast between animal and man. There is a similarity because man, too, has a hypothalamus, the animal center of innate behavior (p. 96); he may sink down so low that he can come to be dominated by that center. "Someone who buries himself in the instinctive or emotional excesses of sensuality . . . is [however] not a real man; [and that because] he reaches the point of using only his lower brain, the one that is closest to an animal's" (p. 161). Normal cultured man, real man, on the other hand, uses essentially his higher centers, and therein rests his contrast to the beast—a contrast which appears, from the point of view of sociology, far greater than the similarity. In man, Chauchard explains, there are two centers, and it is the latter, the higher, which is, and which alone can be, the seat of sociality:

> On the one hand, there is the primitive brain of the rhinencephalon, which is responsible for instinctive and affective manifestations—calm and agitation, alimentary and sexual kinds of behavior, manifestations of pleasure, pain, anger. On the other hand, there is [the cortex] the brain of verbalized thought and awareness, the sensory–motor zone that may be called the noetic brain of knowledge and action. . . . It is the brain of . . . the sense of oneself and of others and the sense of what is human; and it is because of it that social intercourse is not merely verbal dialogue but profound human relationship [pp. 126, 127].

Basing himself squarely on scientific physiology, Chauchard rejects the exaggerated dualism of Descartes. "We now have objective indications that an animal is not an automaton whose activity could be said to be purely reflex. It does not guide itself exclusively by the signals of the moment, but also by what it has in its head." Yet, even in the same breath, Chauchard asserts that the facts warrant and support a dualistic philosophy, though one that is not apodictic but carefully circumscribed. "Does an animal think?" he asks (p. 117), and he answers without hesitation: "If by that we mean human thought, certainly not." He explains that

> Animal thought, the extent of which depends on the complexity of the brain, and the simplest human thought, which is much more complex because of cerebral progress, are thoughts by images. . . . Animals possess only this kind of thought by images, and in elementary form. Thought that is distinctly human is situated on another level. It is a question of verbalized thought, of an inner language [p. 118].

Chauchard's emphasis on growing complexity could be misunderstood; it might be taken as an admission that the difference between animal and man is after all only one of degree. We must therefore be grateful to him that he expressly rejects this interpretation. His thought tallies exactly with one of the basic theses of the present investigation: differences in degree become differences in kind. "Between animal and man there is an important margin," he explains (p. 166), "in which quantitative complexification conditions new qualities, as neurophysiology shows." The dissimilarity between animals and man, he writes (pp. 118, 119),

> is said to be that the former have only a very simple language, a very affective means of alarm signalling, whereas in men language, which is very complex as a result of the motor brain's greater ability to modulate sounds, is the means of expressing a thought independent of language itself. Language thus becomes

a direct proof of human spirituality. The neurophysiological point of view is different: the greater complexity of the human brain does not merely give it the ability to emit much more varied sounds or to understand them; it makes of language, which is a means of communication, a new and more efficacious means of thinking. . . . It was Pavlov who showed that language is a consequence of human cerebral complexity and that it objectifies the superiority and special nature of the human brain by comparison with the animal brain. He saw language as a special variety of conditioned reflexes, a *second system* of signaling. The first system is that of the gnosias and praxias of direct thought by images. Education substitutes for each image its verbal denomination. Since he names everything, man is able, instead of associating images, to associate directly the corresponding names—a system that is better suited to developing the potentialities of abstraction of the human brain.

In the end, Chauchard reaches, from his physiological starting point, exactly the same conclusions as this book, which may be said to have approached man from the very opposite—the purely cultural—angle. This is what he writes:

It would be a mistake to deny the existence of a kind of consciousness in higher animals which plays an active part in directing their behavior, but it would be another mistake to identify their consciousness with ours, which even from the cerebral point of view seems to be of a quite different order. . . . It is the inadequacy of the animal brain that prevents it from rising far enough above determinisms to be able to direct them in a reflective way. . . . What characterizes the normal human brain, thanks to its complexity, is that it is *the organ which permits freedom* [pp. 125, 124].

Such talk of freedom is not metaphysics, it is physics in the strictest sense of the word, as a look at the statistics involved can prove. Chauchard gives the number of the neurons in the cortex—the neurons are the functional units of the brain—as 14 billions and points out that "what counts . . . is not the absolute number of neurons, but the density of the interconnected network" (pp. 53, 57, 58). To this we must add the fact that "any cortical neuron may make up to 60,000 synaptic contacts with its neighbours" (C. U. M. Smith, *The Brain: Towards an Understanding* [London, 1970], p. 318). Which neuron will connect with which is not—so far as the higher cerebral centers are concerned—predetermined; hence we may rightly speak, not only of elasticity, but also of freedom. And that freedom is not only real; it is substantial as well. Let anyone who can, calculate or imagine what the possibilities of a human brain are! To say that they are, in principle, limited is near nonsense, for in practice they are, to all intents and purposes, unlimited.

But we are interested, not only in possibilities, but also in actualities, not only in freedom, but also in order—which means in habit and custom, for it is habit and custom which create, and impose, an enduring pattern on human action and interaction. Our problem at this point is to explain how it is that the brain retains and reactivates the settled modes of conduct which it has encountered in the learning process. Experience tells us in no uncertain manner that it does retain and reactivate them, and this is an entirely simple matter; but to elucidate the cerebral modifications which make this possible is by no means simple; we must assume that there are such modifications for if we did not, we should be left with some such concept as that of an extraspatial mind. What then are the lasting traces which experience leaves on or in the brain?

One theory which has held very wide sway is the so-called pathway theory. The neurophysiologist Ralph W. Gerard reveals its basic idea rather clearly, if somewhat crudely, in the following passage: "The fact that repetition makes for better memory reminds us of the analogy of the river cutting a channel in its bed ("What is Memory," in *Psychobiology*, edd. McGaugh et al., p. 129). The classical representative of this intuition was William James, and it makes its appearance in several contexts of his *Principles of Psychology*—in connection with habit formation, with association, with memory, and with the will. "The brain is essentially a place of currents which run in organized paths," James writes (p. 70).

> A path once traversed by a nervo-current might be expected to follow the law of most of the paths we know, and to be scooped out and made more permeable than before, and this ought to be repeated with each new passage of the current . . . until at last it might become a natural drainage-channel. . . . The entire nervous system is nothing but a system of paths between a sensory *terminus a quo* and a muscular, glandular, or other *terminus ad quem*. . . . The currents, once in, must find a way out. In getting out, they leave their traces in the paths which they take. The only thing they can do, in short, is to deepen old paths or to make new ones; and the whole plasticity of the brain sums itself up in two words when we call it an organ in which currents pouring in from sense-organs make with extreme facility paths which do not easily disappear [pp. 108, 107].

This theory was later somewhat modified by E. L. Thorndike, who, instead of speaking of brain paths (or traces, or impressions, or engrams), spoke of the establishment of "bonds" between nerve cells in the brain—a more verbal than real change. Altogether, James's exposition has worn rather well. Even as late as 1970, C. U. M. Smith could write that, where an action is repeated, the "balance of evidence presented . . . suggests that [an] 'engram' is, in mammals, laid down in the cerebral cortex" (*The Brain*, p. 315). Yet we must distinguish here between general and specific truth. In a general sense, something of the sort James suggests must indeed happen; experiences must somehow be encoded in the brain. But in a specific, in a technical, sense, his exposition may still be erroneous. When one speaks of a treading out of brain paths (or, for that matter, of an establishment of inter-neuronal bonds), he is using metaphorical, not scientific, language, and that is to be avoided, if it can possibly be.

The present author is not the man, and the present book is not the place, to go more deeply into such matters, yet even the sociologist and his literature must try to achieve, and to present, a tolerably reliable idea of how habits— and this is to say, socially approved modes of action, customs, or folkways— gain entry into the physical brain and thereby into organic life. We would like therefore to make two remarks on the brain path theory. The first is that it oversimplifies when it suggests that one afferent or cortico-petal wave releases one efferent or cortico-fugal response, and that the two specific events then bond and thus tend to repeat themselves. For it has been proved that each stimulus received affects a whole array of neurons and thus does not lay down one determinate path. The work of D. O. Hebb, which has been particularly important in this field, has been summed up as follows:

> Hebb believes that even the simplest perceptual learning involves hundreds of neurons widely dispersed in the brain and is established only gradually by the development of neuronal interconnections. The perception of a given event activates a certain *pattern* of sensory, associational and motor neurons. At first the pattern is a comparatively simple one and its durability is precarious. But as the perception is repeated and the neurons involved become more practiced in firing as a team, their functional interconnections become more firmly established. In time additional neurons are recruited, alternate pathways develop and the system becomes less and less vulnerable to disruption [Alan E. Fisher, "Chemical Stimulation of the Brain," in *Psychobiology*, edd. McGaugh et al., p. 73; emphasis added].

This modification of the pathway theory, though certainly significant, is nonetheless not so incisive as the other which we have to bring up, for it leaves the mechanistic simile on which it is based—the making of pathways through an area—largely untouched. Hebb himself admits as much, for in his book *The Organization of Behavior* (p. xix) he says that his theory "is evidently a form of connectionism, one of the switchboard variety, though it does not . . . make any single nerve cell or pathway essential to any habit," and insists later on that "the assumption we must accept is that the memory trace, the basis of learning, is in some way structural . . . ," that there is "a structural reinforcement of synaptic transmission" (pp. 12, 67). Another recent development is a good deal more telling. It has been found that the formation of habits rests essentially on the facilitation of certain chemical processes in the brain, and not on a widening or deepening of current-conveying channels. This shift from the mechanistic to a biochemical style or key of explanation is so fundamental that even the student of social conduct has to take note of it.

Briefly, the present state of knowledge in this field appears to be as follows. If a photographic picture is taken of the brain, it is seen that there is no physical contact between the endpoint of an afferent nerve which transmits a stimulus to the brain and the starting point of the efferent nerve which initiates the proper response to it. There are gaps or clefts between the neurons involved, and therefore comparison with a switchboard, where there is a plugging in, and hence establishment of a firm physical connection between the line carrying the incoming call and the line conveying the outgoing message, is out of the question. "There is never actual continuity between two cells," Chauchard explains (*The Brain*, p. 54), "but contact through close contiguity at the points of interconnection, called synapses." How, then, are the synaptic gaps or clefts bridged? Bernhard Katz explains:

> The motor nerve terminals act rather like glands secreting a chemical messenger. Upon arrival of an impulse, the terminals release a special substance, acetylcholine [or dopamine, or something of the sort], that quickly and efficiently diffuses across the short synaptic gap. Acetylcholine molecules combine

with receptor molecules in the contact area of the muscle fiber and somehow open its ionic gates, allowing sodium to flow in and trigger an impulse ["How Cells Communicate," in *Psychobiology*, edd. McGaugh et al., p. 222].

If this is what in fact happens, then the problem which William James tried to solve with the aid of his pathway theory, the problem of the learning of habits, of their registration in the brain, and above all of the learning and registration of law-abiding habits, may be raised anew and answered anew. Gerard does raise and answer it for us: "What then is the enduring static trace?" he asks, the trace which takes the place of the pathway or engram earlier assumed, and he replies:

> Many suggestions have been made as to what kinds of changes may alter the response at the synapse. They must be structural—either in the fibers and contacts or at the molecular level, where displacement of ions might alter the electric potential or displacement of atoms change the chemistry. One observed change . . . is the swelling of fiber end-bulbs induced by activity ["What is Memory," pp. 129, 130].

Induced by activity: these three words are of the greatest importance for the sociologist. The fiber end-bulbs swell because a particular circuit is habitually used. It is human action, then, which shapes the brain to its purposes, and since human action flows from the human will—in the case which interests us, the will to conformity, to norm-abidingness—it is in the final analysis the will which determines the functioning of the brain as far as social conduct is concerned.

We could well leave the matter here; the essential point has been made. The mode of operation of the cortex in the matrix of social life depends, not only on heredity, but also on experience and education. When we learn what we ought to do, and especially when we do what we ought to do, we take the Ought —the norm—into our brains and incorporate it there. (The word incorporation as used here must be taken in its physical, and not only in its metaphorical, sense.) Yet in order to give a comprehensive as well as a correct picture, it is permissible to add a few more lines. When the physiologist speaks of the swelling of fiber end-bulbs, he is referring not only to a somatic development, but even more to the chemical facilitation of impulse transmission which is connected with it. "Memory might be due to changes in nerve proteins," Gerard writes (ibid.), and he continues very cautiously: "It is far from explained just how the passage of nerve impulses would alter protein molecules at a synapse, or how, in turn, an altered protein composition would aid or hinder the passage of a nerve impulse. Yet some such chemical mechanism cannot be discarded. . . ."

Other physiologists are much bolder, and they appear to be on safe ground. Holger Hydén has proved that in rats which were subjected to a learning process certain brain proteins were produced in greater amounts; here for once the results of animal experiments may legitimately be applied to man since it is a purely organic change which is at issue, and nobody will deny that the human body is an animal organism. In an article which is brief, but rich in content, entitled "Brain Changes in Response to Experience" (*Scientific American*, 226,

No. 2 [February 1972], 22–29), three eminent researchers, Mark R. Rosen-
zweig, Edward L. Bennett, and Marian Cleeves Diamond, have provided a
good survey of up-to-date knowledge in this field, which is much more important for the student of social action and interaction than any other aspect of
biology. Their words speak for themselves:

> We found indications that the level of brain acetylcholinesterase was altered
> by problem solving tests. . . . we found that different experiences not only af-
> fected the enzymatic activity but also altered the weight of the brain samples.
> . . . rats with enriched experience had a greater weight of cerebral cortex [and]
> a greater thickness of cortex. . . . The most consistent effect of experience on
> the brain that we found was the ratio of the weight of the cortex to the weight
> of the rest of the brain: the subcortex. It appears that the cortex increases in
> weight quite readily in response to an enriched environment [pp. 24, 25].

It is not, however, the weight of the brain which is decisive, but its effectivity:
"Measurement of the synaptic junctions revealed that rats from [experientially]
enriched environments had junctions that averaged approximately 50 percent
larger in cross section than similar junctions in littermates from impoverished
environments. . . . there is increased synaptic contact in enriched-experience
rats" (p. 27).

"There can now be no doubt that many aspects of brain anatomy and brain
chemistry are changed by experience" (ibid.), the three researchers conclude,
and the sentence as it stands applies to *Homo sapiens* as well, and as much, as
to the rat. Let us now hear a student of the human cerebrum. "It is known that
active neurons do synthesize protein at a rate considerably in excess of that
found in resting cells," writes C. U. M. Smith in *The Brain* (p. 326). The

> critical points in the conduction of a nerve impulse are the initiation of the
> action potential at the axon hillock [or end-bulb] and the transmission to the
> next cell at the synapse. It is at these points that flexibility occurs. . . . Protein
> P might affect either or both of these points. It might make it more or less
> difficult for an action potential to be "sparked off" at the hillock, or it might
> affect the ease of synaptic transmission. . . . This molecular mechanism en-
> sures that the nerve circuits excited in a learning situation have their resistance
> to impulse transmission permanently . . . altered. . . . the essence of memory
> fixation is the alteration of the resistance to impulse transmission of one or
> more neuronal circuits. . . . memories have a physical basis in the form of low
> resistance "circuits" in the brain, particularly in the cerebral cortex [pp. 326–
> 27, 328].

We saw earlier that Gerard calls the swelling of the neuronal fiber end-bulbs
at the synapse "induced by activity"; we see now that Smith ascribes the low-
ering of resistance to impulse transmission—in other words: the easing of impulse transmission at that point—to the passing through a "learning situation";
the two statements come, of course, to much the same. Activity or, more concretely, learning—hence human, cultural, volitional action—therefore molds
the brain and determines the functioning of it. The implication of this insight is
clear: society is not an epiphenomenon of nature, as materialism has always

asserted. The will of man which has transformed the surface of the earth and which has created in habit, custom, law, and religion powerful and effective guides to conduct, transforms even the recesses of the human brain.

If, as physiologists assure us, even the acquisition of simple skills by poorly equipped creatures such as rats alters the operation and the very chemistry of their brains, how great then must be the effect of human education, an education which is a sustained and sophisticated process of learning and has a highly evolved cortex to work at? It must be remembered here that men as a species are born premature and that their brains are as unready on entry into independent existence as the rest of their organic equipment. Indeed, we may say, more unready. For, as Paul Chauchard informs us (*The Brain*, p. 50), the lower centers develop first; they take shape during the intrauterine fetal period; the higher centers, on the other hand, lag far behind; their maturation occurs only after birth. "At birth, this brain is incomplete and is constructed slowly during childhood and adolescence," the great physiologist writes. Heredity, needless to say, is important, but "more important than heredity is the influence of the environment during the early years, for it becomes a part of the very nature of a human being by contributing to the formation of his brain" (pp. 41, 46). Chauchard explains that there are four factors which are jointly responsible for the construction of the human brain: heredity, the inner environment, the outer environment, and, finally, human conduct. Heredity and the inner environment (factors originating within the organism, such as, e.g., the flow of hormones) are to be classed as natural; the outer environment (especially the extrauterine environment) and human conduct, on the other hand, are largely cultural. The outer environment, a stream of "innumerable sensorial data much more complex than those coming from the inner environment," is called by Chauchard "extremely important in stimulating the growth of the nervous system" (p. 45).

> The fundamental law of cerebral development requires that cerebral maturation always find not only the physical but also the cultural and affective environment that favors it. . . . It is cerebral maturation that makes a baby babble in its cradle, but if the sounds do not become socially interesting as communication, as in the case of the wolf-child, the development of the language centers will be impeded [pp. 52, 51; see also p. 44].

Chauchard's teachings, as can be seen, easily blend with a culturalist sociology, but they even support a specific form of that culturalism, namely, voluntarism. He compares the growth of the human brain with the growth of a plant and explains that there is a decisive difference between the two phenomena. In the case of the development of a plant, there is interaction between a living force and its environment, but that living force cannot intervene, "while . . . the child himself, as his consciousness comes to life, can *intervene on his own* in the completion of his brain" (p. 45). It is no counterargument here to say that the child's will is merely an evolved form of that living force which manifests itself in the vital activities even of a plant. If the theory of evolution is accepted, this assertion cannot be rejected, nor need it be for the purposes of a culturalist–voluntarist social philosophy. For, once again, the difference in degree between the two variants of the *élan vital* is so vast that it undoubtedly amounts to a difference in kind. It is also characteristic that the point of time in ontogeny which marks the completion of brain structures is also the point of time which, as we have seen, marks the period of true socialization. "Anatomically, a human brain is not finished—that is, does not possess a complete nervous network—until approximately the age of seven" (p. 44).

Chauchard makes one further remark in this context which, rightly appreciated, is very enlightening for the student of social—and total—man. "This age," he writes (pp. 44, 45), "marks the moment when the construction of the brain . . . makes way for the acquired art of using this brain, which is a realm in which possibilities are the most durable." Seven is a threshold, and yet "it would be a mistake to regard the brain of a seven-year-old, though anatomically complete, as a mature brain from the functional point of view, and educative errors can still impede this physiological maturation and deprive the adult of important possibilities. It is only toward the age of eighteen that the electroencephalogram becomes that of an adult." The importance of this statement for the sociologist consists in this: that it discusses, by implication, the relation between structure and function. We have repeatedly given it as our conviction that the difference between the animal and the human brain lies in their functioning rather than in their structure—in that specifically human functioning which Chauchard correctly and strikingly describes as the "acquired art" of using the brain, and which shows itself fully from about the seventh year onward. We have now, in conclusion, to introduce a small qualification of our formulation. Even as far as the structure is concerned there is a significant contrast between the human and the animal brain, for unlike that of the animal brain, which receives only marginal modification from learning and experience, the transformation of the human brain owing to these cultural influences is considerable, especially during the extrauterine fetal period, which, as we know, is a formative phase and not a phase of accomplished fixation. A "human social environment," says Chauchard (p. 44), is "necessary for the brain to be normal," to become normal. Indeed—as we have seen—he goes so far as to say that the human brain receives "construction" from the human social environment; in other words: that it is to some extent *made* through the imprints which the human and social environment leaves. This takes little from the fact that the brain is in the first place a natural and physical structure, that it is due to heredity rather than to any other formative influence, that it is genotypic rather than phenotypic. But it does mean that even the cortex, though it is an organ, a material entity, is shaped by cultural factors, that we have even here an interplay of nature and nurture rather than the domination of the one over the other. Popular opinion and even a more sophisticated and academic materialism maintain, for instance, that we can speak because we have linguistic centers in the brain. This is true, of course, but it is no less true that we have linguistic centers in the brain—centers which can do more than release an occasional emotive cry—because we have learned how to speak.

We can now bring this discussion to a close. We started by denying that human sociality grows out of physical nature. We may end by asserting that, on the contrary, human sociality grows into physical nature, that it enters into, and lodges itself in, the very fibers of the brain. In taking this position, we have enlightened scientific opinion entirely on our side. Whoever or whatever may be the First Cause, the *causa prima*, of all that is, man is undoubtedly, as Thomism has so rightly insisted, a *causa secunda*, a minor, but true, creator, the creator, above all, of his own sociality and, indeed, of his very self.

2

The Diversity of Mankind

83. Our whole analysis so far has been based on one implied assumption or, rather, conviction which few sociologists will be inclined to impugn: the assumption and conviction that the human race is one, as far as the need to socialize the individual is concerned. All men, wherever and whenever born, are born potentially, rather than actually, social. If that potentiality is to become actuality, if the self-preferring body is to be inhabited by, and controlled by, a will bent on cooperation with others, the person must undergo a process of education—a metamorphosis, as Ernest Schachtel so rightly calls it—which must center on the internalization of values and norms. Yet these values and norms are not the same the wide world over; indeed, their systems show an amazing, not to say overwhelming, variety. Our investigation of the ontogeny of sociality would therefore be incomplete if we did not pay some attention to the multiplicity of phenomena observable in the field.

In approaching this subject, we must, to begin with, point out that we are concerned, not with the variety of mankind in all its aspects, but merely with the differences in the process of socialization. Much has been said, for instance, about the comparative condition of assignable parts of humanity with regard to native intelligence. Are all human beings equally well endowed or are some better, some worse? Are some more clever and others rather dull? We, too, shall have to express an opinion on this matter, for more intelligent people are likely to be more rapidly and more thoroughly socializable than dunces slow on the uptake. Yet this whole nodus of problems is of comparatively little interest to the student of socialization. The same mental brightness which enables some to grasp and to digest the norms of social life with relative ease is also likely to give them a quicker and more comprehensive idea of their own personal interests; what is gained on the swings may be lost on the roundabouts, and there is no saying where the final balance will lie. Experience proves that societies which rank lower in the scale of formal intelligence, for instance, with regard to the application of the principle of rationality to economics and technology, often do better in the area of cultural tradition and culture transmission. What Aristotle said of individuals is true of collectivities as well: if nature has endowed some more lavishly than others, *art* can step in and even out the odds or, indeed, turn the tables. Social education is precisely such an art.

One reason given for the great differences in the process and, above all, in the content of socialization—for the fact that some societies put much pressure behind their norms and others little, or that some leave the choice of a marriage partner free while others insist on the acceptance of a cross cousin—is the geographical variety of human habitats, of the globe. The school of geographical determinists, started in the middle of the nineteenth century by Frédéric LePlay, asserted that place determines work, work determines the family and its forms, the family determines character, and character in the end determines the social system. In the great plains of Russia, for instance, in the steppe, society is bound to be traditionalistic and authoritarian. This habitat develops, quite spontaneously, cattle breeding, especially horse breeding, as its appropriate economy; but in the tending of herds there is nothing which would lead either to innovation or to the breakup of descent groups. The large family under one patriarch will be the result. Everything will remain the same year-in year-out and through the centuries. The effects of the Norwegian landscape will be very different. Strung out along a rocky shoreline, forced to shelter in narrow fjords, the Norwegians will have to earn their living by the craft of fishing. Children will have to find their own niches as soon as possible. They will therefore be brought up to be independent, daring, full of enterprise. Individuality will be as consistently developed there as it will fail to be developed in Russia. But strong individuals will brook no authoritarianism. They will be inclined toward democratic forms of life.

This pretended explanation of the variety of social life, though it has appealed to many, is in the final analysis unconvincing. Though there may be some poor settings which admit of only one mode of economic life, most areas offer a whole gamut of alternatives. In the Middle West you can grow cereals or raise beasts, or do both in appropriate mixture. The cereals may be wheat or rye or maize, the beasts horses or bovines or sheep; and so on. What will decide then is, not nature, but the will of man. Vidal de la Blache based his anti-deterministic, voluntaristic "theory of regional possibilities" on these sober facts. For the sociologist, the salient point is that the social forms of life are manifestly not laid down in and by the habitat. On the assumption that the ancient inhabitants of Norway did have to look to the sea as their chief source of food, was there any cogent reason, laid on in geography, why they should prefer individual to collective enterprise, fishing on one's own to fishing in cooperation with others? The chain of causation presented by the geographical determinists has no link in it which is not brittle and which will not fail to hold.

But quite apart from the poor logic of the argument, simple observation is sufficient to overthrow it. The same environment harbors contrasting societies. In North Africa live the Moors and the Tuaregs, in Arizona the Navaho and the Hopi, yet Tuareg norms of conduct are different from the Moorish ones and Hopi values different from those of the Navaho. But the strongest disproof of the assertions of the LePlay school, old and new, is a reference to history. Look at any country you like and ask yourself whether social life in it, and especially the socialization to which it has subjected its new citizens, has remained the same over the ages, even though its physical conditions, its climate, its rocks and rivers *have* remained the same? "The most elementary logic teaches us that it is impossible to explain a variable by a constant," writes Robert Bierstedt (*The Social Order* [New York, 1963], p. 42), and he is right. The variety of the earth's surface cannot therefore account for the variations of sociality and socialization.

Geographical determinism had a metaphyical prop, no better, but also no worse, than others of its kind: the doctrine of the monogenetic origin of the human race. There was one cradle of humanity, indeed, one primal pair, and all the races have descended from it. Scientists tell us that this theory cannot be correct for we find in the world many separate gene pools, and genes do not change under the influence of different habitats. We can leave this matter to those who study it *ex professo*; but we brought the monogenetic doctrine up in order to contrast it with its rival: racialism, the dogma of the polygenetic origin of the human race, classically presented, for instance, by Ludwig Gumplowicz. It, too, will not stand up to critical examination. For it invites us to believe that in evolution the dividing line between man's simian ancestor or ancestors and man himself was crossed repeatedly by unconnected hordes, and this is totally incredible—for how can different developments have led to nearly identical results? If the monogenetic metaphysic fails because the differences between the races are too great, its polygenetic alternative breaks down because the differences between the races are too small. Since any healthy human male can produce offspring with any healthy human female, whatever their race—offspring, moreover, who themselves can become parents—it is clear that nature has constituted humanity, physiologically speaking, as a unitary race.

These last statements are, however, introductory, rather than concluding, remarks. There is at least a *prima facie* case for considering racial inheritance as a possible cause of variation in human sociality, for are not the social systems, the values and norms of the cultures built up by the whites in Western Europe and America, by the blacks in Central Africa, by the Chinese and Japanese in the Far East, very different? Are we not confronted with inclusive human types which are different in everything, even in socialization and sociality, and not only in physique?

We have said that there is a *prima facie* case, but we have to add now that there is no more than that. On closer inspection it is easy to see that physical inheritance is as little responsible for the socio-cultural variety of mankind as physical environment.

The weakness of any position derived from polygenism begins with the difficulty of defining and identifying a race. It goes without saying that the popular method of distinguishing races—judging by the color of the skin—is scientifically worthless. Should or could a small detail, namely a relatively high concentration of melanine in the epidermis, make of the Negro an entirely different sort of man, contrasting even in habitual conduct, from the Caucasian? What can it mean, this detail, in view of the proved fact that all the major and decisive traits—skeletal structure, brain, blood vessels, viscera, and so forth—are common to all human beings? Differences in skin color, and in physical type generally, are owing to a few genes only, but most genes, almost all, are the same for everybody—for every human body. "In classifying mankind we witness the end-operation of but a dozen or so pairs in literally thousands of pairs of genes," an outstanding expert has written (W. R. Krogman, "The Concept of Race," in *The Science of Man in the World Crisis*, ed. Ralph Linton [New York & London, 1964], p. 45). "It is upon this dozen or so, the results of which we can actually see—for head, hair, eyes, nose, lips, and so on—that we rely for stock and racial diagnosis; all the others, so far as we know, may be constant for all groups." Even the contrast of black and white turns out, on scientific analysis, to be less marked than it appears to the untutored eye. All human skins contain basically the same pigments; only their relative frequency or concentration is different. There is some white in black skins, just as there is some black in white skins; there can therefore be no question of absolute contrasts. The same is true of other features asserted to keep the races apart. Take the cranial or cephalic index, the relationship of the length to the width of the skull. Mediterraneans— for instance, Italians—tend to be round-headed, brachycephalic; Northerners —for instance, Danes—long-headed or dolichocephalic. Yet there are plenty of dolichocephalic Italians and of brachycephalic Danes. In a sample of 300 Copenhagen girls, all blond and blue-eyed, taken for a different purpose, Rose Franzblau found very few long-headed specimens—only 5% of the total ("Race Differences in Mental and Physical Traits, Studied in Different Environments," *Archives of Psychology*, 28 [April 1935], 35). This may be an accident, but it is a significant one. On the average, Danes are more dolichocephalic and less bra- chycephalic than Italians, but what do averages mean? They mean little in any case, but they mean least where they would have to mean most if racialism is to be supported. In remote and isolated areas, where pure races still exist, if they exist anywhere, for instance, in Scandinavian mountain valleys, the char- acteristics of separate familial descent lines are much more prominent than the unitary features of the Nordic type. But all this is, in the final analysis, irrelevant. Any skull can come to harbor any content, if social education, the internalization of norms, is appropriate.

Much more important for the scientific physiological classification of human types than skin color and head shape are the differences in blood groups of which generally four categories are distinguished (A, B, AB, and O). But their distribution, too, has apparently nothing to do with the socio-cultural variety of the human race. Even here we can see, behind physical multiplicity, a more basic physical uniformity. If we may quote Krogman once again: "The inher- itance of blood groups cuts straight across all stocks, all races; that is, all blood groups are found in all races, though in varying percentage combinations" ("Concept of Race," p. 45). There has been plenty of talk, in racialist liter- ature, of the importance of blood, and especially "pure" blood (which, after centuries of race mixture, does not exist), for human culture and human con- duct, but at the decisive point the argument has always trailed off into a material- istic kind of mysticism, the worst kind of mysticism there is. No proof has ever been presented that populations with a prevalence of one of the blood types has, for this reason, developed its characteristic culture and mode of conduct. But without a strict causal analysis, all assertions to this effect fail to convince.

With the physiological unity of the human race which, as we have seen, shines, on analysis, again and again through the more superficial diversity, why, so we must ask, have racial differences ever developed? The best answer, if not the only answer, which science can give, is still along Darwinian lines. "Variations in skin color may be due to certain processes of differential selection related to the actinic [i.e., chemical-change–producing] rays of the sun," writes Otto

Klineberg in his authoritative article "Racial Psychology" (in *Science of Man*, ed. Linton, pp. 67, 68).

> In northern Europe a relatively unpigmented skin would be an advantage for survival, since such a skin would aid in the absorption of the comparatively weak actinic rays. Conversely, in the tropics a dark skin would have survival value, since the pigment would act as a preventive against too large an amount of such absorption. Given enough time, we would expect those with fairer skins to survive in the north and those of darker skins in the tropics.

This explanation of the origin of races, i.e., hereditarily transmitted physical types, is in contrast both to radical monogenism and to radical polygenism, while preserving the kernels of truth contained in both. It agrees with monogenism insofar as it sees a common starting point of evolution and considers the ensuing diversification of the human species as merely a secondary development. But it also agrees with racialism because it considers the end point of evolution to be the emergence of genetically contrasting subspecies, whose distinguishing marks are real and abiding, and go well beyond the contrast in skin coloration. The races, such as selective evolution has established them, are different in several physical functions. They do not have the same capacities for the output of energy or for resistance to various diseases, they do not have precisely the same glandular equipment and balance of hormones (to mention only a few facts), and some of the innate differences cannot fail to influence, not only physical, but even social, life (for instance, a different degree of nervous excitability). Many of these distinctions, if not indeed all, result ultimately from dissimilar environmental conditions, but that does not make them any the less real.

From the physiological point of view, then, races have to be cleanly distinguished, but that does not mean that the distinctions drawn by the physiologist are important for the sociologist and social psychologist as well. Apart from those very few who still adhere to the crude physiological materialism preached in the middle of the nineteenth century by such men as Jacob Moleschott and today generally abandoned, there is now widespread agreement that physical constitution and socio-moral conduct are not causally connected. "Only in the case of relatively small isolated and inbred communities . . . can one speak with any degree of probability of a racial psychology. For the larger, more heterogeneous populations . . . 'race' and psychology appear, in the present stage of our knowledge, to be unrelated," writes Otto Klineberg (ibid., pp. 77, 66). So far as the bulk of mankind is concerned,

> there has been no acceptable demonstration of any relationship between physique and personality within the normal range of individual variations. The correlations between traits of intelligence or temperament, on the one hand, and anatomical characteristics (stature, skin color, shape of head, size of head, height of forehead, and so on), on the other, have almost invariably yielded results of no predictive value.

Turning the argument more in the direction of the general drift of the present volume, we can express the essential truth by saying that the social potentialities of human beings are not predetermined by their bodily actualities; whatever the color of his skin or outline of his skull, whatever the activity of his secretive glands, any man can learn any kind of discipline and can become an integrated part of any system of social control, for quite generally, as Krogman puts it ("Concept of Race," p. 61), "bio-genetic potentials are shared equally by all stocks and by all races." "There are no known differences among races of men which either interfere with or facilitate the learning of cultural forms" (Margaret Mead, "National Character," in *Anthropology Today*, ed. A. L. Kroeber [Chicago, 1965], p. 646).

At this point it is appropriate, not to say advisable, to cast a short glance at the alleged differences in native intelligence between the races, partly because the discussion around this topic has not yet been put to rest, and partly because a proper analysis and comparison of mental traits will lead us to the true source from which the social variety of the human species ultimately flows. Two introductory remarks are necessary. The one concerns the physiological aspects of the matter, the other its technical (mensurational) aspects. It would be totally unfair to compare the level of intelligence in a well-nourished and an ill-nourished population and to draw inferences from the test results obtained concerning the mental capacities of the groups tested. Surely, a group exposed to nutritional deficiencies, especially deficiency in protein, which is a kind of brain food, is bound to perform less well than a group with a normal, protein-providing diet. Only equally well-fed populations can be validly compared. But this difficulty in the way of a valid comparison appears small when we see it alongside the other which we have mentioned. Interracial comparisons, to be convincing, would have to be based on culture-free tests. If the tests probe for capacities which are well developed in one culture and undeveloped in another —for instance, if they concentrate on mathematical reasoning which is cultivated in America and comparatively neglected in native Africa or Australia —then they measure educational achievement (of a special sort) and by no means general, hereditarily transmitted intelligence. The two points which we have mentioned are apt, between them, to throw most of the statistics alleged to show the superiority of some groups over others out of court.

Let us therefore concentrate, in this brief survey, on comparisons between roughly comparable populations—not on the blacks and whites in America, for the blacks have in the past never been so well nourished or so well taught as the whites, but on the Nordics and the Mediterraneans, more concretely, Italians and Danes. Assuming that the American-born children of immigrant parents have had about the same chances in life (an assumption only partially true since the Danish-American fathers showed, in Franzblau's investigation, a higher occupational level than the Italian-American ones ["Race Differences," 42]), setting aside, for simplicity's sake, such disturbing factors as differential nutrition, etc., what do we find? "The research . . . has almost invariably led to the same conclusions: the North European groups were generally found to be the most intelligent and the South European groups the least" (p. 13).

These statistics passed for a while as supports of racialist theories o' intelligence distribution between the racial stocks until it dawned on the investigators that racialist–hereditarist inferences could only be drawn if the two populations showed the same discrepancies everywhere, not only in America, but also in their European home countries. Applying the International Intelligence Examination to four groups of 300 girls each, 300 Danish-American and 300 Danish in Denmark as well as 300 Italian-American and 300 Italian in Italy, Franzblau found that the assertions of the racialists fell to the ground. "In line with the findings of other investigators in this field, we find the American Danes definitely superior in intelligence to the American Italians," she writes (p. 16). However, she continues,

> when we compare these groups in their native countries, this difference disappears. . . . The average total score of the Danish sampling from Copenhagen is not reliably different from that of the Italian sampling from Rome. The difference is only -.71 times its standard error, proving the Italian to be quite as intelligent, according to the International Intelligence Test, as the Dane. This finding points to the conclusion that the differences which have so frequently been found between samplings of these racial groups in the United States are due to the operation of other factors than inherent racial inequality [p. 16; see also the strong words on p. 41].

What other factors, we must ask? The answer cannot be in doubt: cultural factors. The Dane immigrating into the United States enters a society much closer to his native one—much closer, above all, to the order of values instilled into him at home and handed on, in time, to his children—than the Italian. To pick out just one trait of some significance: North American society is the capitalist society κατ' ἐξοχήν. Its roots lie in the mentality known to sociologists as the Protestant Ethic. Danish Lutheranism is incomparably closer to that mentality than Italian Catholicism. A whole wide range of consequences follows from this fact. It reaches from the tendency of the South Europeans to prefer jobs involving personal contacts and the preparedness of the North Europeans to accept an entirely impersonal climate at work, to the Protestant attunement to more abstract and the Catholic alignment with more concrete or pictorial modes of thought. Clearly, the Dane, even the American-born Dane, is closer to the new country than the Italian, even the American-born one. And this explains both the larger discrepancy in test scores between European-born immigrants and the smaller, progressively more and more marginal, discrepancies in the case of their offspring.

We have quoted only one investigation out of an uncountable multitude, but it must and may suffice in our context. Let us merely emphasize, before passing on, that the case of the blacks and whites is hardly different from that of the long-skulled blondes and the round-headed brunettes. "When American Negroes live under relatively favorable environmental conditions," writes Klineberg ("Racial Psychology," p. 70), "their test scores are correspondingly high, and when whites live under relatively poor conditions, their test scores are correspondingly low. It is apparently not 'race' but environment which is the crucial variable." Other authors, such as Philip E. Vernon (*Intelligence and Cultural Environment*; London, 1972), are more careful, but their final judgment is hardly different: "At the moment we can only hazard the guess that there are some genetic differences involved in some of the mental differences between ethnic groups, though their influence is probably small relative to that of the tremendous cultural differences. . . . Clearly the major barrier to the fuller realization of human intellectual potential lies in the realm of adult values and child-rearing practices" (pp. 13, 232).

There is one small detail which comes repeatedly to the surface in investigations of this kind, which deserves to be mentioned, and indeed to be emphasized, here because it has high diagnostic value. Books like A. M. Shuey's *The Testing of Negro Intelligence* (Lynchburg, Va., 1958) and A. H. Passow's *Education in Depressed Areas* (New York, 1963) go to show that the test performances of blacks fall progressively below those of whites as they grow older; in other words, the closer the subjects tested were to birth, the nearer they were to each other in intelligence. This surely proves that such differences as exist or, rather, emerge are owing, not to genetic factors, but to environmental–educational ones. Even if there were some variations in native acuteness between human descent groups, so we must conclude, they would not be such that they could not be removed by appropriate educational methods.

The upshot of our whole disquisition, then, is that it is not nature which accounts for the socio-cultural variety of mankind—neither the nature which encompasses our bodies from without nor the nature which operates in our bodies from within. We must find the cause of that variety in the socio-cultural condition itself. Durkheim was right: social facts have always to be derived from more basic social facts. But before we turn to this topic, we have to look at a problem which lies, as it were, across our path: the influence of the sex dichotomy on society, and especially on the socialization process. Here, if anywhere, we should see the power of nature at work. Negro men and white men or Negro women and white women are not so different, genetically, that they would constitute radically distinct sociological types; but males and females certainly are.

To say that nature has prepared or destined men and women for different kinds of work and therefore for different social positions is to make a very trite statement, a statement which would be universally accepted. Yet trite and acceptable as it is, such a formulation would be highly problematical. For it must surely be asked how binding nature's arrangements are, whether society must fall in with them or is free to reject them; in other words: whether there is merely predisposition or strict predetermination. It follows from the whole tenor of the present work that it must, at this crucial point, opt and plead for mere predisposition and deny strict predetermination. True, if nature-given tendencies are allowed to prevail, if a culture simply drifts in the directions imparted to it by its physical substratum or substrata, it will give women social roles which are merely annexes, as it were, to their physical roles. That has often happened, but by no means always and everywhere. By nature, women are better equipped to nurse (in either sense of the word) than to fight, but the girl soldiers of King Abeokuta were a formidable fighting force on the battlefield. By nature, men are better equipped to fight than to tend babies, but most pediatricians are males and even mothers must take their cues from them. It is with sex-tied tendencies as with every other body-borne impetus. Culture can countermand them. Our bodies certainly predispose us to prefer, in every situation, our own interest, our own sum total of pleasure, to the interest, the satisfaction, of others; but as cultured personalities we can, and sometimes do, act otherwise.

What precisely are the specific predispositions of men and women respectively? In answering this question, we must start from the simplest fact of sexual life. Males are so made that they are capable of a quick build-up of energy and its equally quick discharge, after which there normally supervenes a stretch of time during which rest, not to say inactivity, is in order. Women, on the other hand, are attuned to the necessity of living through protracted periods of subserviency to their procreational task: gestation lasts nine months. Thus we have an emphasis on activity on the one side, a demand for endurance on the other. This endurance, it is said, is not only demanded by nature, but imperatively imposed by her. Whereas man's life is not structured and dominated by sexuality, woman's is. The differences between a young man and a middle-aged man, or between a middle-aged man and a man of declining years, are nothing as compared to the differences between a virgin and a mother, or a mother and a woman past the menopause. Man is comparatively free, woman comparatively tied—caught, so to speak, in a nearly inescapable condition. The bitter complaints voiced by women writers like Simone de Beauvoir root in these facts. Many societies have accepted them. Sweeping surveys by anthropologists, such as George P. Murdock's "Comparative Data on Division of Labor by Sex" (*Social Forces*, 15, No. 4 [May 1937], pp. 551–53) show that men tend to be hunters, trappers, fishermen, and, above all, warriors, while women are usually cooks and dressmakers or tailors, and the like. These occupations Thorstein Veblen has characterized as "drudgery," while giving the work of males the sobriquet "exploit."

We have spoken of facts and advisedly so, facts which we do not mean to deny or even to belittle. But perhaps it is permissible to distinguish preliminary and final facts; differently expressed: tendencies which may, and tendencies which must, prevail. As we have just said, many societies have accepted the predispositions laid on by nature in males and females respectively and shaped their division of labor and thence of norms accordingly, but others have not. Margaret Mead, in her book *Male and Female*, has given examples on both sides. The Iatmul, fierce head-hunters, use the male bent toward belligerency to the full and restrict the womenfolk to the humdrum tasks of everyday life; the Manus and the Balinese have worked out one style of life and effort which is the same for both sexes. The Manus are rather puritanical; they do not allow sexuality a large share in their lives; they cover it up. The Balinese have embraced a quiet and steady mode of existence. Whatever they do, they do slowly, peaceably and systematically, without discontinuity and without rush, whether they belong to the one sexual group or to the other. They obviously believe that they have found a better mode of being than that of the beast (Harmondsworth, 1967; pp. 162, 166, 167).

It is true, of course, that only the ovum has to be renewed every four weeks, but not semen; that, therefore, only women are subject to menstruation, and the first of the menses is an event of prime importance in a female life. But it is equally true that culture to a large extent bridges the gap which nature has in this way opened up. Psychological investigations show that sexual maturity and social, or, more simply, human, maturity do not coincide. "In summary, we may say," writes Franzblau ("Race Differences," 34, 42), "that our findings fail entirely to support the claims of those investigators who report the existence of definite relationships between mental and physical maturity. . . . No relationship was found between intelligence ratio and age of first menstruation or between mental age and weight–height ratio. There is thus no relationship between mental and physical precocity or retardation." Any materialistic or psychological determinism is therefore unjustified. And if the maturing of the body tends to mature the mind, with its adjunct, social and moral behavior, culture for its part also tends to help the body, even the sexual apparatus, to mature; there is a two-way street, a mutual influence. City girls menstruate earlier than country girls and upper-class girls earlier than lower-class girls (pp. 22, 23). Several factors are responsible for these discrepancies, some purely somatic (heredity), some mixed (quantity and quality of nourishment), but some purely cultural (intensity of mental stimulation).

Calvin P. Stone and Roger G. Barker, in a meritorious study ("The Attitudes and Interests of Premenarcheal and Post Menarcheal Girls," *Journal of Genetic Psychology*, 54, No. 1 [March 1939], 27–71), have entered more deeply into this problem and investigated, not only the relationship of physical and social maturity, but the changes in the order of values coinciding with the first of the menses; they have therefore come much closer to the core of the sociological interest. They have arrived at the conclusion that "premenarcheal and post menarcheal girls of the same chronological ages and social status respond differently to the items of an attitude-interest questionnaire" (p. 61). But this general result (which will surprise nobody) does not give much support to the claims of a physiological determinism, for the authors add: "Certainly interests and attitudes as tapped by our questionnaire differentiate the post menarcheal and premenarcheal groups much less strikingly than do anthropometric measures during these adolescent years" (p. 60).

The authors also have a close look at the general question of causation, asking whether the new attitudes and interests of the ripened girls result from the physical changes which have occurred or, perhaps, as well, totally or partially, from their altered social position and relations; what they say is highly instructive. We make no apologies for quoting the passage in full:

> It is generally known that certain physical changes associated with the menarche are to be accounted for in terms of specific tissue responsiveness to hormones of the anterior lobe of the pituitary and to hormones from the gonads. Perhaps certain behavioral changes as manifested in interests and attitudes also can be accredited to hormones from one or both of these glands. In this connection, however, one must not overlook or underestimate the importance of extrinsic factors, particularly those of an ideational type, which undoubtedly would play a more potent role in man than in lower animals lacking man's cultural background. It is not unlikely that self-evident changes in adolescent physique (accelerated growth, enlargement of the accessory sexual organs, hirsuties, etc.) and the onset of the menses give rise in the adolescent to new interests, new aspirations, and new conception of freedom and restrictions imposed by society on persons who have passed that milestone in development which in all

ages has separated the child from the young adult. . . . there may be differences in the social stimulation directed by adults to post menarcheal and premenarcheal girls. If so, these social pressures could account for new types of interests, attitudes, or other mental residuals that show up in adolescent responses to items of a questionnaire [ibid.].

These words are cautious, perhaps overly cautious, but in whatever light they are seen, they do bring out the importance of the socio-cultural factor present even in the consequences of what is basically a somatic process. The girl who has menstruated for the first time *knows* that she is no longer a child; it is her *knowledge* of the physical fact which changes her order of values, not the fact itself. And because she regards herself as an adult, or a near adult, she will act differently in relation to others and will be differently reacted to and acted at. "You can't treat her now as if she were a baby," people will say, and so there will be a totally new definition of her situation, a totally new set of social circumstances. In other words: different models will now be applied, different patterns of action and interaction followed. Above all, different *norms* will be considered as applicable, new rights conceded, and new duties imposed. All these, however, are human, social, cultural elements, and the physical change is no more than a signal for their entry into operation, an occasion, not a cause.

All this goes to show that a difference in body is not yet, *per se*, a difference in mind and mode of conduct. But nothing which we have said so far would fully justify the phrase which we used above: namely, that the gap between men and women is being "bridged." The time has now come to look at the facts which make it entirely correct. Chief of these facts is the existence, in most societies, of ceremonies which mark the transition from boyhood to manhood as the first mensis marks the transition from girlhood to womanhood: the foreskin is circumcised, teeth knocked out, the face scarified, the arms tattooed, and so on— rites no less bound to affect the body and to alter the mind and the personality than the appearance of the first menstrual blood. Some cultures go so far as to establish a close parallel between the two sexes: men are bled so that they are freed from "bad blood" that may have accumulated within them. Margaret Mead does not hesitate to speak of a "male menstruation" in these cases (*Male and Female*, p. 175). Here, clearly, the gap is indeed bridged.

Of course, a cardinal difference, or the cardinal difference, remains: boys become warriors, and girls, as a rule, do not, and this contrast results from nature rather than culture. Here we behold the area in which the social division of functions has most closely followed the natural distinction in physical equipment, in which society has most consistently pursued the lines of development prefigured in its natural substratum. We are thinking less, at this point, of the fact that men are larger in stature and stouter of muscle than women, or that women would be hampered, on the warpath, by pregnancy and even by menstruation: we are thinking, above all, of the dependence, in nature, of aggressivity on the male sex hormone, androgen. If the materialistic assertion that physical nature determines social phenomena is correct anywhere, it is correct here. Yet even here it is only largely and not entirely correct. If we place ourselves, as we should, on the Darwinian analysis, then survival is the keynote of the arrangements of nature. But the male involvement in and commitment to the defense of the group are hostile to survival because men are in fact not, what they are so often called, the stronger sex. On the contrary. They are lower in vitality. Before birth, more male fetuses are aborted than female; at birth, girls are more fully developed than boys; girls progress more quickly than boys, their teeth, for instance, cutting earlier, and so on; on reaching puberty, girls have an advantage of about two years; and their greater toughness lasts to their dying day. It is generally known that at all ages female life expectancy is superior to male. Therefore, theoretically, male lives are more precious and should receive heightened protection for the sake of survival. (In recent years, advances in pharmacology have improved the survival chances of male babies, but this fact is irrelevant here because we are speaking of what is natural and not of what is purposefully, i.e., culturally, engineered.) The fact that nature has connected aggressivity with androgen seems to contradict Darwinism at this point; nature seems to have made an arrangement which is anti-vital. Yet appearances are deceptive. In nature (and that is a point where nature and culture are different) aggressivity, the fighting spirit, rarely leads to annihilation. Animal males challenge each other, snarl at each other, turn menacingly around each other, in short, play at conflict, but they rarely kill. The weaker retreats before he is destroyed. Only man is different; only his conflicts are man-killing. Intraspecific wars are rare in nature; they are regular in history. What, then, is responsible for this contrast between nature and "culture"? Undoubtedly, it is the presence of, and the intervention of, reason, and especially of that trait of reason, consistency. Man goes to the logical limit, the animals do not. One is reminded here of the words which Goethe puts into the mouth of Mephisto:

> He calls it reason; but, by a strange twist,
> It makes him beastlier than any beast
> [*Faust*, Part 1, "Prologue in Heaven"].

Our main point in this context is, of course, that the division of labor between the sexes, and especially the imposition of the defense role on the male, though basically natural is at the same time also social. Even here, it would seem, nature inclines rather than compels, suggests rather than enforces, social phenomena.

Turning away now from aggressivity and war, we may generalize a little and say that social roles depend not only, or even not mainly, on physical roles, but also, and perhaps predominantly, on a society's ideas about these roles. What men and women do depends only partially on what nature has best equipped them for, or what they *can* do, but partially also on what culture considers they *should* do. Travelers in Russia return often deeply shocked at what they have seen there: women carrying heavy loads. This is against the Western ethos with its traditions of chivalry, with its idealized image of woman as ethereal and fragile, but it is not against basic natural fact. Russian women are potentially capable of carrying heavy loads, and they actually learn how to carry them. No doubt, diseases may spring from this particular occupation if social legislation does not introduce safeguards for health, but so they may from any occupation if rendered unduly burdensome and exhausting; so they may in the case of men.

One particular sex role (in the wider, cultural—not natural—sense of the word) which is almost universally considered as nature-given, but which in fact is nothing of the kind, is paternity. It would be so only if our species were endowed, as some animals are, with an inbred and inborn paternal instinct activated automatically at the appearance of offspring, but of such an instinct there is in reality no trace: witness the reluctance of "natural," i.e., illegitimate fathers, to pay child support. Margaret Mead calls Chapter 9 of her book "Human Fatherhood Is a Social Invention," and gives the facts in so clear and succinct a form that we can do no better than to quote her:

> Male sexuality seems originally focused to no goal beyond immediate discharge; it is society that provides the male with a desire for children. . . . Men's desire for children is learned. . . . Among our structurally closest analogues— the primates—the male does not feed the female. Heavy with young, making her way laboriously along, she fends for herself. He may fight to protect her or to possess her, but he does not nurture her. . . . Man, the heir of tradition, provides for women and children. We have no indication that man the animal, man unpatterned by social learning, would do anything of the sort [*Male and Female*, pp. 215, 212, 181, 182].

From whatever side one approaches the complex of facts with which we are concerned at the moment, even if one starts out from the hard and irremovable physical givens, analysis, provided it is unbiased, will in the end lead to the recognition that culture and ethos, custom and education, are ultimately decisive for the conditions which emerge, in the course of history, from the natural, subcultural bases. Sex differences may be culturally played up or played down; in the one case they will tell, in the other mean but little, at least comparatively speaking. Sometimes the very organizational facts of a society will be responsible for the pattern of sex relationships, sometimes the values which arise from these facts; as Marx would have said, sometimes the substructure, sometimes the superstructure. The former case is illustrated in John J. Honigmann's book *Personality in Culture* (New York, Evanston, & London, 1967; p. 311):

> Sex differences in socialization are . . . marked whenever people live in extended families that contain two or more generations, practice polygamy, or follow other customs likely to build up large, highly cooperative, composite households. However, when each nuclear family of husband, wife and children lives alone, so that each spouse must on occasion be ready and able to assume the other's roles, then differences in the rearing of boys and girls go unemphasized.

We can see that even what Marx calls the substructure has different layers: the constitution of the family—extended *versus* nuclear family—is prior and basic to the elaboration of the relationship between the sexes considered as social groups. The relations which thus take shape may equally well be characterized by equality and inequality, harmony and exploitation; absence or presence of emphasis on the sexual factor does not *per se* prejudge the question as to whether the sexes will be hostile classes rather than cooperative units or vice versa. Which way evolution will go, whether or not it will proceed in a patripotestal direction, will then depend on further (cultural) determinations. Sometimes, however, the valuational, we may even say, the power–political factor may be dominant. It may be the cause of development rather than the effect. "In parts of old Japan, the four-year-old male, because he was a male, could terrorize his mother and the other females of the household," writes Margaret Mead (*Male and Female*, p. 87). "His maleness overrode the difference in size that would have made it possible for any of the females to have given him a sound thrashing." In this case it is not a neutral substructure which creates an appropriate superstructure, but a value-laden superstructure which creates an appropriate substructure, i.e., corresponding forms of social organization. A society has a choice. It can either place the stress on the fact that children—all children, both male and female—are juniors and in need of control, and then the sexual factor will be minimized; or it can give greater weight to the fact that some children are males (and thus prestigious) and others females (and thus not prestigious), in which case the sexual factor will stand out and may even be maximized. This has only remotely to do with nature; it has more to do with a socially established value judgment, partly certainly derived from, partly imposed on, the natural facts.

The informed reader will surely have noticed that, in this discussion, we are taking a very un-Freudian, indeed, an anti-Freudian attitude. It was one of Freud's deeper convictions that nature has established and forever secured the predominance of the male since she has given him, in his penis, a privilege which females are denied and must forever envy. In Paretian language: nature has given the male, along with a physical feature, a *sentiment de domination*, and women a correspondingly opposite *sentiment de submission*. But quite apart from the fact that this alleged privilege is, even according to Freud himself, problematical (since it saddles men with a fear of castration), it is organically connected with a countermanding weakness—barrenness, the inability to bear children. Karen Horney was surely justified when she pitted against Freud's concept of penis-envy her own assertion of womb-envy on the part of the male. The truth is that any such envy is based on social valuations and not on anatomical facts; whether females will think their own fate harder or whether males will (even the latter is observable in some societies) depends predominantly on cultural currents. We range ourselves once again by the side of Margaret Mead: "Sharp envy of opposite sex anatomy . . . may or may not develop. . . . Envy of the male role can come as much from an undervaluation of the role of the wife and mother as from an overvaluation of . . . aspects of achievement that have been reserved for men" (ibid., pp. 96, 102). But whatever alternative applies, one thing is certain: it is *we* who value, and not nature for us.

Many other factors have entered into the social relationships of men and women as they have historically developed and into the socialization processes to which boys and girls are respectively exposed: for instance, the representation of women as temptresses and, hence, disturbers of the peace, and the conception of the menstrual blood as a magically defiling matter. We have no need to discuss such details; we are concerned merely with principles. The two influences which we have mentioned (both, as it happens, inimical to women's interests), are clearly *ideas*, and it was surely their progressive defeat in a struggle of *ideas* which has been responsible, in recent times, for the striking improvements in women's rights which have taken place.

Let us now, before concluding this long parenthesis in our analysis, have a closer look at the socialization process as influenced by the sex dichotomy, and at the parts played, actively and passively, by men and women. Much will depend on who is singled out, by the culture concerned, as the enforcer of norms; more brutally expressed: as the one who thrashes a child when he has been naughty. It may be, and often is, the father; it may be the mother's brother; and it may also be the mother. (Even in decidedly patripotestal societies there are always cases where a father, being tenderhearted, may leave this unpleasant task to his wife.) The tamer will, of course, be feared and resented, albeit often only fitfully, and therefore the father–son relationship may be difficult. It was very difficult in the second half of the nineteenth century when the head of the family was generally considered the absolute master of whom the children had to stand in awe. The intrafamilial conditions which then existed account for the Freudian concept of the Oedipus complex, which we would prefer to describe as a Jupiter complex, since the linkage, asserted by Freud, with a supposed desire, on a boy's part, sexually to possess his mother, appears to us unconvincing—unconvincing for two reasons. The first is that girls can suffer from father-fear and father-hatred as well as boys can. (A classical example, known to lovers of English literature, is the case of Elizabeth Barrett Browning.) The second and much more weighty reason is that boys can develop such fear and hatred as easily in relation to their mothers as they can in relation to their fathers that we find a Juno complex alongside a Jupiter complex wherever the mother is the martinet. "Although [a boy of] six is often described as being 'embroiled with' his mother," write two child psychologists, Arnold Gesell and F. L. Ilg in *The Child from Five to Ten* (New York, 1946; p. 118), "he is actually extremely ambivalent in regard to her. He may say 'I love you' at one minute and 'I hate you, I wish you were dead,' at the next. He is most loving with his mother, yet most of his tantrums are directed against her." And why? Clearly because she takes good care of him, yet at the same time must, even in our culture, help to educate him, that is, frustrate some of his most elementary self-regarding wishes.

Clearly, then, it is not natural sexuality, but the differentiation in the social function of the two sexes—sternness *versus* indulgence—which accounts for the contrasting roles which they play in the economy of socialization. But what about the position of the child within that economy? When we come to consider this aspect, we do find an important difference between boys and girls; we find that there is a crisis—psychologists would speak of an "identification crisis"—which hits the boys, but largely bypasses the girls, so that the process of growing up is somewhat smoother for them. All children identify by preference with their mother, and she remains an entirely appropriate model for her daughters; but, of course, not for her sons. These must, if they are to grow up, break their early identification with a woman and substitute a direction-giving male one, for instance, identification with their father. If they do not achieve this feat, they will become misfits, with homosexuality as one of the dangers which threaten. Talcott Parsons has strongly underlined this divergence between the male and the female in early life: The "girl can, in relation to her mother, repeat on a higher level the infantile identification. She can, to a degree, take over the mother's role, which she does as an apprentice in the household and, in phantasy, in doll-play. . . . The boy, on the other hand, must break radically with his earlier identification pattern" ("Social Structure and the Development of the Personality," p. 184). There is somewhat more to this divergence than meets the eye. The adolescent girl who helps in kitchen and nursery is sure to feel useful and important; she is also, on occasions, likely to be praised; in any case, she continues contact with her mother or even intensifies it. Thus she will have a relatively pleasant life experience. It is not so with the boys. Since the center of men's activities is normally outside the house, they must undergo a rather more radical redirection, with all the unavoidable uncertainties, anxieties, and sufferings connected with it. Some primitive societies smooth the path by instituting young men's clubs, men's houses etc., but some painfulness will continue to cling to the transition from boy to man. Of course, there may also be a valuable compensation. He who has successfully managed to realign himself may, indeed will, find his character strengthened. Women may, to some extent, remain more childlike all their lives, while men will develop decidedly adult traits, such as a spirit of independence and even a Paretian *sentiment de domination*. The stronger position which they occupy in most societies may well be causally connected with these facts.

Now, we must ask, what is the nature of these facts? Are they physical facts or social facts? The answer must be that they are both, but that their power of causation is owing to the social element in them, while the physical basis is more remote and only indirectly influential. What we have emphasized before, must be reiterated here: society is free to arrange its affairs as it sees fit and even in such a manner that its arrangements cut across what we would be inclined to call "natural," and even of what might rightfully be called "natural in itself." The head-hunting Iatmul along the Sepik river of New Guinea give pride of place to the male, the killing male, and every boy is expected to become a killer. Yet Margaret Mead, who knows them well, can write about them:

> Little boys take almost as much care of infants as do girls, and even young adolescent boys spend a good deal of time playing with babies. In manner, they are surprisingly feminine. . . . Later, in their early teens, and long before they wish to go, they are whisked away to be initiated, and then afterwards spend several miserable months, and sometimes years, during which the women chase them away, while they themselves are loath enough to join the men [*Male and Female*, p. 104].

Here the great transition is made more difficult, through cultural conditions, than it naturally need be. But difficult as it is, it is easy in comparison with the realignment expected from, and imposed on, girls among the Manus of the Admiralty Islands. What society has instituted here appears to us quite unnatural and may in fact be objectively so described:

> The small girl first becomes attached to her father, and then, at five or six, must return to the women, because the avoidances and taboos connected with marriages and prospective marriages would embarrass the men and boys among

whom her father and brother move freely. Her identification with the female group is never as happy or as complete as her brother's identification with the male group [p. 101].

All this goes to show, and to show convincingly, that reaching adulthood is not a process like the growing of beards or the budding of breasts, not a process which results from hormonal changes as these developments are, but the work of socio-cultural, truly human forces, and this is the main thesis which the long interlude which we are now bringing to a close, was meant to show.

The good look which we have just had at the problem posed by the physical distinction and the mutual dependence of the two halves of the human race, the sexes, has taught us something, not only about this narrow topic, but also about the unity and the multiplicity of mankind and its culture and cultures in general. There is, to begin with, a natural fact; there is, arising from it, a challenge socially to respond to this fact. On the human level, the relations between the males and females of the species must not only run off and work themselves out according to the laws of nature, they must also be culturally organized. Creatures capable of reflection and foreknowledge realize that the sex act, while offering momentary satisfactions, has in the long run onerous consequences which must be mastered. There is a problem of fairness and justice: the female is saddled with months of pregnancy and years of child care. Nature has in some instances solved this difficulty, in some not. She has either created a paternal instinct or refused to do so. It is by no means clear what she has done or refused to do in the case of our pre- and subhuman ancestors, but in practice this does not matter to the sociologist. If there ever existed a paternal instinct in the hominid, which is highly doubtful, it has disappeared in the course of evolution. *Homo sapiens* therefore had to opt and has opted for a solution which is peculiar to him: he has developed the institution of marriage, of the family. The challenge was posed by nature; the response has come from society. The challenge is always the same; the response is to some extent—basically—also the same, but to some extent—in the concrete—different. And so it is with most social institutions. The need for them is laid on in the physical constitution of things; the answer or, rather, answers to that need are found in and by human, social, moral searching and experimentation. The original problem is universal; so is the necessity of solving it; but the solutions to it may be, and are, very varied.

The institution of marriage or of the family regulates, however, not only the relations between men and women, but also those between men and men, on the one hand, and women and women, on the other; and because this is so, it is truly archetypal for all socio-cultural ordering or form- and norm-giving. In their elemental desire to secure sex satisfactions, men will compete with men for access to women, and women with women for the services of men. In this competition, there lurk dire consequences—the possibility of social strife, and war literally to the knife, to say nothing of the waste of effort and energy which mankind, an ever-hungry species, can ill afford. The challenge presented by nature in this field is, therefore, not only to find a bond which will unite fathers and mothers so that they come to carry the burden of procreation together, but also to discipline and tame the entire sex drive, to moderate its violence, until it is no longer a danger to continued pacific and cooperative existence. The injunctions of Holy Writ "Thou shalt not commit adultery" and "Thou shalt not covet thy neighbor's wife" are culturally created dams against an animalic flood which might well inundate society and destroy it, and other traditions have parallel commandments. Here, too, the problem is universal; the necessity of solving it, equally universal; but the concrete forms of sexual discipline as numerous, or nearly so, as the societies which have sprung up in time and place.

It is hardly necessary to point out that what is true of the sexual drive is true of the instinct of nutrition, the hunger drive, also. Human life has often been described as a continued struggle for access to the trough, and though this expression is crude, it is undoubtedly correct. The crux of the matter is that (as we have shown in the first volume of this work—see esp. p. 83) nature has organized the war for survival, the process of selection, as a contest between individuals, and that she has laid the elementary desire to be only into individuals. In Hobbist language, all men naturally crave what is good for themselves (*bonum sibi*) and so they must "naturally" clash (*homo homini lupus*). If social forms of being are to exist, therefore, natural propensities have to be controlled, and that is a universal necessity. But the discipline which, for the sake of sociality, is imposed on the individual, may take a thousand and one shapes, and so there is one starting point and innumerable issues, one question but innumerable answers, all equally fitting. To give a simple example: to reduce our greed, society has invented and enforces table manners. We must eat our soup not just in any fashion, but with the help of a spoon. But in some countries it is good form to move the spoon toward oneself and in others away from oneself—to speak of only two possibilities. All these techniques are equally efficacious as methods of drive reduction; society has far-reaching freedom in shaping them; but society is under constraint, is absolutely forced, to institute *some* kind of table manners, for the greeds centering in the intake of nourishment cannot go unchecked.

The general diagnosis of the relation between unity and diversity in social institutions which we have outlined often appears in sociological and anthropological literature. Thus Clyde Kluckhohn writes in his essay "Universal Categories of Culture": "All cultures constitute so many somewhat distinct answers to essentially the same questions posed by human biology and by the generalities of the human situation" (in *Anthropology Today*, ed. Kroeber, p. 520). Kluckhohn also quotes from a paper of A. L. Kroeber's, "The Concept of Culture in Science," first published in the *Journal of General Education* (3, No. 3 [April 1949], 182–96): "Such more or less recurrent near-regularities of form or process as have to date been formulated for culture are actually mainly subcultural in nature. They are limits set to culture by physical or organic factors. The so-called 'cultural constants' of family, religion, war, communication and the like appear to be biopsychological frames variably filled with cultural content . . ." ("Universal Categories of Culture," p. 516). This formulation, it is true, contains a problem to which we shall have to revert; but, as the last words in particular indicate, the general attitude of Kroeber's is close to that of Kluck-hohn and to our own.

Many more passages from the literature could be quoted here which are similar in general attitude, and between them they go to prove that there is widespread agreement in this field. And yet it is precisely this field in which particularly violent discussions have raged. Two parties have formed, one asserting that there is unity rather than multiplicity, the other that there is multiplicity rather than unity. Clearly, what we have before us in this regrettable contest is merely a pseudo-problem. Everything depends on clear definitions. Westerners try to preserve the life of their parents as long as humanly possible. Eskimos, on the other hand, and quite a few other peoples as well, apply the principle of euthanasia, dispatching them as painlessly as they can when existence has turned into a burden. We may speak here with equal justification both of uniformity and of variation. There is general comparability but specific divergence. Both cultures contain techniques for the care of the aged, but these techniques are *in concreto* sharply contrasting. And so it is in every area of observation. To express it all in sociological jargon: there is always one functional imperative, but always also many ways of meeting it. Perhaps one may go as far as to say that there is determination of culture content by nature, but then one must add that there is multivocal rather than univocal determination, and that the multivocality is so wide that, paradoxically, the term determination almost ceases to fit. Perhaps one may also borrow a helpful pair of concepts from aesthetics and say that nature sets several universal themes, but societies produce innumerable variations of them.

An anthropological concept which, at one time, held considerable prestige was "the universal culture pattern" which Clark Wissler tried to identify in his book *Man and Culture* (New York, 1923). "Students of cultures find that the same general outline will fit all of them," he asserts (p. 75). "The facts of culture may be comprehended under nine heads . . . viz. speech, material traits, art, mythology, religion, social systems [such as the family], property, government and war." It is, no doubt, formally true that all societies show the traits thus denominated, but *only* formally. As soon as we consider the concrete contents of the "pattern," we recognize that it is anything but universal. Wissler's nine headings constitute no more than a check list. They describe pigeonholes, as it were, which every society must endeavor to fill, but what will be put into them is assuredly different from culture to culture. Thus there is, and at the same time there is not, a "universal culture pattern."

It is time now to turn from this pseudo-problem to a real one: the one raised, by implication, in the quotation from Kroeber given above. Is it in fact true that such universal near regularities as have to date been formulated for culture are mainly subcultural, i.e., dependent on and enforced by the physical constitution of man, society's somatic substratum? We would doubt it. It appears to us that there are three sources of the agreement of cultures in basic theme or themes, not one. The first and foremost is undoubtedly the universality of man's biotic equipment, but this takes us only part of the way. There is, in addition to it, the self-identity of human reason, and, as a third, more elusive, but equally real, factor, which might perhaps be described as the inner fitness of things, a phenomenon to which above all the utilitarian philosophers have drawn attention.

When we said just now against Kroeber that the universality of man's biotic equipment takes us only part of the way toward a pan-human uniformity of societies and cultures, we had two different, indeed contrasting, points in mind. The first has been emphasized throughout this work and need hardly be mentioned again; the other has not yet come into focus and must be brought up at this point, at least for completeness' sake. The strength and the competitiveness of human greeds, we have pointed out, creates a universal necessity for discipline, for drive reduction; but this discipline, this drive reduction, may take many different forms. Now we have to add, in elucidating the variety of mankind, that even the satisfaction of human greeds creates diversity. The point is a primitive one, but it must not be passed over in silence. All men must eat, but some come, for cultural reasons, to prefer wheat to rye, or beef to pork, and others arrive at the opposite decision. Invariably, both specific likes and dislikes, including even taboos, are seen to spring up. Above universal hunger there arise in this way culture-bred appetites (plural), and though the latter are based on the former, they are not determined by it. We may, once again appropriating Marxian terms, call our physical needs a substructure on which a cultural superstructure of need satisfaction is created. That superstructure can be as different from society to society as the houses which may be built on the same plot of land. All societies must allow for the satisfaction of the sex drive, but it may freely assume a serious (almost non-erotic) character as in the Calvinist countries, or a playful and erotic one as in chivalric times. Many cultural flowers may grow from one biotic root.

Let us now look at illustrations of the three causes distinguished above for the world-wide similarity of social institutions. Before we enter into the detail, it is imperative to emphasize with as much energy as possible that the distinction between the three aspects which we have drawn is purely conceptual. In life they form one complex which cannot be broken up. Institutions which are universal because man's physical constitution demands and determines such universality are regularly also universal because they are always and everywhere in agreement with reason and prove appropriate in practice. The fact that the three plies are in effect woven together and form one strand does not make the distinction between them nugatory.

As far as uniformity resulting from the unity of men's physical constitution is concerned, a good example is the ubiquity of the division of labor. In explaining it, Emile Durkheim based himself on the Malthusian principle of population, i.e., on the assertion that, by dint of a law of nature, the number of hungry mouths always tends to exceed the number of loaves and fishes, and that society is therefore invariably forced to think of new methods of escape from overpopulation. One of these methods is precisely the division of labor; in ways which it is not our duty to discuss at this moment, it makes more room on the surface of the earth, room for an increasing volume of population. Durkheim at first thought that, by this theory, he had explained the whole phenomenon—explained it as the effect of natural causes. But he soon came to see that his explanation was at best partial. Some societies, so history taught him, do not help themselves by instituting and evolving a division of labor, but by abortion or infanticide or emigration and the like. There is a choice, then; society, faced with *one* challenge, is free to reply by any and many responses. So far, Durkheim. But even if society chooses not to choose, even if it allows itself to be driven in the direction laid down by the Malthusian principle of population, by population pressure, even then cultural multiplicity will appear and complete natural uniformity. For there are several historical patterns of divided and integrated labor. Modern capitalism splits the stages of production, one man beginning the transformation of the raw material, another and yet others manipulating it in various ways and bringing it ever closer to the finished product, until a last person sells it to the ultimate consumer. Medieval society opted for a different system, the splitting, not of the process of production, but of the professions, the trades, one baker baking black bread, another white, another sugar bread, and so on, but always seeing the raw material through every stage of its passage through production, even to the end point, the point of marketing. As ever: one natural thrust, several cultural adjustments.

In what we have just said we have in fact, if by implication, brought up a second example showing how nature creates comparable—indeed, in one sense, identical—phenomena wherever there is social life, an example too important to be passed over even in a discussion which does not and cannot aim at completeness. If the division of labor, or rather *a* division of labor, is apt to arise because man is strong (strong in his power of procreation), a development of technology, with all that it implies, even for the creation of social norms, even for the educational process by which these norms are inculcated, is mandated by the fact that man is weak (weak in his natural aptitude for food production). Man, as he comes from the assembly line of evolution, is equipped only for that food gathering, that collection of fallen tree fruit or edible sea fruit, by which he has in fact lived in the dawn of time. He must, if he is to live better, or to live at all in increased numbers, fashion tools for himself, from the primitive snare or stick to the sophisticated machines of today. Thus *Homo sapiens* is by natural necessity *homo faber*, whatever the social constitution under which he lives. But not all societies will drive the creation of tools equally far or in comparable directions. Here, too, natural unity is followed by cultural multiplicity.

And yet, there is an element even in that cultural multiplicity which will make for unity, i.e., for uniformity as between otherwise different societies, an element which cannot be called natural, at least not in every sense of the word. That element is reason. It is present in, and operates within, the cultural response to natural challenges, and not in these challenges themselves. Because of it, we have to disagree with Kluckhohn's proposition that the generically human is identical with the physically-somatically universal. No, even in the mind, not only in the body, there is a common pan-human factor. (We are aligning ourselves here with Franz Boas, or rather with his "doctrine of psychic unity.") All the formal structures of the human understanding, including the Kantian categories, such concepts as time and space within which we apprehend reality, are common to all human beings. Two times two equals four in all cultures. The assertion sometimes heard that there is a specific bourgeois mathematics different from feudal or socialistic mathematics is nonsense, and obviously so. Yet the question is how far the influence, the identity-inducing power, of the formal structures of the mind can reach. Certainly not all the way. The vision of a system of social relationships totally dominated by the formal *ratio* and hence apt to be recommended for adoption to all societies, is less a utopia than a nightmare; it is not worth wasting printer's ink on. Besides formal logic, there is what has been called "the logic of life" (see Stark, *Sociology of Knowledge*, p. 287). To those who know only one kind of reason and truth, namely, the reason and truth revealed by the exact sciences, this whole concept may appear suspect or even objectionable. Yet in the social sciences it has long been established. "What I have attempted to do is to bring rationality back to a certain type of conduct, the type of conduct in which the individual puts himself in the attitude of the whole group to which he belongs," writes George Herbert Mead in *Mind, Self, and Society* (p. 334). "What we term 'reason' arises when one of the organisms takes into its own response the attitude of the other organisms involved. . . . When it does so, it is what we term 'a rational being.' " If this kind of rationality is declared to be rationality itself, exclusive rationality, and there have been tendencies in this direction, then we get a radical relativism which cannot be maintained. Such imperialism is to be resisted, but so is the imperialism of the formalists who claim that there is only so much truth in a proposition as there is mathematics or formal logic in it. We would plead for a sane dualism even here. Some things we string together on the basis of absolute and inescapable laws, others only on the basis of habitual association. The former, or formal logic, is binding on all men; the latter, or logic of life, a logic only in a wider and vaguer sense of the word, is different from culture to culture. Yet even within the logic of life there are structures, or at least tendencies, which are generically human and not only temporal or local—the striving to eliminate self-contradictions, for instance.

Far more difficult to fathom than the relationship between formal logic making for racial unity and the logic of life making for diversity is the question whether there are also universal structures of emotion. Hobbes asserted that fear is a sentiment which belongs to man as such in precisely the same way as reason does, and if it is often dormant, so too is reason, or so may reason be. Any natural catastrophe such as an earthquake, or even a simple thunderstorm, may awaken it in any human being. If we think of the tremendous power of the forces of nature and of the deplorable weakness of the individual in relation to it, and if we further think of the possible release of men's mutual enmity, precariously held at bay by socio-cultural arrangements, of a possible breakdown of law and order, an outbreak of anarchy, we can understand why Hobbes considered fear as a constitutive trait of the human race. Yet the salient question here is: Is the experience of fear, of anxiety, the same for all men? Differently expressed: Is there such a sentiment as archetypal fear, fear-in-itself, or is fear in every society different from fear in any and every other? It is impossible to decide this issue, but we may and must say that if there are universal, simply human, pan-human sentiments as there are universal, simply human, pan-human propositions of reason, the unity of the race results from them in the same way as it results from the formal laws of logic; and then both emotion and intellect, and not only the human physis, underlie such generically human features as exist.

While leaving this question to some extent open at this point, it is necessary to give a warning in connection with it. Mikel Dufrenne speaks, in *La Personnalité de base* (p. 74), of *drives spirituels*, and he would not use this English term in his French text if he did not wish to indicate a real drive, a universal tendency parallel to, say, the sex drive. He gives as his main example *le désir de justice*. Yet such a mental desire, such a supposed psychological need, if it exists at all, cannot possibly be considered a drive; historical observation shows that it is nothing of the kind. Western societies indeed, such as the one in which Dufrenne himself lives, are deeply concerned about justice and see to it that it is done when a conflict breaks out between neighbors, but other societies think, feel, and act differently. Eskimo society—which, as we know, is anything but an ill-ordered system—is much more insistent on the termination of the conflict than on the meting out of justice between the parties involved. The Eskimos will accept suppression of the quarrel, even if a just claim remains unsatisfied, without being unduly disturbed. We cannot therefore speak of the desire for justice as a universal drive; we are forced back, from this specific concept, toward one much more general and therefore also much more nebulous. We may perhaps assert that there is a general desire for stability, peace, neighborliness, and the like in settled societies, but we may not go much further without clashing with the fact of observable multiplicity.

Indeed, we are forced even further back when we continue to search for the psychologically, as against the physiologically, universal. What all human beings have in common is less the concrete contents of the psyche (though there are some) than the *capacities* of the psyche—less that which is than that which may be. Dufrenne mentions in this context four human faculties—perception, memory, judgment, and will (p. 75)—and here he seems in fact to be pointing to the truly and generically human, as far as the mind is concerned. Many emotions which are said to indicate or to demonstrate the psychic unity of mankind indicate and demonstrate such a unity *in posse* rather than *in esse*. Thus Robert Redfield writes in his essay "The Universally Human and the Culturally Variable" (*Journal of General Education*, 10, No. 3 [July 1957], 158): "All people feel shame or guilt, or, probably, some combination of these; all take satisfaction in or feel dissatisfaction with regard to their enterprises and productions; all dislike, under some conditions, public humiliation and enjoy recognized success, and so on." This is, no doubt, true. The tendency to feel shame is no doubt universal, yet what will bring it on, or how far it will intensify, and, above all, what coloration it will carry, will be different from society to society. The shame which a medieval page felt when he dropped a plate in court is different from the shame which a waiter feels when he drops a plate in a modern restaurant. Yet it remains true that both feel ashamed—humiliated—at their clumsiness.

Among the capacities which link all men and make them truly equals, there is one which a book like the present should strongly emphasize: the capacity to learn; more specifically: the capacity to internalize norms and values. Murdock is never more correct than when he asserts that "the common denominator of cultures is to be sought in the factors governing the acquisition of all habitual behavior, including that which is socially shared" ("The Common Denominator of Culture," in *Science of Man*, ed. Linton, p. 142). These factors, however, are faculties; they are potentialities rather than actualities, and the actualities which arise from them are apt to be contrasting rather than common.

It has often been said that an institution such as monogamy is both natural and reasonable, but assertions to that effect are rather shallow. The tendency of males and females to get together is natural, but by no means is the habit of staying together. All nature cares about is that ovum and sperm should meet, that the species should be preserved, and that purpose may as well be served by fleeting encounters as by legally organized and lasting unions. As for reason, it can certainly bring up arguments, even convincing ones, why legally organized and lasting unions are superior to fleeting encounters, but these would be *ex post facto* rationalizations rather than antecedent and causal considerations. Here, for once, Pareto would be right: a rational defense of monogamy would be a set of *derivazioni*, with little in animal nature to back them up. Why then has monogamy appeared in so many societies, and why have other forms of marriage so much in common with it and even the tendency to give way to it? Not because it is natural or reasonable, but because it is purposive, because it has proved its superiority in practice. Its root in life is neither instinct nor intellect, but experience.

The insight that social life, considered as a process, is a sustained and, as a rule, successful search for purposive solutions to the problems posed by common existence belongs to the securest achievements of the science of sociology. Its classical exposition is William Graham Sumner's book *Folkways*. What Sumner saw at work, in the lap of society, was a process of selection separating, by way of trial and error, useful and disappointing expedients, and leading to the adoption of the former and the discarding of the latter. The guide in this never resting and never ending stream of experimentation is, not pure, but practical, reason, not ratiocination, but, rather, common sense. General principles of action may and do in the end emerge, but they are merely abstract formulations, summings up, of concrete experiences. The answers to the needs of life are given by life itself, and this is in the final analysis the reason why they are sound. The third volume of the present work will attempt to rethink and to reapply—to modernize, as it were—the Sumnerian approach and therefore no more will be said about the folkway-forming process at this point. But our topic at this point is not really that process itself, but its issue, seen under the aspect of unity and diversity. Does it lead up, so we must ask, to institutions which are universally applicable and purposive, or to local and temporal solutions which distinguish societies rather than unite and unify them?

We have seen already that sometimes universally applicable and purposive norms do emerge. Our example was marriage. "Every society affiliates a child with a group of relatives through a rule of descent," writes George P. Murdock ("Common Denominator of Culture," pp. 139–41).

Complex family forms, such as polygamous and extended families, are variable, but all known societies have the same fundamental form, the nuclear family of father, mother and children. . . . In all societies the nuclear family is established by marriage, and the relationship between its adult members is characterized by a division of labor according to sex. Sexual intercourse is always permitted between father and mother, but invariably prohibited as incestuous between father and daughter, mother and son, brother and sister. Seeming exceptions, such as dynastic incest, pertain only to small groups of peculiar status, never to an entire society. The nuclear family is always an economic unit, and it is universally charged with the functions of child rearing, socialization, and early education. . . . The particular constellation of relationships [in the nuclear family] provides individuals with such powerful rewards and solves at once so many problems of vital importance . . . that once made, the responses are certain to be fixed and perpetuated. Man has never discovered an adequate substitute for the family. . . .

This example of the family certainly proves that the spontaneous process of folkway formation may in the end lead to universal, or nearly universal, patterns of norms, and other parallel illustrations might easily be adduced (such as the development of that great social institution and integrator, money). But there are also counter examples and counter illustrations, and their number is great; nor do they necessarily concern institutions of lesser importance. Undoubtedly, the most crucial instance is language. The possibility of a universal idiom need not detain us, for it is no more than music of the future. More weighty are the theories which assert the presence of universal elements in the existing languages. If the literature is surveyed, two such elements are seen to be in the focus of interest, one physical, the other logical. "Not only does every culture have a language, but all languages are resolvable into identical kinds of components, such as phonemes or conventional sound units, words or meaningful combinations of phonemes," writes Murdock (p. 124), illustrating the first point; Anthony Wallace says, bringing out the second:

The Whorfian and other hypotheses of extreme cultural relativism . . . assert a radical dependence of the very form of rationality upon the local structure of language. But it seems more likely that the elemental notions which are the common base of the various logical and semantic calculi—notions of "not," of "and," of "and/or," of "identically equal," of "equivalent," of "order," and the like—are symbolic representations of processes intrinsic to such evidently universal psychic functions as discrimination, conditioning, and the generalization of learning ["The Psychic Unity of Human Groups," in *Studying Personality Cross-Culturally*, ed. Kaplan, p. 142].

In these two passages we have illustrations of the theses considered earlier according to which the unity of the race and the uniformity of its social arrangements result from either the universality of bodily structures (here, the ear) or the universality of the laws of logic. Both undeniably play their part in the linguistic field, but obviously only a minor one. For who would deny that, as far as language is concerned, our race is riven, multiform, and not united, uniform? Who can forget the Tower of Babel? Though there are common elements, nobody can be blind to the fact that their influence is little or nothing in comparison with the factors making for diversity. As William D. Whitney showed some forty years before Sumner (see *Language and the Study of Language*; New York, 1867), languages develop as customs (i.e., folkways) do, but in their case the spontaneous search for ever more appropriate means of expression and communication has led to several sharply contrasting systems; there is little likelihood that, apart from some very partial mutual borrowing, a common idiom will emerge from them and supersede them. The reason for this persistence of division is the fact, emphasized by Benjamin L. Whorf in his essays "Science and Linguistics" and "A Linguistic Consideration of Thinking in Primitive Communities" (both *ad finem*; see *Language, Thought and Reality*, ed. John Bissell Carroll; Cambridge, Mass., 1956), that there exists an overall functional equality of all languages. None is necessarily better, i.e., more expressive, than any other. Of course, not all of them are at present equally far evolved and therefore in actuality equally effective; but all carry within themselves the same potential and not only may be, but will be, perfected as the need for more sophisticated conversation appears. Here then we have, arising from the same basic process of sociality, an end result which makes for diversity, even ultimate and irreducible diversity, as we have seen the nuclear family making for essential unity in the species *Homo sapiens*.

The whole discussion which has gone before unavoidably leads to the question *which* specific areas of social ordering show a stronger tendency toward convergence than toward divergence, and which drift or drive in the opposite direction. This query may, and perhaps must, be raised, but it cannot be answered. In the homely phrase, the proof of the pudding is in the eating. Only the practical outcome can decide. It is not given to the sociologist to prophesy. All he can do, in discussing the unity and the diversity of the human race, is to point out that both have their roots deep, deep down in the reality of life.

DIVERSIFICATION AT THE SOCIETAL LEVEL

84. The grand formula of geographical determinism which we considered at the beginning of the last section—the thesis that environment determines the ways of breadwinning, these form the family, the family in turn education, and education finally the social structure—contains two assertions, not one. We have already dealt with, and rejected, the one—the idea that geography is the ultimate cause of all social institutions. We must now consider the other. It is to the effect that the family is placed, in the chain of causation, before the social system; that, to say the least, the social system depends more on the family than the family on the social system. Needless to say, this conception has been widely criticized and replaced, by many, by the opposite idea. The basic consideration of those who say that the family is ontologically prior to the inclusive society is the observation that the breeding pair exists in many departments of animal life, that it is created by nature before culture ever dawns, and that cultured coexistence "must," therefore, have started with the clustering of institutions around this core. We have already shown wherein the decisive weakness of this deduction lies. Nature ensures only the performance of the sex act, the breeding contact, so to speak, but not the continued coherence of the breeding pair, the social bond among the partners. A male and a female in sexual partnership are not yet husband and wife; it is culture which transforms them from the former into the latter. An older, but very wise, sociologist saw this rather clearly: Franklin H. Giddings. He showed how improbable it was that culture began with the formation of isolated pairs. The cement of their union was in his opinion (which we fully share) the development of a division of labor, but that development is part and parcel of a broad, indeed comprehensive, process, the settling down of human interaction into stable and ultimately lawful forms. "Though transient relations of the sexes may be an important factor in the phenomenon of population," he writes in 1896, "they do not create the family as a unit of social composition. . . . The stability of the family increases as the division of labor between the sexes becomes perfect. . . . It seems to be an economic condition then which, in the lowest communities, determines the duration of marriage" (*The Principles of Sociology*, repr. ed. [New York & London, 1970], pp. 257, 266). Everything seems to indicate that it is not true that the tribe formed as a kind of protective enclosure around the breeding pair —this would, once again, be an indefensible form of biologism—but rather that the tribe, heir to the primal horde, created a condition of relative stability and order within which the marriage bond and the family could form, along with similarly abiding social institutions.

We have just mentioned the tribe, and this brings up the question, implied in all that we have already said in this section: *Which* society is it which must be considered as ontologically prior to the family, i.e., the society whose diversity accounts for the diversification of mankind? The answer is at the first stage rather simple, but complications arise when the matter is followed further. We can say that the inclusive society is the *causa causans* of all social institutions, and we may add that it comprises all those who are subject to the same norms, or, what comes to the same, all those who share the same social traditions, meaning by tradition, above all, an integrated set of values, an *ordo amoris*, as St. Augustine would have called it. That much is clear as well as certain. But it is not easy to grip, as it were, this society in real life. It cannot be identified with the state even though the state is the guardian, the enforcer, of the core norms; it cannot be identified with the linguistic group even though language, with its subtle overtones and undertones, is the most essential *traditor* of values. Of course, in primitive societies the tribe, and in evolved societies the nation, tends to coincide with the inclusive society, but it would be wrong simply to equate these groupings. The reason for the whole difficulty lies, not in the weakness of our definitions, but in the complications of life. We have no need to apologize here. The borders of real societies are floating even if we may, with Talcott Parsons, speak of border maintenance. Border maintenance—the habit of distinguishing those who act and feel like ourselves from those who do not, and the effort to intensify interaction with the former and to diminish it with the latter—is but a tendency, and often a weak one at that. Scholarship has no choice but to acknowledge this fact.

Perhaps we can drive our analysis further by taking our cue for once from the Marxists or those who follow them in this particular. "Apparently each type of social system cultivates those personal attributes which its technological system demands for successful adaptation," writes John J. Honigmann in his important treatise *Personality in Culture* (p. 193), and he refers in this context particularly to an investigation by D. R. Miller and G. E. Swanson, *The Changing American Parent* (New York, 1958), authors who assert "the existence of two highly divergent modes of child training in the United States—one exercised by entrepreneurially oriented mothers who emphasize control, hardening, and strictness, while the other, practiced by bureaucratically inclined mothers, leans towards encouragement, reward and affection." Since the two types of education must necessarily produce two different types of man, the source, or at least one source, of the diversity of mankind appears to be indicated in this analysis—provided, of course, that the writers concerned are right.

Are they right? Yes and no. If they imply that the technological, economic, and administrative system determines the type of man characteristic of, and prevailing in, an inclusive society, they are wrong. They then preach an ontology which cannot be sustained; differently expressed: they then commit the error which, in logic, is known as the *pars pro toto* fallacy. What Honigmann calls the technological system is in truth only a subsystem of the inclusive society, and it is hard to see why it should be conceded a privileged status. Historical observation teaches that one kind of economic life is consistent with several kinds of education, character formation, and style of human relationships. "Among the populations who live by hunting and fishing," writes Dufrenne (*La Personnalité de base*, p. 98), "the Eskimos are individualists (and the threat of famine makes them cooperate, while it produces the opposite effect among the Ojibwa), whereas the Kwakiutl are competitive and the Dakota cooperative." Yet the error which Honigmann, following Miller and Swanson, commits, consists only in a confusion of levels. If the levels are cleanly distinguished, if it is realized that the substratum tends to produce its own appropriate type of man for an enclosure, and only for an enclosure, within the wider confines of the superordinated system which lays down the universal frame, then the main assertion of Honigmann may indeed be rescued. It is wrong to assert that "each type of social system cultivates those personal attributes which its technological system demands," but it is correct to maintain that each type of prevailing technology cultivates those personal attributes which it demands for its functioning, just as it is correct to maintain that each type of social ordering cultivates those personal attributes which it needs to operate and to survive. In saying this, it is not our intention to deny or even to belittle the vital connections which exist between technological, economic, or administrative subsystem on the one hand and the inclusive supersystem on the other. They determine each other, indeed, in a sense, they are one. But they determine *each other*; the mutuality of determination must be emphasized; in other words, one-sidedness must be eschewed. Of course, a society like the one known as capitalism will create for itself men of an appropriate mentality and mode of action, for instance entrepreneurs; but men of an appropriate mentality and mode of action, for instance entrepreneurs, are needed before a society like the one known as capitalism can come into existence. That much has surely been proved by Max Weber's classical analysis (see also Stark, *Sociology of Knowledge*, passim).

Each society has an ethos, and that ethos is at the same time a style of conduct and a style of thought, simply because it is in the final analysis an inclusive style of life. If we want to know why the human race has produced the great variety which we find in history and geography, why it has diversified in spite of a common physique, in spite of a largely common psychical constitution, in spite of the fact that independent experimentation has often led to identical results and recommendations, we must remember that habits and customs with their coordinated mental modes—and these make up what is called an ethos—are not the same. It is as if developing mankind had struck out, from one point of inception, in divergent directions, as innumerable radii issue from one and the same origin. Robert Redfield was surely correct when he said in *The Little Community* (Chicago, 1955; pp. 68, 69): "A code of conduct; a kind of human being: two things. But the code or system of values dominates the culture and so controls the type of behavior of the people, makes the type of human being, and corresponds to character in the individual."

Honigmann, too, appears, in most contexts of his book, to agree with this position. Thus he writes:

> Through time a community unconsciously selects certain temperamental traits and dispositions as desirable, selecting them from possibilities inherent in human nature. Everyone must learn the socially desirable traits and dispositions regardless of his own, personal proclivities. . . . A nation's culture . . . is embodied in the intrapsychic structure of its individual members . . . [*Personality in Culture*, pp. 42, 96; see also p. 78].

If he had critically considered the assertions of Miller and Swanson from this wider point of view, he would have seen that the decisive shift which changed education and in consequence man in the United States was not the transition from one type of industry (that under an individual entrepreneur) to another (that under a bureaucratically administered company)—though this development was certainly concomitant and co-causative—but the transition from an ethos, the puritanical ethos, to another, the ethos of hedonism.

All this could be summed up by introducing some such concept as Abram Kardiner's "basic personality structure" or Cora DuBois' "modal personality structure." In adopting such concepts, care would only have to be taken to tone down the overheavy emphasis, characteristic of all who ultimately derive from Sigmund Freud, even if the links with him have already become tenuous, on the influence of the earliest years, the effects of the "techniques of child treatment" ("The Concept of Basic Personality Structure as an Operational Tool in the Social Sciences," *Science of Man*, ed. Linton, p. 111). As this particular aspect will be considered in the next section, we bypass it here and merely quote, and support, Kardiner's contention that "there are different basic personality structures for different societies" (p. 110). But the terms used—most clearly perhaps DuBois' " 'modal' personality structure"—indicate the presence of a problem which must be cleared up. Modal means "abstracted from life" rather than "observed in the concrete"; its opposite is "directly given," "individually identifiable," etc., and hereby hangs a difficulty. It comes out very clearly in a statement of Honigmann's (*Personality in Culture*, p. 95) in which we italicize the salient words: "any culturally distinctive aggregate of individuals, if suitably studied with the help of psychological concepts and techniques, can be made to reveal *a fairly general system* of overt and covert behavior—a personality— *which, however, no particular member of the aggregate need reveal in its entirety.*" Kardiner himself has raised this problem directly (see "Concept of Basic Personality Structure," p. 114): "How is it possible," he asks, "to reconcile the idea of basic personality with the known fact that each individual in a given culture has his own individual character?"

This difficulty is often waved away—and certainly not without good reason —by pointing to the undeniable truth that multiplicities of men do in fact have common characteristics. Ruth Benedict's studies, for instance, have shown that Plains Indians are, by and large, distinct from, even in contrast to, Pueblo Indians—*modally* distinct, even if some individuals in the two camps appear, as individuals, comparable. Nor can books like Salvador de Madariaga's *Englishmen, Frenchmen, Spaniards* (London, 1928) or André Siegfried's *L'Ame des peuples* (Paris, 1950) be simply thrown out of court. They are often derided as "mere impressionism," but this taunt shows their strength as well as their weakness. Is an impression perhaps not derived from reality? Does it not reflect that reality? Is it not also a form of observation?

Still, most books on national character show considerable vagueness, and the question arises whether this vagueness cannot be replaced by more precision. It not only may be, but it certainly should be. The only query is, How?

Unfortunately, modern sociology has become so much identified with one form of precision, namely, mathematical exactitude, that all other forms of it have been declared taboo, if they are not simply unknown. Not without reason has Pitirim Sorokin spoken of "quantomania," not without reason has the sobriquet "nosecounters" become attached to the whole profession. Even Margaret Mead, a scholar with deep roots in descriptive and analytical anthropology, could assert that "ideas like that of modal personality structure . . . imply a statistical model" ("National Character," p. 654). This is, however, a grave misconception which has to be removed and overcome.

To get the problem clearly into focus, let us concentrate for a moment on a simile—the comparison of a culture spread over many individuals with the musical form of "theme and variations." Composers like Max Reger, with his "Variations on a Theme of Mozart," usually present their themes in their first movements (in this case a quotation from one of Mozart's piano sonatas) and then append a series of variations, some close to, some far from, the general theme. So far are these variations sometimes from the general theme that it is very difficult to discover it, but it is always there, however hidden it may be. It takes a good ear to hear it within the welter of deviating sense impressions. The student of a culture faces an even more daunting task. He is supposed to identify the common theme though he has nothing to go by but the variations: there is no open statement of the basic melody anywhere. The archetypal man exists only in theory, never in practice. And yet, even the problem of the student of a cultural mode must, in principle, be soluble, for the common theme or themes are as fully contained in the individuals he studies as they are in the variations which a music lover or musicologist has to comprehend.

Attempts at counting will not take him very far. A society is not like a basket of eggs which can simply be added up because the variations between them are so small that they can be disregarded. It is an assembly of personalities very different from each other, and yet all connected—subjectivities with an element of intersubjectivity in them. This intersubjectivity is not as easy to grip as the visible forms which characterize an egg. We are here in an area where we may compare, but cannot count. The unity of a society is a stylistic unity, not a sum total of identities. If we wish exactitude, we must seek it in a direction different from statistics, however sophisticated.

The fact that statistical methods do not lead us to our goal in this particular exploration becomes obvious as soon as we consider any major effort of this kind. Sorokin (who often practiced what he condemned) wanted to show that modern society—the society which had developed out of, and in consequence of, the French and Industrial Revolutions—was "sensate," i.e., regarded only the human senses as reliable guides to truth and only sensual enjoyments as values to be striven for. He analyzed the personalities listed in the *Encyclopaedia Britannica* and found that those active between 1800 and 1900 were dominated by sensate empiricism to the extent of 42%, those active between 1900 and 1920 to the extent of 53%. The geometrical average for type of historical person included in the *Encyclopaedia Britannica* belonging to the half-century from 1800 to 1849 was: ideational (the opposite of sensate), 9%; sensate, 41%; mixed, 50%. What a miserable result! On the basis of it, one could not even call the supposed heyday of sensate culture truly "sensate."

The avenue toward quantification appears therefore blocked. But precision need not be sought in this direction: it may be conceptual as well as numerical. The sociologist will do well, in this context, to remember Max Weber's concept of "ideal type." If we wish to know what capitalism really is, we must follow the principle of analytical and not that of naïve empiricism. We should not describe a concrete country, even if it is, without doubt, highly capitalist, but separate out what is capitalist in it, or in any other society for that matter, and exclude what is alien to its social nature. We must aim at a conceptually "pure" image. Even what economic historians call classical capitalism was not in fact pure capitalism; even in the period so denominated there existed traits which did not really fit in, which were, for instance, pre-capitalist (like the small retail trader who did not compare cost and profit) or post-capitalist (like cooperative societies which did not consistently pursue the minimization of costs and the maximization of profits). The truth is that "pure" capitalism or "pure" feudalism or "pure" communism is as little to be found in history as chemically pure water is to be found in nature. But the truth is also that history shows tendencies—strong, undeniable, unmistakable tendencies—toward the realization of the principles of these various types of social organization, and they are nonetheless significant for being unable to occupy the *whole* field, to dominate life *completely*. The concept of ideal type is not a useless construct; it is no more useless and no less helpful than extrapolation in statistics.

These considerations give us a chance to clarify the concept of "modal personality structure." The modal personality is the ideal–typical concomitant of contemporary society in its essential aspects. Its attributes are such that, if they are allowed to work themselves out without hindrance or falsification, they will make the given social system work optimally. What we are presenting is a functional definition of typical man. It is in the final analysis commonsensical for, as anybody knows, capitalist society cannot possibly operate without capitalist man, or caste society without caste-bound man, or any other society without an appropriate culture internalized, i.e., realized, in the individuals belonging to it.

It may perhaps be objected here that these deductions are very clever in theory but not a great help in the effort to understand practice, that they belong more to the world of textbooks than to the arena of life. But this is decidedly not so. For the ideal–typical or modal man, as we have defined him, is a model powerfully operative in the processes of history. It is a *norm* which certain very real forces offer out to, and try to impose upon, the concrete personalities which populate its orbit. For instance, "Be thrifty and enterprising!" was an injunction which rising capitalism propagated, and insofar as it got men to accept it, it realized itself. Other preachings are in the same vein. "Be a good American!" "Be a good Britisher!" "Become what you are!" The list would be endless. And because the modal personality structure is a norm as well as a fact—indeed, a norm more than it is a fact—it is nowhere 100% realized. All norms meet with resistances; none is ever completely victorious. The cry "Be competitive" characteristic of ideal capitalism is no easier to accept (because it implies risk and pain) than the cry "Be altruistic" and "cooperative" characteristic of ideal communism (because it implies discipline and self-abnegation); and even the cry "Be patriotic" will not appeal to everybody.

The reason just revealed why it is not easy to focus the psychological concomitant to the unity of society applies to all societies. Some societies, however, show a second cause of serious complication: the norms, the forms of conduct, thought, and feeling which are offered to, and instilled in, the individual, are themselves ambiguous, indeed, divided. We must think here in the first place of the nations. Somebody has written a book under the title *Germany Is Caliban*, and if the mentality of traditional German militarism is remembered, the famous *furor Teutonicus*, the harshness of this judgment can be understood. But it would be as easy to present, not only a different, but even a diametrically opposed, picture: Germany is Ariel as well. There is no finer manifestation of pacifism anywhere than Kant's *Zum ewigen Frieden*, nor a more humanitarian vision of man than that of Wilhelm von Humboldt. France, too, is split. There has always been a tradition rejecting, and another accepting, the great Revolution. And there have appeared innumerable reconciliations and combinations of these two aspects. One of them is imaginatively, yet convincingly, portrayed by Anatole France in *La Rôtisserie de la reine Pédauque* and *Les Opinions de M. Jérôme Coignard*. What Ruth Benedict says in *The Chrysanthemum and the Sword* (Boston, 1946; p. 304; see also pp. 2, 3, 171) of one nation, "The Japanese have an ethic of alternatives," applies to them all. There are plenty of scholars who will regret this mental condition of the modern nations, regard it as a pathological state, and recommend a dose of logic for a cure. But an understanding sociology will be inclined to argue that such two-facedness, though intellectually and morally problematic, has high pragmatic value: it allows a people to switch tracks at a moment's notice, as Germany did when she turned from Hitler to Adenauer in 1945 and France when she turned from Léon Blum to Philippe Pétain five years earlier. We are not concerned with the consistency and the morals of such events; all we wish to show is that the modal personality—the good German, the good Frenchman—is in itself complex. Such is life!

There are other difficulties as well, in addition to the two which we have paraded: there is, for instance, the fact that a society is less a structure than a process and that its mentality, as offered to and established in individuals, is always in flux. But we need not pursue these complications further. It will be more fruitful to ask whether the whole concept of a modal personality retains its significance if we are dealing with a multivocal phenomenon. There can be no doubt whatsoever that it does. For the salient question is not whether the sociologist or statistician, an outsider, can come to grips with it, but whether it plays a role in practical life, and that it certainly does. When we act, and more especially when we learn how to act, we meet with the modal personality in no uncertain manner. We must adjust our modes of conduct to it; it is our guide and also our censor. Of course, it meets us through intermediaries who themselves are concrete, highly personalized individuals, not walking types, but these concrete, highly personalized individuals—these significant others, as George Herbert Mead has labeled them—are precisely what we have just called them, intermediaries, agents, so to speak, of a more impersonal and supra-individual reality, the social code. When Mead introduced, not only the term "significant other," but also the term "generalized other," he aimed in exactly the same direction in which we are aiming here. "Generalized other" and "modal personality" are more than kindred conceptions; they are two words for the same thing. Basing himself on similar considerations, Mikel Dufrenne writes: "To be a Kwoma, a Manu, or an American . . . is a task. . . . The basic personality appears to be a norm, partly because it is produced in the individual by his socialization, but partly also because it is more or less confusedly discovered by him on the part of others. . . . It is not only a result in him, but also a guiding image for him" (*La Personnalité de base*, p. 207).

In view of the tremendous importance of the basic personality in life and especially in the process of socialization, the difficulties of the scholar in handling it are but dust in the balance. But even the scholar, the outside describer, can come to see its reality. If he wishes to meet it, he must descend toward those basic conceptions which are more of the nature of culture premises than of culture contents and which constitute a kind of submerged metaphysic, binding all individuals in a culture together and setting them in contrast to the carriers of other cultures. (Studies of the national character often come to grief because they deal with surface phenomena, the floating mist, instead of digging for the deeper structures, the bedrock base.) We shall give, by way of illustration, two instances which show with all desirable clarity that there are in truth and in fact features constituting a modal personality, an intersubjective cultural unity.

Our first example is taken from the field of thought, our second from the field of emotion. As far as thought is concerned, its framework is, of course, a definite idea of time and space. In our modern world, we structure time neatly into the three categories of past, present, and future, and we are all agreed that whatever was is no longer, and that whatever will be is not yet. The tenses of our grammar make it impossible for anyone of us to stir out of this pattern. Yet there are other societies which have produced other grammars, other tenses, and, hence, other time conceptions—conceptions which stamp their modal personalities as our dynamic stamps ours. Idioms as different as Hebrew and Hopi have forms which indicate an abiding present. Such a redefinition of time is among the revolutionary changes which came with the Reformation. Catholics believed that Christ's sacrifice on Mount Calvary could be enacted over and over again (one feels tempted to write: re-enacted, but this would already constitute undue modernization), whereas Calvinists considered it as an event fixed to a definite moment of time, so that the rite of communion could only be a memorial meal. We may use the category of space to draw attention to other differences which establish distinct modal personalities. In our modern world, our attitude to space is characterized by what Talcott Parsons calls "affective neutrality." A place is a spot on a map located where two lines, latitude and longitude, intersect; one spot or place is in principle no different from any other; both are thought of as empty. But in other societies places have emotional —affective—aspects, as it were: one is good, for instance, safe; another evil, for instance, threatening. What Emile Durkheim has to say about this matter in *The Elementary Forms of the Religious Life* has been amply confirmed by anthropological research.

For our example from the sphere of the emotions, we can go to A. Irving Hallowell's excellent essay "Fear and Anxiety as Cultural and Individual Variables in a Primitive Society" (*Journal of Social Psychology*, 9 [1938], 25–47). In the area along the Berens River in Canada, wolves and bears are to be found as are snakes, toads, and frogs. Westerners would be afraid of the former, but not of the latter. It is the other way round with the Indians of the region. "The creatures they fear most are snakes, toads and frogs, animals that are actually among the most harmless in their environment. Indeed, the only species of snake that occurs is a small variety of garter." Why then the terror these animals inspire? "It is the identification of actual snakes with the mythical variety that accounts in part for the attitude of the Indians. . . ." It is no good arguing here that the phobia described is unreasonable and unnecessary. For the belief in an unseen world and in the power of evil, the belief also that snakes, toads, and frogs are creatures of ill omen, harbingers of bad luck, is as deeply established here, as common and universally compelling a culture content, as our own conviction that night will follow day and day, night. "With respect to the emotions," Hallowell sums up, "culture defines: (*a*) the situations that will arouse certain emotional responses and not others; (*b*) the degree to which the response is supported by custom or inhibitions demanded; (*c*) the particular forms which emotional expression may take" (pp. 27–29). There is thus an emotional framework embracing all *socii* as well as an intellectual one, a standard mode of feeling as well as one of thought.

Speaking of Indians brings to mind another aspect of modal personality, or of the national character: the amplitude of the swing allowed to moods. The Kwakiutl, as for instance Franz Boas has described them, change easily from exultation to depression, and all reports of the cultural life of Imperial Russia agree that there, too, radical and lightning redirections in feeling tone were common. Not so among men whose character was formed by Calvinism. Calvinism, Puritanism, has always tended to stabilize people midway between the extremes of emotion, never to feel exulted, never to feel abashed. The Englishman's traditional "stiff upper lip," i.e., self-control even in very trying situations, is one part of that syndrome. Excitability or the relative lack of it thus becomes an inclusive trait which informs the children of a culture and makes them all, though with significant variations, conform to one model.

These are just illustrations, no more. A systematic investigation of modal personality, that psychological counterpart to socio-cultural integration, would demand a tome, not to say a library, of its own. It would do well to start out from Talcott Parsons' pattern variables, those alternatives among which a society must choose as it tries to settle down into abiding forms of life, into a stable system. Should human relations be affective or affectively neutral? Which should be the one, which the other? Should they be kept narrowly defined, or should they be allowed or encouraged to broaden out, to become diffuse? It is by answering, *via facti*, such questions that a social whole gains a contour, a face, a character, which is then internalized, that is, realized, in the personalities which it brings into its life process through socialization. Here we can wind up our discussion by stating that the establishment of socio-cultural unity and the effective mirroring of it in individual minds is in theory almost a matter of definition, and in practice certainly a matter of necessity. For if there were not a common language (in the very widest sense of the word) permeating a society and filling each and everyone included in it, how could its members communicate with each other, cooperate, and coexist?

The statement which we have just made is, however, likely to be attacked from the political left. Those who move the fact and the concept of the class struggle into the center of sociological thought will argue that a society is, not a unity, but a duality, that it is class-divided, and that the class has more personality-forming, mode-creating influence than the inclusive society. It is not necessary to quarrel about this point. Everything depends on the given circumstances. If the classes are very sharply divided, if they constitute circles of life closed against each other, with only minimal interaction, it may well be true that the decisive modal personality owes little to the inclusive society and much to class affiliation. An example which immediately springs to mind is France shortly before 1789. Louis XVI and Maximilien Robespierre were assuredly not of the same human type. On the other hand, even an objectively crass contrasting of the classes may go with a deep sharing of subjective mind contents; differently expressed: even a sharp distinction between the classes may be compatible with their coordination and integration in an over-arching, complex system. While Indian caste society was still intact, the distance between a Brahmin and a Mahar or a Mang was very great, but both believed in metempsychosis, and both accepted the necessity of *dharma*, obedience to the duties inherent in caste membership, if ascent on the social pyramid was to be possible in another incarnation. This mutual adjustedness of the classes goes often further than meets the eye. If, in a society, the upper classes are arrogant, and the lower cringing, these attitudes are not only complementary, but in part even identical in psychic content. For cringingness no doubt implies resentment, hence (submerged) aggressivity of which arrogance is a more open form, and arrogance carries within it an (overcompensated) feeling of uncertainty, the sentiment which is the root of cringingness. The most orthodox Marxists would hardly dissent from this analysis.

But not only is it unnecessary to engage in polemics with Marxism, classical Marxism can even be used to support the insights contained in these pages. It certainly taught that bourgeoisie and proletariat are locked in combat, but it also asserted that the terms of that combat were set by the social system comprising them both, the reality of capitalism. It never forgot that adversaries are both opposed *and* tied to each other. The fated struggle of the day was seen as a contest for the control of the means of production, and on the centrality of that issue the warring parties were said to be agreed. It is certainly true that the classes of high capitalism shared the conviction that material values were the decisive ones and that property was the institution of institutions—enough to give them a similar *ordo amoris*, a mutual kinship. Marx thought of the relation between the world view of the capitalist and that of the working class as parallel to the relation between a positive and a negative, a white and a black photograph, *of the same reality.* Contradictory in one sense, they are yet identical in another. Proof of this is the fact that Marx regarded his own economic theory displayed in *Das Kapital* as a version of classical economics and, as the unfinished last part (*Theories of Surplus Values*) in particular shows, he shared many conceptions with such exponents of capitalism as Adam Smith and David Ricardo, especially the basic labor theory of value.

Yet we can draw still more support from the Marxist tradition. Georg Lukács' uniquely important book, *Geschichte und Klassenbewusstsein* (1923), is based on a concept similar to that of modal personality structure, if not indeed identical with it. Like all Marxists, Lukács considered that the only "true" proletarian was the workingman who was subjectively aware of the objective condition of his class under the capitalist dispensation, and who was determined to fulfill the "historical task" of that class, namely, the abolition of the capitalist order, the termination of a system which rested on the exploitation of man by man. But he emphasized more than any other Marxist that not all proletarians were in fact what they should be: class-conscious. There was also "false consciousness," and it existed on a large scale. Therefore it was imperative that the atypical proletarian be transmuted into a typical one, false consciousness replaced by the modal mentality (we may obviously call it that without deviating from the substance of Lukács' doctrine); that was to be achieved by the Communist Party, the educational organization of the world proletariat. Clearly, Lukács' call to the workers of the world was parallel to the behest of all societies to their new incoming members: "Become what you are!"

Considered in our context, a class is simply a subsociety. Its existence introduces a complication into the analysis, but not a particularly severe one. The modal personality of a class is a variant of the modal personality of the inclusive society, just as an individual is a variant of the complex made up of the modalities characteristic of both inclusive society and class. And what is true of the subsociety called a class is true of other subsocieties as well, for instance, of religious affiliations where they are vital and effective. H. J. Gans's book *The Urban Villagers* (New York, 1962) shows that the inhabitants of the West End of Boston, Italian-American workingmen, are both Americans and Italians and wage earners and Catholics, and that life has molded all these influences into a modal whole of which many individuals are typical representatives, though each one of them in his own personal manner. "There are as many different kinds of education as there are different milieux in a given society," writes Emile Durkheim in *Education and Sociology* (trans. S. D. Fox [Glencoe, Ill., 1956], p. 67). This is undoubtedly true; but the term "milieu" applies to no subsociety more than it does to the family, to the study of which we must therefore turn.

DIVERSIFICATION AT THE FAMILIAL LEVEL

85. It is necessary to begin this section with a statement that is so trite as to be almost absurd: the family is of all subsocieties by far the most important for the formation, and hence also for the diversification, of character because it is in its confines that basic education, the decisive first steps on the road to socialization, take place. "There would be neither common personality characteristics within a society nor a continuing culture, were it not for common childhood experiences," writes Theodore M. Newcomb in his *Social Psychology* (New York, 1950; p. 488), and if there is any truth to be accepted without demur, it is this. Yet it is a truth which can be, and has been, greatly exaggerated, and if it is so, it turns into a serious error which has to be combated.

One striking illustration of the length to which some are prepared to go, and of the absurdities which result if the influence of intrafamilial child-care techniques is overemphasized, is afforded by Geoffrey Gorer's study *The People of Great Russia* (New York, 1950). In the first years of this century, on the eve of the Bolshevik revolution, the empire of the Tsars harbored two very different types of man, the peasantry and the intelligentsia, and most of us would feel that it is not difficult to explain the psychological contrast between these two strata. Terms like "traditionalism and rationalism," "religiousness and atheism," "rural existence and urbanization" spring to mind at once and would appear to account largely, if not fully, for the observed phenomena. But for Geoffrey Gorer the last cause of the difference between the strata lies somewhere else: the peasants were swaddled when they were babies, the children of the intelligentsia were not. Looking back over his exposition, Gorer himself is in the end appalled by the unconvincingness, not to say the ridiculousness, of his theory, but that does not prevent him from developing it on a broad front and from presenting it as a

serious analysis of a historically relevant revolution-producing class contrast.
   This is how Gorer describes the aetiology behind the psychological characteristics of the muzhik population:

> except during the short periods when he is being fed or bathed [the Russian
> infant] is completely inhibited in the free movement of his limbs. . . . it is as-
> sumed that this inhibition of movement is felt to be extremely painful and
> frustrating and is responded to with intense and destructive rage, which cannot
> be adequately expressed physically. . . . These feelings of rage and fear are
> probably made endurable, but also given emphasis, by the fact that the baby
> is periodically loosed from the constraints, and suckled and petted while un-
> swaddled. This alternation of complete restraint without gratifications, and of
> complete gratifications without restraint, continues for at least the first nine
> months of life. It is the argument of this study that the situation outlined in the
> preceding paragraphs is *one* of the major determinants in the development of
> the character of adult Great Russians [pp. 123, 128].

   Several features of ordinary Russian life are derived, by Gorer, from the habit
of swaddling the babies: for instance, the sharp contrast and alternation, within
the calendar, of periods of semi-starvation and periods of overindulgence, e.g.,
"the prolonged ritual fasts [of Lent and Advent] and the Gargantuan feasts with
which Christmas and especially Easter were celebrated. I think it is legitimate to
trace a connexion between the total pleasure of the orgiastic feast, &c., and the
total pleasure which the infant can be supposed to feel when it is unswaddled,
nursed, and loved" (p. 139). But even the philosophy and theology of the Orthodox Church are, if Gorer is to be believed, to be explained in the light of
early child-handling. Two intellectual pillars of that church were the traditional
emphases on the deep sinfulness of man and on the inescapable collectivity of
salvation, the famous *sobornost*. This is how Gorer explains the formation of
these doctrines:

> For several months, at least, the Russian infant experiences intense but rel-
> atively undirected rage and fears deriving from his projection of this rage on
> to the external world; as a result . . . he develops a feeling of pervasive though
> unfocused guilt. . . . This feeling of diffuse guilt presumably underlies the
> Orthodox dogma of the universal sinfulness of human beings. . . . The inhibi-
> tion of exploration of the surrounding world during the swaddling period
> would seem to be one way in which the lack of sharp distinctions between
> other people in the environment and (on an unconscious level) the distinc-
> tion between the self and the not-self is perpetuated [pp. 129, 130, 134].

Because of this failure to distinguish ego and alter, "in the Orthodox Church the
central experience is *sobornost*, the Pentecostal descent of the Holy Ghost on
the whole congregation simultaneously" (p. 134).
   The revolutionary forces which gathered after the middle of the nineteenth
century were made up of very different personalities, and the personalities concerned were different from the muzhiks because, as babies, they were not swaddled: "Together with other 'Westernizing' ideas the intelligentsia imported (at
least, to the best of their ability) Occidental ideas of the proper way to bring
up children. The children of the intelligentsia were not, as a rule, swaddled;
older informants will explain, 'We were not swaddled because we belonged to

the intelligentsia' " (p. 119). Because of this, the Russian masses and the Russion élite had very different styles of revolutionary activity. Only the élite could make revolution a persistently pursued program, the masses could not. "For the latter the proper response to the identification of an enemy is an attack of destructive rage, *zloba*, which may involve the exercise of violence, but which is quickly over. For the intelligentsia and the Soviet élites the proper response is hatred—persistent, conscious, cold negative feelings which should not be allowed to lapse" (p. 162). This mental tendency seems to Gorer to explain Russia's foreign policy since 1917; but the inner condition of the Soviet Union, too —the alienation and distance between the ruling few and the ruled many—appears to him as explicable in the same way:

> The analogy of swaddling illustrates very clearly the relations that exist between people in authority and people under authority. . . . Just as those in positions of authority abandon their feeling of "oneness" with the mass of the people over whom they are placed in authority, so do the mass of the people apparently feel that those in authority are "apart" from themselves. This would seem to be a derivative of the fact that the earliest constraining "authority"— the swaddling—is not part of the self, and is not personified [p. 174].

After these samples of his argumentation, it is impossible to give credence to Gorer's assertion that to him swaddling "is a clue, not a cause, of Russian behaviour." It is far easier to accept his admission "I have undoubtedly overemphasized the importance of swaddling . . ." (p. 198). To judge his whole attitude, it is, of course, necessary to look at his other works, such as *Exploring English Character* (New York, 1955), and though we find no reference there to the feature or features which he has presented as responsible for Great Russian culture, we see parallel traits right in the center of his analysis. One of them, for instance, is toilet training, i.e., the imposition of bowel control on the infant. A great deal seems to him to depend on this particular (see, e.g., p. 31). But preoccupation with this matter is no personal characteristic of Geoffrey Gorer alone. It is a central interest of the whole Freudian tradition, and we find it fully developed in the writings of Erik Erikson whose prestige in his school probably surpasses that of Gorer by a considerable margin.

Writing of the Sioux Indians and their handling of material wealth, Erikson has this to say: "there is an intrinsic relationship between the holding on to and letting go of property and the infantile disposition of excrement. . . . In general, it can be said that the Sioux attitude toward feces does not contradict that concerning property. In regard to both, the emphasis is on free release rather than on rigid retention . . ." (*Childhood and Society*, pp. 124, 125). The words chosen are careful; no causal connection is openly claimed. But what else can "intrinsic relationship" mean, especially in view of the fact that toilet training is imposed before proprietary ideas are developed? In his analysis of Yurok culture, Erikson lays no emphasis on elimination, but again it is a similar complex of facts—namely, alimentation and, in particular, weaning—which is presented as a key to the entire system of the life and thought of the tribe: "As far as we know, the Yurok does not seem to focus any interest, pleasurable or phobic, on feces; and such reaction formations as regularity or compulsive or-

derliness do not apparently exceed what could be expected of people with crafts-
manship of Yurok level. Yurok retentiveness seems alimentary rather than
anal." Why precisely do these people become economical, indeed, stingy? "The
Yurok child is exposed to early, and, if necessary, abrupt weaning before or
right after the development of the biting stage." Therefore not only does he show
constant anxiety over being left without provisions, but the whole culture becomes attuned to this preoccupation. For instance,

> ceremonial behavior was designed to further dramatize that nostalgic need for
> intake which may have been evoked by the early weaning from the breast. . . .
> The ceremonial represents a grandiose collective play with the themes of earliest
> danger in the individual life cycle: the individual loss of the mother's breast
> at the biting stage corresponds to the possible loss of salmon supply from across
> the ocean [pp. 158, 151, 152, 156].

The very last words are an apt opening for a criticism of the whole Freudian
tradition incarnated in such men as Erikson and Gorer. Why make the fear
that the fish supply may fail secondary to the memory of the refusal of the
mother's milk which, however painful it may have been originally, is in the life
of all adults a fact over and done with? Does Erikson not place the cart before
the horse? Why search for the dominant trait of an ongoing culture in the past
instead of finding it in ever-present, ever-actual circumstances? If Gorer is
correct, then Americans suffer throughout life from the same trauma as do the
Yurok. They, too, are too abruptly weaned. But Dufrenne rightly considers that
Gorer is not correct, at least not entirely correct, and he criticizes him as follows:

> If it is possible, as Gorer does, to attribute the adult's taste for milk observable
> in America and the obsession there with the image of the female breast to a cer-
> tain awkwardness of maternal care, is it necessary to trace the general chase
> after security to the same psychological origin? Is it not more convincing to
> connect it with the adult's experience of a social system where illness is ruinous,
> competition a permanent menace, an economic crisis always possible? No
> doubt, the basic anxiety is economic [*La Personnalité de base*, p. 296].

Certainly, childhood experiences explain a great deal, but they do not explain
everything. In *Exploring English Character* (see pp. 122–24), Gorer gives it as
his opinion that the Englishman's general Puritanism results from the fact that
he is very soon, and very strictly, subjected to toilet training. There is, he says,
a "relationship between early training in cleanliness and general rigidity of
character." The two undoubtedly belong together; they form what the Germans
call a *Sinnzusammenhang*. But is it not a general Puritanism, the deep conviction
that the beast in man has to be repressed, which leads in the first place to such
marginal phenomena as an educational emphasis on sphincter control, rather
than the other way round?

There are several weighty reasons why the theoretical suggestions put forward
by Erikson and Gorer have to be relegated to a rather marginal position in any
balanced and truly realistic attempt to explain the diversification of the human
race. One is that they stem, not from psychology, but from psychiatry, i.e., not
from the study of normal man, but from the analysis and treatment of the sick

personality. In *The People of Great Russia*, Gorer gives an interesting account of the way in which he formed and developed his basic style of theorizing, and in the course of it he writes: "I thought I saw an analogy in the misery of motionlessness to the misery of depressives, . . . and I then produced the . . . hypothesis of infantile depression as a result of exhaustion from unassuaged rage" (p. 218). Here we see a wide open door through which error could, and did, enter into Gorer's thought. In the case of Erikson, we have no similar open admission, but we have an even clearer, even more precious proof: his book *Young Man Luther* (New York, 1950). In spite of the copious historical, philosophical, theological, and generally cultural materials with which this study is laced, it is a typical case study, the study of a neurosis, and all the instruments of psychiatry are paraded and used: the Oedipus complex, the adolescent identity crisis, inhibition, explosivity, etc. (see esp. pp. 58, 73, 77, 122, 164, 247, 255–58)—and anality, in particular. Late in life Luther made an unfortunate remark to the effect that his central theological conception, justification through faith alone, came to him in a latrine while he was engaged in defecation. Erikson makes this absurd statement the pivot of his account. "His total being," he says of the Reformer (p. 205), "always included his bowels." Luther was plagued all his life by both physical and mental constipation; his liberation from plaguing religious doubt was therefore not unnaturally connected with liberation from compacted fecal matter. Whatever the merits of such considerations in the framework of medicine, physical or mental, it is manifestly absurd to transfer them from the clinical to the cultural context. Of course, it is not to be denied that the infant's meeting, and especially his first meeting, with social disciplines, such as the demand of bladder and bowel control, creates tensions which are not without danger of degenerating into obsessions or other abnormalities, and this would bring psychiatry into the picture. But the salient point is that such unfortunate incidents and accidents are the exceptions, not the rule. Apart from a few deviating cases, anthropological research has proved that societies by and large manage to wean and to clean and generally to discipline their infants without crippling them for life (see Dufrenne, *La Personnalité de base*, pp. 114, 115) and it makes little difference that some modern Western civilizations, in their foolish abandonment of time-tested and long-established techniques, have here and there maneuvered themselves into difficulties. The principle remains—and it is unimpugnable—that abnormal conditions must not be made the key to the explanation of normal and healthy sociality.

Besides, though it is true that, in Wordsworth's words, the child is father to the man, that childhood experiences remain with us through life and even leave permanent scars on our selves, infancy is only a passing phase and is bound to be overcome. On this point we can with profit quote Mikel Dufrenne (pp. 288, 289):

> It is possible to explain the conduct of some sick persons by going back to certain crises of their babyhood, but they are sick, and their sickness consists precisely in their inability to free themselves from their earliest years. The normal man is he in whom infancy survives in the form of a memory and not of an obsession. . . . No doubt, even his personality preserves traces of his early history, but these traces give a style to his personality without haunting and

without ossifying it: man carries his past with him without becoming its slave. ... To assert that the adult can be fully explained by the child, and that which belongs to man, like his culture, can be fully explained by childhood, is in the final analysis tantamount to suggesting that what is normal has to be understood in the light of what is pathological.

This is entirely wrong. "It is, after all, the task of man to free himself from his infancy; and even in primitive societies man grows into a manly mentality."

We have noticed, on one or two occasions, that the representatives of the Freudian tradition are reluctant to claim that childhood experiences, such as swaddling and weaning, are the causes of adult character (taking the word "cause" in its proper and fuller sense), and that they prefer to speak of correspondence rather than of causality, even though it is clear that they do, in their heart of hearts, believe in the existence of a causal nexus. The reasons for this inhibition are obvious. It is clear that, if the prevailing child-care acts determine culture patterns, culture patterns for their part determine the prevailing child-care acts. Nobody can and nobody will deny this; the question is only which is the ultimately decisive variable. We believe we are in full accord with the vast majority of anthropologists and sociologists when we assert that general culture conditions child care rather than the other way round. We pointed out, in the preceding section, that the inclusive society creates the nuclear family rather than the nuclear family the inclusive society, and here we have to take the same line, and we take it with even more assurance. The truth has worked to the surface even within the Freudian school. Speaking of the "analysis of the relation of infantile attitudes to adult adaptations," Kardiner wrote in 1943 in *The Individual and His Society* (New York, p. 348): "This analysis demonstrates that once the basic personality structure is established, any change in primary institutions will lead to personality changes, but that these changes will move only in the direction of the already established psychic constellations." Yet in his 1945 essay "The Concept of Basic Personality Structure" (p. 119) he raises what he himself calls "the crucial question": namely, "What determines the parental attitude toward children and hence the specific influence to which the child is subject?" and answers it entirely without ambiguity: "In general, one can say that these parental attitudes are determined by the social organization and the subsistence techniques."

Needless to say, the final arbiter in this general quarrel must be the facts, and we are fortunate in that we have a whole number of apposite investigations. We are fortunate, too, in that able observers have summed them up for us. Let us hear three of them. John J. Honigmann writes in *Personality in Culture* (p. 299): "Comparative studies of U.S. children don't consistently confirm that the balance of early gratification and frustration encountered, for example, in the oral zone affects learned personality characteristics. Confidence, self-assurance, or optimism don't consistently vary between children fed on demand or by schedule, or weaned early rather than late." Similarly Justin Aronfreed (*Conduct and Conscience*, p. 304): "The available evidence offers no reason to think that any index of internalization will be related consistently to specific practices of care and feeding during infancy, or to the pace at which weaning and control of eliminative functions are introduced into the socialization process." Finally, Philip Vernon (*Intelligence and Cultural Environment*, pp. 53, 218):

> Even within western culture, follow-up studies seldom give any confirmation for apparently plausible hypotheses regarding the long-term effects of treatment of infants. . . . Infant rearing practices and maternal deprivation may cause temporary emotional traumata. . . . But their long-term effects on personality . . . are more dubious. . . . Socialization practices and the home "climate" during preschool and school years are more influential.

One special investigation ought to be expressly mentioned here not simply because it is competent observation but because it approaches the character of an experiment: Stephen T. Boggs's work on the Ojibwa Indians, and more especially on their Manitoba branch, known as the Saulteaux (see "An Interactional Study of Ojibwa Socialization," *American Sociological Review*, 21 [1956], 191ff., and "Culture Change and the Personality of Ojibwa Children," *American Anthropologist*, 60, No. 1 [February 1958], 47–58). Boggs started out from the results of an earlier researcher whose name has already appeared in these pages, A. Irving Hallowell. Hallowell, "by comparing the projective test responses of representative samples of persons in three contemporary Ojibwa communities, each representing a different degree of acculturation . . . found . . . that the historic type of personality structure . . . was not altered." Boggs then asked "whether the persistence over time of some adult personality characteristics . . . can be traced to personality formation in childhood" ("Interactional Study," 191, 192). If the Freudians are correct, then we must expect a persistence of the basic child-care techniques, for instance, a continuing use of the cradleboard, which was as characteristic of original Ojibwa culture as close swaddling was of Great Russia. But the correlation to be looked for simply was not there. Boggs's summing up is terse and clear: "The persisting characteristics of Ojibwa personality do not appear to be maintained by the formative influence of parental care, insofar as this can be observed in the interaction within Ojibwa homes" ("Culture Change," 54). Honesty forces us to add that Boggs's material is not as full as might be desired, but there is no reason to doubt the reliability of his overall result.

The hypothesis of Gorer and Erikson would be much more attractive if it were possible to sustain an assumption of theirs which they obviously made without being in the least aware of it—the assumption that the family is a more or less closed society. If it were indeed a whole world, so to speak, everything which happens within it would be of decisive causal significance. But the family is in fact a wide open society. The broad stream of culture flows freely through it and only because this is so have we described it, in the opening sentences of this section, as the most important locus of character formation. There is, in this connection, one point which is of surpassing importance, and we can best bring it out if we use philosophical terminology. According to Freud and his successors, we should conceive the relation of child and adult in terms of cause and effect. "Freud's emphasis on the ontogenetic past was so strong that he

tended to see in man nothing but the power of his past over his present life . . . ,"
Schachtel says (*Metamorphosis*, p. 8), and even the most orthodox Freudian
would hardly dissent from this statement. But there is also an inverse relationship, a power of the future over the past, and in saying this, we are not proposing
an idle paradox. For we must, if we wish to be realistic, conceive the relation
of adult and child in terms of finality. In all societies (we need make no single
exception) society has so organized the educational process, including even
the earliest child-care acts, as to insure that the adult will ultimately emerge
from the infant, and the adult is thus the guiding image which is ever before the
educators' mind, whether they be aware of it or not. St. Thomas Aquinas would
have said that education is "ordered to" maturity, and this formulation makes
the finalistic purpose in the process, which totally dominates it, manifest. A
holistic argument is entirely appropriate here. We can say that the inclusive
society allots to the family the function, or imposes on it the duty, of producing
a future full-grown member, and this undeniable fact cuts the ground from under the Freudian *vis a tergo* theory and the elevation, by Freud and his disciples, of intrafamilial events, and especially intrafamilial techniques, to the
position of an ultimate cause of personality formation.

If the handling of the infant is realistically considered, it soon becomes obvious that it is imperative to make a distinction between the cultural norm and
the individual, idiosyncratic, implementation of it. The cultural norm—babies
ought to be swaddled, they ought to be forced to control their sphincters as soon
as it is physically possible, etc.—is developed and pressed on the population
because of certain societal needs and values. Thus the swaddling may—in given
historical conditions—be an effect of restricted home space and the early toilet
training of society's call for highly self-disciplined men. The appropriate techniques are therefore imposed upon the family from above. But every family
will carry them out in its own way. Even where swaddling is the rule, one mother
will tie the bands close and another will leave them relatively loose; even where
all will try to drive dirtiness out of a child, one mother will be more patient and
gentle in the training process, another less. What decides, then, is less the family
than (the inclusive society and) the personality of the mother, or other educator.

Margaret Mead has distinguished three basic attitudes of the mother to her
child (see *Male and Female*, pp. 77ff.) which we shall enumerate here in inverse
order because that inverse order, as will appear immediately, is more appropriate: (*a*) reciprocal (mother and child exchange services); (*b*) complementary (the
child is conceived as different from the mother, as weak, in need of care, and
so on); (*c*) symmetrical (the mother considers the child as a human being exactly like herself). Though different societies may emphasize one of these alternatives to the detriment of the others—according to Margaret Mead, for
instance, the Manus reciprocity and the Arapesh complementarity—they are
surely all three always present. At first, reciprocity seems to prevail. During
breast feeding the child receives milk and provides relief from glandular pressure. Later complementarity supervenes. The child is an object of care rather
than a subject properly so called. In the end symmetry wins out. Yet symmetry
is laid on already in reciprocity, and reciprocity remains present in symmetry

for love is exchanged—given and received. The reason why we brought up the Meadian typology is to show that what decides is, not a child-care technique, but a human attitude. Reciprocity, complementarity, and symmetry are laid on in thought and will; they are inspired by culture and variable according to personalities. Causal patterns of explanation are not really applicable in the analysis of intrafamilial child treatment and its influence on diversification. Diversification results from the variety of cultures and the variety of selves.

One important aspect which must not remain unmentioned is the influence of social stability and social change on the treatment of children. In societies which are relatively stable, each generation faces more or less the same contingencies and, hence, the same difficulties. The mother will know, and will be able vividly to realize, what her boy or girl has to go through. There will therefore be much sympathy, and rough transitions will be smoothed. In dynamic societies, on the other hand, a gulf will open up between parental and infantile experiences. Socializers will be less able to understand and to sympathize with the problems of the socializees, with resulting frictions and, in particularly unfavorable cases, the emergence of deviancy, be it mental illness, be it crime.

We spoke, a moment ago, of the mother "or other educator," and thereby hangs a further important cause of diversification. In the modern West, the burden of child handling falls squarely on the parents and especially the mother, but other cultures have differing arrangements. The grandparents or older siblings may have to take a major share, or even the major share, of the duties, and this will undoubtedly make a difference. It would be easy to hypothesize that grandparents, who have lived a long time under the existing system of norms and values, will be more determined to inculcate them in the oncoming generation than older siblings on whom these norms and values sit as yet very lightly, but this assumption might be misleading. Grandparents are often indulgent; it may be that they are enfeebled; it may also be that they have a bad conscience because they fear that they have been hard earlier on on their own immediate offspring; older siblings, on the other hand, may be strict; it may be that they enjoy the power given them over weaker creatures; it may also be that they apprehend that they may be punished if their wards misbehave. We shall not attempt to develop and to display a specious typology here. Certainly there are in fact types of society in accordance with the differing division of educational labor; but what will *in concreto* decide is once again the character, the individuality, of the specific individuals involved. A grandparent may be grumpy or kindly, an older brother or sister fond of their junior or filled with ill will. Our next and final section, which will deal with the emergence of individuality, will cast some light back on the aspects which we are discussing here, the aspects of intrafamilial conditioning.

We have now brought the general structure of the family into the picture and we have thereby shifted the focus of our investigation rather radically—much more radically than might appear at first sight. We have in fact changed over to a new topic. If we have so far had to reject the suggestions of one psychologist, Sigmund Freud, we may now utilize the findings of another, Alfred Adler. Adler's theory, badly misnamed *Individualpsychologie* (misnamed because it emphasizes the social character of the individual more than the individual character of the *socius*), regards the family not as an institution which does violence to the child by swaddling or weaning him, but rather as an environment in which he may develop and mature. The end point of the process—full integration into society and culture—is ever before Adler's eyes, but he emphasizes that the road lies through a specific subsociety, the family, which is the approach, the entrance gate, as it were, into the wider field of adulthood. While the Freudians see little difference between the inclusive society and the family insofar as the family is to them merely the *locus* of particularly harsh processes, the Adlerians draw attention to the true specificity of the home, to the fact that—unlike the market place—it is divided into male and female, parent and offspring, older sibling and younger. Because it is so divided, it contributes after all powerfully to the diversification of the human race.

First, a word of warning. By suggesting that the generational structure of the family—its sex division and birth order—has a not inconsiderable influence on the character of the persons within its orbit, we do not wish to introduce a kind of biologism—the theory which we have rejected throughout this work. It is not the fact that there is a contrast between male and female and between older sibling and younger which matters, but the cultural meaning which society connects with this fact. Until recently the prevailing principle of inheritance in European agriculture was primogeniture (*droit d'aîné, Anerbenrecht*) whereby the oldest son came into the peasant holding and the younger sons and daughters were merely "paid out." The senior had a privileged position, but he did not receive it from nature; he received it from human arrangement. In some areas, the opposite principle, that of ultimogeniture, was in force, and there being the first-born meant being disadvantaged, not being preferred, tending toward resentment and depression, not toward pride and optimism. The Code Napoléon, which introduced the law of free divisibility, under which all children are treated equally, created yet a different situation. Thus birth order and sex are not important as mere physical facts; they become important if and when society makes them the bases of statuses and roles.

These statuses and roles were classically described by Alfred Adler (see *The Individual Psychology of Alfred Adler*, edd. Heinz L. Ansbacher and Rowena R. Ansbacher [New York, 1956], pp. 376–83). Adler begins by emphasizing that "It is not, of course, the child's number in the order of successive births which influences his character, but the situation into which he is born . . ." (p. 377). This situation is at first highly favorable for the first-born, but it is apt to become rather abruptly changed for the worse. The crown prince or princess may be dethroned. "Another child is born and he is no longer unique. Now he must share the attention of his mother and father with a rival. We can often find in problem children, neurotics, criminals, drunkards, and perverts that their difficulties began in such circumstances" (ibid.). But even if a first-born does not become a deviant, if all goes well with him, he will be marked for life by his specific position in the birth order of the nursery. Adler ventures far forward in assessing the aftereffects of primogeniture:

> Oldest children generally show, in one way or another, an interest in the past. All their movements and expressions are directed towards the bygone time when they were the center of attention. They admire the past and are pes-

simistic about the future. Sometimes a child who has lost his power, the small kingdom he ruled, understands better than others the importance of power and authority. When he grows up, he likes to take part in the exercise of authority and exaggerates the importance of rules and laws. Everything should be done by rule, and no rule should ever be changed; power should always be preserved in the hands of those entitled to it. Influences like these in childhood give a strong tendency towards conservatism [p. 378].

Other authors have added further details, for instance Edith Neisser, in *The Eldest Child* (New York, 1957):

An eldest child has only adults for his models in his early years. For that reason, only and oldest children tend to be more serious. . . . The first child in the family, in trying to be adult beyond his years, may develop a burdensome conscience. . . . That the eldest, especially during the years he is the only child, is likely to bear the brunt of his mother's and father's inner conflicts to a greater extent than the younger children do is a point on which authorities seem to be agreed. . . . Because of the hurdles he has been forced to surmount, an eldest may become a person of unusual sensitivity, able to respond to and identify with the troubles of his fellow man to a greater degree than could one for whom life had gone more smoothly [pp. 32, 33, 39, 40].

It is obvious that these assertions about the developmental directions taken by first-born children indicate no more than tendencies which may be easily countermanded by other influences. "If the parents have allowed the first-born to feel sure of their affection [even after the appearance of the next in line], if he knows that his position is secure, and, above all, if he is prepared for the arrival of a younger child and has been trained to cooperate in its care, the crisis will pass without ill effects" (*Individual Psychology of Alfred Adler*, edd. Ansbacher & Ansbacher, p. 378).

The parents' power is not, however, the only fact and feature which puts a decided negative on any deterministic interpretation. The situation which arises for the first-born when he receives a younger brother or sister is indeterminate, or at least dichotomous, in itself, the possible breeding-ground for two very dissimilar attitudes. "Among such oldest children we find individuals who develop a striving to protect others and help them. They train to imitate their fathers or mothers; often they play the part of a father or a mother with the younger children, look after them, teach them, and feel themselves responsible for their welfare. . . . These are the favorable cases"; but a senior may also become bossy, a martinet: "a striving to protect others may be exaggerated into a desire to keep those others dependent and to rule over them" (ibid.). "There are those who say 'I was the oldest and I was top dog.' Others insist 'It's tough having a bunch of little ones trailing after you whatever you do,' " writes Edith Neisser (*Eldest Child*, p. 30).

You can find eldest brothers all the way from Tom Tulliver in George Eliot's *Mill on the Floss*, who tormented . . . his younger sister, expecting everything and giving nothing in return, to the central figure in J. D. Salinger's *Catcher in the Rye*, who adored his little sister and found in her the one stabilizing force in his life. You can find eldest sisters who are kindly, responsible, and com-

petent like Meg in *Little Women* or who are possessive, domineering, and un-
bearably self-righteous like Alice in Rebecca West's *Salt of the Earth*. There
are many shades of generosity and protectiveness, selfishness and bad temper,
in fiction as you can observe around you in twenty years [pp. 17–18].

Even this ambiguity is not, however, the only or even the main cause of indeterminacy on the part of the child. There is another, equally potent or even
more potent source of it, which Adler mentions without, unfortunately, emphasizing it as energetically as it should be emphasized. The child's character is
influenced, he writes (*Individual Psychology of Alfred Adler*, edd. Ansbacher
& Ansbacher, p. 377; emphasis added), by "the situation into which he is born
and the way in which he interprets it." Thus there is not only an objectively defined condition, but also room for a subjectively chosen strategy. There is not
only the possibility of parental steering, but also the possibility of self-steering,
of reacting to the shock of dethronement with good grace or with ill grace. True,
a child under, say, three has only a half-developed character and cannot be expected to be particularly generous or moral in his attitude. But he already possesses a rudimentary self, and that self will, to some extent, evolve further on
the basis of the decisions which it makes. Even a tiny tot can throw the switch
and maneuver the train of his development onto different tracks. We must remember this truth when we turn, in the next section, to a study of the emergence
of individuality.

The character of the last-born is not likely to be similar to that of the first-
born. This is how Adler (p. 380) describes him:

All other children can be dethroned, but never the youngest. . . . He is always
the baby of the family, probably the most pampered, and faces the difficulties
of a pampered child. But, because he is so much stimulated and has many
chances for competition, he often develops in an extraordinary way, runs faster
than the other children, and overcomes them all. The position of the youngest
has not changed in human history; the oldest stories of mankind tell how the
youngest child excelled his brothers and sisters.

In our context it is particularly interesting to note that we find, once again, a
deep ambiguity laid on in the circumstances of the youngest as it is in those
of the oldest. An archetypal youngest was Joseph of the Bible (his brother Benjamin was born when he was already seventeen and so not in the picture when
he was a child). Joseph, however, had a grand idea of himself. "Even in his
dreams he asserts his superiority. The others must bow down before him; he
outshines them all." Yet it is by no means impossible or rare that the youngest
develops a deficiency, and not an excess, of self-confidence. "Sometimes a youngest child may suffer from extreme inferiority feelings; everyone in the environment is older, stronger, and more experienced" (p. 381).

Different again is the case of the second child, or another child somewhere
in the middle. "A typical second child is very easy to recognize. . . . From the
time he is born, he shares attention with another child, and is therefore a little
nearer to cooperation than an oldest child." But it is as a rule cooperation with
a twist to it.

Throughout his childhood he has a pacemaker; there is always a child ahead of him, and he is stimulated to exert himself and catch up. . . . He behaves as if he were in a race. . . . In his later life, the second child is rarely able to endure the strict leadership of others or to accept the idea of eternal laws. He will be much more inclined to believe, rightly or wrongly, that there is no power in the world which cannot be overthrown. . . . the typical second child is beautifully portrayed in the story of Jacob. He wished to be the first, to take away Esau's position, to best Esau and excel him [pp. 379, 380].

Adler does not mention, in this chapter, the ambiguity of the intermediate child's position, but this is surely obvious: the child in the middle is both younger and older than another sibling and thus unavoidably facing two ways psychologically.

The picture becomes a good deal more complicated if the siblings are not of the same sex. In analyzing situations of this kind, Adler stresses the indeterminacy of the outcome of childhood experiences particularly strongly:

An only boy brought up in a family of girls has a hard time before him. He is in a wholly feminine environment, since the father is absent most of the day. Feeling that he is different, he may grow up isolated. On the other hand, he may fight strongly against this atmosphere and lay great stress on his masculinity. He will feel that he must assert his difference and his superiority; but there will always be tension. His development will proceed by extremes, he will train to be either very strong or very weak. In a rather similar way, an only girl among boys is apt to develop very feminine or very masculine qualities. Frequently she is pursued through life by feelings of insecurity and helplessness [p. 382].

With regard to the last-mentioned issue, Walter Toman, whose book *Familienkonstellationen* (Munich, 1974) continues and expands Adler's analysis, is considerably more optimistic, as his chapters "The Youngest Brother of Sisters" (pp. 155ff.) and "The Youngest Sister of Brothers" (pp. 171ff.), in particular, indicate. We are not concerned with these differing estimates, for our task is only to show why the human race, which has one nature, becomes so diversified, so split and splintered, in the process of socialization. Toman's study also adds to Adler's analysis by pursuing the influence of the birth order into the marital field. An oldest son with at least one younger sister will make a good husband, we are told, for he is (*a*) prepared to lead, and (*b*) not unacquainted with the ways of womanhood. For parallel reasons a youngest daughter with at least one older brother will make a good wife. The matter has its importance, for if some combinations, like the matching of oldest brother and youngest sister, are better than others for family life, they will create superior environments for education and thus produce more stable personalities—an additional way in which diversification is brought about.

We refrain from presenting more of Toman's casuistical survey. It goes to show, with all its detail, how nursery life and early intrafamilial experiences generally turn some individuals this way and others that. We would only like to mention Toman's distinction between complementarity and identity or identification. An oldest brother of brothers and an oldest sister of sisters would not be so good a match in marriage as an oldest brother of brothers and a youngest sister of sisters (see pp. 93ff.). The reason, somewhat crudely expressed, is that both have learned to be the boss, the strongest among the siblings, and therefore identity of familial position, though it fosters identification and perhaps even mutual sympathy, can also bear the seeds of conflict.

The most important concept which Toman has to offer is his "duplication theorem." He formulates it as follows (p. 81; see also pp. 78, 79, 136): "New social relations are, under otherwise identical conditions, the more successful and the more lasting, the more similar they are to earlier and to the earliest (intrafamilial) relations of those concerned." The salient idea seems to be that the family allots roles to its members, for instance, the role of leader, controller, model, and so on, to the oldest son, and that the oldest son will then tend, not unnaturally, to play the same role throughout life and in every setting which he enters. In his chapter on "The Oldest Brother of Brothers," Toman suggests that appropriate careers for such individuals are: captain of industry, bank manager, financier, naval or staff officer, teacher, judge, architect, and the like (p. 148), whereas he lists under the heading "The Youngest Brother of Brothers" (p. 151) such comparatively humble avocations as entertainer, advertising agent, commercial traveler, assistant to leading men in industry, politics, or science, etc. Under "The Youngest Sister of Brothers" (p. 173) he enumerates as suitable for a "kid sister" the following: typist, secretary, nurse, laboratory assistant, "admiring companion of an artist," etc. But here we surely see that the whole disquisition overreaches itself (to express it mildly) and leads to generalizations which can hardly be defended with any confidence. Common experience tells us that a person is often unhappy with his intrafamilial position —an older sibling with his responsibilities, a younger with his limitations and subjection—and that outside the family he will then try to play a part very different from that forced on him inside. Where then is the duplication hypothesis? This possibility is lightly touched on in the book (see p. 144), but not further considered. The assertion (pp. 176, 216) that an only child, especially a girl, is comparatively little interested in founding a large family—"an only child, preferably a girl, is often enough for her"—seems particularly unconvincing. Remembering her own loneliness, she may on the contrary well try to fill her nursery so that her offspring do not have to suffer as she did. Many generalizations in this study, we can see, are rather suspect. Toman, it is true, brings some inductive–statistical evidence to buttress his assertions (see pp. 96ff., esp. p. 105), but it is too feeble to leave one entirely convinced. This does not mean that his whole analysis (or Adler's) is unrealistic. Far from it! The tendencies he describes are real enough; older siblings do, as a rule, wish to be as dominant in the wider world as they were in the narrower sphere of their parental home, but they are only tendencies, tendencies easily blocked or even turned around by the manifold winds of life.

The truth is that what it means to be an older or a younger sibling, a brother or a sister, a parent or a child, depends less on one's formal position within an objective scheme than on the living interplay of individuals on the basis of that scheme, less on ascribed status or even prescribed function than on the actual functioning of the family. Wherever human beings are together, and especially where they are in constant and close contact, personal sympathies and antipathies spring up which often cut across the usual, to-be-expected pattern of relationships (p. 73). Not all parents are neutral in their attitudes or equally loving to all their offspring; not all older brothers are equally bossy to all their cadets, and so on. We have to make distinctions. We have in fact to return once again to our artistic simile of theme and variations. In the second act of Puccini's *Tosca*, the heroine, having killed the villainous Scarpia, has to say the words *E avanti a lui tremava tutta Roma!* It is well known that every great diva has had the ambition to pronounce these words in her own inimitable way. So it is also with other and less dramatic, more ordinary roles. All are comparable, all have the same text and context, but all are also different in the performance. Therefore even Adler and Toman bring us to the same conclusion as Gorer and Erikson—to the conviction that individuality is produced by, more than anything else, the pre-existence of individuals and individualities. We must close the circle of our investigation by showing why and how highly profiled personalities emerge incessantly from the process of socialization which is yet the avenue to adulthood for all.

THE EMERGENCE OF INDIVIDUALITY

86. Every human being is unique. This statement is by no means irreconcilable with the apparently, but not really, contradictory assertion that every society, and indeed the human race, is a unitary whole. Many leading sociologists have emphasized and developed this truth, each in his own characteristic way. One of them was Emile Durkheim. His classical distinction between "mechanical" and "organic" coherence, which is relevant here, belongs among the most precious, but also the most secure, possessions of the science of sociology. Where all pursue the same ways of breadwinning—for instance, where everybody is an agriculturist who produces his own wheat and meat—there the neighbors are not vitally dependent on each other: they live side-by-side rather than together. Their coherence is merely mechanical, like that of pavement stones which happen to lie close to each other. But where labor is divided, where a baker needs a butcher to secure his roast and a butcher needs a baker to secure his loaf, they cannot do without each other. Such men live together, and that in a very strong sense of the word; they do not live merely side-by-side. Their coherence is organical, like that of the organs of the human body which cannot survive without mutual support, and which are what they are only because they belong to an integrated organism. Thus diversity appears to be a condition of unity, and not a contradiction to it. Actually, Durkheim's theorizing, asserting that there is, in history, a transition from mechanical to organic ordering, and hence an increase in social integration, is less true than he fancied. For early society—say, the Celtic or Germanic village—had developed a strong pattern of custom and culture which held everyone securely within its grip, even if food-getting efforts merely ran parallel, and modern society—say, the capitalist West —is so permeated with competition and strife that the division of labor and the exchange of its products means far less than it otherwise might or would. But this fact does not diminish the basic truth of Durkheim's analysis, the conviction that multiplicity is conducive, rather than prejudicial, to social unity.

Why are the individuals constituting a society as different from each other as we invariably find them to be? The answer lies in three directions: (*a*) human beings are different because of the physical differences in their bodies; (*b*) human beings are different because of the experiential differences in their life histories; (*c*) human beings are different because of the moral differences in their personal reactions to the socialization process in the widest meaning of the term, to social pressures and social demands. The first two influences are generally recognized and accepted, the third is not. Yet, on analysis, it turns out to be at least as important as the other two.

As far as the body is concerned, which an older philosophy liked to describe as the *principium individuationis*, i.e., the beginning as well as the principle of individuation, Talcott Parsons gives us, in one of his happiest formulations, a precious lead. This is what he writes (see "Social Structure and Personality Development," p. 172): "while the main content of the structure of the personality is derived from social systems and culture through socialization, the personality becomes an independent system through its relations to its own organism and through the uniqueness of its own life-history experience. . . ." The passage is interesting, not only because it omits the third factor mentioned in the last paragraph, but also because it draws a distinction between the other two. A man's life history is "his own," but to his organism he stands in a "relation"; a relation, however, is always a link between two entities. May we then sever the person into body and (say) mind, or body and will, or body and action center? The modern materialist is appalled at this suggestion, yet older modes of thought (which, let us not forget, were also based on observation) accepted it without demur. "The law is spiritual. But I am carnal," St. Paul writes in his Epistle to the Romans (7:14, 18, 22–23). "I know that there dwelleth not in me, that is to say, in my flesh, that which is good. For to will [what is right] is present with me; but to accomplish that which is good, I find not. . . . For I am delighted with the law of God, according to the inward man. But I see another law in my members, fighting against the law of my mind. . . ." Let nobody take exception to this classical quotation because of its religious background and its moral tendency. It incorporates an insight which is universally human. If two men are imagined together, both hungry, but one with bread in his pockets and the other without, would not the first, whoever he is, be torn between the desire to eat the bread himself and the knowledge, based on duty, that he should share it? The case which we have just posited is no specious piece of fiction. All material values imply the dilemma which we have described. If one enjoys them, others cannot. It is only cultural values, such as music, which can be shared without sacrifice; food cannot be divided in the same way. The inner conflict so movingly portrayed by the great Apostle can be easily expressed in psychoanalytic language as well. Man is torn, and that inescapably, between the id and the superego (about the ego in a minute). To be man is as undeniably connected with this self-contradictoriness according to Freud of Vienna as it is according to Paul of Tarsus.

The sociologist must in this matter take his clue from Cooley who maintained that man *has* a body but *is not* simply a body. Yet Cooley was inclined to dismiss the body in somewhat too lighthearted a fashion, and we must underline that the body is much more than merely a set of mechanisms operated by the mind, the will, or the self, as he at times seems to think, but rather, as Parsons suggests, an *independent system* with which the mind, the will, and the self have to come to terms. By system we must mean, in this context, action system. The hungry body says: eat; the moral person says: share. The digesting body says: defecate; the person trained to cleanliness insists: wait. The body says: do what is good for yourself; conscience pleads: take your neighbor into account. Actual conduct is always a compromise between physical and social man. Physical man is far more sharply divided from his fellows than social man. The chain which ties the highly socialized personality to his organism, to his id, is therefore the first and foremost reason for the individual's individuality.

But not only are men different from each other because each has his own body; these bodies, too, are constitutionally different from each other, and this fact powerfully increases the contrasts between the individual incarnations of the species. A comparative study of neonates shows that one has more, another less, sensitive lips; that one sucks with energy, another with languor; that one has a regular rhythm of hunger and discharge, another a wayward one; and so on and so forth. The compromise which has to be achieved between physical man and social man—between what Parsons calls man's motivational and his value orientation—will therefore never be quite the same; there will be as many variants as there are people. What a moralizing psychology and pedagogy are wont to call "animal spirits" will be more easily tamed in one child than in another, and in this way the physical inheritance will, so to speak, even break into the sphere of character and conduct.

One special problem which arises here, and which we must mention even though we cannot hope to offer a solution to it, is the nature of temperament. What is involved? "To describe somebody's temperament," writes a very able psychologist, John J. Honigmann (*Personality in Culture*, p. 72), "is to cover such qualities abstracted from his behavior as dullness or alertness, torpor or vigor, gentleness or brusqueness, passivity or assertiveness, apathy or readiness to flare into anger and into other emotions, emotional stability or restlessness, and so on. Temperament is also used to denote the strength, vividness, and other qualities attached to the senses and to basic drives, like hunger and sex." The question is: Is temperament simply an aspect of organic inheritance or is it also due to social living? It seems almost impossible to give an assured answer. Nature does not make such sharp distinctions as science does; things blend into each other. There are, of course, some who assert that temperament is an effect of hormonic balance and more especially of the level of epinephrine in the body, but Honigmann is more careful. This is what he writes:

> Temperament points to activity level and to emotional reactivity, with the implication that those things are partly inborn. Not that a child inherits temperament as a single entity, the way he acquires brown hair or blue eyes. He inherits a constitution, including a range of metabolic and endocrine functions, sensory sensitivity, and drive strength, in which his temperamental qualities are implanted. Prenatal and postnatal experiences inextricably infuse the in-

herited, and probably largely bio-chemical, bases of temperament, so that even in early life temperament partakes of both heredity and environment and is by no means totally fixed or arrested.

This seems to be as balanced and as reasonable an account of common scientific opinion at the present moment as can be given. For us the main conclusion to be drawn is that temperament—more of a borderline phenomenon—is, along with the existence of the body and the different constitution of bodies, a third factor making for individuality.

We come even closer to a borderline—we move, as it were, into a border belt—as we begin to study the individual adjustments which every organism has to make to his life conditions. According to Freud, these adjustments are, in man, achieved by the ego, guardian of the "reality principle," a term which comes close to the meaning of the word "reason." Yet reason is to him not simply conscious reason; the ego is part of the cortical layer of the brain, or at least located there, so that adjustments may be conscious, semi-conscious, and unconscious. In the animal and in the neonate, they are of the latter two varieties. But even the merely semi- or unconscious ego already pursues a life policy. Above all, it constructs for itself an image of the world, which can and will serve as a basis for its dealings with the world, and these constructions are again different from body to body, brain to brain, and mind to mind—yet a further and very powerful cause of differentiation between man and man. George Herbert Mead understood this matter particularly well, and we make no apology for transcribing two lengthy passages from *Mind, Self, and Society*. The reader will notice that the great psychologist uses language which indicates that he is thinking of animal man as much as of man as a mind. "The influence of environment," Mead says,

> is exercised over the form, and the adaptation of the form results from the influences of the environment on it. Spencer conceived of the central nervous system as being continually played upon by stimuli which set up certain paths, so that it was the environment which was fashioning the form. The phenomena of attention, however, give a different picture of conduct. The human animal is an attentive animal, and his attention may be given to stimuli that are relatively faint. One can pick out sounds at a distance. Our whole intelligent process seems to lie in the attention which is selective of certain types of stimuli. Other stimuli which are bombarding the system are in some fashion shunted off. We give our attention to one particular thing. Not only do we open the door to certain stimuli and close it to others, but our attention is an organizing process as well as a selective process. When giving attention to what we are going to do we are picking out the whole group of stimuli which represent successive activity. Our attention enables us to organize the field in which we are going to act. Here we have the organism as acting and determining its environment. It is not simply a set of passive senses played upon by the stimuli that come from without. The organism goes out and determines what it is going to respond to, and organizes that world. One organism picks out one thing and another picks out a different one, since it is going to act in a different way [p. 25].

These last words speak so clear a language that we have no need to go out of our way in order to explain what they mean in the context of a study of the diversification of the species *Homo sapiens*. *Homines sapientes* are different from each other, not only because each has his own body, because each body is physically unique and connected with a unique temperament, but also because they make themselves unique by constituting, each of them, his own *imago mundi*.

Later in the work, Mead returns to this topic, and his words again are well worth quoting:

> A statement of evolution that was common in an earlier period assumed simply the effect of an environment on organized living protoplasm, molding it in some sense to the world in which it had to live. On this view the individual is really passive as over against the influences which are affecting it all the time. But what needs now to be recognized is that the character of the organism is a determinant of its environment. We speak of bare sensitivity as existent by itself, forgetting it is always a sensitivity to certain types of stimuli. In terms of its sensitivity the form selects an environment, not selecting exactly in the sense in which a person selects a city or a country or a particular climate in which to live, but selects in the sense that it finds those characteristics to which it can respond, and uses the resulting experiences to gain certain organic results that are essential to its continued life-process. . . . That sort of a determination of the environment is as real, of course, as the effect of the environment on the form [pp. 214–15].

Before closing our discussion of the influence of the somatic factor, let us add very briefly that even the process of maturation (considered at the moment exclusively in terms of physiology) is different from man to man. True, the stages a "form" has to run through are very similar, but not so the "when" and "how." There is one *élan vital* toward maturity, but here it is faster and there slower, here smoother and more continuous, there rougher and more punctured by crises—here also carrying further forward than there. And so the diversification of the species, already initiated by nature in the play of heredity, in the spontaneous mutation of the genes, is further increased by the elaboration of the material in the course of ontogenetic development. The conditions of that development inside the maternal organism are still fairly uniform, at least relatively so, but when the extrauterine period follows the intrauterine, the new creature is propelled into a much richer and much, much more differentiated environment which will assuredly leave its precipitation in the character of that individual.

The process of maturation, however (considered now in all its width and breadth), takes place in a setting which is not only a constellation of things, but also a circle of men, and this makes all the difference. It changes even the physical facts, not of course in themselves, in their material constitution, but certainly in their meaning. An organic weakness, for instance, becomes easily, not to say regularly, an inferiority complex, that mental trouble which, Alfred Adler tells us, is the cross of all competitive societies and marks many individuals, each of them in a different way. Yet there need not be an organic weakness to start with; any physical feature will do. A bent toward obesity will lead to depressive conditions in our culture where a "fatty" is looked down upon or at least teased, and to pride and exultation where aesthetic ideas are such that baroque body forms rank as beautiful. Somatic inheritance in this way produces, working through the medium of society, further diversification.

But, in the circle of men, the child meets with a kind of inheritance which is a far greater cause of diversification than somatic heredity, either considered in itself or as an element in social life: he meets with socio-cultural inheritance, and this is not simply received as are the qualities of the body, but has to be acquired by learning. Animals learn mainly, not to say exclusively, from experience—experience with their own bodies. Human beings learn also, and certainly predominantly, from others. "Culture is a great storehouse of ready-made solutions to problems which human animals are wont to encounter," write Clyde Kluckhohn and H. A. Murray (*Personality in Nature, Society, and Culture* [New York, 1967], p. 54). "This storehouse is man's substitute for instinct. It is filled not merely with the pooled learning of the living members of the society, but also with the learning of men long dead and of men belonging to other societies."

The process of culture transmission makes for multiplicity, not only because culture itself is multiform, the fact of which we spoke at length in Section 84, but also because its own methods—the methods of teaching and learning—are almost infinitely modifiable and varied. A distinction should perhaps be drawn here between culture in the wider sense of the word, which includes the arts and religion, and culture in the narrower sense of the word, which describes the socialized, civilized ways in which men deal with each other. Even culture in the wider sense of the word has strong influence on the individuality of the individual. Modern readers have been greatly puzzled by the insistence of the Greek philosophers that youngsters be trained in music, a necessity which the twentieth century does not see, but a brief consideration will surely show that Plato and Aristotle had their point. Quite apart from the fact that for instance the acquisition of a sense of rhythm has social significance as a means of coordinating movement, an aspect of practical importance in some lines of production, it simply refines the person and thus molds him—molds him into a more sensitive type of man.

More important, however, as a factor in character formation, meaning by character now exclusive personality, is the transmission of the socio-cultural principles of conduct. Civilized conduct has to be learned, and its inculcation is broadly resisted by the child because it necessitates the curbing of many natural tendencies. There is a protracted battle, and in order to win it, the educator has to be a clever strategist. These strategies, however, are not the same with any two men. Each father, each mother, each teacher, has his own. "Even in small-scale, homogeneous social systems, contrasting temperamental bents from one parent to another confront a child with contrasting influences," writes John J. Honigmann (*Personality in Culture*, p. 159), and Kluckhohn and Murray say: "Concretely, not the group but group agents with their own peculiar traits determine personality formation" (*Personality in Nature, Society, and Culture*, p. 61). There is as little fault to find with this latter formulation as with the former, yet it must be emphasized that nowhere are parents simply group agents; they are individuals in their own right, and it is for this reason that they produce individuals and not stock types. The socialization process, so we may sum up and express the salient truth in the closest possible compass, produces not only social but also individual men. It does so because it confronts the child to be educated with the end products of a process of individuation, and not only with group agents. It is they who press their wards to develop socio-culturally acceptable habits and convictions, each his own, and these then form a person's character, for, as the device of a great English school expresses it, "Manner makyth man."

The last paragraph, pointing out that established individuality is the cause, in every concrete case, of individuality in the course of formation, is the main truth (admittedly a very trite one) which this concluding section of our book has to establish. A broad-based study of the making of men as unique selves would have to enter deeply into the details of the art of education and its fateful implications. It is not our avocation to discuss it. Our duty was merely to indicate the factors which make for multiplicity in the face of, and in spite of, social unity, and that task we hope to have fulfilled. We can close, as we started, with a bow to the philosophical principle of duality. The self, says George Herbert Mead, is both a "me" and an "I." "The 'me' is a conventional, habitual individual," he writes (*Mind, Self and Society*, pp. 197, 196). "It has to have those habits, those responses which everybody has; otherwise the individual could not be a member of the community." But "Over against the 'me' is the 'I.' . . . The 'I' is the response of the individual to the attitude of the community as this appears in his own experience." The complete self is both an "I" and a "me," both an incarnation of his society and culture, and an independent, unrepeatable and unrepeated soul.

Before leaving this topic, it is necessary to draw attention, in a kind of appendix, to yet another factor making for contrasting developments among members of the same society: namely, accident. This influence is not so much forgotten as suppressed in the bulk of the literature because it does not fit into a rationalistic world view such as that characteristic of most scholars and scientists, and art has made more of it than scholarship and science. Yet if a realistic approach is pursued, it appears that accident is often a cause of further and often fateful evolutions. We meet men, and we enter circles which touch our wonted ambit only marginally. There was no need that this should happen, yet the consequences of such encounters, for good and ill, may be momentous. The sociologist will, in this context, think, above all, of the charismatic personality. If such a one crosses our path, we are apt to be changed for the rest of our lives. But it is unfortunately as possible to run into people or groupings which pull us down as into others which lift us up. In any case, accident—events which are not necessitated by the major causal influences within which our existence is set—helps at times to make us different, or more different, from our fellow-men.

Though we have now virtually reached the end of our road, there yet remains one last mistake to be combated and destroyed, and it is by no means unimportant. Few would deny that the character of the adult is the product of a dialectical explication between the self and society, and only because it is so may we truthfully describe it as a synthesis of the antithetic principles of "I" and "me." But there has been a tendency to think of society as stronger then the self, and from Robert Owen via Emile Durkheim to John Dewey and beyond, the inclination has been to see society as the seal and the self as the wax, the plastic matter which receives, and more or less mechanically accepts, the imprint of a stronger force. This is an error, and it results, less from the desire of social scientists to play up their subject, than from their optimism, from a kind of wishful thinking which would fain believe that education is omnipotent. Mikel Dufrenne has, in several contexts of his book, drawn attention to the *will* of the socializee, its significance and its strength, as a factor in the formation of the character, and we range ourselves by his side. Most elegant of his formulations is the following, which we quote in French before translating it, to give it its full impact: *La cause ne détermine que ce qui se détermine à être déterminé*— "Causation can determine only him who is determined ["resolved," we would rather say in English] to be determined" (*La Personnalité de base*, p. 129). He also writes: "The individual gives the social forces a grip on himself by opening himself to them" (p. 48), and "The ego defines itself essentially by the manner in which it accepts or rejects the social discipline" (p. 140). These statements are entirely correct. Socialization, like all truly social processes, is a process of interaction, and though it is not necessarily a synallagmatic process, i.e., a meeting of equally potent forces, the power of the self involved in it is assuredly never nil.

Mikel Dufrenne is a philosopher rather than a psychologist, a thinker rather than an observer, and it is important to hear what a pure empiricist has to say on this issue. What we find is, not surprisingly, that he says virtually the same thing. John J. Honigmann (*Personality in Culture*, p. 166) goes so far as to speak of "a person's autonomy in socialization," a phrase perhaps a little too extreme, and he writes in other parts of his distinguished work: "When a person accepts and embodies a culture pattern into his own system of behavior, he invariably modifies it, leaving his own stamp on the cultural heritage according to how he interprets and evaluates it" (p. 165). And again: "Even when influence flows only one way, socialization amounts to more than slavish copying, passive obedience, or total surrender. . . . It may be the only avenue a poor person's straitened circumstances, a political prisoner's rigorous confinement, or a child's powerless situation allows, but whether he is aware of it or not, the decision to comply behaviorally is his" (p. 200). And yet again:

> The first principle of development states that the way an individual responds in a given situation depends on all previous events in his life which held significance for him. . . . The principle of cumulative influence doesn't claim [however] that early events determine what happens later; far more modestly it asserts that significant events influence and limit what a person later becomes. One way events gain their power to act is by becoming part of the dynamic inner world of meanings which a person draws upon to appraise later situations; such meanings guide him to pick his later course of action, by which, in turn, he modifies his personality anew [pp. 171, 172].

He modifies his personality; a person has therefore at least *some* autonomy in socialization. The question therefore arises: How much of it? The answer to this query must be that two factors are mainly responsible: the one is the manner in which the social forces, the agents of socialization, press the norms and values of their society on the developing personality; the other is the multiplicity of these forces, the number and nature of the influences which impinge on him.

As to the first point, history teaches that there are relatively restrictive and relatively permissive societies, some which care greatly, and some which care but little, for conformity. It should not be thought, however, that societies which put strong energy behind their norms and values will be more successful in producing a conforming type of man. Excessive pressure will provoke determined resistance. There is, theoretically, an optimal combination between restrictiveness and permissiveness, and this will ensure, *uno actu*, the maximum of law-abidingness and the maximum of liberty. This may seem surprising to a superficial view of the matter, but it is true nonetheless. We have before us merely an application of the principle of the golden mean. Where restrictiveness and permissiveness are optimally combined, everyone will internalize society's values and norms, but appropriate, obey, and act them out *in his own way* and thus "me" and "I," sociality and individuality, will be reconciled.

The second point concerns societies which are composed of several subsocieties, each of which offers the developing individual variants of the basic norms and values of the inclusive, superordinated whole. (If these norms and values are more than variants, if they are irreconcilable, we can hardly speak of a society any more, and an integrated personality can arise only if there is affiliation with one of the alternatives in contention, to the exclusion of the other.) In multiform societies of this kind, the self becomes more complex. George Herbert Mead speaks, where he touches upon this matter, of a complete self and of elementary selves within it. "The unity and structure of the complete self reflects the unity and structure of the social process as a whole," he says (*Mind, Self, and Society*, p. 144),

> and each of the elementary selves of which it is composed reflects the unity and structure of one of the various aspects of that process in which the individual is implicated . . . these aspects being the different social groups to which he belongs within that process. . . . The organization and unification of a social group is identical with the organization and unification of any one of the selves arising within the social process in which that group is engaged, or which it is carrying on.

These words have their measure of truth, and yet it is necessary to take exception to them. They sin on the side of sociologism; that is, they exaggerate the influence of the societal factor. Mead, as we have seen, speaks of the individual part "reflecting" the social whole, as if he were a passive mirror, but this metaphor is misleading. In a multifaceted society, such as we are considering it here, the individual is not simply exposed to differing influences but has a chance to *choose* between them, and thus to build a self out of materials which he can freely select.

It is, however, not Mead alone who underplays the self-determination, the self-creation, of the individual; even Dufrenne and Honigmann do so, though to a lesser extent. For what they mainly talk about, and insist upon, is the fact that the person in the course of formation is able to accept and to reject the influences impinging upon him, and this is not the whole story. Not only is the will a kind of gatekeeper deciding what to admit and what to shut out, it is an active principle in a far more pregnant sense of the term, able to go out to assert itself on the stage of life. Honigmann comes twice fairly close to the truth, once when he writes that "Man is what he makes of himself. His character structure, too, belongs to what he makes of himself through the way he acts" (*Personality in Culture*, p. 69), and once when he quotes from Sartre's *Saint Génet* (trans. Bernard Frechtman [New York, 1963], p. 49): "We are not lumps of clay, and what is important is not what people make of us but what we ourselves make of what they have made of us." Yet, by and large, even he keeps to his basic definition of the personality, according to which it is "a system that selectively stores past events to define present choices" (p. 73). There is no need to quarrel with this conception, but there *is* a need to go beyond it. We should like to oppose to it a passage from the pen of one who was no academically trained psychologist, but who knew more about the human psyche than many a professional psychologist—Mary Ann Evans, better known under her pseudonym, George Eliot. "Our deeds determine us, as much as we determine our deeds," she writes in *Adam Bede* (New York, 1947; p. 302), and in this sentence, which enshrines a profound truth, the word "deeds" must necessarily carry the heaviest emphasis.

In order to appreciate the truly momentous issue involved here, we do well to descend to the lowest level of realistic description, to the everyday aspect of the process of socialization. As everybody knows, it consists of frequent and repeated appeals of the educator to his ward: "Don't push your little sister!" "Give that old lady your seat!" "Behave yourself!" Whatever the sanctions which might be brought to bear in case of non-compliance, and whatever the other reasons in the case of spontaneous compliance, one thing is clear: namely, that the *will* of the child appealed to is the predominant cause of his response. One child conforms and another refuses to conform; one conforms at once and with good grace, another but slowly and with a sour face; there are once again innumerable variations. But these reactions and subsequent actions build up into abiding attitudes and habits, and abiding attitudes and habits make the man; indeed, we are exaggerating very little if we say they *are* the man. "Handsome is as handsome does," as the old English proverb puts it. In this way the self is self-produced, even if its self-creation takes place amid given and not amid freely chosen or freely set conditions. Conditions, according to a justly famous formulation of Gabriel Tarde's, incline, but they do not compel. He who drifts along also asserts his will: he wills not to will; and this, too, is a cause of responsibility, a fact all too often forgotten, especially in penal practice.

What the last paragraph maintains is that there is a moral element in the dialectical encounter between society and individual, educator and child, and that everyone is to some extent responsible for his own character, for that which he becomes. The reason why this is so often overlooked, if not indeed expressly denied, lies partly in our habits of thought, determined as they are by the natural sciences which operate exclusively in non-subjective terms, but partly also by the fact that our self-determination and self-creation take place in tiny, so to speak infinitesimal acts, each of which is in itself but a bagatelle. But a thousand petty acts of obedience to the commands of the social code will build up a character very different from a thousand petty acts of disobedience. Our freedom is rarely consummated in great, heroic deeds: we use it in small installments, and it is these small installments, too, in which our moral self is activated and in which our moral responsibility resides.

Such ethical considerations are unsympathetic to the brand of positivism prevailing today, but they are mandated by the nature of reality. Hallowell is correct: "If the individual did not have the capacity for identifying the conduct that is his own and, through self-reflection, appraising it with reference to values . . . , how would a moral order function in human terms? . . . A human social order [however] is always a moral order" ("Culture, Personality, and Society," in *Anthropology Today*, ed. Kroeber, p. 614). The maintenance of social life presupposes a sustained moral effort, and with regard to that moral effort, and perseverance in it, individuals are very different from each other. The factor which we may call ethos also throws a new light on the relation of "I" and "me," actor and role, personal and socialized self. It is only in the limiting—the ideal case—that the two coincide, that the "I" completely adjusts to the "me" and the actor is swallowed up by the role. "Human beings are not passive recipients of their culture," writes Bert Kaplan (*A Study of Rorschach Responses in Four Cultures* [Cambridge, Mass., 1954], p. 32). "They accept, reject, or rebel against the cultural forces to which they are oriented. In many cultures, including our own, there exists a pattern of outward conformity and inner rebellion. . . . It is probably correct to say that individuals seem a good deal more similar than they really are." These striking words clearly reveal the last cause of the diversification of mankind which we have to indicate: the differences between man and man in moral fiber, in the will to act in accordance with the social code, or at least with the minimum standards which it sets.

The ultimate proof of the fact that even extreme individuation can and does go hand in hand with social integration is the existence of deviance, a topic which we need not take up in detail. The deviant—whether he be a criminal or a psychopath—pursues his own way without heeding his neighbors, and this passing beyond the outer limits drawn by normalcy clearly defines him. But it is precisely a study of deviance which shows, and shows most convincingly, that the process of socialization leaves an indelible mark on every self. Both forms of lawbreaking and forms of mental disorder are different from society to society: each has its own. And if there are also similarities from society to society, if psychoses and felonies are comparable the world over, this, too, is attributable to the parallel structuring of social wholes rather than to the physical uniformity of the human race. The truth is, and the truth remains: "Deviant no less than nondeviant behavior is socially patterned" (Honigmann, *Personality in Culture*, p. 102). This is not surprising, for even in sleep, when everything is distorted, we dream in terms of our own culture and regularly comply with the group norms which we have imbibed. In spite of the very wide variations which it allows, our parent society yet holds us firmly in its grip.

Index

238

Commerce, 26, 84, 93
Communal living, 80–82, 93
Communication, 13, 52, 78, 97, 98, 101–105, 155, 159, 166, 171, 192, 200, 209; *see also* Language; Sympathy
Compassion, *see* Altruism; Dunant, Henri
Competition, 49, 73, 76, 81, 82, 85, 93, 120, 137, 139, 143, 214; among siblings, 81, 82, 140, 141
Comte, Auguste, 48, 156
Concepts and conceptualization, 42, 43, 53, 60, 108, 149, 151
Conduct, Human, 9, 19, 67, 69, 70, 196, 203, 206, 207, 226, 227, 230, 235; Strictures on, 65
Conflict, 71, 72, 74, 78, 79, 82, 92, 93, 112, 120, 148, 186, 196, 197, 224; *see also* Competition; Quarreling
Confucianism, 14
Conscience, 69, 91, 92, 126, 143, 156, 160, 161, 162, 221, 227
Consciousness of body, 60–63
Consciousness of self, 59–65, 77, 153, 154, 171; *see also* Knowledge of self
Constraint, Moral, 91, 92, 120–22, 126; *see also* Discipline
Cooley, C. H., 13, 19, 21, 24, 25, 30, 54, 55, 63, 66, 68–80, 83–86, 91, 92, 98, 109, 110, 112, 114, 148, 163, 226, 227
Cooperation, 71, 77, 79, 93, 112, 120, 122, 148, 223
Cortex, 8, 10, 11, 14, 15, 37, 144, 163–66, 169–72; *see also* Brain
Cottrell, L. S., 65, 68
Crime and criminality, 67, 85, 92, 110, 117–19, 122, 123, 126, 127, 219; *see also* Punishment
Crime, Juvenile, 122
Cry and cries, 50, 98, 99
Culture pattern, Universal, Theory of, 193, 194
Custom, 49, 114, 115, 134, 135, 164, 166, 167, 171, 187, 200, 203, 225

Darwinism, 178, 185, 186
Davis, Allison, 137
Dependency, 56, 57, 72; *see also* Child care; Spoiling
Depth psychology, 3
Descartes, René, 146, 163, 165
Determinism, Geographical, 176, 177, 200
Deviance, 66, 67, 138, 219, 220, 235
Discipline, 49, 57, 58, 71, 77, 96, 97, 100, 110, 114–16, 119, 121, 123–25, 129, 132, 135, 147, 162, 180, 192, 194, 232; *see also* Authority; Constraint, Moral; Punishment

Displacement phenomena, 95, 96
Dogs, 40, 50–52, 153, 160
Dorfman, Josef, 3
Drives, 197; Reduction of, 20, 57, 58, 67, 92, 137, 191, 192, 194; *see also* Discipline; Freud, Sigmund
Drug addiction, 122, 137
Dualism, 1, 9, 10, 12, 13, 23, 24, 56, 58, 86, 147, 148, 160, 163, 165, 196, 209, 231
DuBois, Cora, 203
Dufrenne, Mikel, 17–20, 108, 109, 197, 202, 207, 214, 215, 232–34
Dunant, Henri, 79, 80
Dunlap, Knight, 16, 17, 113, 163
Duration, *see* Bergson, Henri
Durkheim, Emile, 94, 96, 112, 121, 122, 124–27, 132, 133, 142, 162, 182, 194, 195, 208, 211, 225, 232

Eating, 9, 10, 20, 94, 194, 213, 214
Egalitarianism, 115, 116, 126
Elan vital, 45, 172, 229; *see also* Bergson, Henri
Eliot, George (Mary Ann Evans), 234
Envy, 6, 30, 70, 81, 82, 139, 140–44, 188
Epistemology, 108; *see also* Knowledge
Erikson, Erik, 56, 159, 213, 214, 215, 217, 225
Eskimos, 93, 193, 197, 202
Ethics, 108, 117, 118; *see also* Norms, Internalization of; Values

Family, The, 48, 49, 83, 109, 110, 125, 129, 132, 136, 176, 187, 189, 191–93, 199–201, 211, 216–25; *see also* Marriage
Fear, *see* Anxiety
Fetal condition, Yearning for, 3, 4, 7, 56
Fetus, 1–4, 7, 8, 39, 44
Feudalism, 31, 205
France, Anatole, 206
Frank, L. K., 114
Franzblau, Rose, 178, 180, 181, 184
Free will, 7–9, 14, 15, 17, 34, 36, 37, 44, 45, 51, 55, 58, 68, 71, 75, 94–97, 113, 123, 147, 157, 161, 162, 166, 171, 235; *see also* Will and willing
French Revolution, The, 5, 121, 205, 206
Freud, Sigmund, and Freudianism, 2, 9, 10, 15–17, 19, 36, 39, 49, 56, 57, 59, 66, 70, 87, 113, 133, 137, 145, 154, 188, 189, 203, 213, 214, 216–20, 226, 228; *see also* Neo-Freudianism
Fromm, Erich, 5
Frustrations, 70, 71
Function, 11, 12, 14, 15, 33, 34, 36, 88, 145, 172, 185, 206; *see also* Role, Social; Structure